Creative Paint Finishing Techniques

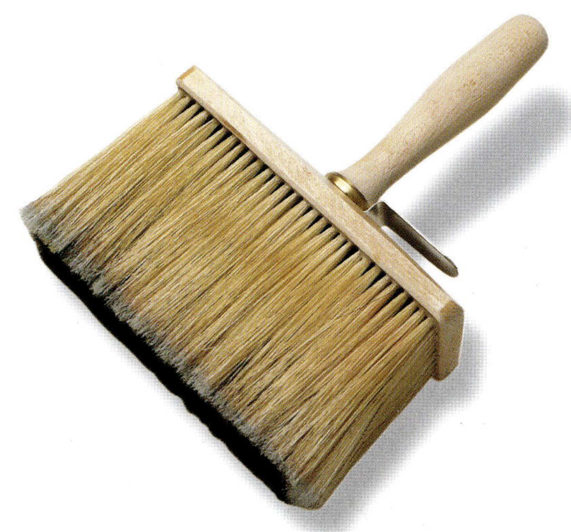

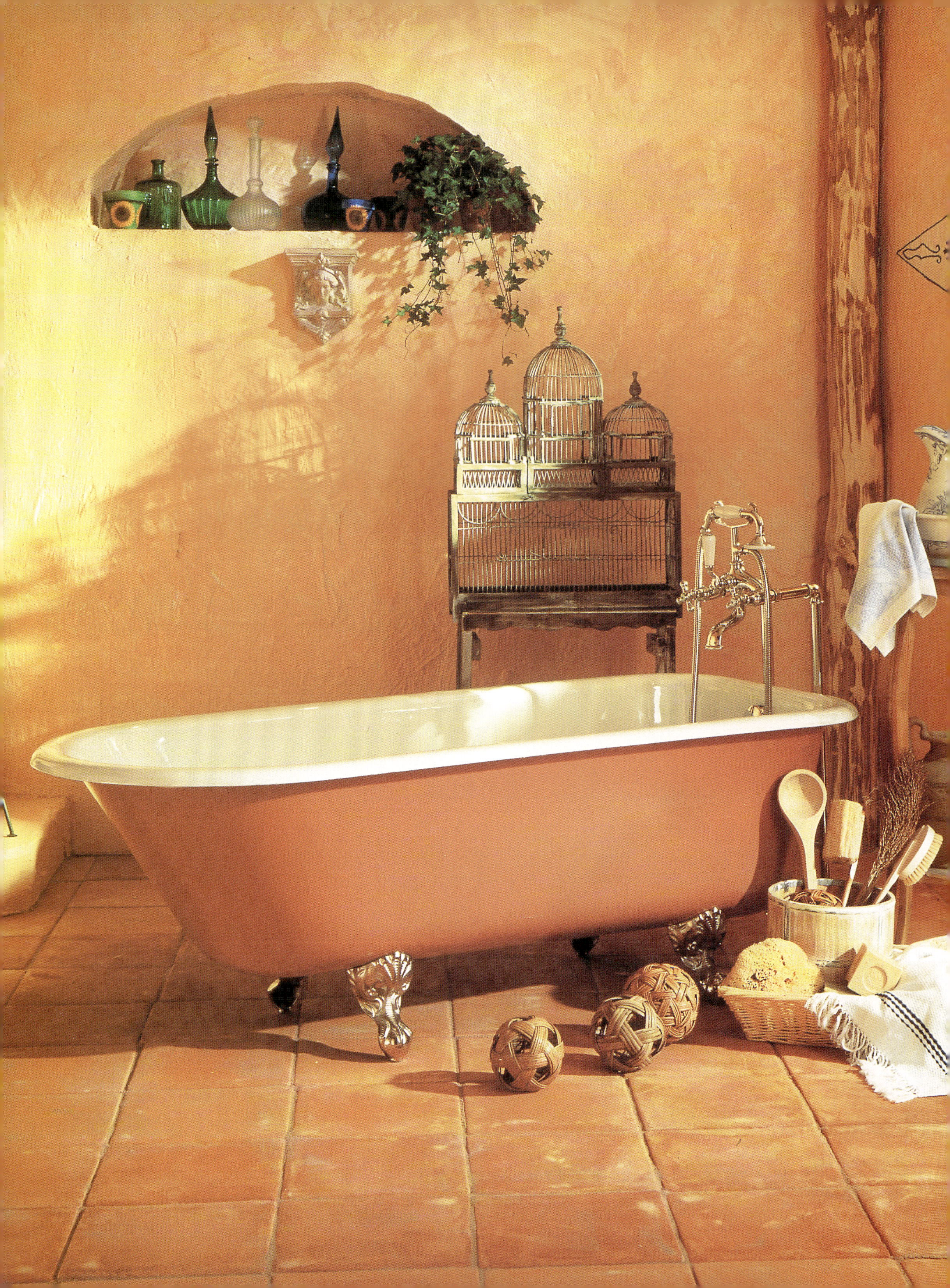

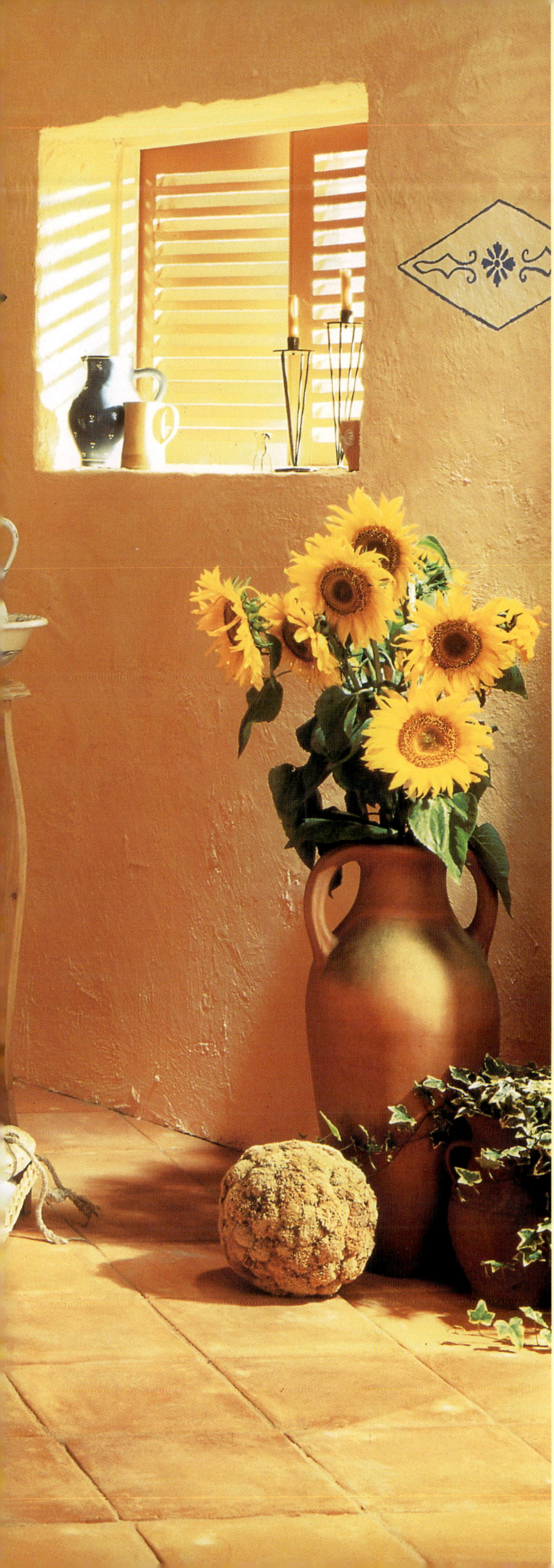

Creative Paint Finishing Techniques

Transform your home from floor to ceiling with these 45 easy-to-master decorative finishes

Ray Bradshaw

CHARTWELL BOOKS, INC.

A QUARTO BOOK

Published in 2005 by Chartwell Books
A division of Book Sales, Inc.
114 Northfield Avenue
Edison, New Jersey 08837, USA

ISBN 0-7858-1946-0

This book was designed and produced by
Quarto Publishing plc
The Old Brewery
6 Blundell Street
London N7 9BH

Senior Project Editor: Gerrie Purcell
Copy Editors: Honor Head, Jean Coppendale
Art Editor: Sally Bond
Designer: James Lawrence
Photographers: Martin Norris, Paul Forrester, Colin Bowling
Illustrators: Ian Sidaway, Dave Kemp
Picture Research: Henny Letailleur
Editorial Director: Pippa Rubinstein
Art Director: Moira Clinch

Typeset by Type Technique, London
Manufactured by Regent Publishing Services Ltd, Hong Kong
Printed by SNP Leefung Printers Ltd, China

PUBLISHER'S NOTE

The author, copyright holder and publishers have made every effort to ensure that all instructions in this book are safe and accurate, but they cannot accept legal liability for errors or omissions or for any resulting injury, loss or damage to either property or person whether direct or consequential and howsoever arising. They would like to draw particular attention to the following:

When handling, using or storing paints, mediums, implements or any products mentioned in this book it is strongly advised to always follow the manufacturer's instructions; always store chemicals or similar products securely in their original containers, or clearly marked non-food containers, and keep them well out of reach of children and animals. When using sprays or aerosol cans ensure eyes and exposed skin are protected. Always work in a well-ventilated area.

CONTENTS

Introduction

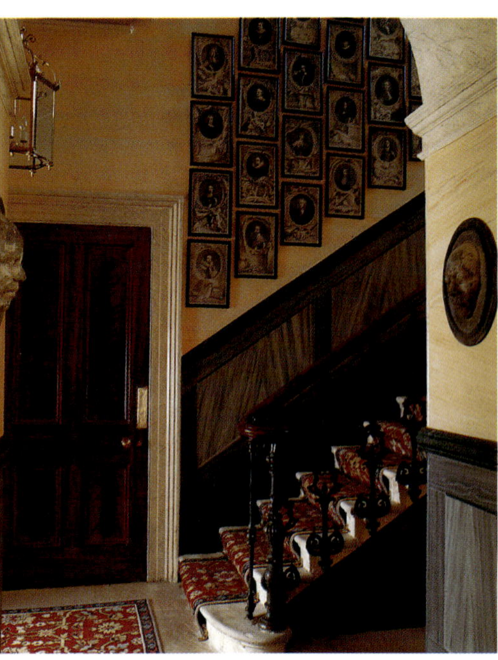

▲ *In this hallway several different effects create a feeling of warmth and richness. The door has the look of flame mahogany, while the frame and the area above the picture rail has a faux marble effect. The walls have the look of sandstone and below the dado rail are faux woodgrain panels.*

Over the centuries the use of paint effects has become more and more widespread. Today they can be seen not only as beautiful decorative additions to the interiors and exteriors of many of the world's great palaces, stately homes, hotels and commercial buildings, but they are also being used more and more in our homes. The re-creation of the most beautiful marbles, rich, sumptuous fabrics, exotic woods and semi-precious stones is often combined with simple creative effects such as colorwashing, sponging and stenciling.

As you progress through this book you will begin to understand the versatility of paint and will be ready to start creating your own paint effects. Use this book as a guide to choosing appropriate techniques or finishes, to preparing your particular project and the way to obtain the best results. The main requirements for success when dealing with any broken colorwork are confidence, understanding, versatility and initiative. We hope that this book will help to create inspiration and make these exciting paint effects readily and easily achievable.

Before starting on any of the techniques we show you the tools, brushes and basic equipment that you will need to produce these fantastic effects as well as some of the less expensive alternatives. Care and maintenance of your tools is essential and good results will make it worthwhile. Understanding the uses and properties of paints and glazes is also important and tables and diagrams have been included to help make some of the rather technical data more understandable. The color wheel is included and this will help you to understand the uses of color and differentiate between tints and shades. Although color is a very personal choice, it can easily make or break a decorative scheme. Color can create illusions both wanted and unwanted unless you have a basic knowledge of its uses. The final quality of the effect is also dependent upon the preparation of the surface to which it is applied, as well as the way it is carried out and ultimately finished.

▶ *This formal dining room has been given a rather gothic look by the use of distressing to the walls and doors, and colorwashing to the ceiling.*

We have chosen around 45 broken-color effects that can be applied to ceilings, walls, floors, doors, units and window frames as well as architectural embellishments, moldings, dado rails and baseboards. They have been graded as basic or advanced according to ease of application and length of time needed to complete them. Each technique has been broken down into step-by-step procedures with comprehensive instructions and an accompanying picture to help you see what you are aiming at. In addition there are variations enabling you to gather more ideas on how to mix and match each technique with variations of itself or with other separate finishes. Remember mixing and matching can lead to some wonderfully vibrant, individual and elegant schemes which can be very satisfying.

Throughout the book you will find selections of photographs which show many of these techniques in actual settings. These have been produced by some of the world's top interior designers and decorators and show what can be done with practice, understanding, patience and above all confidence. Nothing is beyond reach.

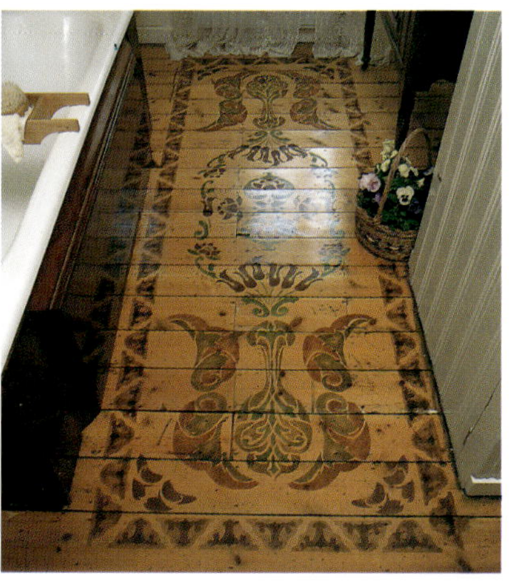

▲ *The use of woodstain inlay on this bathroom floor has created a truly exotic look.*

Read the book, understand and enjoy it. and do not be afraid to experiment with ideas of your own. We hope that by using it as a guide for producing many wonderful paint effects in your home you will be inspired to carry out many more hours of decorative work which will provide you with lasting pleasure and satisfaction.

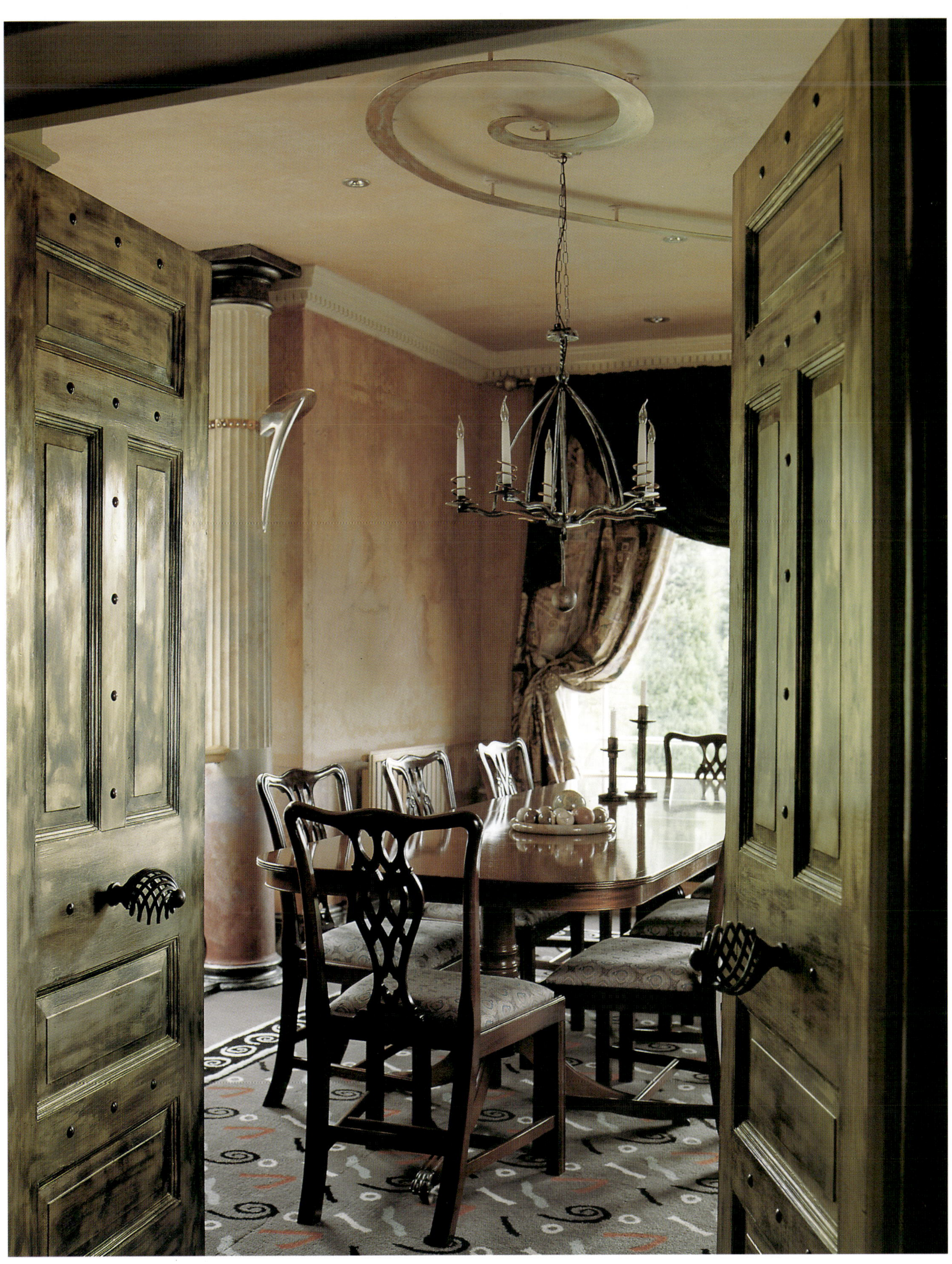

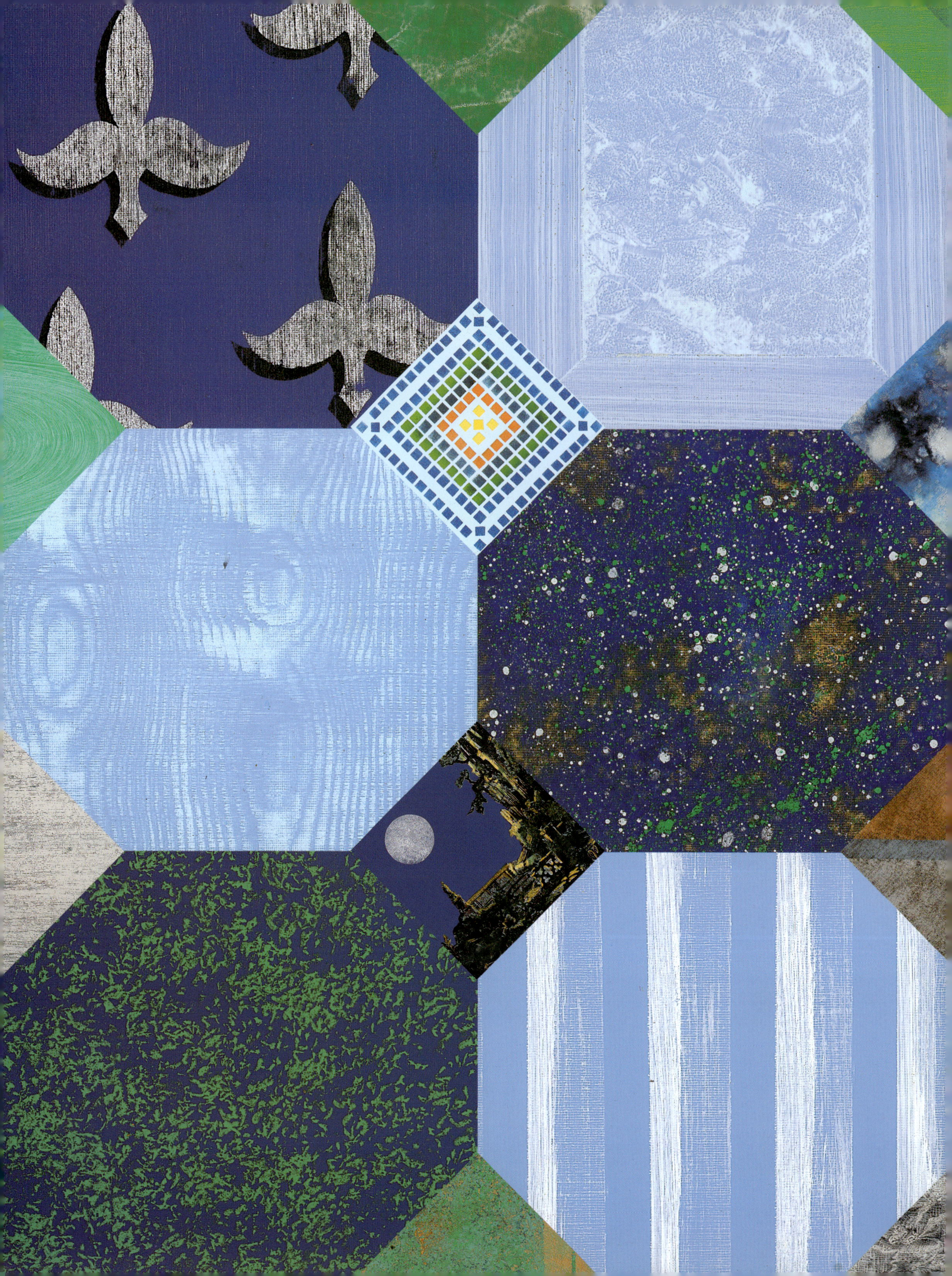

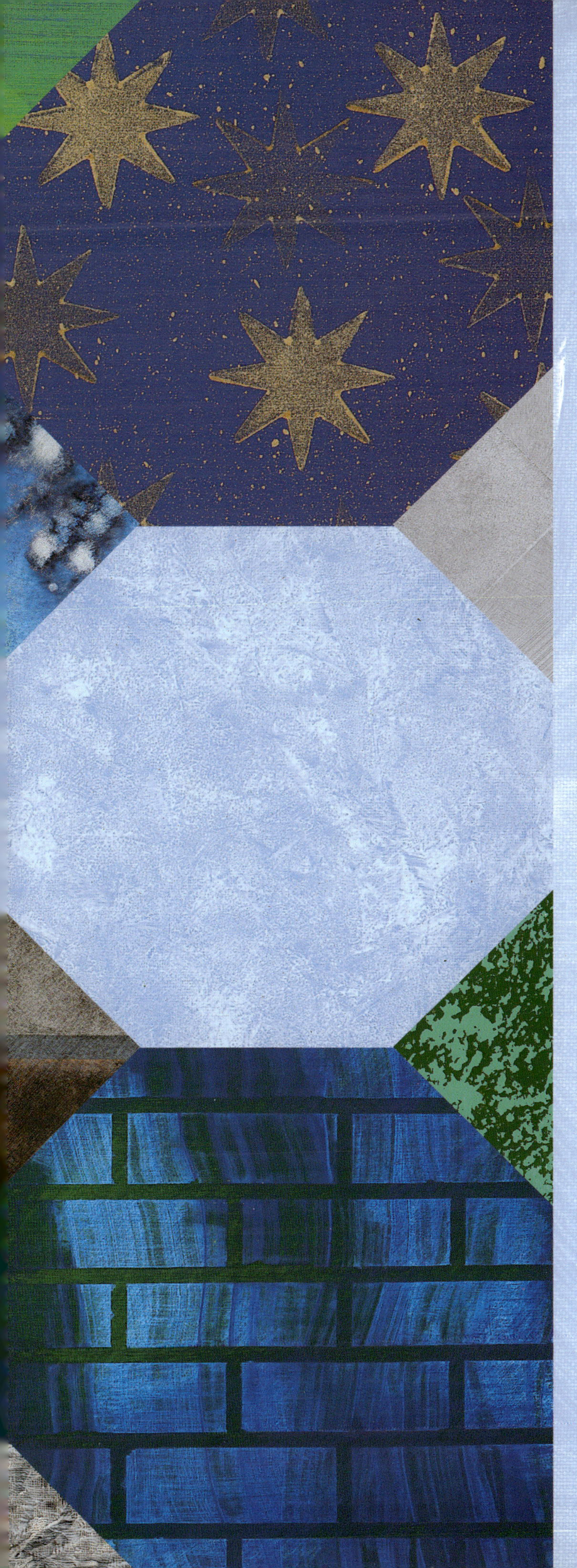

Before you Start

After much deliberation with friends and family you have decided on the paint effect that you want and it is time to start. Allow enough time to complete the project and check that you have at hand the correct equipment and materials to achieve the required finish. Can you work from a ladder if necessary with a paint pot in one hand and a brush in the other? Is the room being decorated empty at the required time? If the answer to these questions is yes, then start by practicing on a small area or a prepared board first. This will eliminate any mistakes that may happen while working on the real thing. If things go wrong do not give up, simply wipe away the mistakes and start again. Above all be patient, relax and enjoy what you are doing. Creating these simple finishes will hopefully give you endless years of pleasure and satisfaction.

Basic equipment

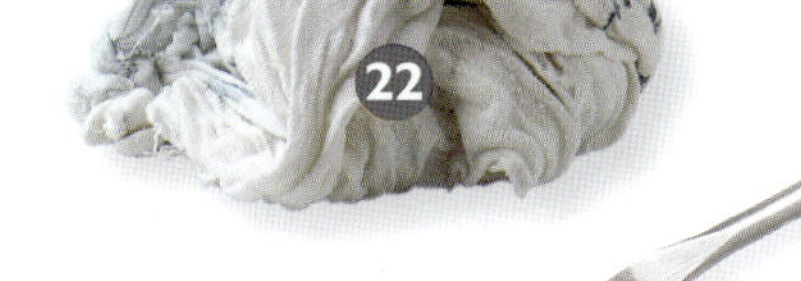

The equipment you will require for each technique can be categorized under five separate headings from protecting and preparing the surroundings and surface, to the final finishing and cleaning up once the job is complete. Most of the terms are also illustrated. By reading these next few sections carefully and noting the safety instructions for each piece of equipment (safe fixing of ladders and so on,) your own safety and that of your surroundings is ensured.

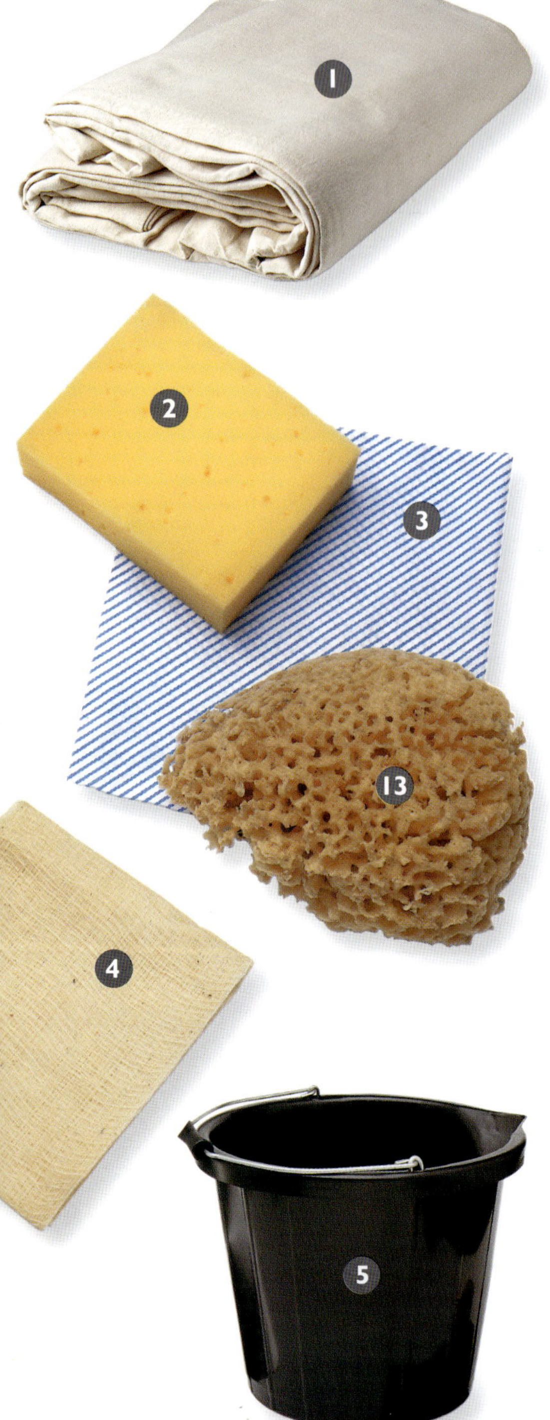

Preparation and cleaning

Before starting any job make sure that you are wearing some type of protective clothing appropriate to the job.

1 Dust covers *To protect all vulnerable areas or furniture or use plastic sheeting available from decorator stores. This should prevent any accidental and possibly irreversible damage to the room and its contents. Old newspapers can be used as an alternative to sheeting but newsprint does not cover larger areas so easily and can leave marks.*

2 Synthetic (cellulose) sponge *This is always good for wiping down the surface that you are preparing and is easily rinsed out.*

3 Lint-free cloths *These are cloths that will not shed their fibers during use. You will need them to wipe down and remove dust from any surfaces before you start work. They will also be used to dampen in the relevant solvent, and to remove quickly any mistakes or mishaps that may occur in the course of applying the technique.*

4 "Tack cloth" *This is cloth impregnated with linseed oil. It will free the surface of any dust particles safely and completely.*

5 Bucket of fresh water *This is a good idea to have nearby as it can be used to clean up any accidents that may occur when you are using water-based or oil-based products, as well as removing any splashes to your skin or eyes or clothes. if you are using products that have a solvent other than water, have a supply handy in case of accidents but always follow all manufacturers' instructions.*

Preparing surfaces

For any technique to be completed easily and professionally thorough preparation is essential. This part of a project is not very exciting, but it must always be done really well to ensure an excellent result, and also to prevent any chance of unwanted reactions between stages that will spoil your final effect.

6 Cleaner or a proprietary degreasing agent (sugar soap) *This type of cleaner should be applied to the surface before you start work. Rinse thoroughly afterward.*

7 Sandpaper *Existing paint or varnish must be removed completely or at least any flaking sections removed. You should stock various grades of sandpaper for different tasks.*

8 Sanding block *This will make the job of sanding larger areas a great deal easier as equal pressure is applied over the surface of the flat block.*

9 Steel wool *Available in various grades can also be used to "key" the surface before you start to paint and this will also help to remove any flaky paint or varnish.*

10 Scrapers *These are another essential tool for both stripping off paint and varnish (when using proprietary stripping products), and for eliminating larger flaking areas. They are also ideally suited for filling any cracks and holes when using store-bought fillers.*

11 Wire brushes *Depending on the type of surface and its condition, wire brushes (both stiff and fine) are also ideal for preparing the surface as well as removing any rust and so on, from metallic surfaces.*

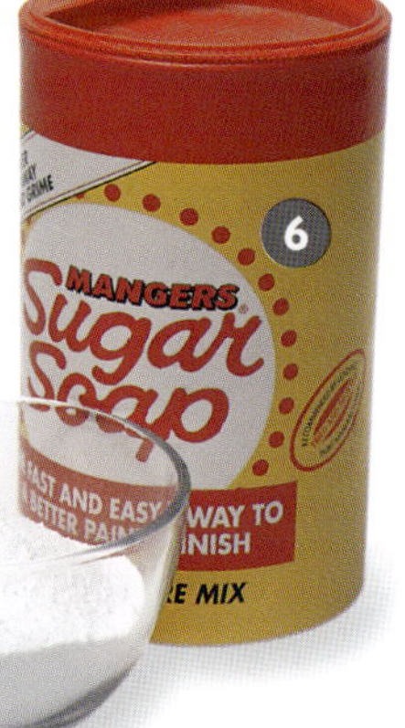

General equipment

Ladder *This is an essential piece of equipment if you are doing a ceiling, wall or picture rail. For most average rooms this would be a 3 to 4 step-ladder. These are available from most general stores. A lightweight aluminum ladder is most suitable as they are strong yet easily portable. When using ladders make sure that they are fixed securely before climbing.*

12 Masking tape *Used to mask off areas which need to be protected from the paint finish being applied. Also used to create stripes and for creating perfectly straight lines. Low-tack is best.*

Brown paper tape *A self-adhesive strip along one side makes this tape useful for protecting ceilings and corners as well as carpet edges.*

13 Natural or marine sponges *Necessary for the sponging technique and which can also be used for stenciling, texturing surfaces and for breaking up glazes.*

14 Sharp scissors, craft knife or scalpel *Essential when applying découpage, but also for creating stencils and for cutting straight edges.*

15 Quality steel tape measure *Important for precise measuring (available in both imperial and metric and in most cases both).*

16 Pencils *For accurate measurement and for for achieving fine straight edges as in stripes. Remember that pencil marks are harder to remove than chalk and can damage the surface. They are ideal when masking tape is used and they can be painted over as part of the technique.*

17 Chalk *Used for drawing in lines. Chalk is easily removed and will not mark the surface.*

18 Straight edge or steel ruler *Required for lining and obtaining accurate lines.*

19 Plumb-bob or plumbline *Essential for obtaining perfect vertical lines.*

20 Buckets *A range of suitably-sized buckets for washing brushes in or for mixing paints (this may include old plastic containers such as those used for ice cream).*

Palettes *Preferably white, to show accurate color is used for mixing small amounts of paint or glaze, and can also be used for resting brushes.*

Paint tray and roller *As an alternative to brushes. Makes painting larger areas easier and quicker.*

21 Paint tin opener or a flat-head screwdriver *For opening paint tins. Do not use keys or a coin as this can cause accidents as the grip pressure is not correct.*

22 Paper (kitchen) towel, cottonrags *For cleaning up and wiping down drips etc., from the paint tins.*

Measuring

Many of the effects shown in this book require accurate measuring both vertically and horizontally. If this is not carried out correctly, disappointing and costly mistakes can happen.

Cleaning up

Dust particles should be totally removed by vacuum after preparation is complete. First, dust should not be inhaled and second, if you are working in a well-ventilated area the particles will adhere to the surface of the wet paint.

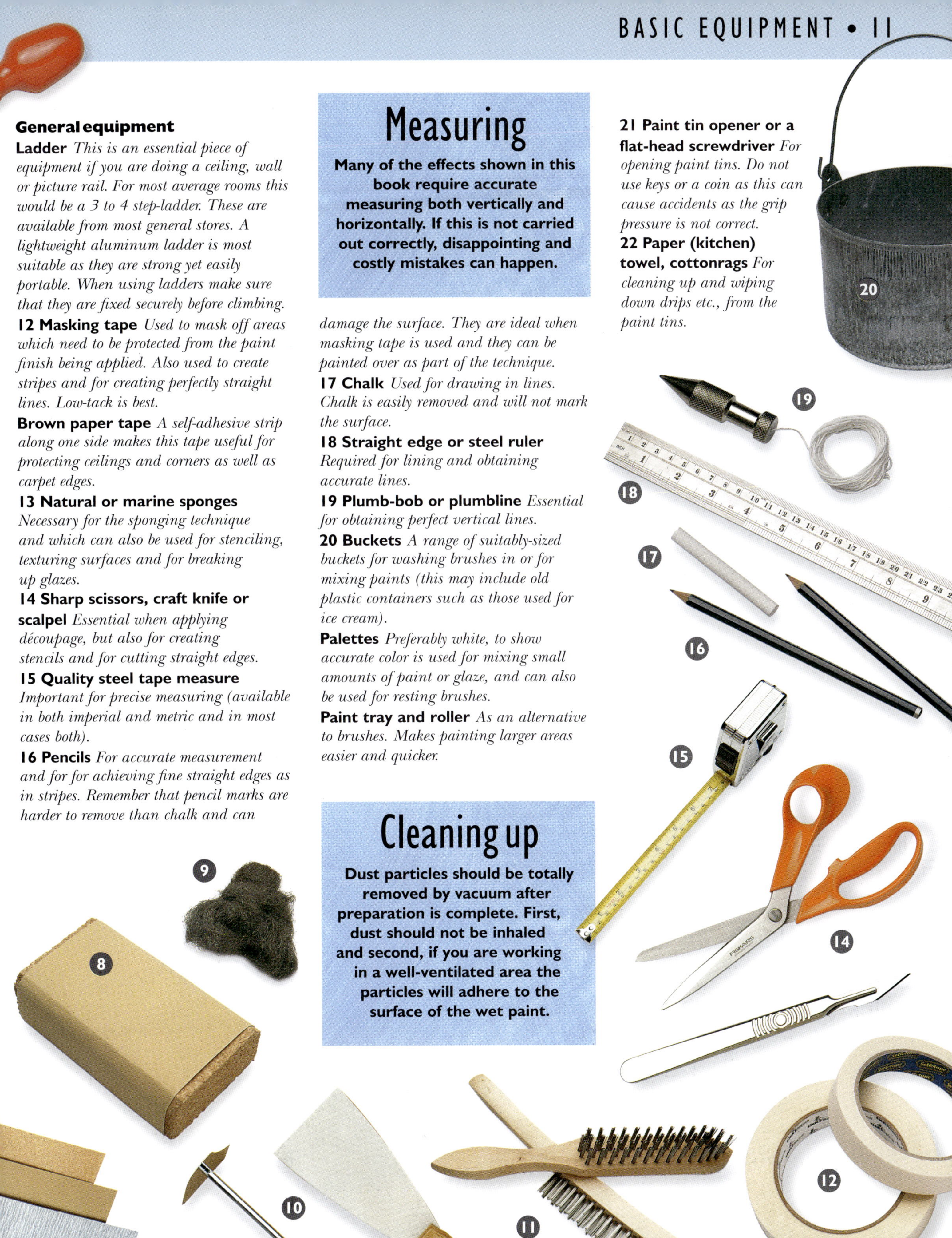

Brushes

The secret of success when applying paint techniques is controlled by the use of the correct or best brush for the particular finish being applied. Is it the correct size for the job? Will it easily reach into corners or produce a straight edge if required? Will it produce a fine line?

A good basic rule when choosing brushes is to go for the best brush you can afford for the particular job. It will pay for itself in the end, especially if it is cared for correctly! Remember also that brushes are composed of different materials. Nylon or synthetic brushes are generally for use with water-based paints while the oil-based paints are generally used with bristle or hair brushes.

Some brushes, especially those made of natural bristle, can be expensive, but they are well worth the outlay! Stippling brushes and badger hair softening brushes can be extremely expensive, and although cheaper alternatives can be used it is not advisable. Always buy the best quality you can afford to ensure quality results.

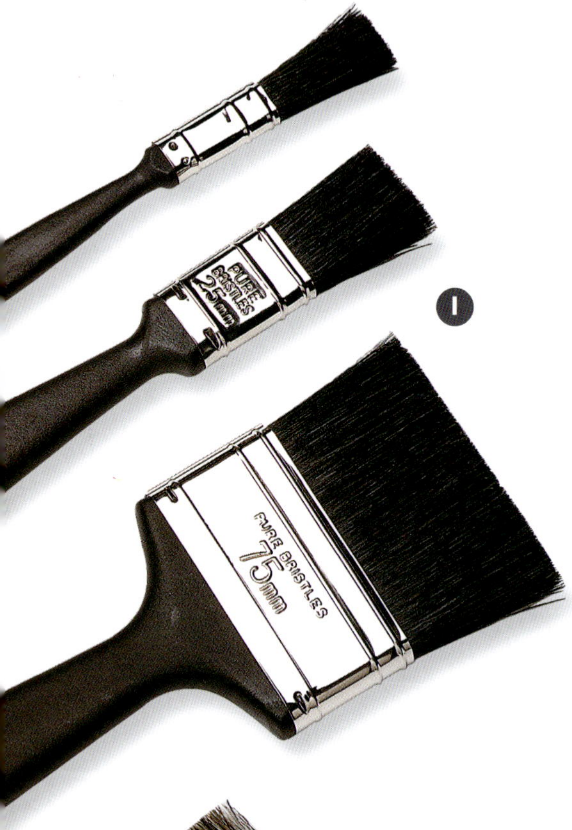

1

3

2

4

Types of brushes

1 Bristle basecoat brushes *come in a wide range of different sizes. For priming and undercoating it is best to use a straight-edge brush and for cutting in edges, a chisel-edge brush. Choose the size that is most suitable to the job—the largest that you feel comfortable with. A good range to purchase would be ½ in. (1.3 cm.), 1 in. (2.5 cm.), 2 in. (5 cm.), 4 in. (10 cm.), or 5 in. (12.5 cm.).*

2 Softening brushes *such as the high quality, badger hair softener are very expensive. A hog hair softener or dusting brush is a cheaper alternative but its primary use is to remove excess dust before you start painting.*

3 Dragging brushes *are long-bristled brushes that are used for the dragging and graining techniques. An alternative would be an ordinary basecoat brush but the effect is less subtle.*

4 Sponge applicators *are ideal for small areas as they show no brush strokes. They are excellent for cutting in on panels and for working in tight corners.*

5 Lining brushes *e.g. sword liners, are an essential tool for line and other decorative applications. They hold the paint in long bristles and allow easy flow. They are also ideal for marbling. Good after care is essential as with all these brushes. Build up a collection starting with sizes 0, 1 and 3.*

6 Fitch brushes *are usually made of hog hair and come in shapes such as round, oval or flat, and can be chiselled or flat. They are well suited to cutting in and for applying primary veins when marbling etc. Start with ¼-½ in. (0.63-1.3 cm.) round and ½ in. (1.3 cm.) flat, and possibly a ½-¾ in. (1.3-1.9 cm.) chiseled.*

7 Varnishing brushes *come in a wide range of sizes. They are thickly bristled and can be flat or domed. Ideally purchase a 2 in. (5 cm.) flat brush.*

8 Mottling brushes *come in squirrel or hog hair and are used in graining techniques. A good starter would be a 2 in. (5 cm.) brush.*

9 Stenciling brushes *come flat or domed and in many sizes. Flat brushes work well when a stippling motion is used. The domed variety are good for soft, exquisite shading. Begin with a ½ in. (1.3 cm.) flat and a ½-¾ in. (1.3-1.9 cm.) domed.*

10 Toothbrushes *are excellent for use in spattering techniques. Good stiff bristles help to control the paint flow.*

11 Stippling brushes *come in a variety of shapes and sizes that produce different textural effects. They can be made of bristle or rubber and this dictates price.*

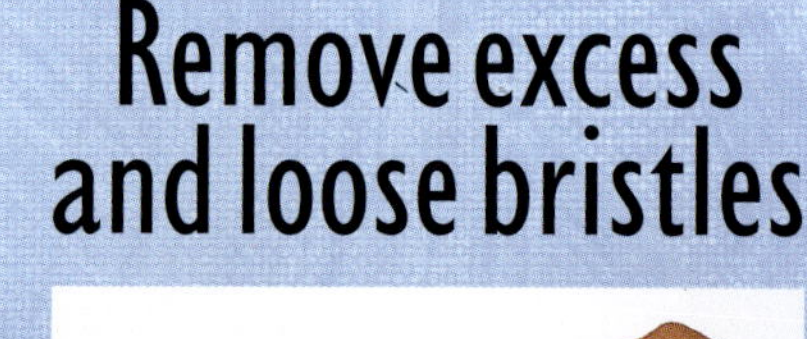

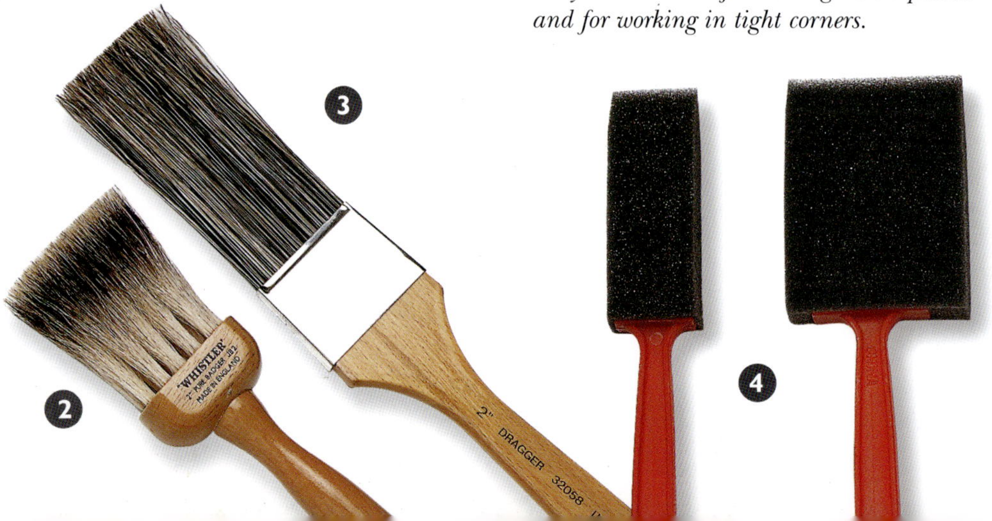

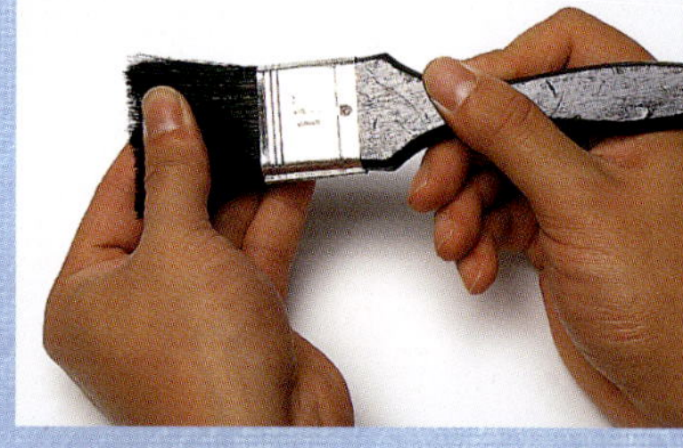

Remove excess bristles by gently brushing the bristles with your fingers from the ferrule downward, or use a comb and gently pass it down the bristles.

Care of brushes

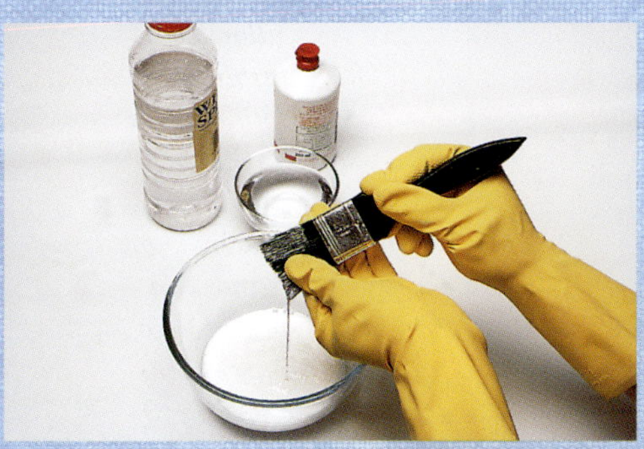

Cleaning *Oil-based paint: Use two containers of solvent and wear protective gloves. Dip brush in and work out paint from ferrule downward until clean. Use second container of clean solvent and repeat. Wash brush in detergent and rinse in fresh water. Water-based paint: Use same technique as above removing paint under running water. Apply soap and rinse.*

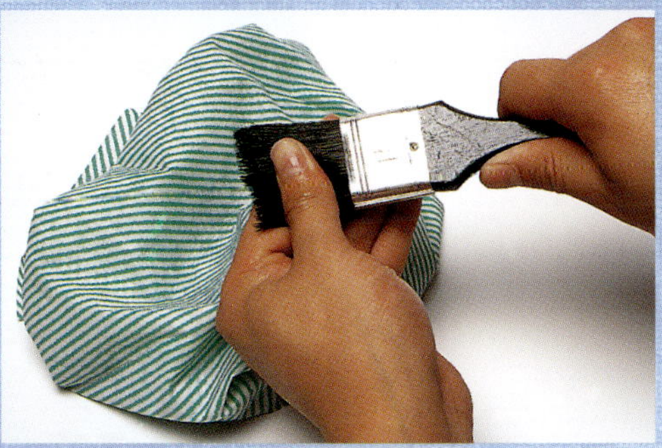

Drying *Carefully squeeze along bristles from ferrule down with your finger to remove moisture. Do not work up or against bristles as it can cause damage.*

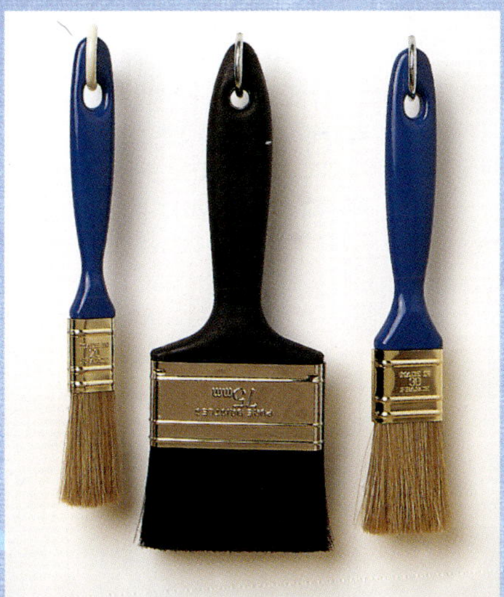

Storing *Hang brushes, bristles down, from a suitable rail or sit them upright in clear containers. Do not over crowd as this will damage the bristles.*

Loading a paintbrush
After decanting a small amount of paint into a clean container, dip the brush into the paint up to about ⅔ of the bristle length. Wipe off all excess paint on the inside rim of the container.

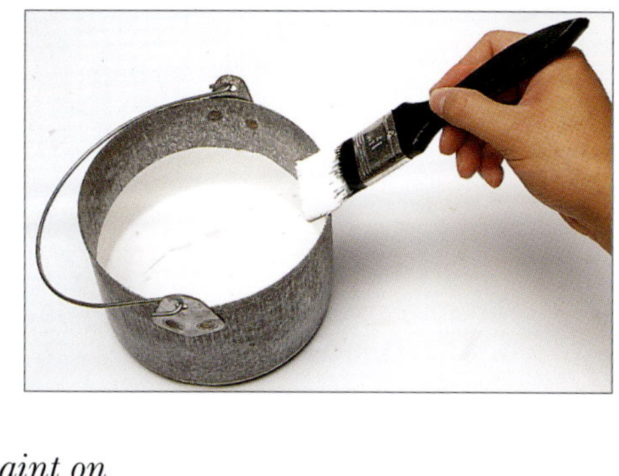

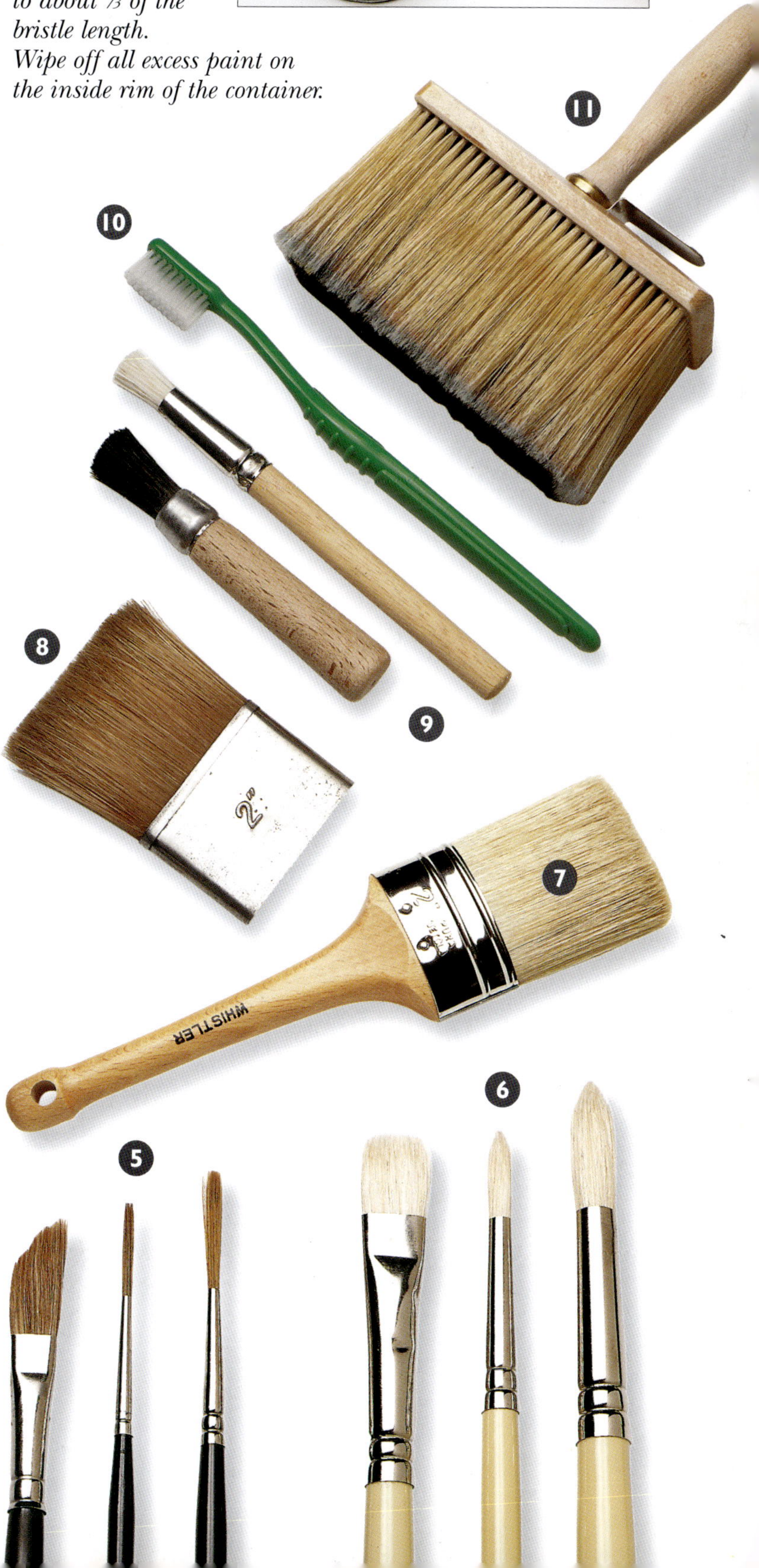

Paints

The techniques described in this book use a variety of paints, both oil- and water-based depending on the finish required. Paints such as acrylic eggshell are now much more user-friendly. However, always read all the manufacturer's information about use and content before you buy. Water-based paints such as latex (vinyl silk emulsion) and simulated milk paint, are more eco-friendly and can be cleaned off brushes with water instead of turpentine or mineral spirits (white spirit). However, each type of paint has its own merits and for this reason specific paints have been chosen specially for each technique.

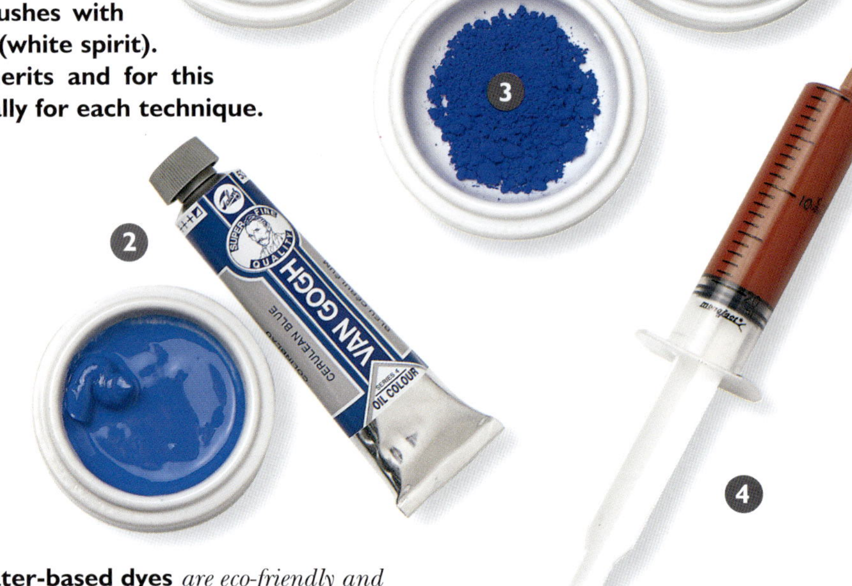

Types of paint

Oil-based undercoat *is available as an undercoat and primer combined. It is used before applying a basecoat, especially on raw wood (depending on technique). It is now available with no added lead.*

Oil-based eggshell paint *is mainly used for woodwork and walls. It is slow drying and gives a wipeable mid-sheen finish. It is particularly good for covering color surfaces. When working with this paint be sure there is adequate ventilation. Solvent: turpentine or mineral spirits (white spirit).*

Oil-based gloss paint *is used as a finishing coat on woodwork. Unsuitable for use with paint effect work. Solvent: turpentine or mineral spirits (white spirit).*

Latex *(Vinyl-silk emulsion) is an ideal base for walls to be given a decorative paint finish. A vast range of colors is available and it is quick drying. It gives excellent coverage but is easily damaged.*

Water-based acrylic eggshell paint *is a user-friendly version of oil-based eggshell. It gives good coverage.*

1 Artists' acrylic paints *are available in strong colors and are ideal for tinting water-based glazes used for broken color effects.*

2 Artists' oil colors *are used for tinting oil glazes for broken color work and oil-based marbling effects, but can be expensive.*

3 Powder pigments *are used for tinting glazes and paints and give intense color.*

4 Pigment syringe, *available from DIY stores, is used for tinting paints.*

5 Simulated milk paint *has a very soft, flat finish similar to limewash, and gives a "dusty" appearance. It is water soluble. It will need an additional protective coat if it is to be subject to a lot of wear and tear. Excellent for use on furniture and walls.*

6 Water-based dyes *are eco-friendly and are excellent for woodstaining and colorwashing. They do need varnishing.*

7 Stencil paints *come in a good color range, are quick drying and can be used for tinting acrylic glaze. Solvent: water.*

Metallic paints *are for interior and exterior use. Water-based paints will need two to three coats. The spirit-based and lacquer-based paints dry very quickly.*

Woodstain *highlights the grain of wood and is available in either spirit- or water-based versions. Plain woodstains are available, as well as a range of colors.*

Solvents

The solvent of a paint or varnish is the base which is used for diluting the paint and cleaning the tools used. Solvents can be water, mineral spirits (white spirit), turpentine or methylated spirits. Read all manufacturer's instructions fully before buying or using any solvents. The solvent for all water-based and acrylic products is water. Mineral spirits (white spirit) or turpentine are the solvents for oil-based products, and methylated spirits is the solvent for shellac (knotting solution) and enamel varnishes.

Rules for mixing paint

Paints can be mixed mechanically at your local decorator store. But although there is a vast range of colors to choose from, you may not find the exact shade you want. By buying the closest color and tinting it with stainers, artists' colors and other tinting agents, you can achieve the shade you require. Always make sure that the solvent base in both paint and tinting agent is the same. When tinting or mixing add a little color at a time and stir thoroughly. You may find it easier to dilute the tinting agent with a little of the relevant solvent first as this will help to achieve an even color. Always mix enough paint to complete the job as matching will be almost impossible.

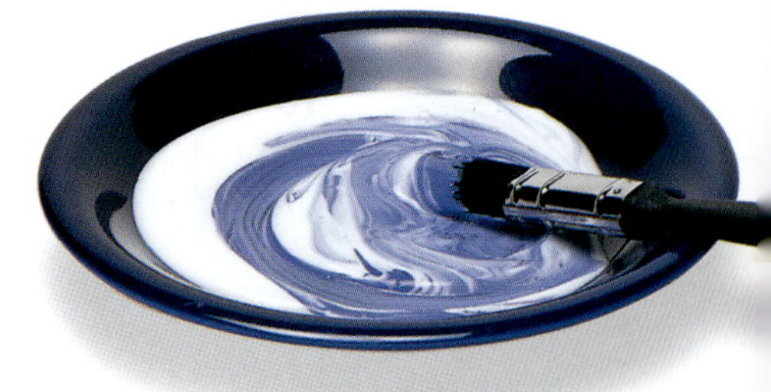

PAINT TYPE	SOLVENT	COVERAGE PER LITER	DRYING TIME	USE ON	COLOR RANGE
latex (vinyl-silk emulsion)	water	46-52 square feet (14-16 square meters)	2-4 hours	walls and furniture	extensive
simulated milk paint	water	32-43 square feet (10-13 square meters)	very quick 1 hour	walls and furniture	limited
oil-based eggshell	mineral spirits (white spirit)	49-55 square feet (15-17 square meters)	touch dry 4-6 hours dry 18-24 hours	woodwork and walls	extensive
acrylic eggshell	water	39-46 square feet (12-14 square meters)	4-6 hours	woodwork and walls	extensive
metallic paint	water/turpentine mineral spirits (white spirit)	see instructions on product	very quick	metal, walls and woodwork	limited
stencil paint acrylic	water	excellent	almost immediate	walls and furniture	extensive
gloss paint	mineral spirits (white spirit)	49-55 square feet (15-17 square meters)	touch dry 4-6 hours dry 16-18 hours	woodwork	extensive
oil-based undercoat	mineral spirits (white spirit)	46-52 square feet (14-16 square meters)	touch dry 2-6 hours dry 14-16 hours	bare wood prior to basecoating	limited

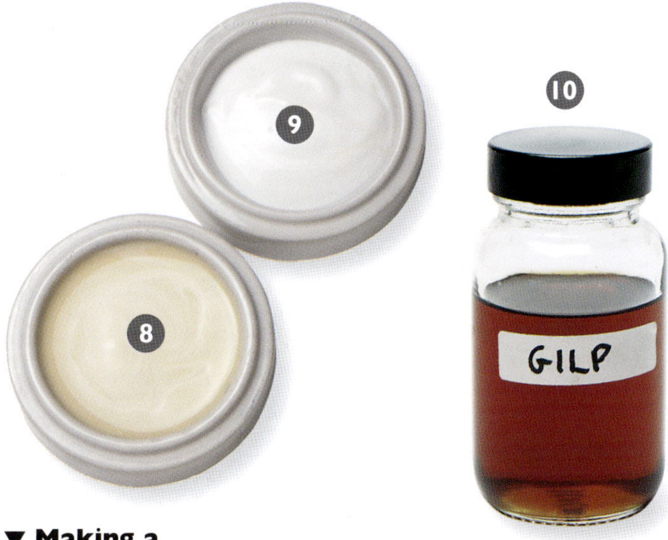

▼ Making a glaze
The glaze is the transparent layer of color used over a basecoat. You can use oil- and water-based mediums. or thin the paint with the relevant solvent to the required consistency. Apply as a glaze.

Glazing mediums

8 Transparent oil glaze *used for oil-based paint effect glazing. Gives more working time but tends to yellow with age. Dilute glaze with mineral spirits (white spirit). Add tint with oil colors or universal stainers.*

9 Acrylic glazing medium *is non-yellowing and water and heat resistant. it is tinted with acrylic colors for decorative glaze work. It gives a short working time, about 15 to 30 minutes.*

10 Gilp *is used as the floating medium for marbling. Mix together 1 part boiled linseed oil, 1 part pure mineral spirits (turpentine or white spirit) and 1/20th liquid driers. Store in an airtight container.*

Safety procedures

As with all paints, varnishes and glazes, always read the manufacturers' instructions before starting work. Certain products advise the use of protective clothing such as overalls, old shirts, goggles and dust masks, and in some cases protective footwear and gloves. You should also work in a well-ventilated area. This is particularly important when using spray paints. With techniques such as simple gilding with metal leaf and powders, ventilation can be a nuisance, but masks should be worn especially when dealing with very fine, bronzing powders. Do not throw crumpled rags soaked with volatile liquid substances into the bin – lay them out flat to dry before discarding. Always keep a bucket of water handy in case of accidents or splashes to the skin and eyes. Be careful and do not hurry—this is when accidents happen.

Safety tip
When using chemical strippers, both goggles and a mask are advised as well as other suitable protective clothing. Never hurry as this will lead to mistakes which can cause unwanted accidents.

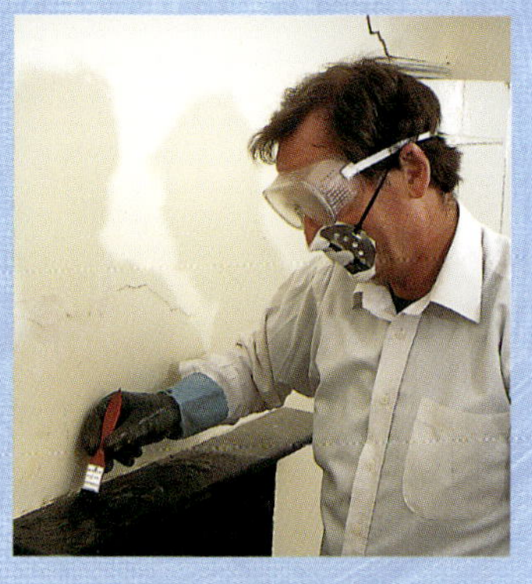

Using color

A great many words over a great many years have been spoken and written about the theory of color. The color you choose can make or break a project but the final choice should always be your own. Color creates moods, it can change the whole ambience of a setting—even the same color used as a solid block or as a broken color effect will vary immensely. Light from different sources will also change a color quite noticeably. When a color is used in conjunction with others it can easily change—blues can become gray or mauve, greens can become yellow or shades of blue. Different people view particular colors in very different and individual ways. A particular color scheme that works for one person may not work at all for another. Pursue your own ideas and do not be led by fashion trends or the opinions of friends and neighbors.

The color wheel

Discovered by Sir Isaac Newton in the 17th century, the color wheel comprises 12 colors. The primary colors are red, yellow and blue. The three secondary colors are formed by mixing equal parts of the three primaries for example, green (yellow and blue), violet (red and blue) and orange (red and yellow). Lastly there are the tertiary colors, which are obtained by mixing each primary color with its closest secondary. This mixing results in the six tertiaries as follows: yellow and orange, orange and red, violet and blue, violet and red, green and yellow and blue and green.

Red
Red-orange
Orange
Yellow-ornage
Yellow
Yellow-green
Green
Blue-green
Blue
Blue-violet
Violet
Red-violet

The use of tone

By varying the intensity of a pure color or "hue" we obtain a tone of that color which is lighter or darker. Some people find "pure" colors too overpowering; they find it easier to live with a tone. Tone is the lightness or darkness of a pure color. By adding white to a tone you obtain a tint, and by adding black you obtain a shade. A green or a blue or a red may all have the same tonal value if the same amount of white or black is added. When planning a color scheme it is easier to coordinate colors of the same tonal value unless you want to create a particularly vibrant and powerful look.

▼ *Color swatches help you to decide which colors coordinate well and work together in your particular room*

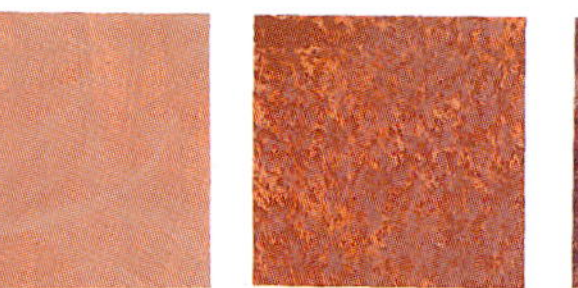

▼ **Different tones** *By the use of different colors, or hues, chosen from the same area of the color wheel, very powerful and exciting moods can be created. Warm and cosy, cool and enticing—the possibilities are endless.*

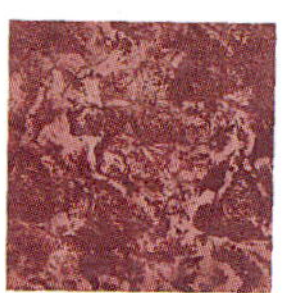

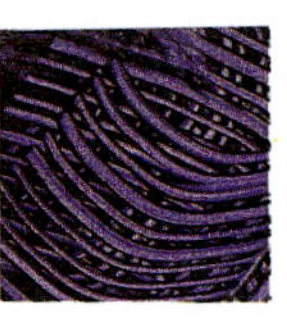

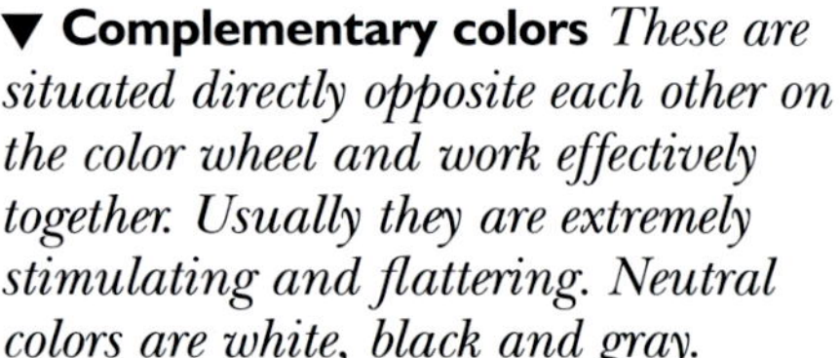

▼ **Complementary colors** *These are situated directly opposite each other on the color wheel and work effectively together. Usually they are extremely stimulating and flattering. Neutral colors are white, black and gray.*

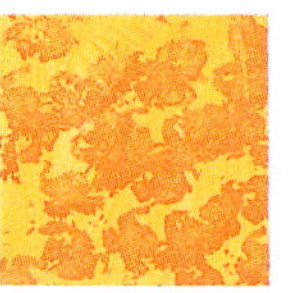

How color effects a room

The classification of colors into warm and cool does not necessarily stand true. Generally reds, yellows and oranges are classified as warm colors, and blues, greens and grays as cool. But there are warm blues, which contain more red, and also cool yellows which contain more green. Two blues together can be seen as both cool and warm.

As a general rule, warm colors will make a room seem smaller, whereas cool colors will give a more spacious feel. For example, a pale lemon will create a very soothing, airy and open feeling, whereas a dull yellow, although warm and vibrant, will reduce the apparent size of the room.

The amount of proportion of color used in a room, together with its position, will also affect both mood and space. Darker ceilings will substantially reduce a room's height, and dark walls will close them in, making the room more intimate. Dark color above a dado rail with light color below will reduce the height of the ceiling and may cause the overall affect to seem a little top heavy. By using the darker color below the dado, although it will "enclose" the room the lighter top walls and ceiling will give a feeling of the room being open and airy.

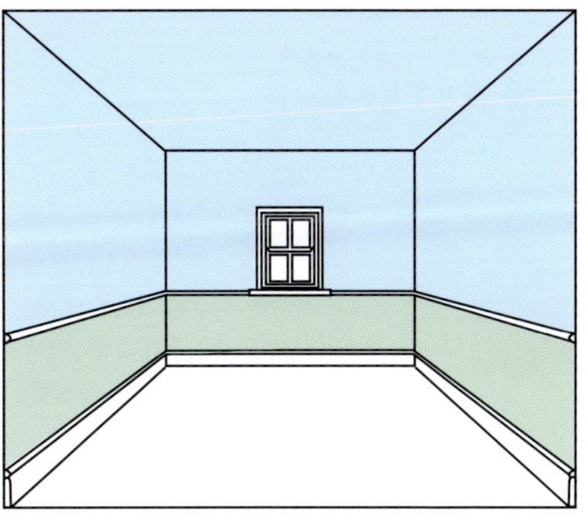

▲ *The use of two cool and light colors can create a feeling of spaciousness.*

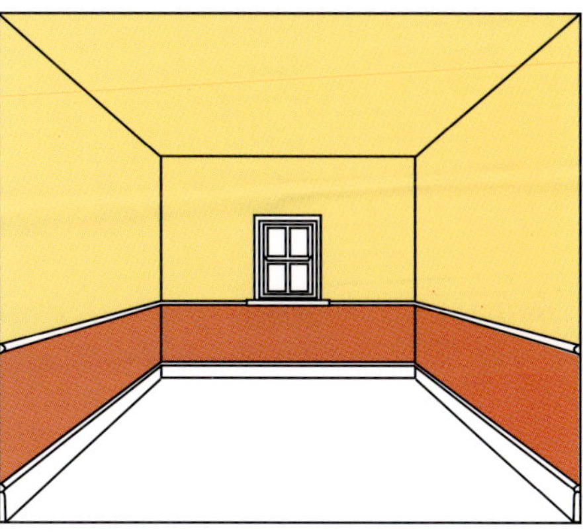

▲ *Using two warm colors together can create an intimate atmosphere.*

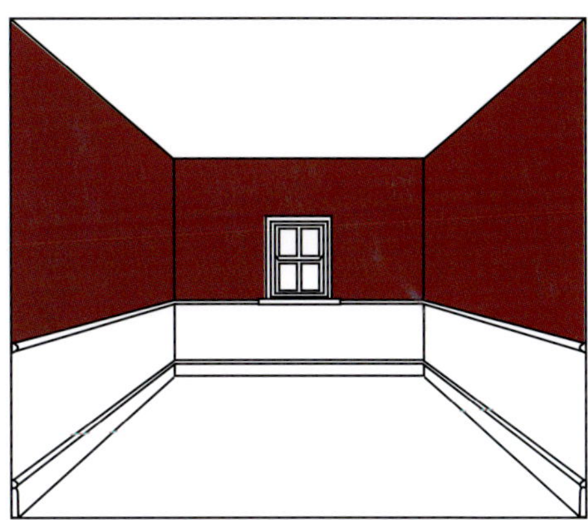

▲ *A dark color above a dado rail can make a room look a little top heavy.*

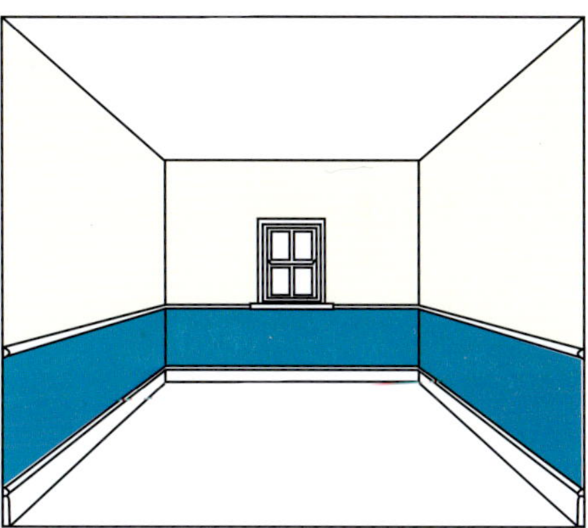

▲ *Dark colors below a dado rail enclose a room, light colors above give balance.*

Using color to create mood

Color means different things to different people. The moods or feelings it conjures up in someone depends on personal influences, up-bringing and geographical location. In general, the following guide may be of help. Bold and vibrant colors, such as reds, orange and yellow, are both warm and inviting, but can signal fear and danger. Yellow is the color of sunshine—it glows and brings light and happiness into our lives. Green conjures up images of woods and valleys, serenity, peace and tranquility, while the blues evoke the mystery of rivers and oceans. The earthy, subdued colors of sienna and ocher are soothing and comforting, solid and warm.

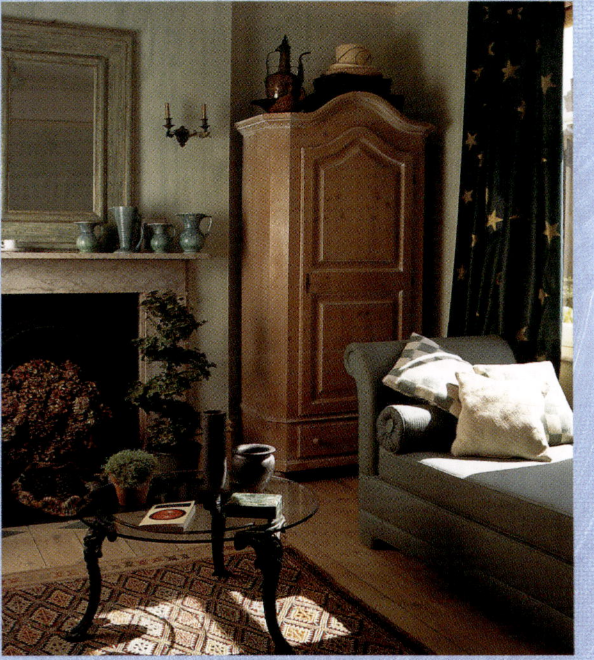

The soft, cool greens of the colorwashed walls together with the blending tones of the furnishings help give this room a feeling of calm tranquility.

How to choose a colorway

Ultimately the final choice of colors is a personal one. It may depend on various factors—personal preferences, the direction the room faces and the amount of natural light it receives, the overall function of the room, its size, and whether it is used often or very little. Do you want it to appear larger or smaller, intimate or airy. Finally, the existing furnishings may limit your color choice to a certain extent. A large budget will open up a whole range of possibilities, but if, however, the furniture and or the drapes are staying then possibly the choice of color or style of decor is a little more limited.

Preparation

The final result of any decorative technique will depend on the quality of the preparation work. Unfortunately most of us find this a nuisance, but hard work and dedication at this stage will only lead to a successful final finish. Some techniques do benefit from a less than smooth surface, colorwashing in particular, but this does not apply to most of the broken color work techniques.

Tidiness and keeping the work surface and surrounding areas clean and clear is essential. Make lists of all the tools and materials needed, and use only those that are required. Remove any unnecessary items from the area, including furniture if possible. Make sure you understand the technique and the products that you are going to be using before you start. Good preparation will save time and will eliminate costly and unnecessary mistakes.

Cleaning

It is important that the surface to be painted is cleaned thoroughly before any work is done. Grease should be treated with either a de-greasing agent (sugar soap) or similar cleaner following manufacturers' instructions. All dust and stray particles should be removed with a dusting brush or tack cloth and any excess vacuumed away completely before the job is started. This is crucial as dust will be blown around and may affect the wet paint surface. Wash the surface with clean water and allow to dry completely before beginning the work.

The use of strippers

All existing paint should be removed from the surface before beginning the work. If the surface is in good condition then sanding will be adequate. Begin by using coarse grade sandpaper and work down to fine-grade sandpaper. A sanding block will help. Fold the sandpaper to get into moldings. Rough paint or varnish should be removed completely with chemical strippers and a scraper, following manufacturer's instructions. A gel stripper is easier to use than liquid caustic soda.

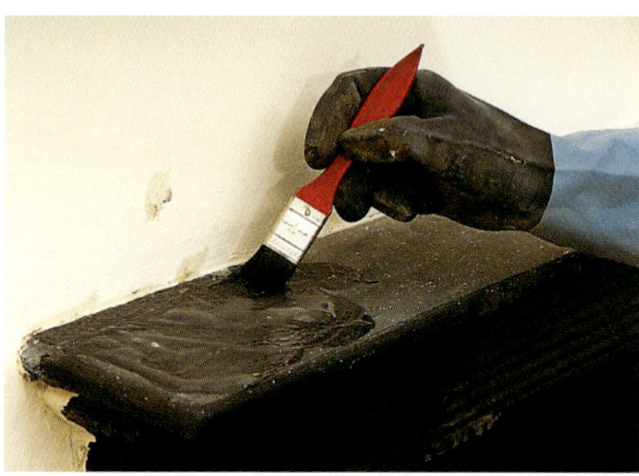

Chemical strippers

When using store-bought chemical strippers always wear adequate protective clothing, including acid-repellent gloves. Always work carefully and be sure that you do not splash yourself or damage any other surface.

Preparing a wall

The type of effect required will determine the exact preparation necessary to a wall, but whatever you are doing, old wallpaper should be removed completely and any cracks filled with filler and, when dry, sanded to a smooth finish. An undercoat or primer should be applied to seal the surface before basecoating. Paint quick drying shellac (knotting solution) over any newly-filled cracks to avoid color imperfection when applying the basecoat. If the walls are very damaged, apply lining paper before priming and basecoating.

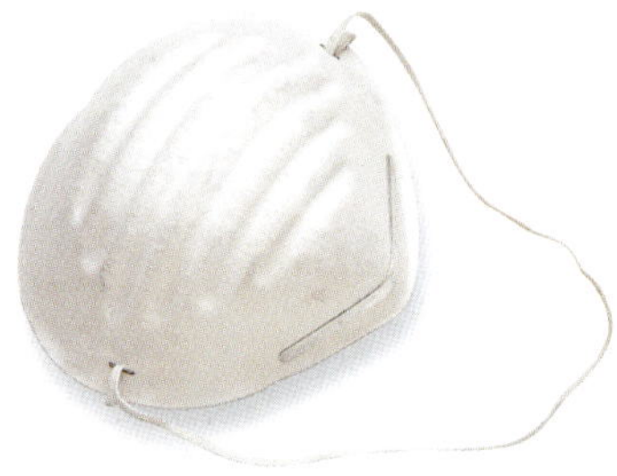

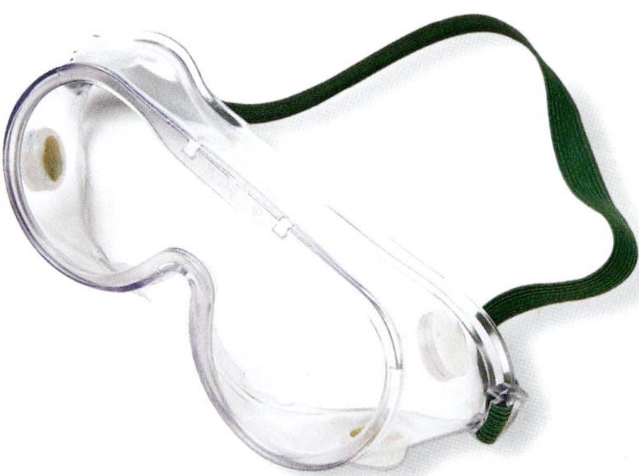

Extra protection

Wear a protective mask and goggles when applying chemical strippers to any surface.

Preparing metal

When preparing a metal surface, it is important that all rust is removed using steel wool or, if the rust is particularly bad, a wire brush followed by steel wool. Once sanded, remove all traces of dust before applying a coat of de-rusting solution (follow all safety guides. Allow to dry completely before applying at least one coat of metal primer. When dry, apply two or three coats of an oil-based paint such as eggshell in a basecoat color. You are now ready to continue with the paint effect. For small metal objects, you may find it easier to use spray paint. New metal may have a greasy layer to protect it from rust and this should be washed off with detergent.

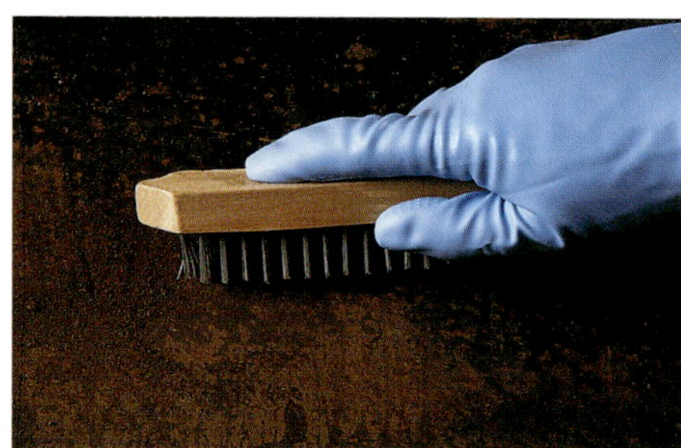

Cleaning

When painting metal, particularly old or rusty metal, always use adequate protection. With a stiff wire brush carefully remove all loose paint and rust from the surface before brushing away excess with a soft cloth.

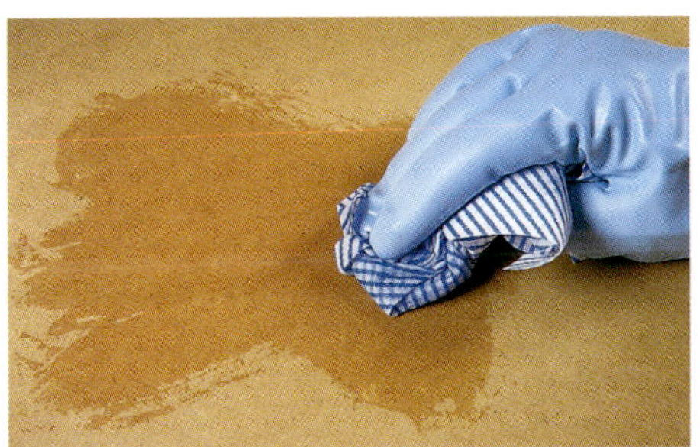

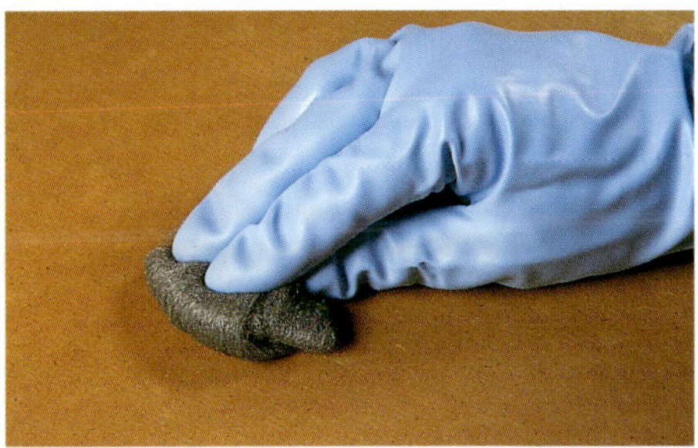

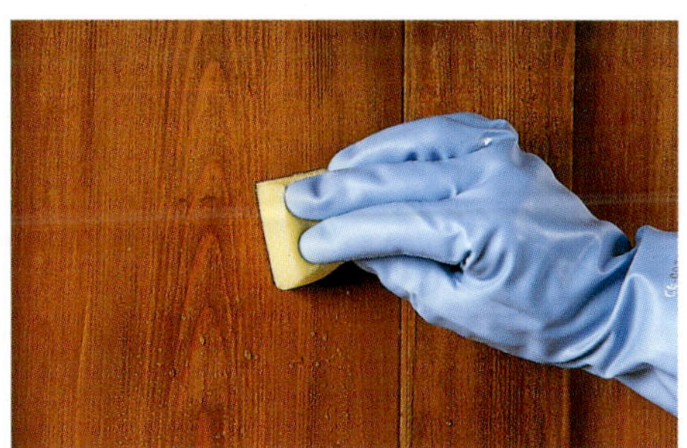

Using a de-greasing agent

1 *A store-bought de-greasing agent (sugar soap) should be used with care following manufacturers' instructions. It is ideal for cleaning or distressing.*

2 *Always wear protective clothing and rubber gloves. After each application clean down the surface with water. Steel wool can be used in combination with a de-greaser for particularly difficult jobs.*

General cleaning

For cleaning down surfaces such as cupboards and units, a kitchen scouring pad is as good as anything. If using toxic materials always wear adequate protection.

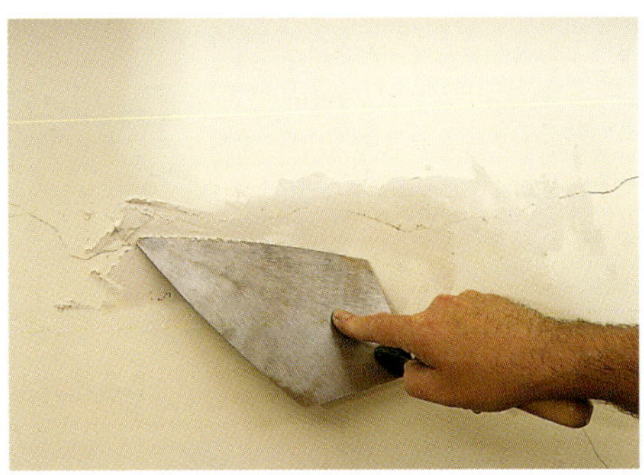

Filling cracks

When filling cracks in walls use a good quality filler and always follow manufacturers' instructions. Carefully fill the entire crack pushing the filler in with a trowel. Remember to leave a little excess on the surface to allow for shrinkage when drying. Sand smooth.

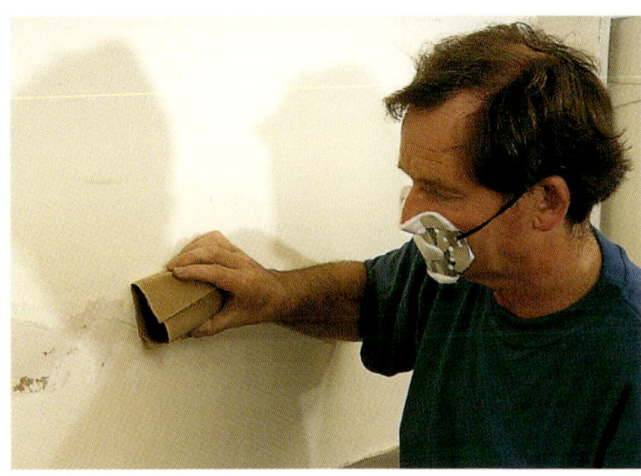

Safety

Always wear suitable protective clothing when carrying out any surface preparation. When sanding down surfaces it may be necessary to use a face mask to avoid any danger from the inhalation of fine dust.

Skimming

Certain techniques that require an extremely smooth surface, such as lacquering and marbling, may mean that skimming is necessary after priming. This is done with skimming plaster (spackle) and is extremely difficult to perfect. Using a skimming blade, pass the plaster across the surface filling all indentations. Use even, smooth movements. Wipe the blade clean and pass again over the surface. Slightly dampen the blade if necessary. Depending on the size and condition of the wall, it may be better to call in a professional plastering and decorating firm to do this.

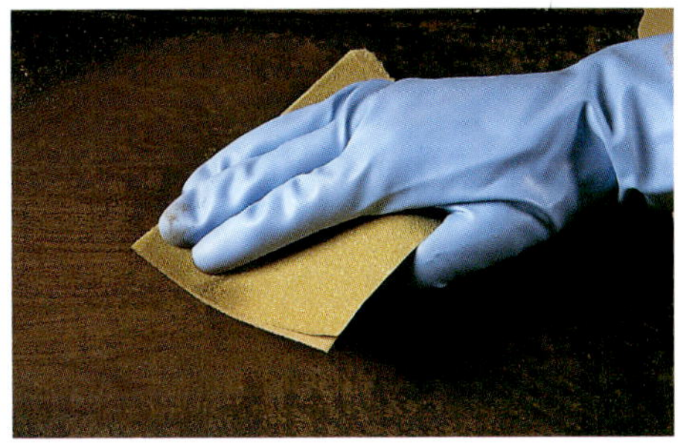

Sanding metal

Use a coarse grade sandpaper and work down to a fine grade sandpaper. Completely sand off any remaining rust or paint making sure not to miss any awkward areas. Wipe away any excess dust using a soft cloth.

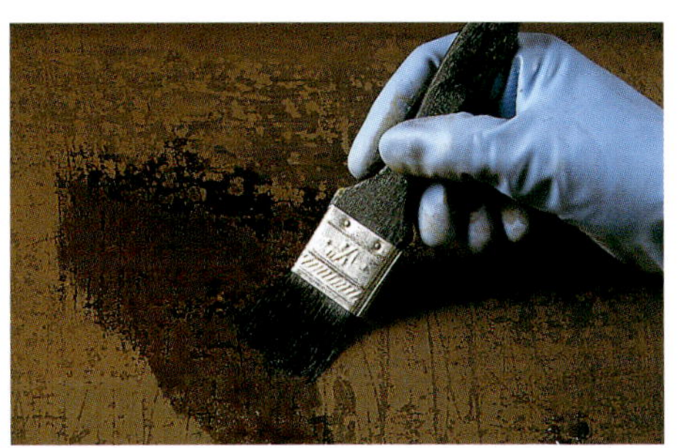

Applying rust remover

Use a bristle brush to apply a coat of rust remover or inhibitor, following manufacturers' instructions, and allow to dry completely. These products form a protective film over the surface which inhibits any further oxidation.

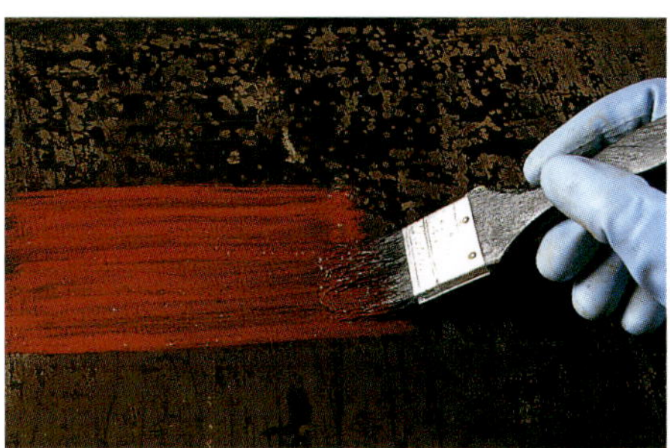

Undercoating with red oxide

With a bristle brush apply an undercoat of sealant such as red oxide. This will seal the surface and also provide a good base for applying your chosen basecoat. Apply two layers of the basecoat.

Preparing wood

The preparation depends on the final look required, a weathered look requires possibly the least amount of preparation. Remove all nails and fill and sand all holes before priming, undercoating and basecoating. Always sand between coats. Raw wood containing knots should be sealed with a knotting solution or shellac (to avoid the chance of resin staining the paint work) before being primed or undercoated and basecoated. Again, sand between coats to obtain a really smooth surface. Remove all traces of dust with a tack cloth before continuing. Reprime if the surface is still uneven and apply a second basecoat.

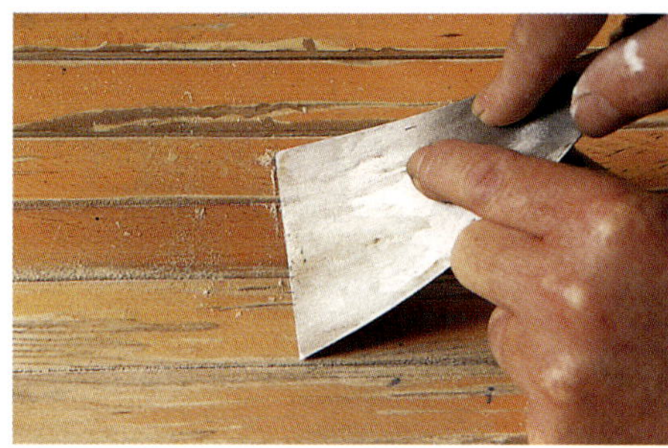

Removing excess paint and varnish

When treating old surfaces that have seen a lot of wear and tear, remove any excess flaking paint or varnish with a good, sharp scraping tool. Be careful not to gouge the surface as you work. Always work with the grain, not against or across it.

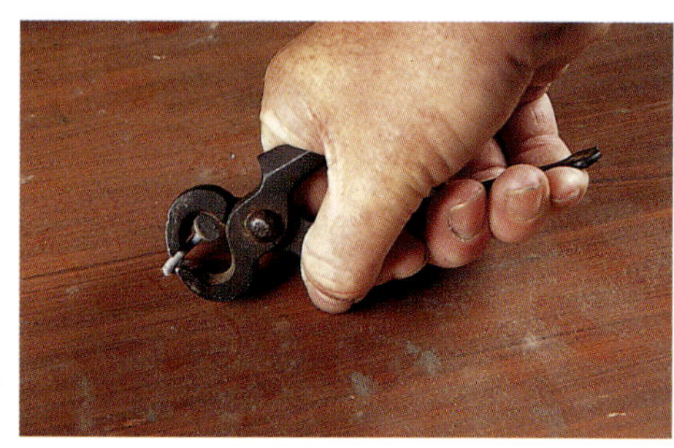

Removing nails and filling

When preparing surfaces, using the correct tools for the job helps to avoid accidents and makes the job easier. Here pinchers are being used to carefully and safely remove nails and other unwanted items from the surface.

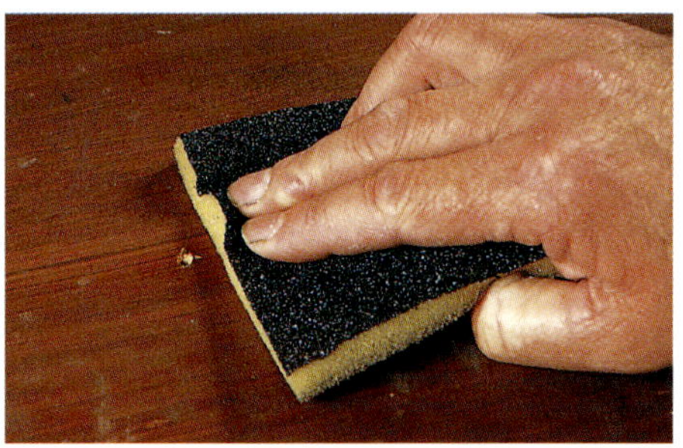

Rough sanding

Once the nails have been removed, sand the surface gently to remove any excess splinters. This will also prepare the surface for filling.

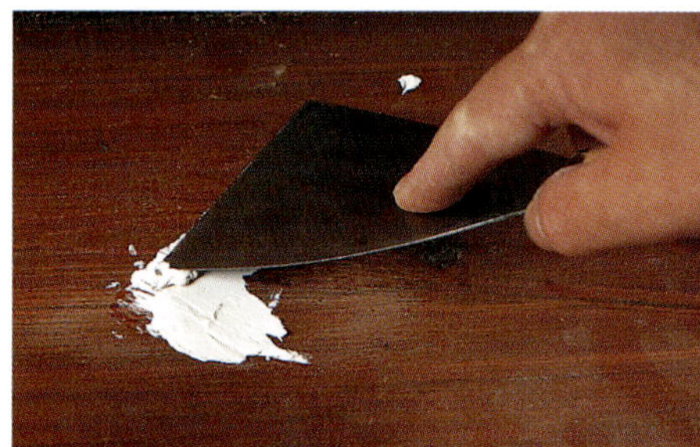

Filling

Any holes should be overfilled with store-bought filler. This is to allow for shrinkage during the drying process. Smooth the filling paste out as much as possible but still leave a little excess.

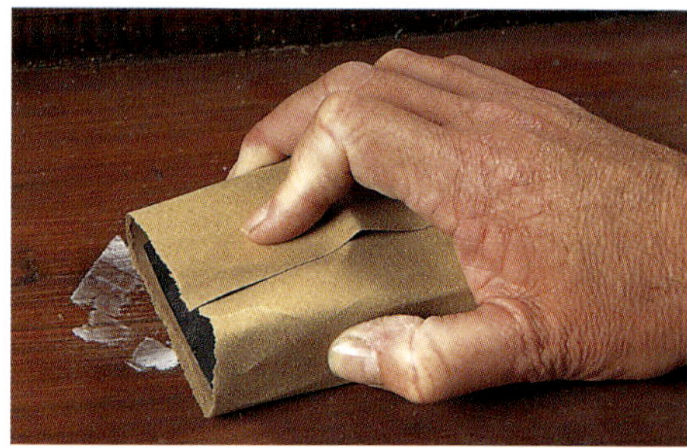

Sanding

To obtain a smooth finish, use different grades of sandpaper, from coarse to fine. Always finish with a fine grade sandpaper. The use of a sanding block helps to achieve an ultra-smooth finish. The bought sanding block could be substituted with a simple block of wood. Always sand with the grain.

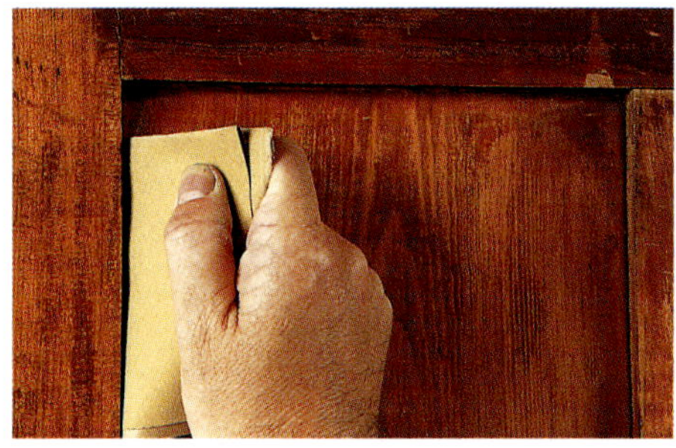

Sanding in corners

Some jobs require access to corners and recessed areas. Fold your sandpaper in half to create a sharp, firm edge. This helps access to the most awkward spaces. Always work with the grain and never too harshly.

Priming wood

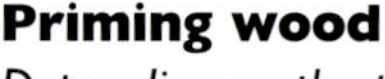

Depending on the paint technique being applied, new wood and/or newly stripped wood needs to be primed with an appropriate primer. Seal all knots with a knotting solution such as shellac, and then prepare the surface, finishing by sanding with a fine grade sandpaper. The surface should be as smooth as possible. Apply a coat of primer working along the grain of the wood. Follow all safety instructions carefully. Allow to dry and then apply your undercoat followed by your chosen basecoat. Sanding may be necessary between coats to create a good, smooth surface. Primer and undercoat combined is now available from good decorator stores.

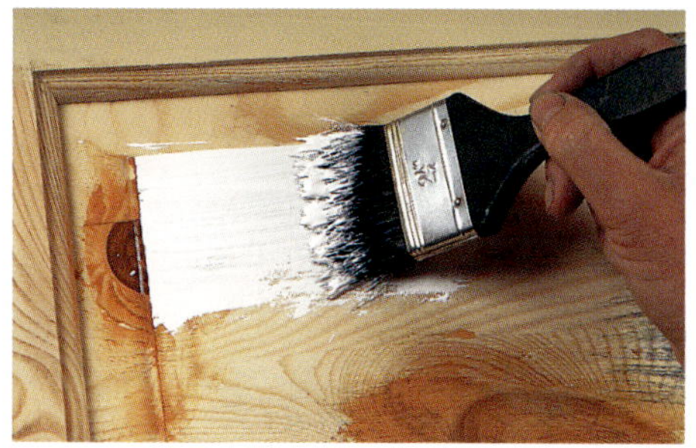

Using primer

The main use of a primer is to seal the wood. It creates a surface where a long-lasting adhesion of undercoat and topcoat is both necessary and advisable.

▼ Preparing plasterwork

Old plaster needs to be well prepared, all cracks filled and sanded, dust removed, undercoated and basecoated. New plaster is different, moisture will keep escaping for up to 5 to 6 months so this is the ideal "drying out" time. Once dry, raw plaster should be sealed and undercoated before applying two basecoats of either eggshell, or latex (vinyl silk emulsion) depending on the requirements of your paint effect.

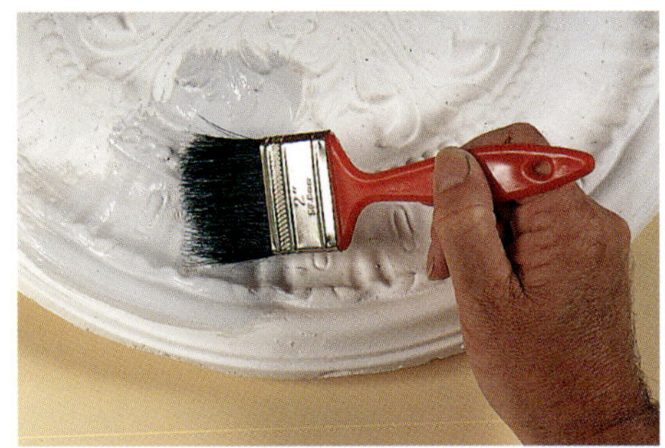

New plasterwork must be sealed or sized with a proprietary size or diluted paint.

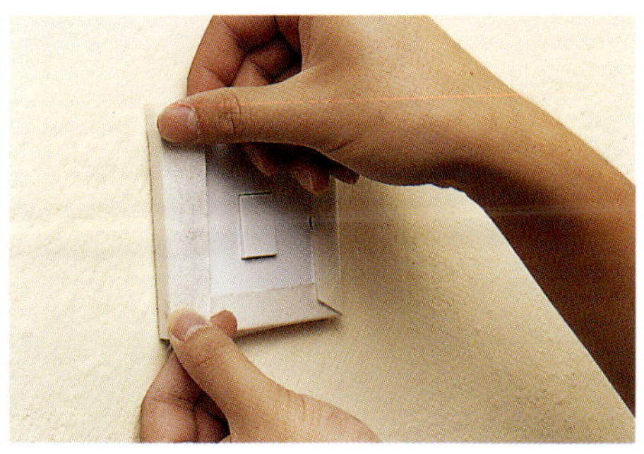

To save time and work later, it is advisable to mask off areas such as light switches and plugs.

▲ Masking off

Areas next to that about to be worked on must be masked off to prevent splashing and accidental overpainting. This applies to areas around door frames, windows and so on. Masking tape can be applied to a painted surface but remember to use low-tack tape as this will stop any paint from being pulled off. Apply the tape carefully with not too much pressure!

If you are using spray paints, plenty of newspaper should be used to mask off any area that is not to be painted – remember spray paint will find its way into the most surprising of places. Good decorator stores will sell a paper strip with one sticky edge. This is particularly easy to apply and remove and very effective for protecting glass as well as carpets and walls.

Handy tip

When undercoating or painting at any stage, never load the brush to more than two thirds up the bristles. This avoids accidental drips and messy mistakes which will need extensive cleaning up afterward. Always work along the grain of the wood as much as possible.

SURFACE	PREPARATION	TREATMENT	BASECOAT
WALLS	Clear dust if necessary. Wash down with a de-greasing agent (sugar soap) and rinse with clear water.	Fill all holes and cracks with filler. Allow to dry and sand. Skim if required. Prime if necessary (appropriate primer for chosen technique).	Basecoat with appropriate paint that is compatible with the primer used.
NEW WOOD	Remove all traces of dust and wipe down with a clean damp cloth.	Paint knots with shellac. Prime, allow to dry, and sand. Remove dust.	Basecoat with oil-based eggshell. Latex (emulsion) may be used with acrylic primer.
PAINTED AND VARNISHED WOOD	Sand surface if in good condition. Otherwise remove paint and varnish. Sand and clean up.	Paint with suitable (oil- or water-based) undercoat suitable for technique.	Basecoat with appropriate paint for undercoat.
METAL	Remove rust with wire brush or sandpaper. Wipe away excess with damp cloth. Dry.	Paint with de-rusting solution. Dry.	Apply two coats of oil-based eggshell or can spray.
OLD PLASTER	Clean down with detergent. Dry. Fill all holes and cracks. Leave to dry.	Sand and remove all dust. Skim if required. Prime with suitable primer.	Basecoat with paint that is compatible with the undercoat/primer.
NEW PLASTER	Dry completely (up to six months). Sand, remove dust. Seal with proprietary sealer.	Prime with shellac (knotting solution) or suitable primer.	Basecoat with appropriate paint for chosen technique.
MELAMINE PLASTIC	Clean thoroughly with mineral spirits (white spirit) and follow with detergent. Wash down with clean water.	Sand with medium sandpaper. Remove all dust. Prime with appropriate primer.	Apply an oil-based basecoat (e.g. eggshell).

Planning

Even if you are not an artist, sketch out a few preliminary ideas in pencil. Do you want to apply the effect to just one wall? Will it be paneled or plain? Do you want to create a false chair (dado) rail which combines two or more effects? Always remember which items are staying in your room—for example, the drapes, or carpet and furniture—as a result you may be restricted in your choice of color or pattern.

If you are lucky enough to be starting from scratch ask for some color samples of the paint that you like from your local decorating store, together with some carpet samples, and drape and blind samples. Then place them together and make sure that they work for you. Pattern, style and color are all very personal things and ultimately you should always rely on your own intuition. Do not let yourself be persuaded by others.

Color testing

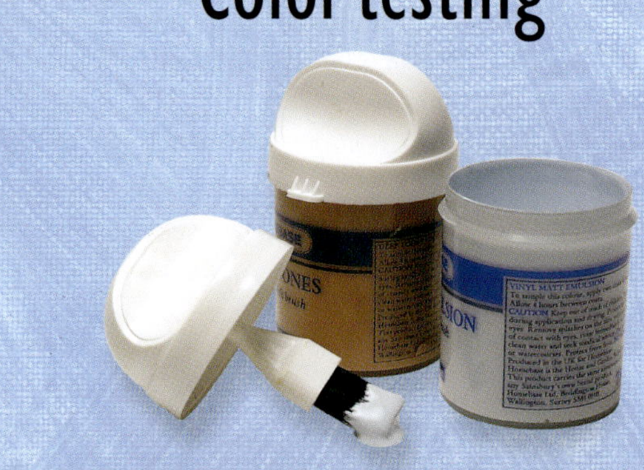

Although there may be only a limited range of colors, sample pots are really useful as testers, otherwise purchase the smallest pot available and use it on a small part of your chosen wall or room. View the effect by day and by night, and arrange the room lighting, making a note of the contrasting effects that it will produce. In particular, view the color sample at a time when you are most often going to be using the room. All these suggestions will ultimately save you time and expense in the future.

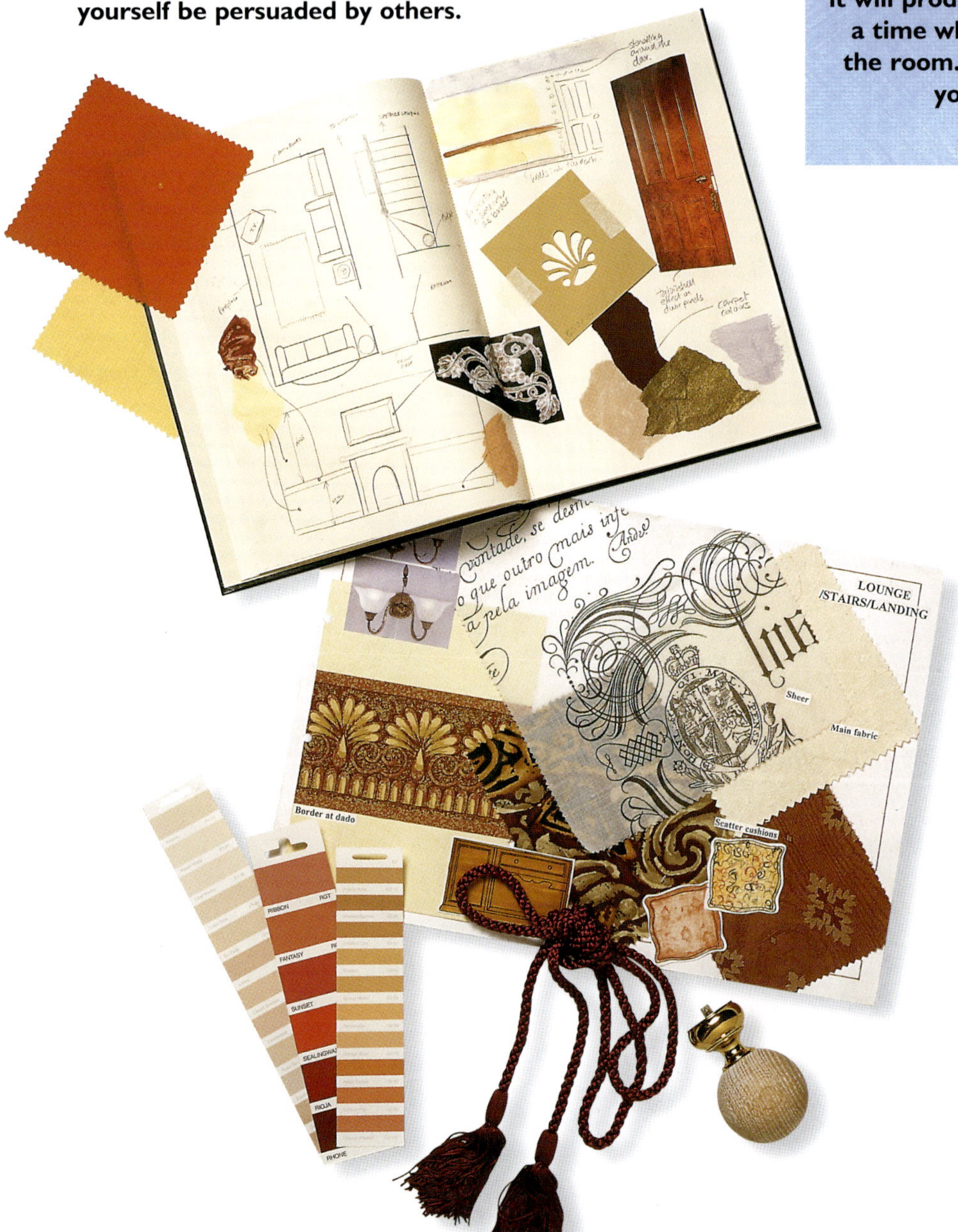

◀ Make a book of rough sketches of the basic ideas that you have for your room. It is also useful to make short notes of any specific details or items that you want to include. A swatch board of fabrics, wallpapers, paint colors etc., that you particularly like will serve as a visual reminder. A mood board is a valuable device on which to pin pictures from books or magazines of styles and designs that you would like to copy.

Setting up

Clear the room as much as you can including the furniture and light fittings. Vacuum up all dust and carefully protect all vulnerable areas with dustcloths or other suitable coverings, including all electrical sockets and wall lights if necessary. From your checklist gather all the materials and tools you need to complete the project. Lay them out, possibly on a pasting table keeping them in an orderly group. Do not forget to wear protective clothing and always keep a bucket of clean water nearby in case of any accidents. Finally, complete any outstanding tasks that may interrupt your work schedule and avoid answering the phone! You should now be ready to begin.

Walls

First cut in with a brush around all the corners and the edges of door or window frames and chair (dado) rails. Do not forget to mask off all areas that require protection. Next, work from the ceiling down in strips of about 3 ft. (90 cm.) wide being very careful not to overlap the edges, causing darker lines—this is particularly true when using glazes. Paint opposite walls first and allow them to dry and paint the remaining walls last after masking down corners. You might begin with the wall opposite the windows as the natural light will show clearly the results that you can expect. If you are working as a team never do the same job as your partner. When glazing, one person should paint the glaze on, while the other stipples or drags the glaze. Even though the effect is the same, each person works in a slightly different way and these differences will definitely show in the final result.

▼ Wooden and paneled doors

The diagram below shows the recommended order in which to paint a door. Regardless of whether the door is glazed, paneled, or plain the order of painting is the same. First prime or undercoat the surface. When dry, paint a topcoat with the appropriate paint for your chosen technique (wood usually requires eggshell). Priming may not be necessary if you are going to colorwash or distress the door so check the technique requirements before you begin. Work with even strokes and do not use too much paint. Crisscross to create even coloration.

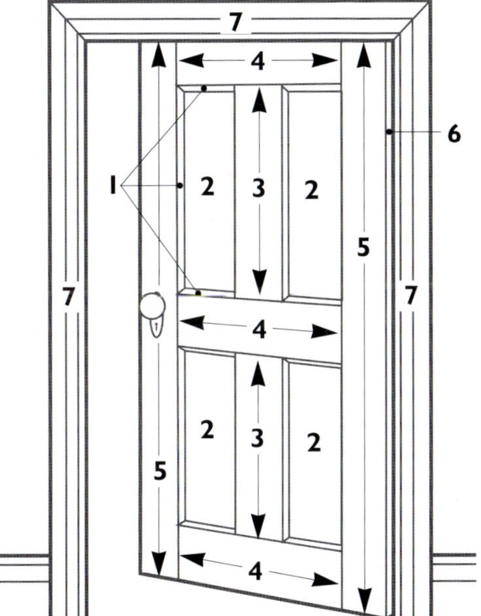

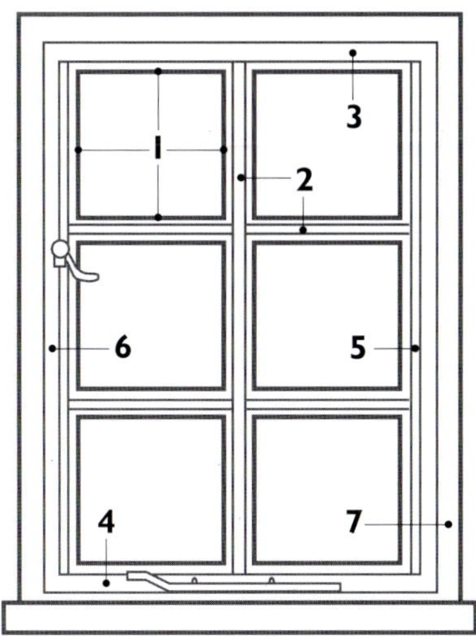

▲ Windows

The diagram above shows the recommended order in which to paint a window frame. Complete all window frames, sills etc., first beginning with priming and undercoating using a good bristle brush. Do not forget to mask off any nearby walls to avoid splashes or over painting. Once they are dry, paint a topcoat with the appropriate paint for the undercoat—for example, eggshell together with oil-based primer. Paint brushstrokes in one direction, following the grain of the wood. Take care not to close windows while the paint is still wet.

Using and loading the paint roller

Before attempting to use the roller, cut in all edges (where the roller will not reach) with a brush and mask off well any areas that will be vulnerable to spray or paint damage. Next, half fill the roller tray with paint and carefully wipe away excess from the tin. Dip the roller in the paint and work back and forward on the top part of the tray to spread the paint evenly. Apply to the wall and roll in as evenly as possible. Crisscross to create even color.

Ceilings

Always begin with the ceiling. It will eliminate the possibility of splashes onto your finished paint effect work. You will find a large area such as a ceiling easier to paint with a roller, but always wear protective goggles as rollers tend to give off a fine spray of excess paint during use. For the basecoat begin by painting in one direction and then paint at 90 degrees to your first stroke. Work in manageable areas and if using a brush remove brushstrokes by going over the area again with a clean roller. Two coats are better than one and each coat can be thinned slightly with the relevant solvent (around 1 part solvent to 10 parts paint). Follow the ceiling with the cornice. Be extremely careful when using ladders—do not step backward to admire your handiwork!

Finally, the floor

Try to visualize the overall effect of the floor on the rest of the room. Remember any rugs and where they are going to be placed so that they do not cover up your design. Many of the techniques described in this book can be applied to floors, but first the floorboards must be repaired, filled, secured and finally sanded and all dust removed. After your chosen technique is applied seal it well with at least three coats of a proprietary floor sealant or varnish. Do not forget that some varnishes may discolor with light so always check manufacturer's instructions carefully before you buy.

Finishing and protecting

A great deal of love and hard work goes into all broken paintwork techniques and to spoil them at this or a later stage would be a shame. Certain techniques need protection for a variety of reasons, but notably for general wear and tear such as susceptibility to the elements, or the fact that they may be exposed to steam or water as in bathrooms and kitchens. Floors will need to be particularly hard wearing and therefore suitably protected. Gilding with metal leaf is prone to tarnishing and should be sealed. Techniques such as faux marble, malachite and steel need the final varnishing as an integral part of the technique. This gives the surface a highly polished finish that is characteristic. However there are certain finishing techniques that do not benefit from or need any final protection.

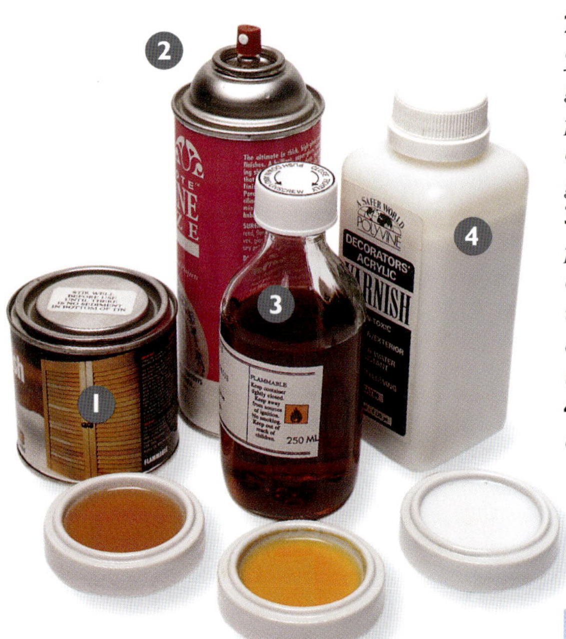

Available protective finishes

1 Oil-based varnish *Many products are available on the market and they are always changing and improving. Oil varnish is more sturdy than its water-based equivalent. Most oil-based varnishes tend to yellow in sunlight or are naturally slightly tinted so always check before you use them as they can change the coloration of a finish quite noticeably. Polyurethane tends to be the most popular, but it is quite yellow and can be brittle. It is available in three finishes: flat, satin and gloss.*

2 Spray varnishes *These are non-yellowing and they need to be treated with great care. They tend to offer only limited protection and work better on water-based effects. They are available in matte and gloss finishes.*

3 Shellac/knotting solution *This provides a barrier between the wood knots and the painted finish. It stops the resin in the wood from bleeding through and discoloring the paint. It is not resistant to water or alcohol.*

4 Water-based varnishes *The acrylic or resin-based varnishes do not yellow, are reasonably heat and water resistant, and more user friendly. Finishes available are flat and satin.*

Tinting varnishes

To get an even tint, add a little of the relevant pigment stainer or the color you are using to a small amount of the varnish first. Mix well in a clean container. Do this carefully to avoid air bubbles. Pour a little varnish into another container and add the previously mixed color. Stir carefully. Do not shake. Add enough of the remaining varnish to complete the job and gently stir.

Finishes for protective sealants

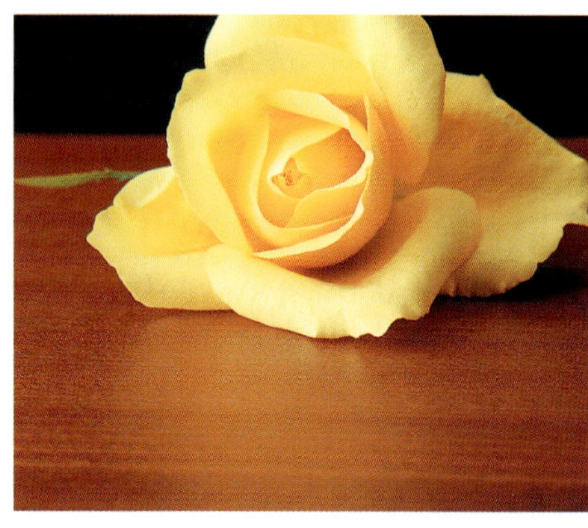

Matte *Otherwise known as flat, or dead flat, which provides protection with little or no shine. The results are mellow and very pleasing.*

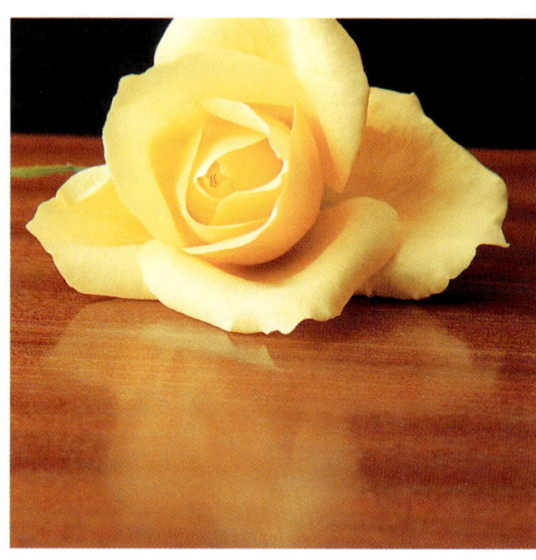

Satin finish *Also gives a pleasing affect and offers protection as well as a little reflective depth and softness.*

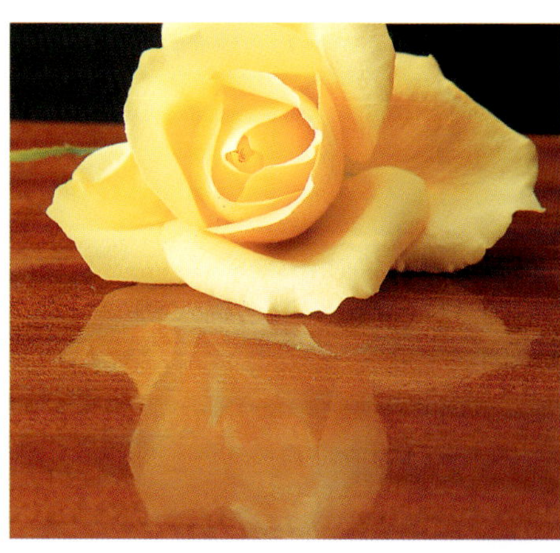

Gloss *Enables you to create a mirrored final effect with an excellent glass-like appearance and reflection.*

The varnishing procedure

Correct preparation is extremely important when applying varnish, and an extremely clean, dust and lint-free area is vital. The ease of application is increased by warmth, so a warm constant temperature to work in is best. Check that the surface is free from grease before you start, use a tack cloth to remove any stray dust. Stir the varnish well and decant enough varnish slowly into a clean container. Then load the brush carefully and wipe off any excess. Pass the brush once over a clean, dry board or a piece of greaseproof paper to help remove any air that is contained within the varnish. If the varnish is too thick, dilute it a little with the relevant solvent. You are now ready to proceed.

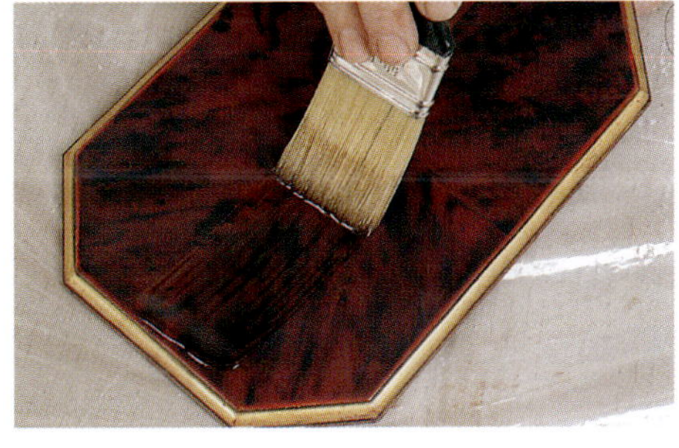

1 *Brush on the varnish in clean strokes across the whole surface in one direction, holding the brush at a slight angle to the surface. Once you have finished, and with your brush free of varnish, gently remove the brush strokes. Dry. Apply a second coat in the same way.*

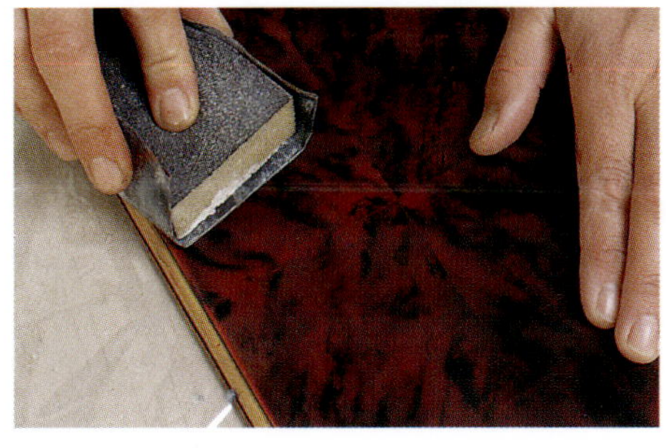

2 *Using wet and dry sandpaper, smooth down surface after dipping paper in a little water. Do this gently so surface is not damaged. Wet-and-dry sandpaper is excellent for rubbing down paint as it is gentle and gives a smooth finish.*

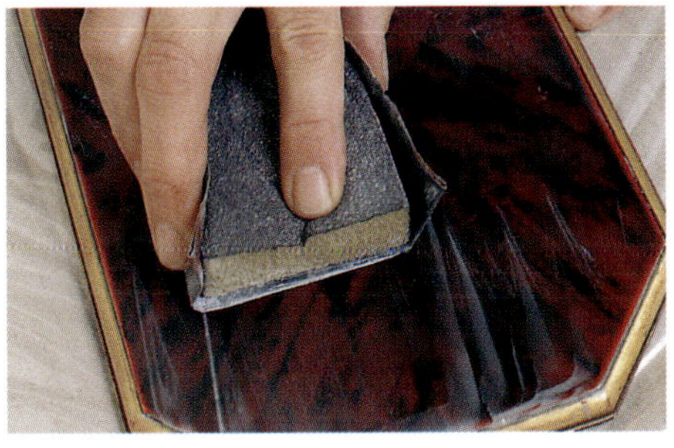

3 *Wash the surface with clean water and a soft cloth when you have completed the area. Allow to dry completely and reuse the tack cloth.*

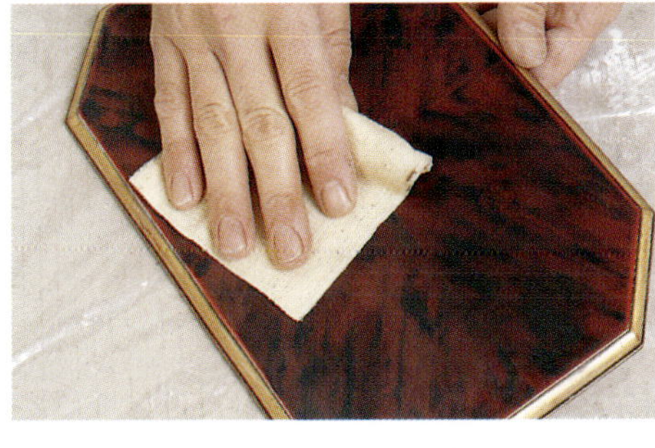

4 *Apply another coat of varnish repeating steps 1 to 3. Let dry and then continue as necessary until you apply the final layer of varnish which should result in a mirror-like finish.*

Waxes

The best are furniture waxes that come in a soft form and in varying colorways, although they can be tinted with stainers or powder color. When they are applied with 0000 grade steel wool and carefully buffed up, they produce a delightful soft sheen. Wax should not be applied to glossy surfaces, such as plastic, and is used as the final protection for some techniques. It must be removed before starting any technique as it creates a barrier that will not take paint (see Waxing, p. 34.)

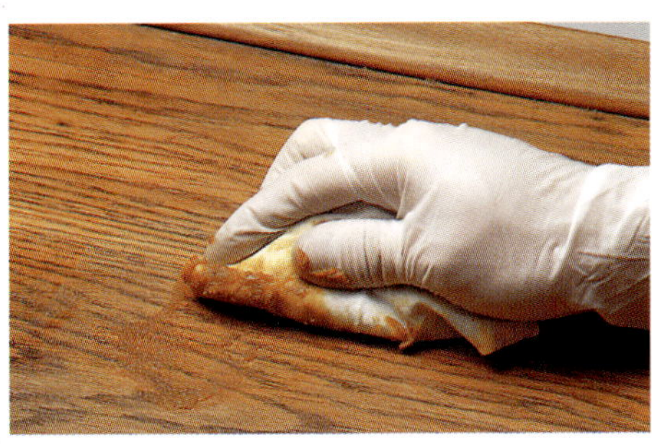

Waxing

Wax is always the final finish whether it is natural beeswax, tinted furniture wax or gilding wax. Additional decorative layers of paint will not take over wax finishes so remember to complete all your detail and final work before applying the wax finish. Try to avoid the use of spray silicone waxes, they tend to smear and can be less protective than their paste counterparts.

When you have completed the ceiling, walls and floors of the room it is time to apply your chosen technique to the coving, ceiling rosette (rose), pilasters and corbels. This is done more easily before they are fixed into position. Once dry, and the relevant protection has been applied, carefully fix them in place. Begin with the coving, followed by the ceiling rosette (rose) and then any pilasters, corbels or panel moldings and lastly dado rails. Finally, touch up any damage with fresh fixing plaster and paint. Clear away all rubbish and mess, and carefully vacuum away excess dust. Then return all furniture and light fittings to the room. Clear away all tools and materials making sure to clean and store your brushes until next time.

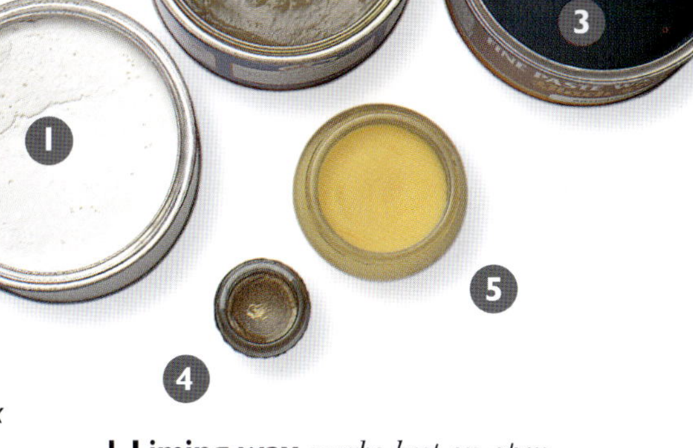

1 Liming wax *works best on open-grained woods.*
2 Clear wax *gives final protection for furniture creating a warm, soft sheen.*
3 Antiquing wax *is used over paint effects to create a mellow antique look. Golden brown is the most popular color.*
4 Gilding wax *is mainly used for high-lighting moldings and edges.*
5 Beeswax *is a traditional wax for protecting oak and pine against dryness.*

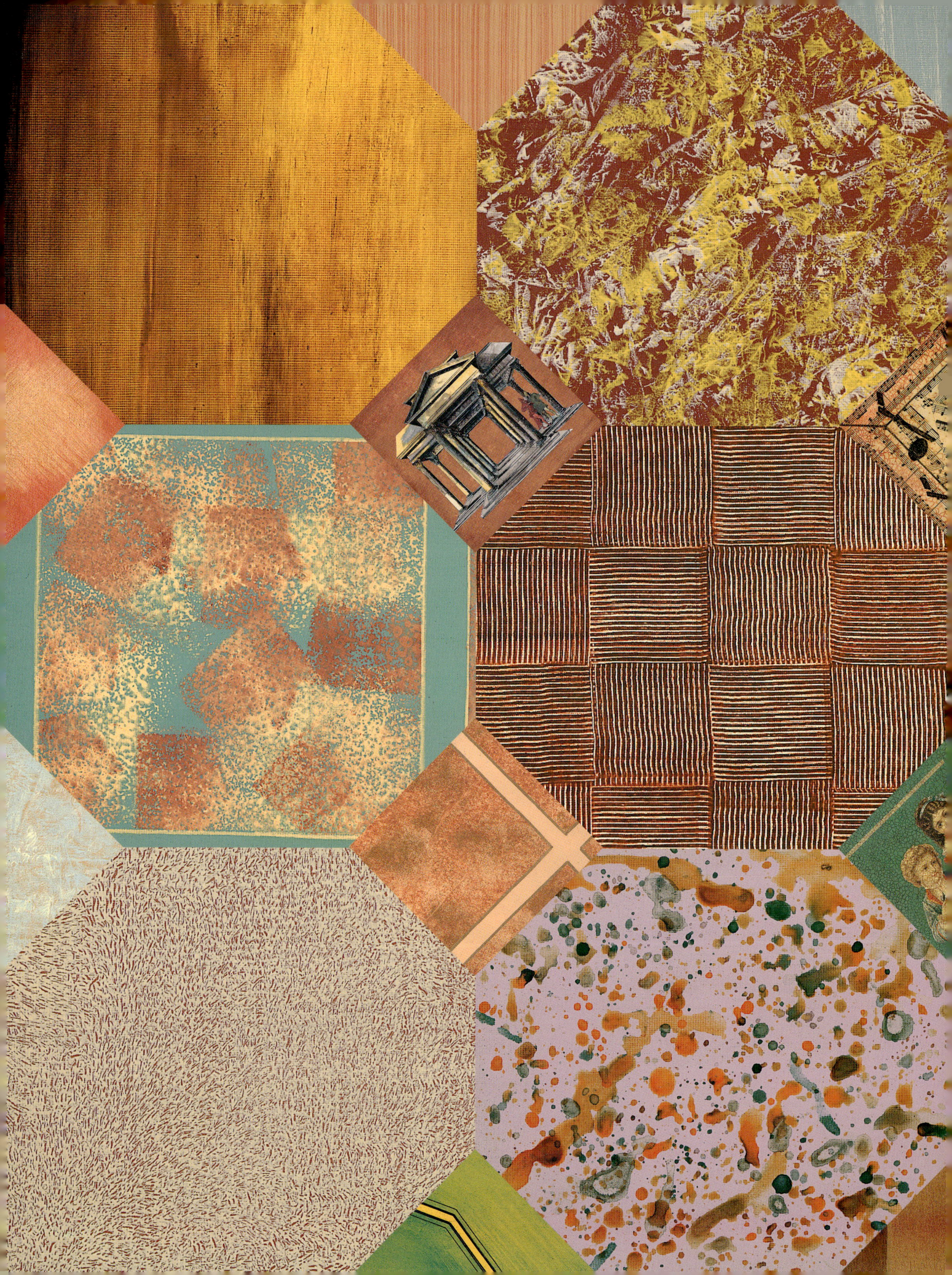

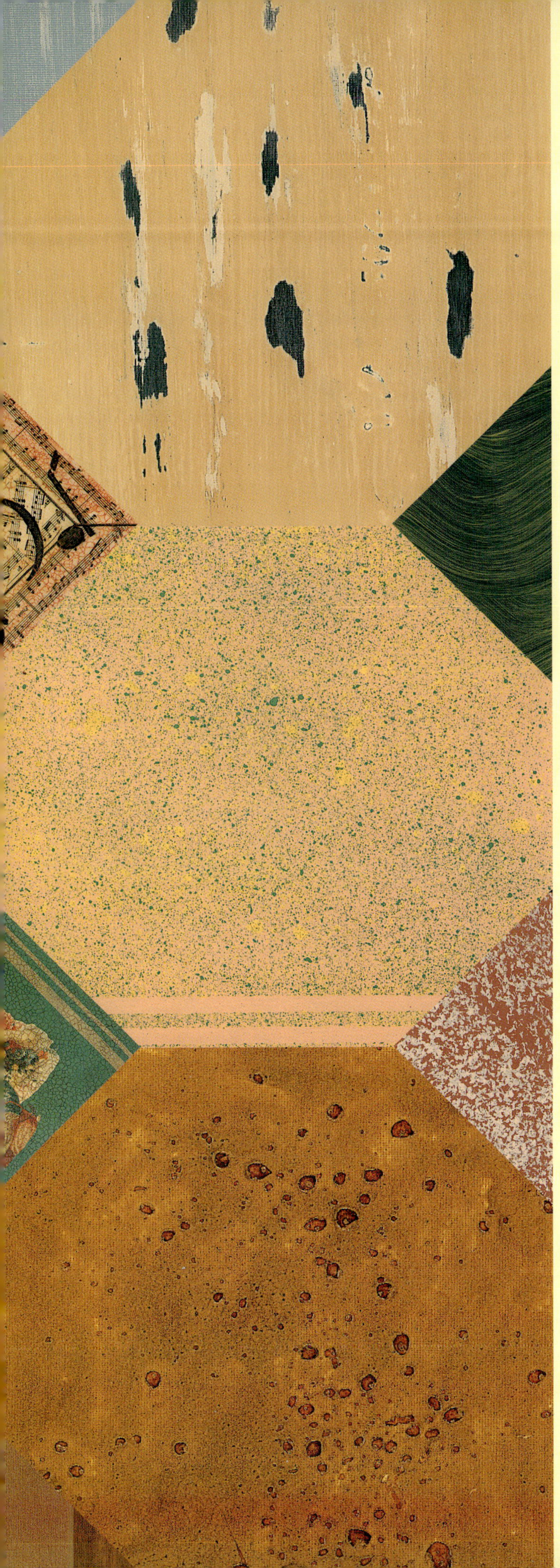

THE BASIC TECHNIQUES

In this section of the book many of the techniques can be achieved with the minimum amount of time and with a basic understanding of the technical aspects and the physical properties of the paint and glazes. They are effects that produce excellent results when applied by both the professional and the amateur decorator. Once the basics have been mastered you will feel more confident about moving on to more advanced levels of broken paint work. As you proceed the possibilities become endless and you will find yourself becoming more and more adventurous.

Frottage

Frottage creates a bold textural effect that is suited to almost any surface and item, from walls, ceilings, windows and doors, to smaller, decorative items such as tables, boxes, lampbases and picture frames. Choosing color combinations is great fun and experimenting with different color ranges will result in attractive and unusual results. Since few tools are required, your initial outlay is minimal.

The most common mistake is allowing the topcoat to dry too quickly. This means that the newspaper cannot create its characteristic pattern. To avoid this, work on small areas at a time. However, if the topcoat does dry too quickly, remove it with a soft, wet cloth, add a little more glazing medium and reapply. For large areas it is safer if two people work together, one applying the topcoat and the other creating the pattern.

If you are working on a large area you will need a good supply of fresh newspaper and dust covers to protect your furnishings from the discarded newsprint. Preparation is easier as the finish, in its own right, tends to cover most minor surface defects such as cracks or flaws. But for a good, professional finish, thorough preparation will always result in a top quality end product.

You will need

Tools

• 2–3 in. (5–7.5 cm.) bristle basecoat brush • 2–3 in. (5–7.5 cm.) glazing brush • Stippling brush

Materials

• Semigloss latex (vinyl silk emulsion) for basecoat • Topcoat of semigloss latex (vinyl silk emulsion) • Acrylic glaze (if a transparency is required to the topcoat; this will also extend drying time) • Plenty of old newspapers

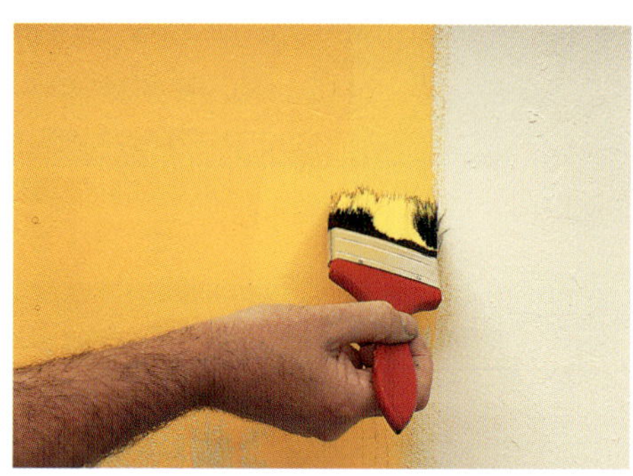

1 Frottage works well on a less than perfect surface as it disguises any faults. Start with a basecoat of yellow semigloss latex (vinyl silk emulsion) using a bristle basecoat brush. Allow to dry. Apply a second coat and allow to dry.

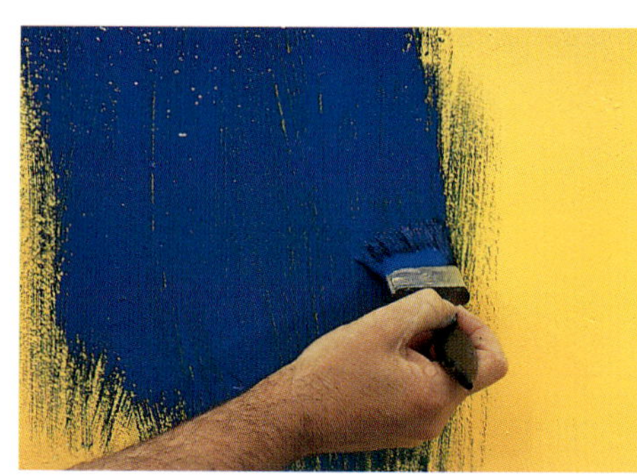

2 Mix a glaze of bright blue from semigloss latex (vinyl silk emulsion) and an acrylic glazing medium, following manufacturer's instructions. Leave fairly thick to create a textured finish. Apply with a glazing brush.

Variation 1

Using two or more colors adds depth and definition to frottage. Here a pale terracotta glaze over a basecoat of pale blue is allowed to dry thoroughly, and the process repeated with a glaze of lemon yellow.

Variation 2

By varying the colorways, and by using vibrant colors, definite statements can be made. Here a glaze of bright purple over a basecoat of vivid red creates an illusion of rich, crushed velvet, which is both warm and exciting. It would look very good in a dining area.

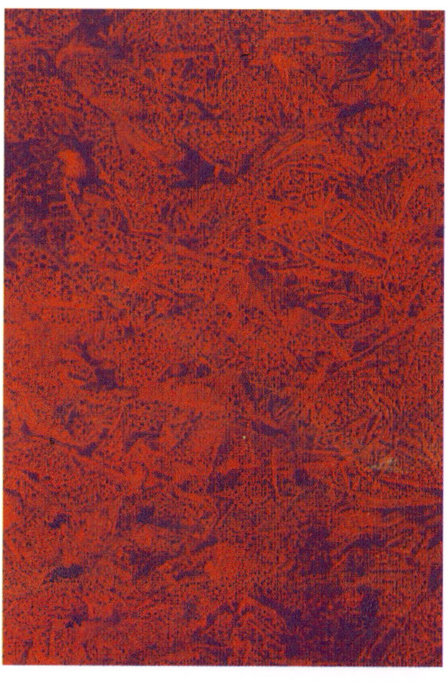

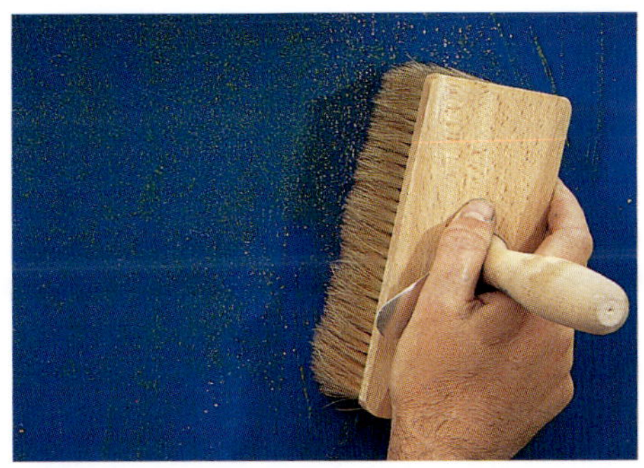

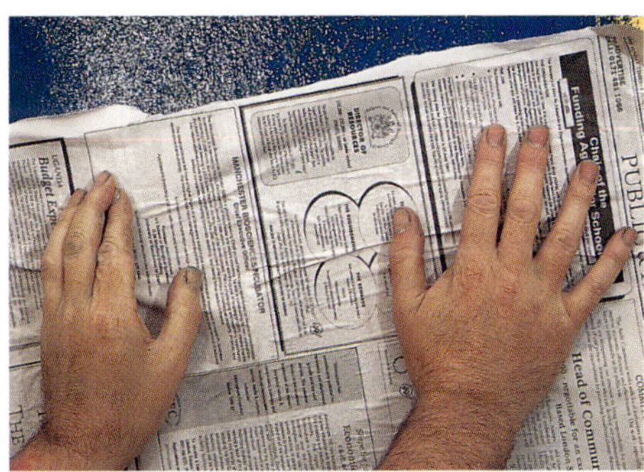

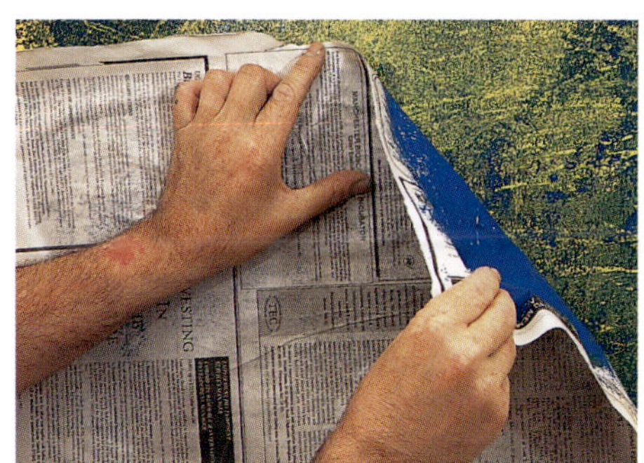

3 With a stippling brush, stipple out all the brushstrokes (see *Stippling, p. 30*) to create an even coverage of the glaze. If a large area is to be covered work on one manageable area at a time. Leave a wet edge to line up with the next worked area.

4 Apply a sheet of clean newspaper over the wet glaze lightly smoothing it down onto the surface. Avoid using too much pressure as this will show handprints. Creases in the newspaper will serve to add to the detail of the surface.

5 While covering the surface with newspaper be careful not to tear or cause the paper to slide. Carefully remove it with one smooth movement and discard the used paper. Continue in this way across the entire surface area.

6 The wonderfully tactile nature of the frottage technique is shown to advantage here—enhanced by the use of two vibrant colors that work extremely well together. Frottage is a simple and quick technique which can be used to achieve perfect results nearly every time, as mistakes are almost impossible.

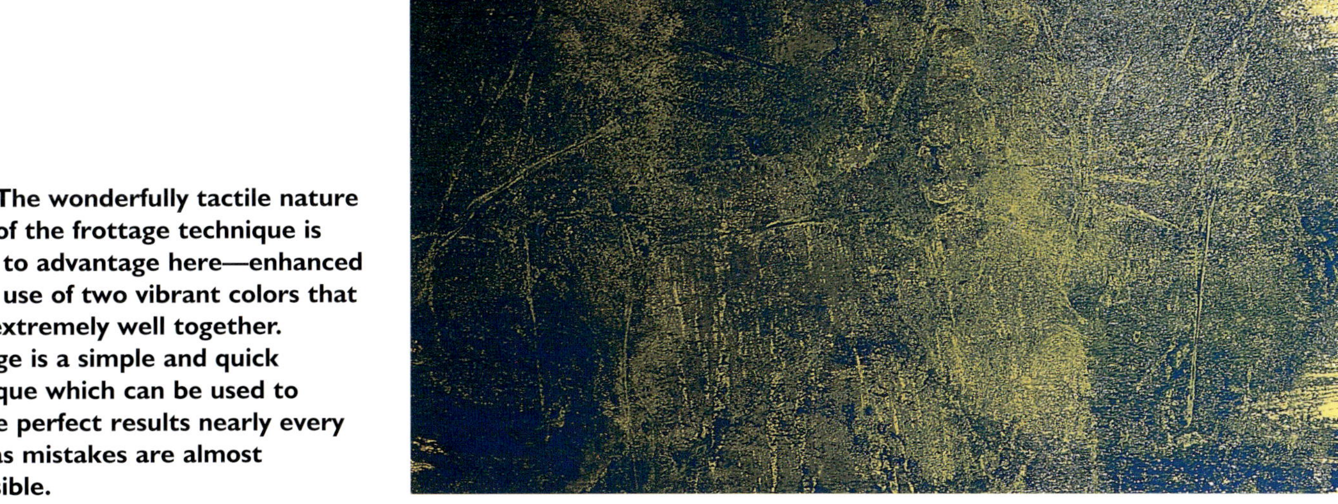

Variation 3

Changing the basecoat color to a dark green, but still using the bright red in glaze form, has created a completely different look. Used below a chair (dado) rail with plain green walls above and some stenciling (see p. 78), or photocopying (see p. 58), this will produce a very dramatic effect.

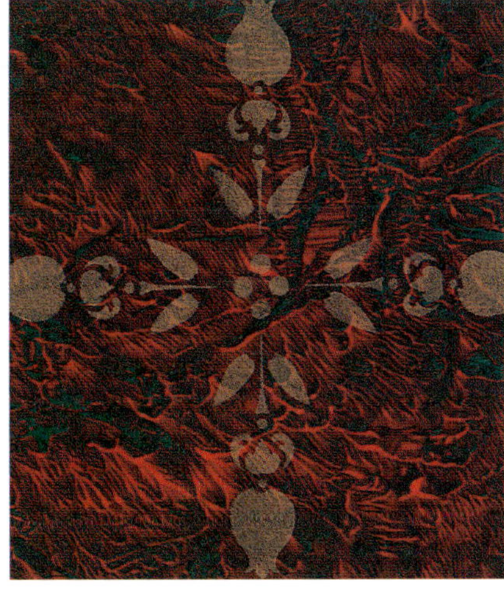

Variation 4

A glaze of white has been applied over a black basecoat. This was allowed to dry completely, and then followed with a glaze of pale blue. The effect conjures up pictures of rippling waves and would look particularly good in tile form on a bathroom or conservatory floor.

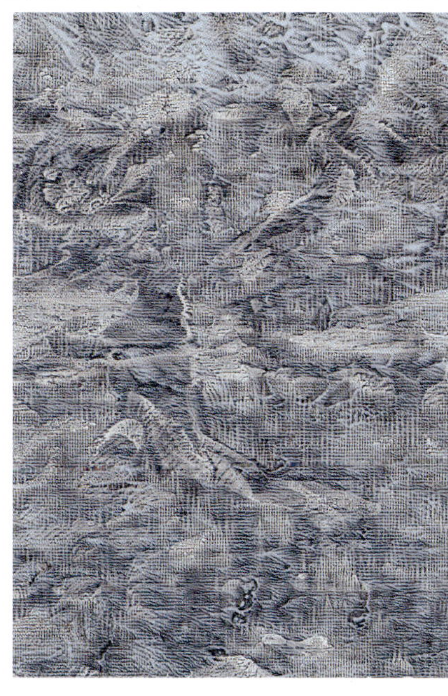

Stippling

Stippling, as a technique, creates an elegant and simple finish, and is ideal for highlighting and aging effects (see p. 32). Used in both period and modern settings, it works well with other techniques, such as dragging (see p. 62) and rag-rolling (see p. 52). Stippling is done with a special brush to produce graded textures on surfaces throughout the home to create visually interesting features.

Stippling is ideal for walls and ceilings as well as cupboard doors, paneling, window frames and shutters. A well prepared and smooth surface produces a quality result. Oil-based glazes are best because of the time needed to work the final finish. Acrylic glazes (see p. 15) dry quicker and are suited to smaller items.

Stippling brushes are not cheap. However, an alternative is to use a large stenciling brush or a shoe brush, depending on the final look required. For quality work, you should try to use the best tools possible. Once you have chosen a color, a sample board, painted with the same basecoat, will give you an idea of what the effect looks like. By using sample boards, later mistakes can be avoided, although if you have to remove some of the glaze when you are working on the actual surface, wipe it off with a soft cloth dampened with mineral spirits (white spirit) and reapply the glaze and stipple again.

You will need

Tools

• *2–3 in. (5–7.5 cm.) basecoat brush* • *2–3 in. (5–7.5 cm.) bristle decorators' brush* • *2–3 in. (5–7.5 cm.) varnishing brush* • *Stippling brush* • *Fine sandpaper* • *Soft, lint-free cloths* • *2 in (5 cm.) foam applicator*

Materials

• *Pale cream eggshell paint* • *Glaze (transparent oil)* • *Universal stainers or artists' oil colors for tinting glaze* • *Mineral spirits (white spirit)* • *Varnish for protection*

1 Prepare the surface (see *Preparation*, p. 18). Sand with a fine-grade sandpaper along the natural grain to avoid cross scratching on the surface. Wipe the surface with a soft brush or a damp cloth. Allow to dry.

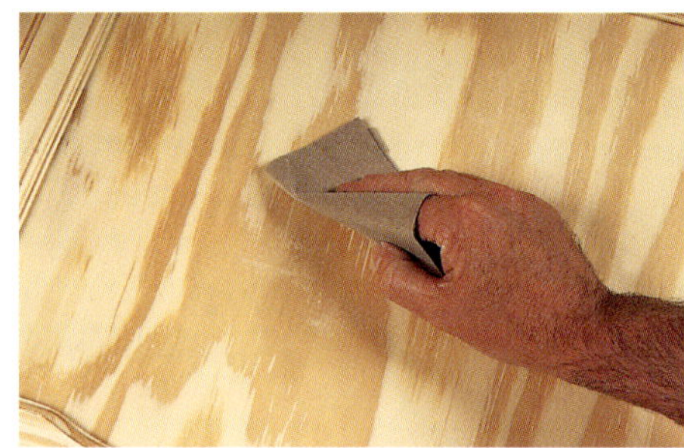

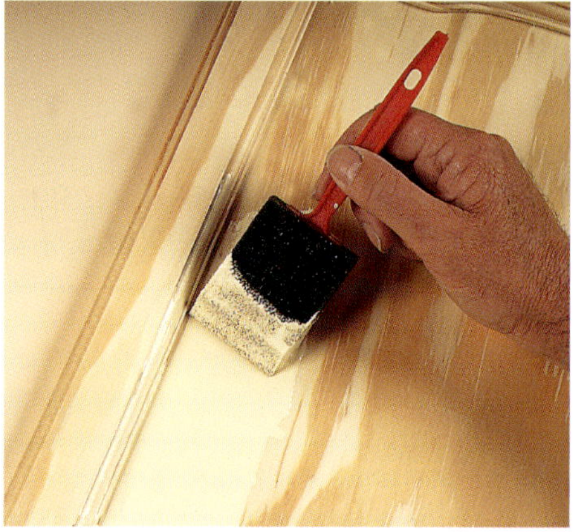

2 Apply two coats of pale cream eggshell using the basecoat brush and a foam applicator for edges.

Variation 1

By using a rubber needled stippling pad the glaze has been broken up into a more "coarse" texture instead of the more subtle effect used on the cabinet door in the step-by-step. Over a basecoat of terracotta a stippled glaze of mid-cream has been added. This creates depth but still maintains a little subtlety.

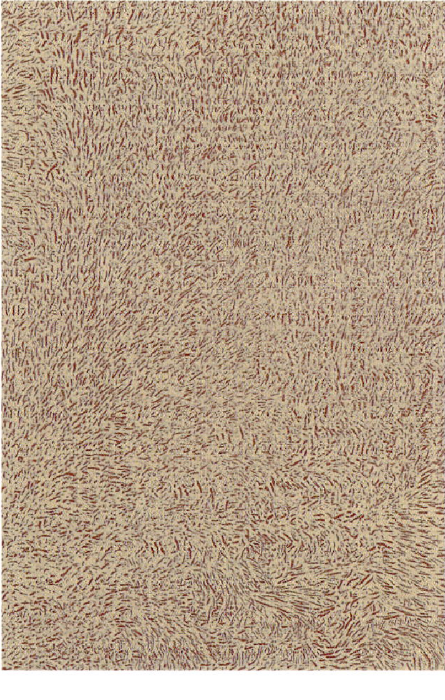

Variation 2

Here a particularly interesting textured finish is created by stippling with an ordinary household brush through a layer of kitchen towel. The colors are purple glaze over a basecoat of mid- to bright blue.

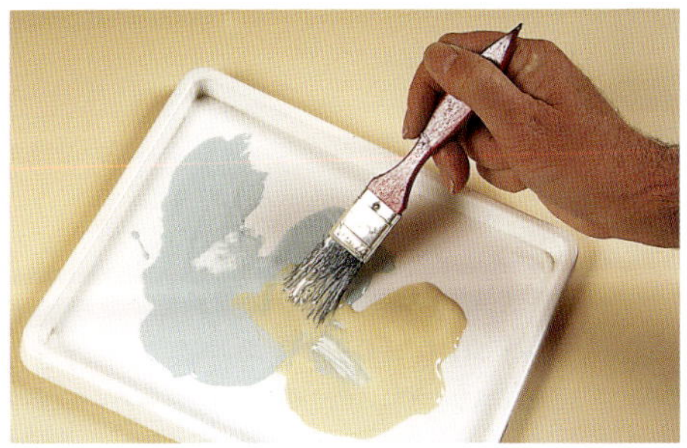

3 Mix together turquoise artists' oil paint (or a store-bought eggshell) with transparent oil glaze, following the manufacturer's instructions. Ensure that the color and glaze are well mixed. Add mineral spirits (white spirit) until the consistency of light cream is achieved.

4 Paint the mixed glaze over the door surface with the glazing or bristle brush. Brush in one direction only. Work on a manageable area and keep a wet edge if painting over a large area (see *Finishing and Protecting*, p. 24).

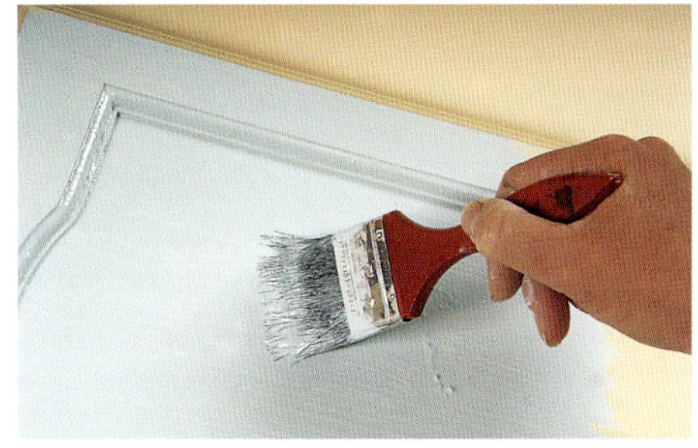

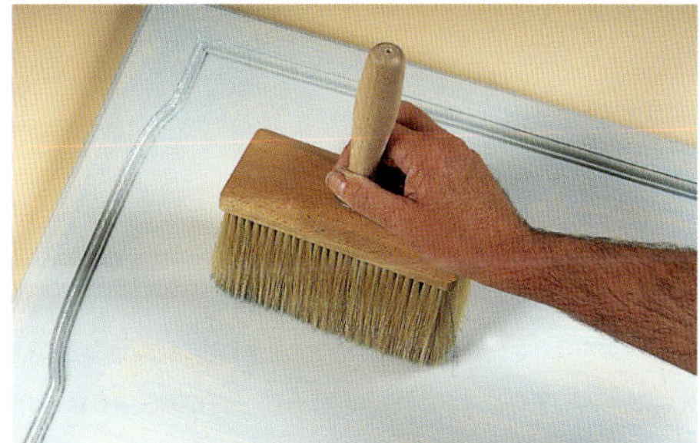

5 To create the stippled effect, use the stippling brush vertically and "pounce" it across the surface. Be careful not to disturb the glaze by using too much pressure. As you work, remove excess glaze from the brush with a clean, lint-free cloth. Allow to dry.

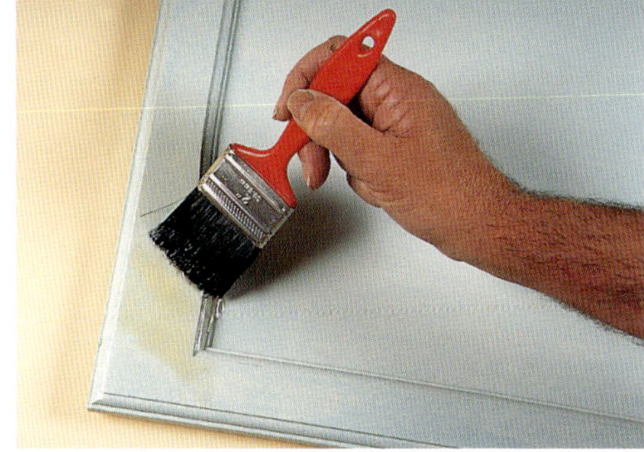

6 Using the varnishing brush, apply an even coat of clear acrylic varnish (non-yellowing), brushing in one direction only. Allow to dry and apply a second coat for extra protection.

7 The subtlety of the stippling technique is clearly shown here by the use of two pastel colors, which create a relaxed and elegant result. This technique is particularly recommended for beginners as it is straightforward to do and gives high-quality and pleasing results.

Variation 3

A glaze of olive green stippled over a basecoat of cream has created a fresh yet mellow look. An effect and colorway such as this would work well in a country or Victorian style kitchen. Stippling could be applied to the unit doors and possibly used in conjunction with dragging (see p. 62) as a border (surround) on the unit shells or casings.

Variation 4

The warmth and romance of a beautiful sunset has been created here by combining the effects of fading (see p. 104) and stippling. Color is very important and a crimson red has been "faded" by stippling over a basecoat of deep peach resulting in a finished effect that would look good in any dining or living area.

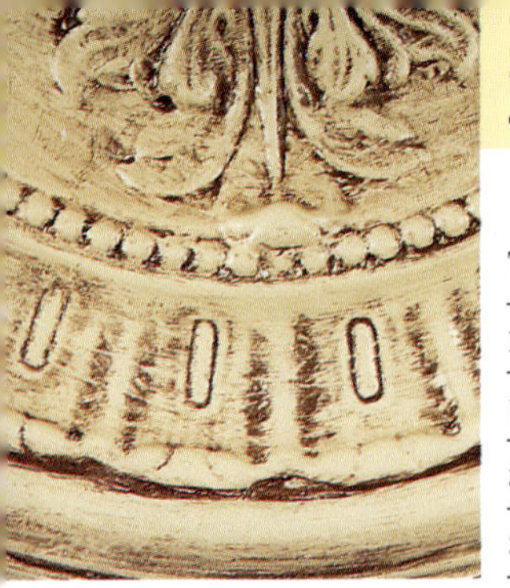

That beautiful mellow patina that was once attained only after many years can now be lovingly created in your own home in a matter of days, producing an aged and authentic look. Antiquing is a paint effect that mixes well with the old and the new. One special "antique" can look as much at home in an ultra-modern setting as it would in period decor.

Antiquing

Every surface is ideal for antiquing, whether it be walls and ceilings, or smaller items such as tables, candlesticks and boxes. Antiquing is an easy effect to achieve requiring only a little time and effort and an eye for detail. However, when aging or antiquing with glazes, it should be remembered that the colors used should look as authentic as possible. Using shades of umber and ocher will look more realistic than very bright, "modern" colors.

To create an authentic finish, work on areas that are most prone to wear and tear, such as around door frames, and that would most obviously age naturally. In other areas the finish would look contrived rather than real. Mistakes may occur, but these can be removed easily with a soft cloth. Years of wear and tear mean knocks and repairs as well as the mellowing of the patina, so if something does go wrong, see if it can be used to enhance the final antique effect.

You will need

Tools

• 2–3 in. (5–7.5 cm.) bristle basecoat brush • 1–2 in. (2–5 cm.) glazing brush • 2 in. (5 cm.) varnishing brush • ½ in. (1.2 cm.) Fitch brush • Plenty of clean, lint-free cloth (see p. 10)

Materials

• Basecoat in oil-based eggshell paint • Artists' oil tube in raw umber • Oil-based transparent glaze • Mineral spirits (white spirit) • Suitable varnish for protection

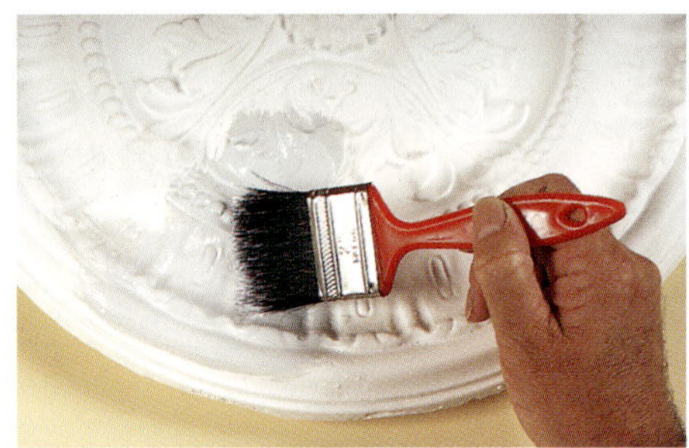

1 Make sure the surface is completely dry and seal it with one or two coats of diluted latex (emulsion) (see *Preparing plaster, p. 21*) using the bristle basecoat brush. Allow to dry.

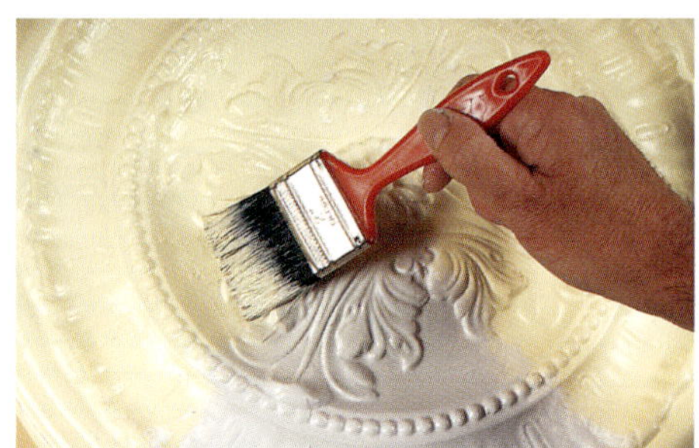

2 With the bristle basecoat brush, apply the basecoat making sure that any intricate carved areas are not missed. Allow to dry for at least 24 hours and then apply a second coat. Allow the surface to dry overnight.

Variation 1

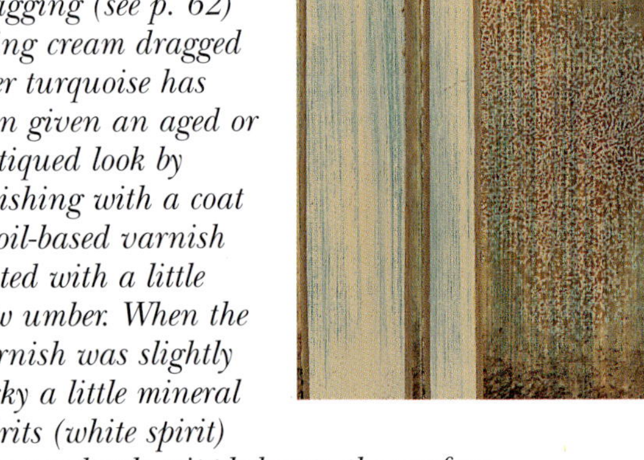

A base of random dragging (see p. 62) using cream dragged over turquoise has been given an aged or antiqued look by finishing with a coat of oil-based varnish tinted with a little raw umber. When the varnish was slightly tacky a little mineral spirits (white spirit) was randomly stippled onto the surface and the whole finish allowed to dry.

Variation 2

Having stenciled (see p. 78) yellow ocher and Wedgwood blue over a basecoat of pale green, the antique effect has been created by rubbing a store-bought antiquing or graining fluid onto the surface with a soft, lint-free cloth.

3 **On a clean dish mix a little artists' oil paint (raw umber) with a little transparent oil glaze (follow manufacturer's instructions.) Add a little mineral spirits (white spirit) to the oil paint before mixing with the glaze to avoid stray pigment streaks later. With mineral spirits dilute the glaze until it has a pouring consistency.**

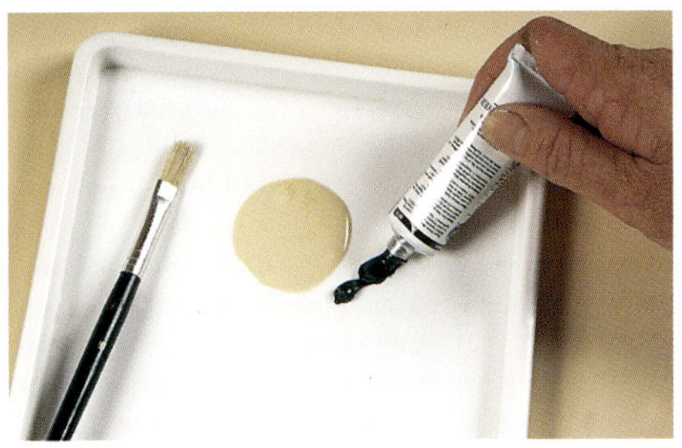

4 **With the bristle or glazing brush cover the surface with a generous coat of the tinted glaze. Make sure all molded and carved areas are covered.**

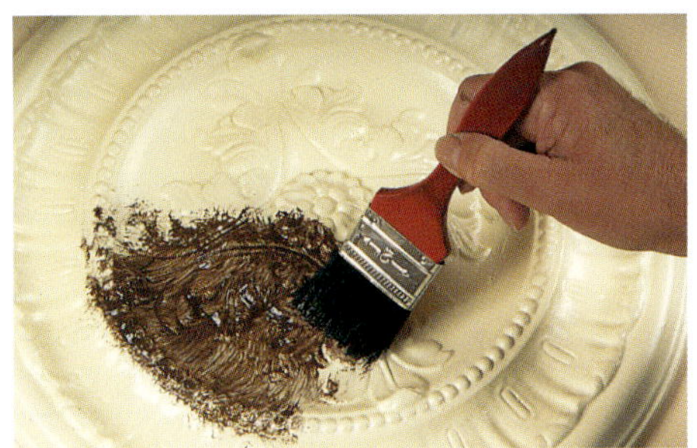

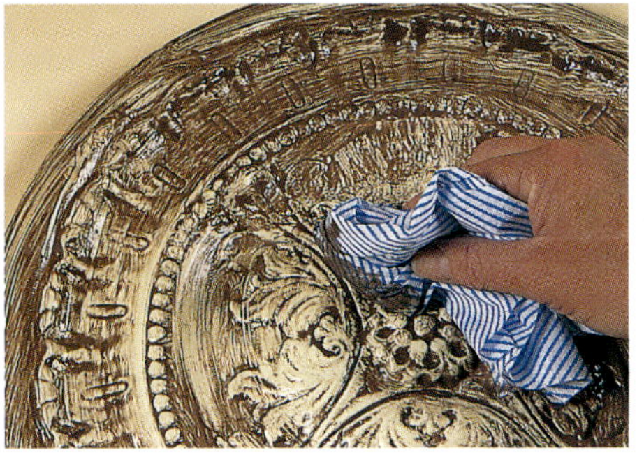

5 **While the glaze is still wet carefully wipe the surface with a soft, lint-free cloth to remove the excess glaze from the raised sections. Do not remove the glaze from the molded areas. When the glaze builds up on the cloth, use a fresh one.**

7 **The texture and molded surface of this ceiling rose has been effectively aged and mellowed creating a patina in only a few hours that would have taken years to achieve naturally. Applied to most surfaces, antiquing will result in an eye-catching finish.**

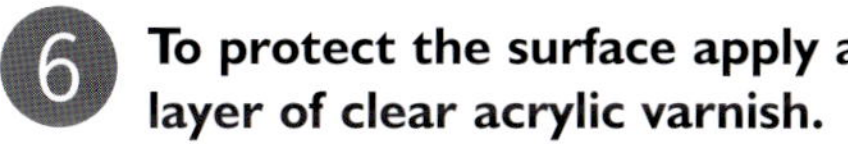

6 **To protect the surface apply a layer of clear acrylic varnish.**

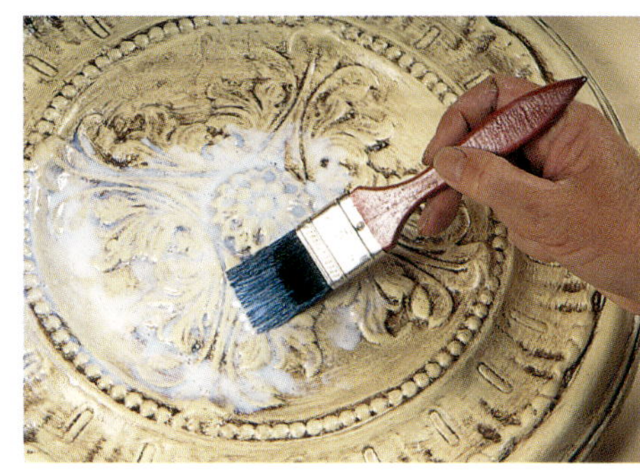

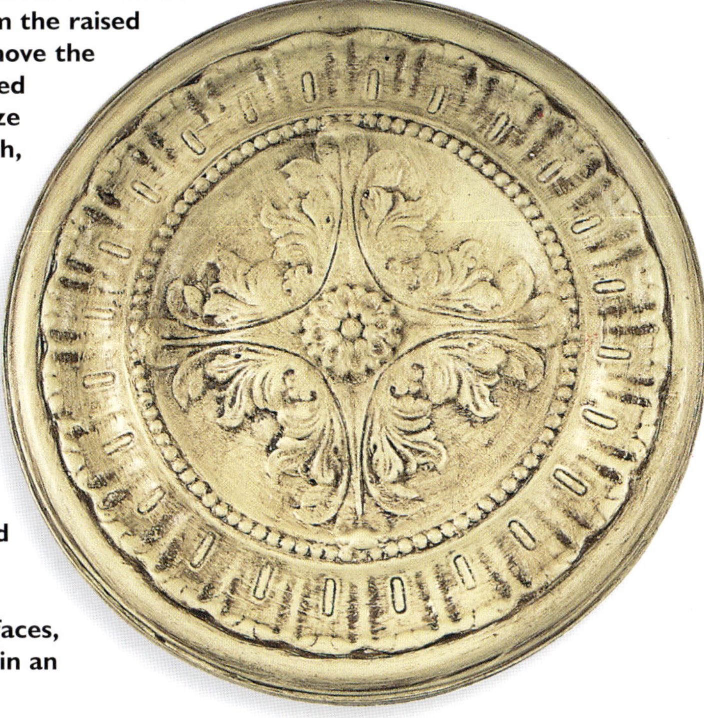

Variation 3

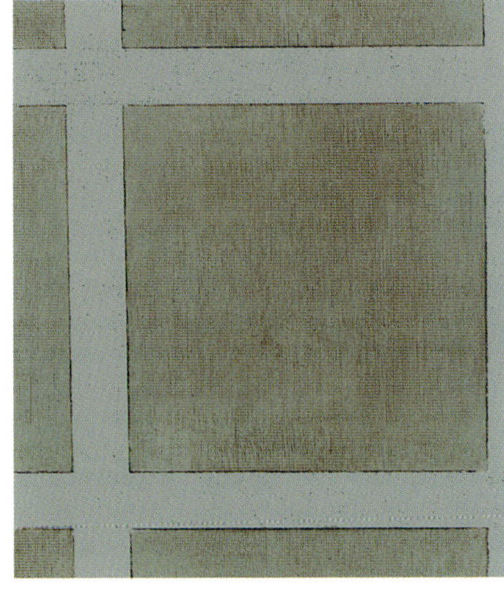

One of the simplest and yet most effective ways of antiquing is to wax the surface with an antique brown furniture wax. As an alternative you can tint a clear wax with some powder color of your choice to achieve your own variations and colorways. Wax works very well over a flat (matte) basecoat, creating some pleasing and special results.

Variation 4

Here, the intense yellow basecoat has been aged randomly with a layer of medium oak varnish. The effect was achieved by constant brushing to help spread the varnish in different directions, and with varying depths of color intensity. A finish such as this would be most effective when used in paneling below a chair (dado) rail, possibly in conjunction with stippling (see p. 30) along the panel edges.

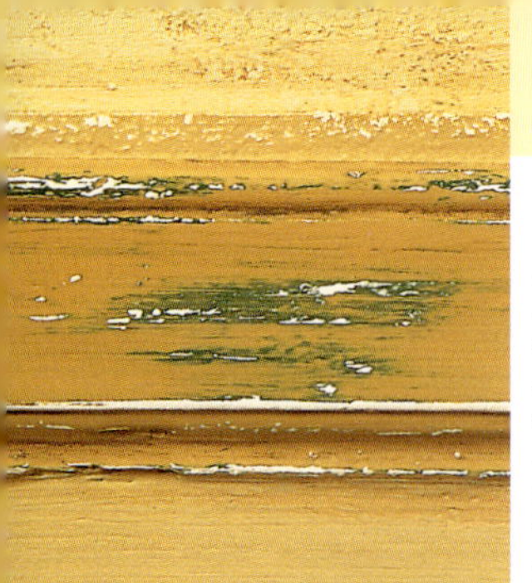

Waxing

Over the years wood develops a warm, mellow glow that comes after being treated with a great deal of loving care. This beautiful patina can be easily created through waxing, a rewarding and inexpensive technique that can be applied to many different items and areas of the home. Waxing is a very simple technique to carry out, and can result in satisfying effects requiring little or no practice.

Furniture, cupboards, chair (dado) rails, floors, picture frames, decorative sconces, pilasters and even walls and ceilings, can be waxed. The surface to be waxed must be absorbent whether it is natural or painted, and waxing should not be applied to vulnerable areas subject to great wear and tear. Although waxing is a good sealant, areas such as bathrooms and kitchens should not be waxed as water will mark wax surfaces even though wax is water resistant.

Many types of furniture wax are available in a variety of colors, from neutral through the wood tones to verdigris, blue and black. You may also tint the waxes with powder pigment to create a special shade that complements your own decor. Waxing is an effect that works well with other effects, such as colorwashing (see p. 60) and stenciling (see p. 78). When applying waxes over stenciling, make sure that the stencil paints have dried completely. Some waxes may tend to dissolve the stenciling, so always test a small area first.

You will need

Tools

• *1–2 in. (2–5 cm.) bristle decorators' brush* • *Fine-grade steel wool* • *Soft, lint-free cloth* • *Sandpaper* • *Rubber gloves*

Materials

• *Furniture wax* • *Low-tack masking tape* • *Simulated buttermilk paint*

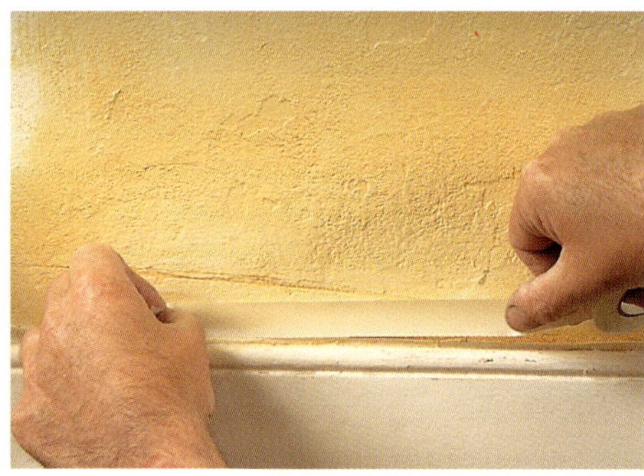

1 Use the low tack tape to seal off the area surrounding the surface to be waxed.

2 Prepare the surface by sanding. Remove all dust with a damp cloth. If the final effect required is one of heavy distressing, leave most of the imperfections to help accentuate the final look.

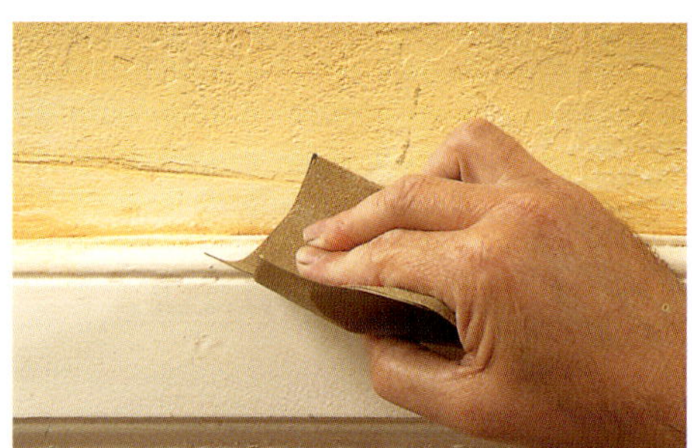

Variation 1

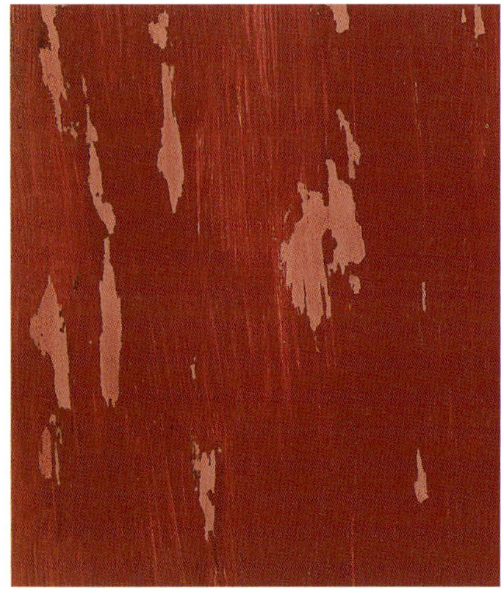

Here, over a basecoat of yellow ocher, smears of wax have been applied using a soft cloth wrapped around a finger. The wax was put on liberally and allowed to dry overnight before the topcoat of burgundy was added. After drying, the surface was heavily rubbed with antique brown wax and fine-grade steel wool (see p. 10). It was then buffed to a dull sheen.

Variation 2

Here, a more even and subtle effect has been created by the use of a more subdued colorway, a basecoat of Mediterranean blue under a coat of white. The effect was achieved by rubbing an ordinary household candle up and down the basecoat following the natural woodgrain, and then applying the topcoat. Finally, the top coat was removed with fine steel wool before finishing with a clear furniture wax.

3 Apply a basecoat of blue/green simulated buttermilk paint using a bristle brush. Make sure that any edges and recessed areas are not missed. Allow to dry for at least 24 hours.

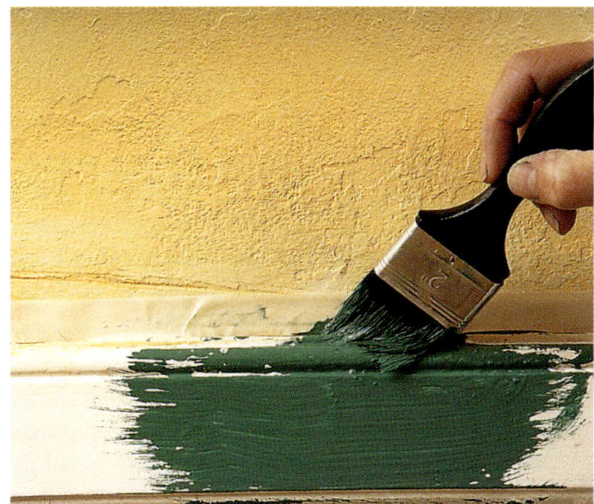

4 With a clean bristle brush apply a topcoat of yellow ocher simulated buttermilk paint. Allow to dry.

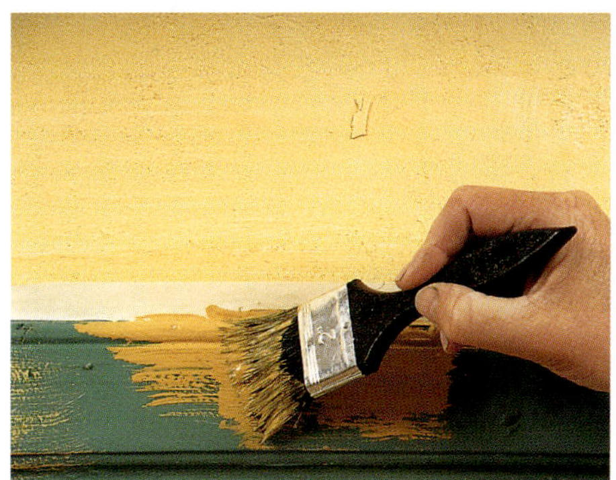

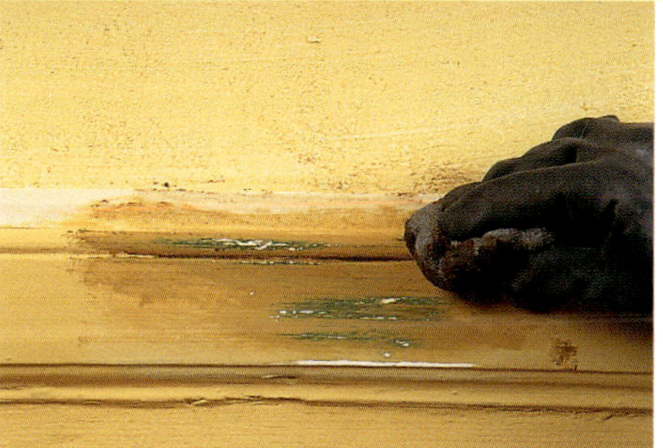

5 Apply antique brown furniture wax to the surface using fine-grade steel wool (0000 grade). Work backward and forward along the grain. Use enough pressure to gradually remove sections of the top and basecoat layers of paint. Coarser steel wool may be used for a more distressed look or to reveal underlying wood.

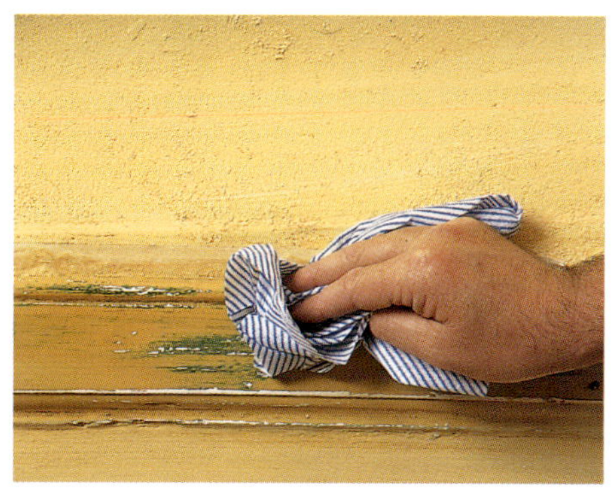

6 Once the final effect is achieved, allow the wax to dry. Apply another layer of wax. Allow to dry. With a soft, lint-free cloth buff the surface to a soft, mellow sheen. If a deeper color is required, add further layers of antique brown wax.

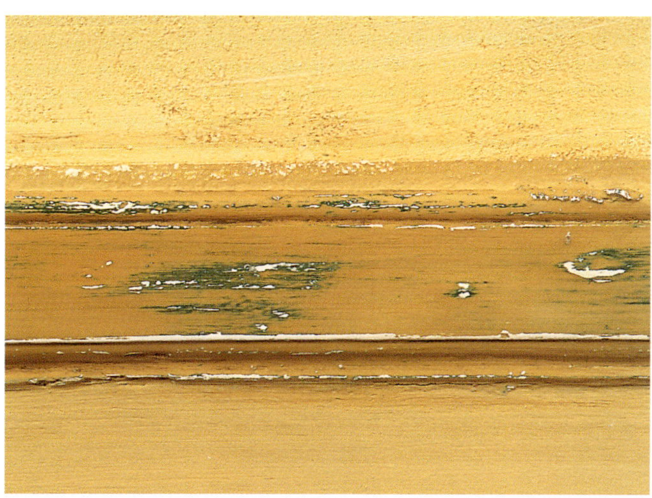

7 The simple technique of using wax and paint has transformed an old and well-worn chair (dado) rail, thus avoiding the expense of replacing it. This versatile effect looks extremely attractive and can help to create a country look with ease and simplicity.

Variation 3

Any number of colored layers can be used in this finish. Here, a basecoat of dark green was applied and allowed to dry, smears of wax were applied using a soft cloth wrapped around a finger, a layer of pale cream added, followed by more wax, and the final layer of dark cream. Finally, the whole surface was lightly sanded with a fine-grade steel wool, and clear furniture wax applied and worked in one direction.

Variation 4

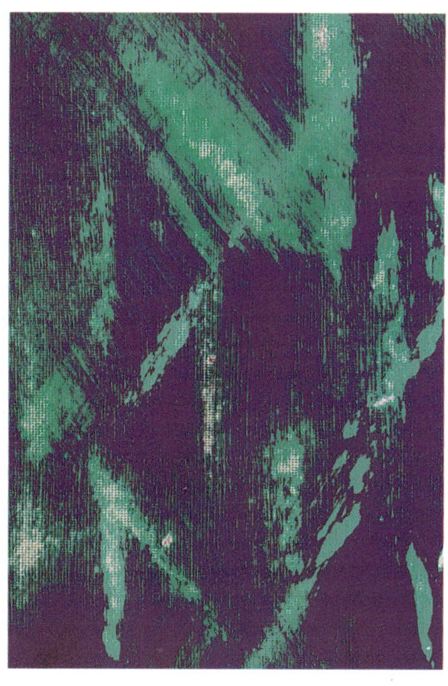

Here again three colors have been used: a basecoat of white, a second layer of peacock green and finally a bright purple, with layers of wax applied in between. The final effect was achieved by randomly applying wax with fine-grade steel wool and rubbing in alternate directions.

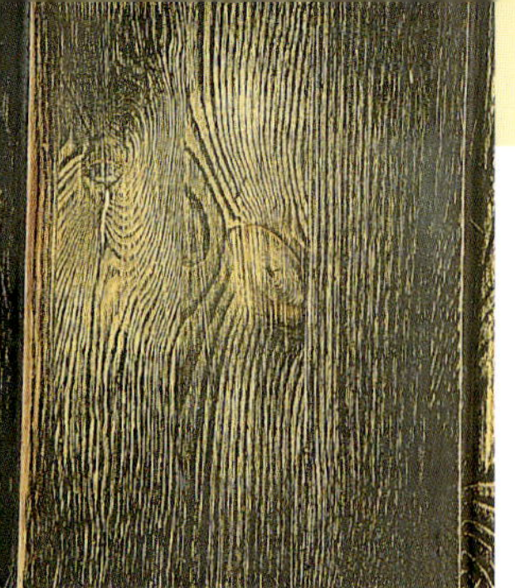

Distressing

Distressing is one of the most effective paint finishes. It can create that valuable antique look from the simplest of everyday items or, when used in larger areas, that mellow, relaxing atmosphere of the "country look." You can distress subtly or noticeably. The choice is up to you. Distressing works well in settings of period charm or country simplicity, and it is very inexpensive to complete.

Ideally suited to wooden units, window frames, doors, chair (dado) rails, and baseboards (skirting boards) this effect also looks good on smaller pieces such as boxes, tables and chairs. For the novice mistakes should be impossible, as the essence of distressing is creating that "time-worn" look! Any mistakes often add to the "authenticity" of the project and should be incorporated rather than removed. Creating different color schemes opens up endless possibilities. Strongly contrasting colors can create vibrant and stunning effects, while more muted colors can create charm and aged elegance. Remember that the distressed look involves the simulation of natural damage as well as the ravages of time or the elements. The possibilities are endless.

You will need

Tools

• *Medium and fine sandpaper or sanding block* • *½–1 in. (1.2–2.5 cm.) bristle basecoat brush* • *2 in. (5 cm.) bristle basecoat brush* • *3 in. (7.5 cm.) basecoat brush*

Materials

• *Shellac (knotting) solution* • *Simulated buttermilk paint* • *Mahogany wood stain (water based)* • *Lint-free cloth* • *Furniture wax*

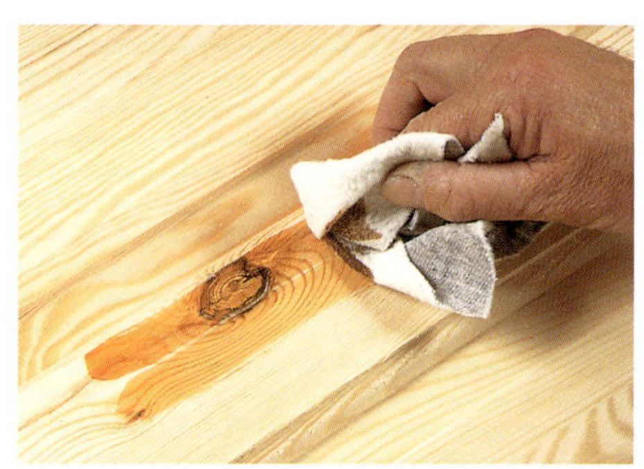

1 Thoroughly sand the surface and seal any knots with shellac (knotting) solution applied with a clean paper (kitchen) towel or a soft, lint-free cloth. This helps avoid discoloration later caused by resin seepage.

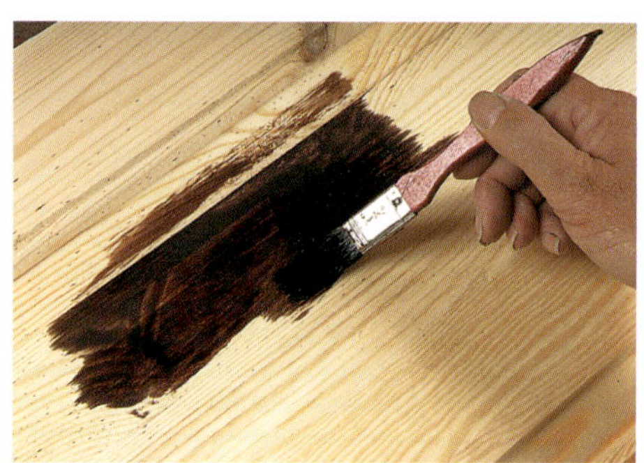

2 Using the ½–1 in. (1.2–2.5 cm.) bristle brush, stain the surface with a coat of mahogany wood stain. Brush in the direction of natural grain of the wood. By using a brush instead of a soft cloth, you will be able to get into the corners more easily. Allow to dry.

Variation 1

Metallic finishes are extremely versatile and well-suited to distressing. Here metallic silver spray paint has been applied over a basecoat of yellow ocher in a flat latex (matte emulsion) paint. The surface has been distressed with fine-grade steel wool (p. 10), rubbing quite hard and with the grain.

Variation 2

Varying colorways works well, as with the case of gold sprayed over a base of deep cream. A layer of dark blue and red acrylic paint was then applied in patches, allowed to dry, and finished with a heavy rubbing with fine-grade steel wool.

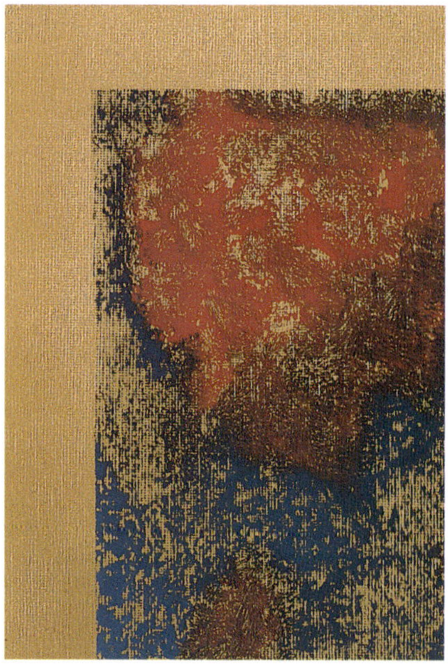

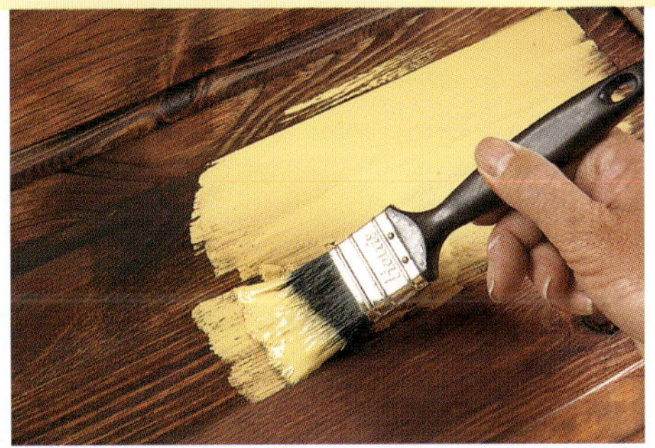

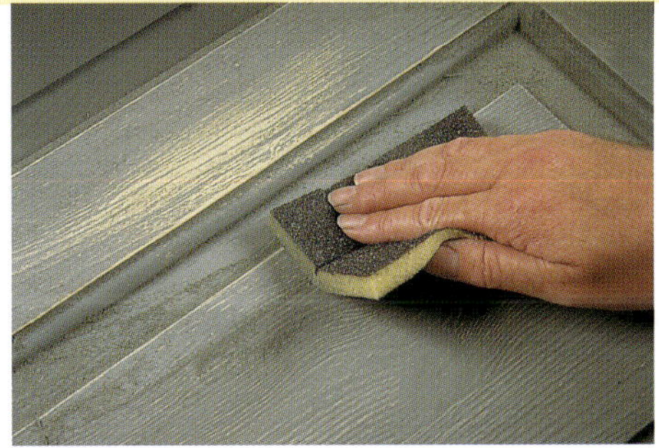

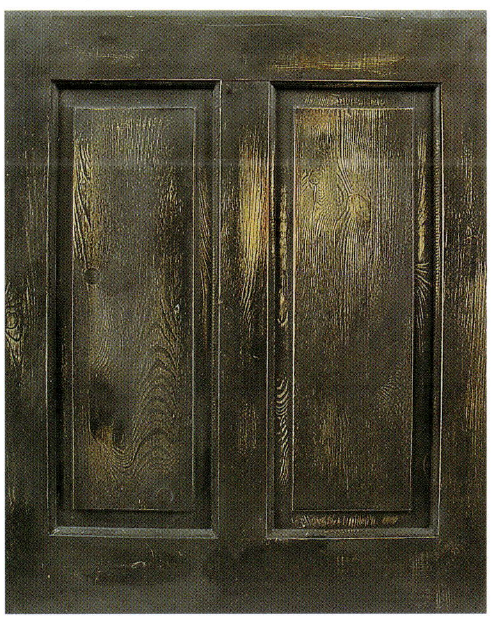

3 **Using the 2 in. (5 cm.) bristle brush apply a coat of ocher colored, water-based paint. Here we have used simulated buttermilk paint (see p. 14). Work along the grain of the wood and make sure that the surface is evenly covered. Allow the paint to dry and then lightly sand it. Remove excess dust.**

4 **Using simulated buttermilk paint in a dark green color, apply a top coat using a 2–3 in. (5–7.5 cm.) bristle basecoat brush. Do not cover the surface completely but make sure that less vulnerable areas are covered. Dry for 24 hours.**

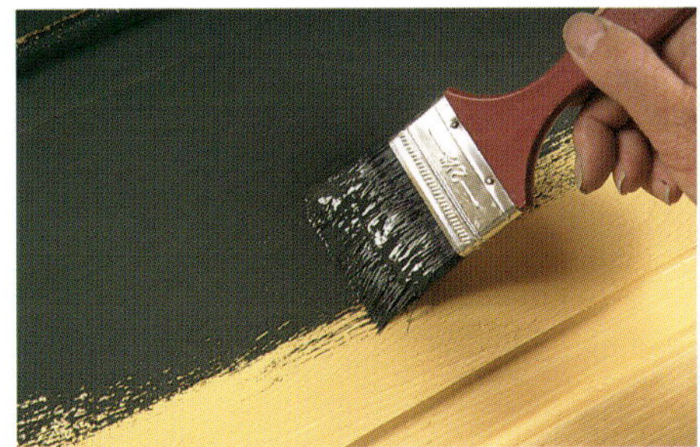

5 **Sand the topcoat in the direction of the grain in the areas which would naturally wear away over time to expose the ocher underneath. Continue to sand vulnerable areas such as the edges and behind the doorknob until you achieve the look you want.**

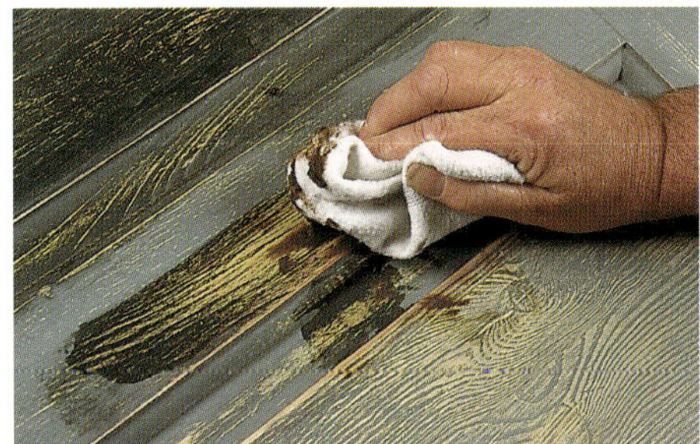

6 **Apply two coats of antique pine furniture wax with a soft, lint-free cloth, following the manufacturer's instructions. (Use a soft bristle brush for any awkward areas.) Allow to dry and buff with a soft cloth for a soft sheen. This wax is used only for internal finishes.**

7 **This door has been distressed to show the natural wood, the knots and the grain which has given the panels an aged beauty usually only possible after years of exposure to the elements. The soft sheen, wax finish will protect the surface but does not detract from the feel and look of the final effect as some protective finishes would.**

Variation 3

The effect of paint peeling and blistering has been achieved by sponging (see p. 54) over the basecoat of aqua with masking fluid and allowing it to dry. A coat of dark green, semigloss latex (vinyl silk emulsion) paint was then applied to cover the surface, allowed to dry, and rubbed down with fine-grade sandpaper. It can be further enhanced with a coat of an antique brown-tinted furniture wax.

Variation 4

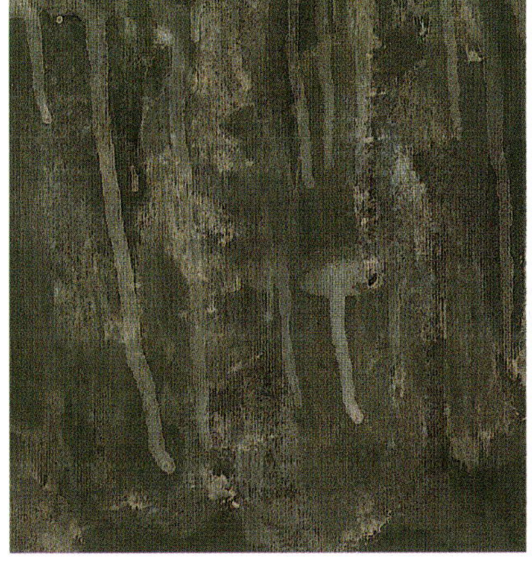

Here a basecoat of flat latex (vinyl matte emulsion) in dark green has been applied and allowed to dry before randomly applying "puddles" of diluted white latex (emulsion). Using a hairdryer to dry the wash has created a hazy effect. Finally, a slightly stronger whitewash was dribbled down the surface, allowed to dry and distressed with furniture wax tinted with raw umber powder.

In context

Broken colorwork paint techniques can be used to create areas or rooms that have a unique look of opulence and grandeur. Here the effects of antiquing, stippling and distressing/colorwashing show how this can be achieved in a variety of settings—from a glorious look of faded grandeur to the warmth and excitement of the Mediterranean. These simple effects can change a very plain and ordinary room into one that has its own special ambience and magic.

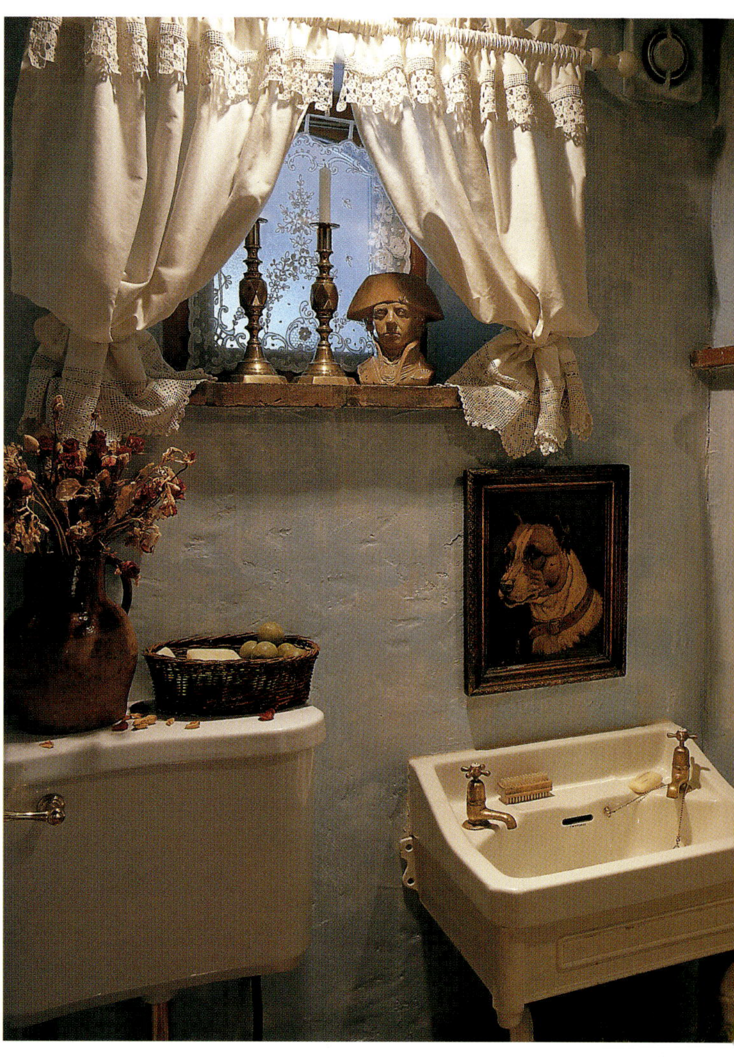

Distressing/colorwashing

▼ Mediterranean-style dining area

This dining area shows the perfect assimilation of the colorwashing and distressing techniques. The choice of warm terracotta over pale terracotta for the walls has a wonderfully warm and inviting effect. The imaginative and very appropriate addition of verdigris effect accessories serves to pull the whole scheme together. Fantasy marble on the shelves and door frame completes the look.

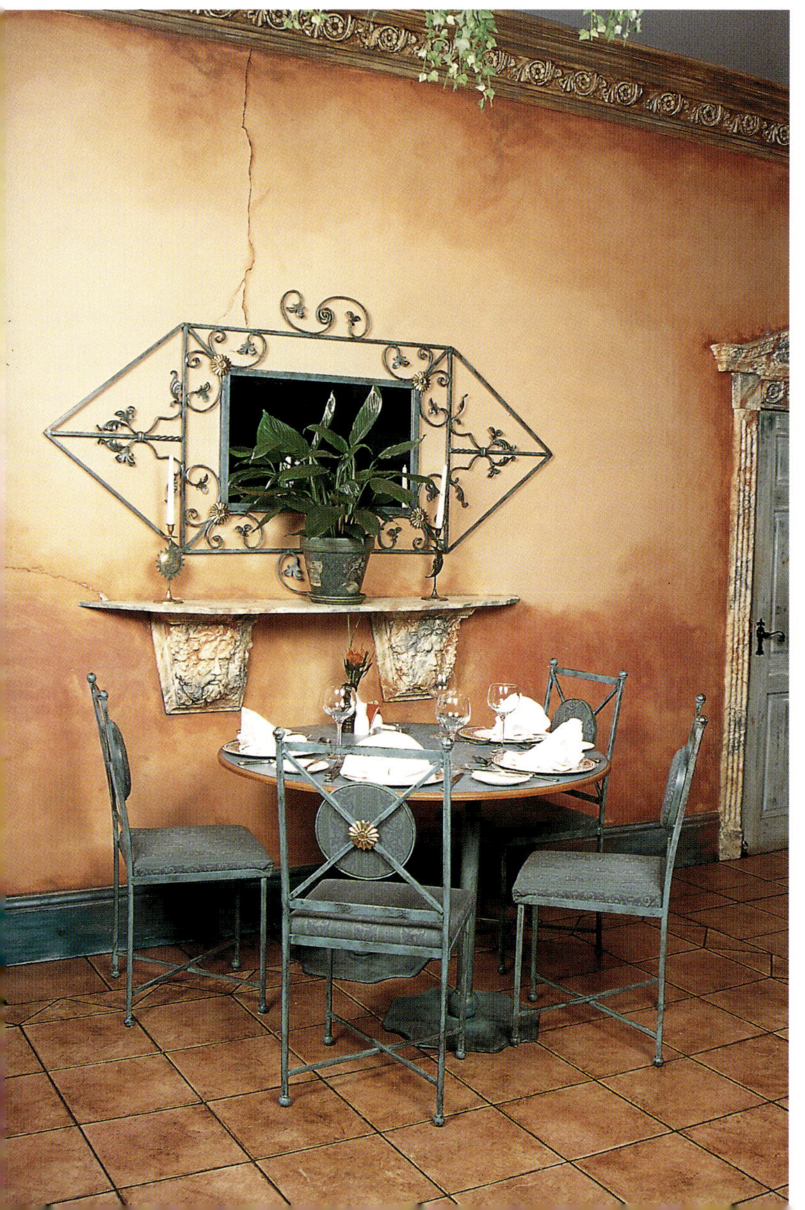

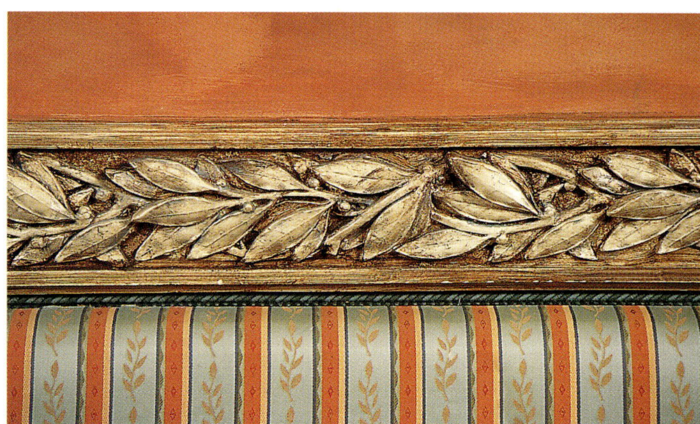

Antiquing

▲ Heavily molded plaster border

This extremely elegant vine of leaves and berries molded in plaster really benefits from being antiqued in umber glaze over a pale cream basecoat. Its true depth has been shown to great advantage and is complemented by the glow of the deep terracotta colorwashed walls and the blues and terracottas of the silk sofa back. The overall effect is one of sheer simplicity and elegance.

Distressing on plaster

▲ Period bathroom

This pure white porcelain bathroom suite has been used to full advantage by drawing on the heavily colorwashed/ distressed blue and white plaster of the walls to create a simple yet inviting mood. Varied accessories in earthy colors of terracotta and brown are accentuated by brass to complete the scheme and add a personal touch.

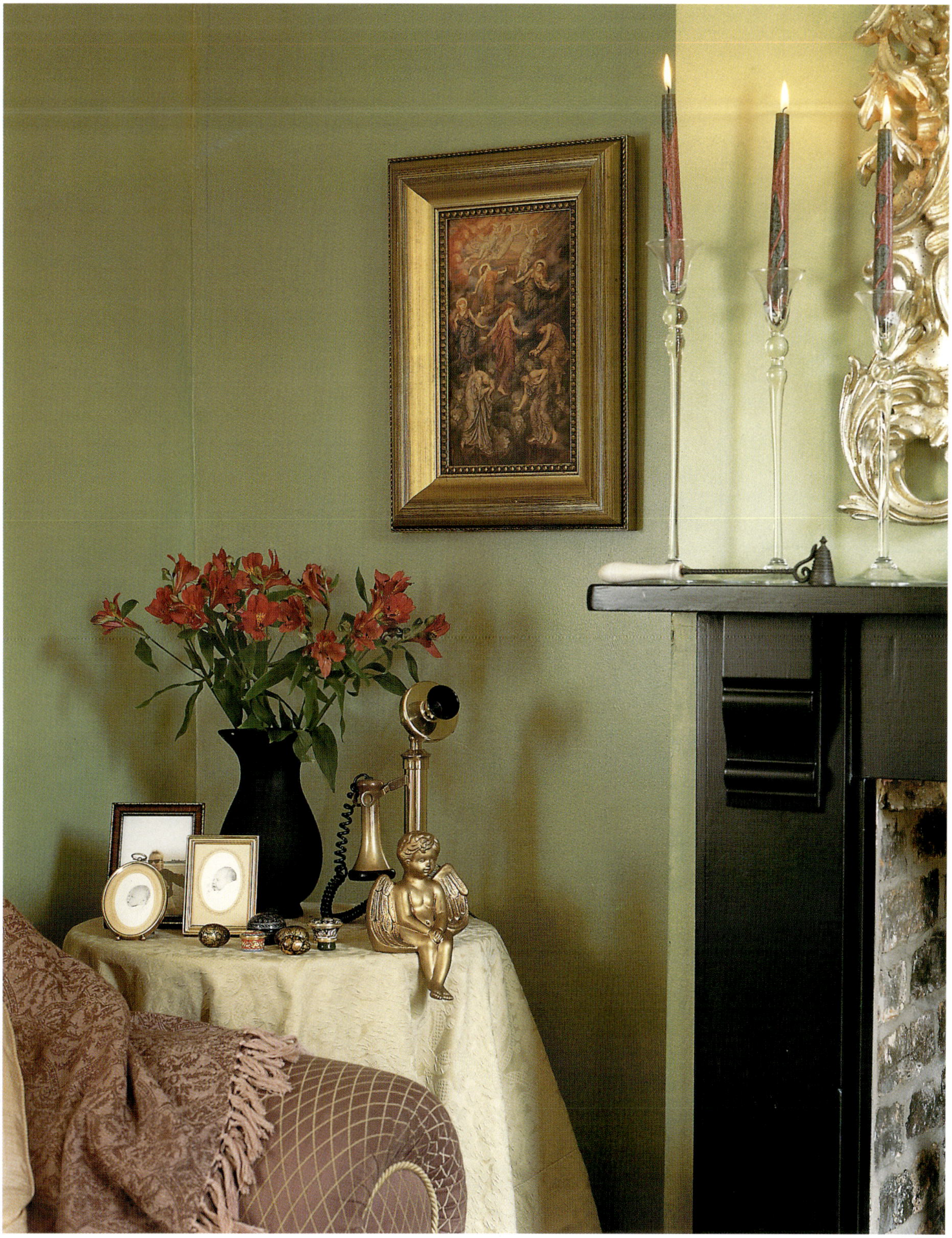

Stippling

▲ Elegant drawing/living room

Here the strength of the solid slate fire surround has been emphasized by the use of some carefully chosen colors in the subtle and elegant stippling of the walls, creating an ambience that is both inviting and relaxing. The uneven nature in which the stippling has been applied has given the walls a look of greater depth and interest.

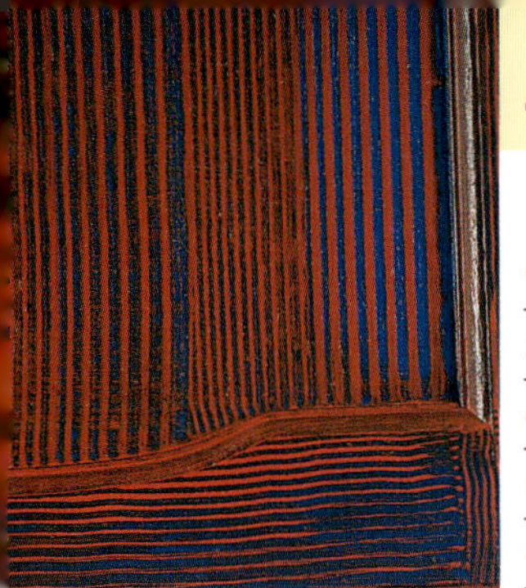

Combing

Combing is a simple and yet effective technique that can be used to create striking and individual patterns. It is a technique that has endless design possibilities enabling you to put your own stamp on any decorative scheme. Combing works better in a modern or country setting than in traditional Victorian or Georgian styles; but a smaller item will, if well placed, enhance any setting.

You will need

Tools

• 2–3 in. (5–8 cm.) basecoat bristle brush • 2–3 in. (5–8 cm.) glazing brush • Stippling brush • 1 in. (2.5 cm.) bristle brush • Paper towel or lint-free cloth • Comb • 2 in. (5 cm.) good varnishing brush

Materials

• Oil-based eggshell paint for basecoat • Transparent oil glaze • Artists' oil color, eggshell or universal stainers for tinting in your chosen colors • Mineral spirits (white spirit) • Oil-based varnish for protection

Combing works best on very smooth surfaces such as walls, floors or furniture, but should not be attempted on irregular surfaces such as chair (dado) rails.

Because your initial outlay for glazes and tinting colors is rather high, combing can be expensive, but the tools required are comparatively few. All the materials you will need are available in good decorator stores, but you can make up your own glaze (see p. 15) and create your own combs (also see malachite p. 98), which will help to save some of the expense. Combing offers a very animated finish and works well with contrasting colors. One pitfall is that it can look very "busy," so it is best kept to smaller areas. More subdued colors will work better on larger areas, but as always you should experiment to obtain the best effect.

Practice will help you to master this technique. It is very hard, although not impossible, to go over your work while combing. Care should be taken when creating the required patterns. If something does go wrong, immediately remove the glaze with mineral spirits (white spirit), allow the surface to dry, and then reapply the glaze. Depending on the vulnerability of the combed area, a final protection of oil-based varnish is advisable, as the oil glaze does dry to a very soft finish.

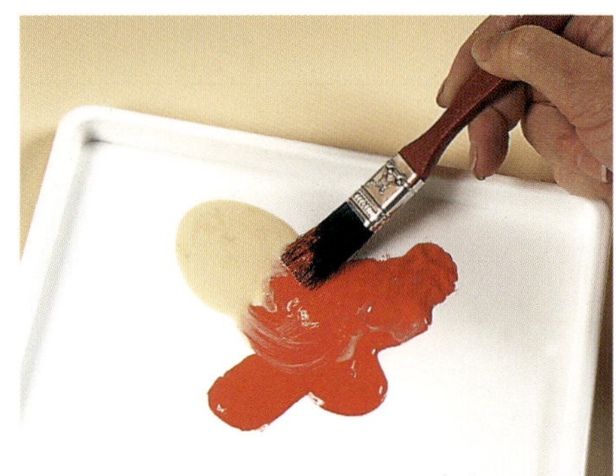

1 Prepare the surface (see *Preparation*, p. 18). Apply the basecoat of bright blue eggshell using 2-3 in. (5-8 cm.) bristle basecoat brush. Allow to dry. Mix a glaze of bright red artists' oil paint with the transparent oil glaze and thin it down to the consistency of pouring cream. Make enough for the entire surface. Use 1 in. (2.5 cm.) bristle brush for mixing.

Variation 1

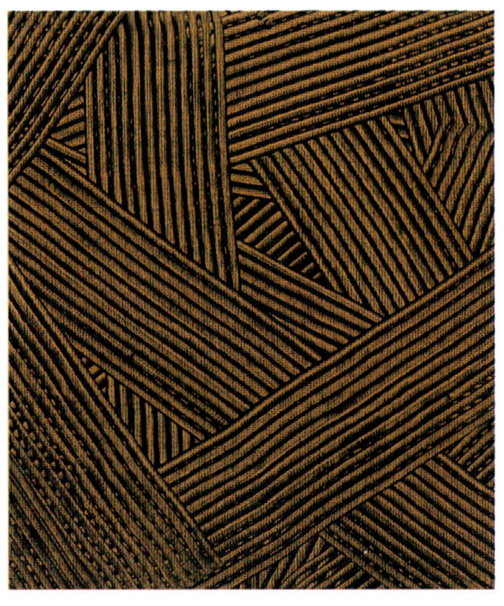

The basecoat of this sample panel was applied using two coats of bright orange, eggshell paint. Drying time was allowed between coats. A glaze was mixed up of transparent oil glaze and artists' black oil paint, following the manufacturers' instructions. The glaze was applied to a dry surface and randomly combed with a 2 in. (5 cm.) wide-toothed, metal comb. The final effect was sealed with a satin, oil-based varnish.

Variation 2

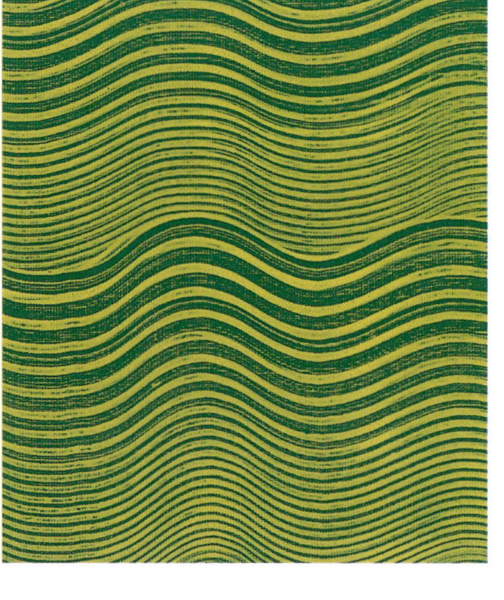

The wild and wonderful has been created in this sample by first using contrasting colorways. A basecoat of bright yellow has been stippled over with a glaze of dark, emerald green. Next, a variegated rubber graining comb was pulled in a "waving" action through the glaze, creating the optical illusion of motion. This is certainly not an effect for the more conservative decorator, but it is great fun.

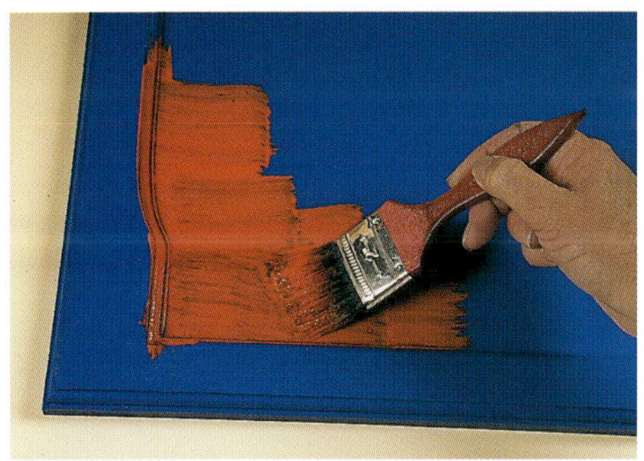

2 Paint the panels of the door frame with a generous coat of mixed glaze using the glaze or bristle basecoat brush. Brush in one direction only.

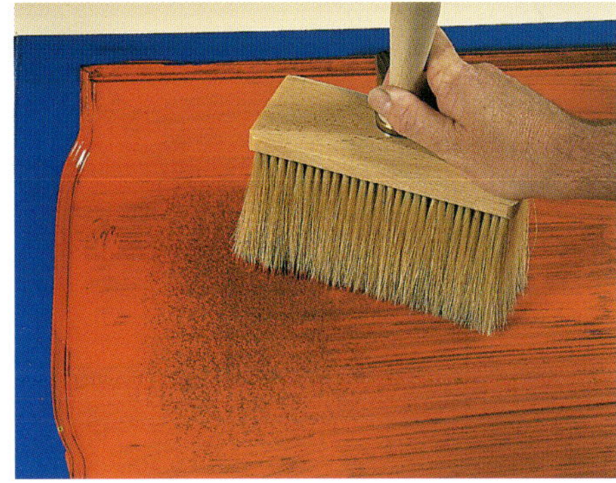

3 "Pounce" the stippling brush over the painted areas to remove all of the brushstrokes. Wipe any excess glaze from the brush with paper towel or lint-free cloth. Remove any excess glaze from the raised area around the door panel.

4 Start combing slowly and carefully through the wet glaze from the top of the panel down. Clean the comb teeth after each complete stroke. Continue across the panel keeping your strokes as parallel as possible. Remove any build up of glaze at the bottom of the panel with a clean, dry bristle brush as soon as you have completed the combing. Allow to dry overnight.

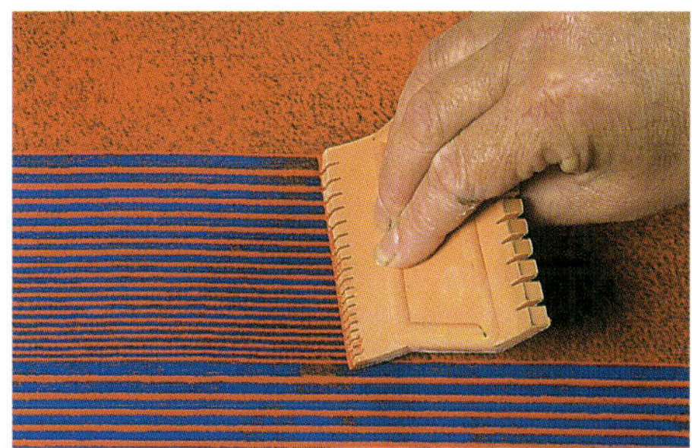

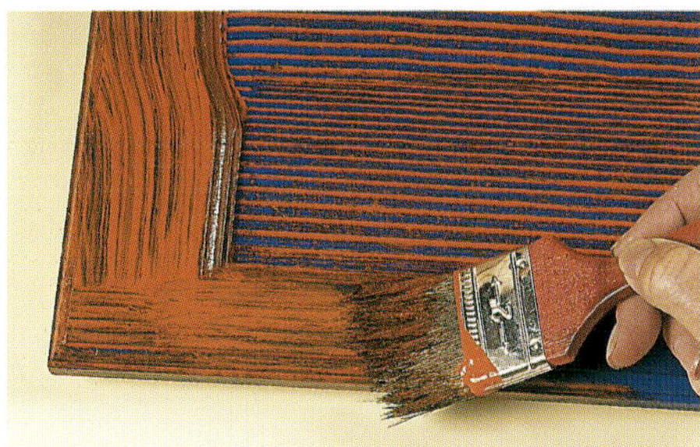

5 Apply the glaze to the outside raised edge of the door panel using the glazing brush.

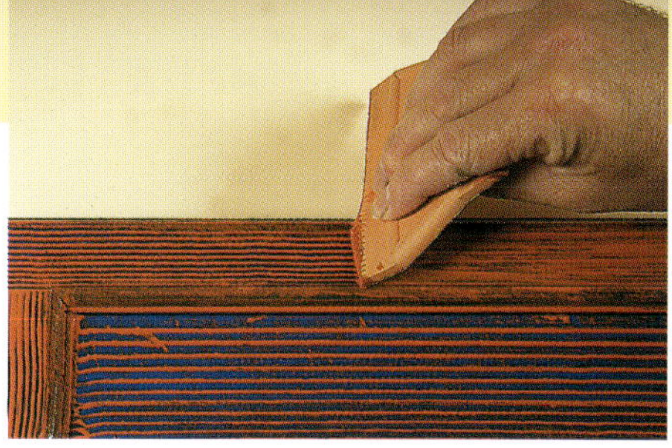

6 Stipple out the brushstrokes and comb through the wet glaze along the top and bottom edges of the panel. Remove glaze from the comb after each stroke. When the edges are finished, comb down the sides from top to bottom. Dry overnight. Seal the surface with at least two coats of oil-based varnish.

7 This technique has given a flat door (below) a new lease of life by the simple use of a comb and some glaze. Whether the colors chosen are strong and vivid or pastel and subdued, combing can revitalize the old or enhance the new with only the minimum of effort and practice.

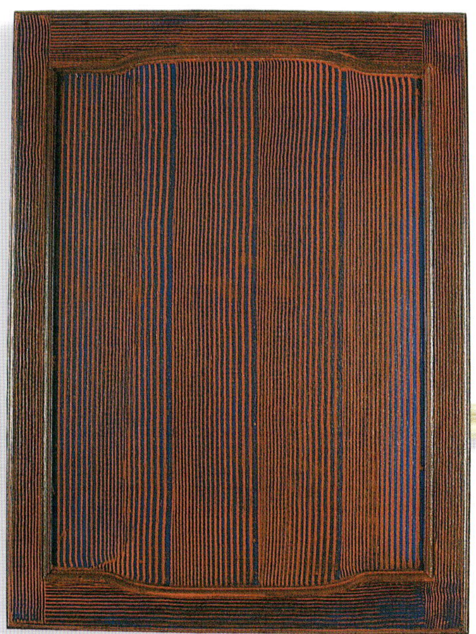

Variation 3

This time a glaze of lemon yellow has been used over a basecoat of dark green, and an evenly graded, rubber-toothed comb pulled through the glaze, first in one direction, and then at 90 degrees to the first part, creating an interesting but subdued checkered (chequered) or plaid effect. This would look good on units in a country kitchen.

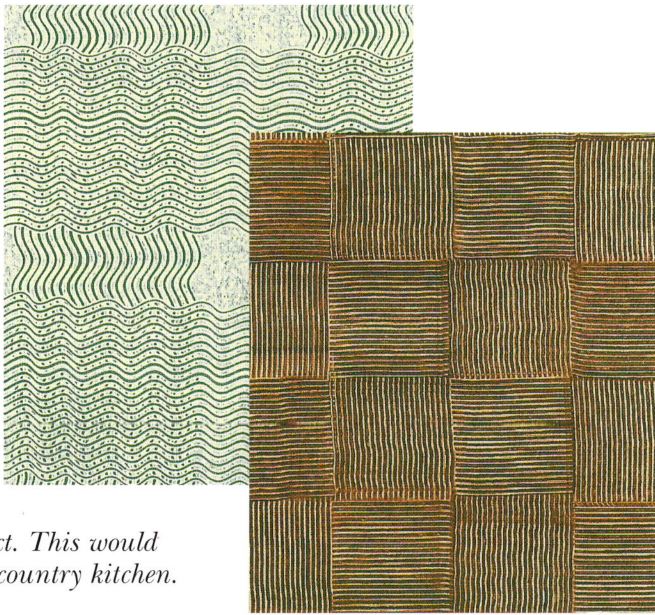

Variation 4

One very popular effect is basket weave (left). Here a 2 in. (5 cm.) fine metal comb has been pulled through a glaze of deep saddle brown over a basecoat of mid-cream. The comb has been slightly "waved" in the glaze to create a characteristic country or hand-done effect.

Dry brushing

Dry brushing is ideally suited to aging techniques (see p. 32) but it is versatile enough to create really interesting results in both period and modern settings. Dry brushing gives you the scope to experiment and be adventurous with color. So do not be too inhibited when it comes to color choice as the final results could be very exciting and individual.

Dry brushing can enhance furniture, walls, ceilings and floors as well as decorative objects such as picture frames, candlesticks or boxes. Creating tactile textures and incorporating them in both traditional and modern settings is extremely easy with this technique, requiring only a little practice.

Dry brushing involves the use of brushes with very little paint, and the most common mistake is overuse of paint. You can solve this problem by practice and by using less paint on the brushes than you think necessary. Go over the surface a few times rather than applying too much paint initially and having to remove it. If you have applied excess paint and cannot remove it, allow it to dry and use the dry-brush technique again, but use the basecoat as the topcoat.

You will need

Tools

• *Fine, soft brush* • *2–3 in. (5–8 cm.) bristle basecoat brush* • *1–2 in. (2.5–5cm.) varnishing brush*

Materials

• *Artists' white acrylic paint* • *Mid-blue eggshell paint* • *Paper (kitchen) towel* • *Fine sandpaper* • *Flat (matte) acrylic varnish*

1 Prepare your surface (see *Preparation*, p.18). (Top) Sand the surface until smooth with very fine sandpaper. Fold the sandpaper in half to reach the areas between the slats of the louvered doors. With a fine, soft brush, remove excess dust from the surface area.

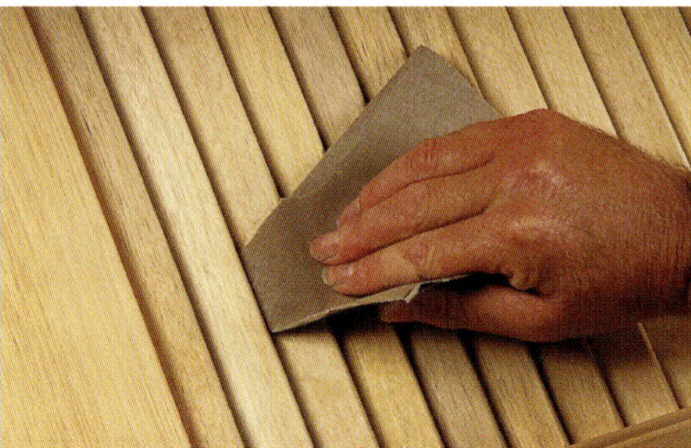

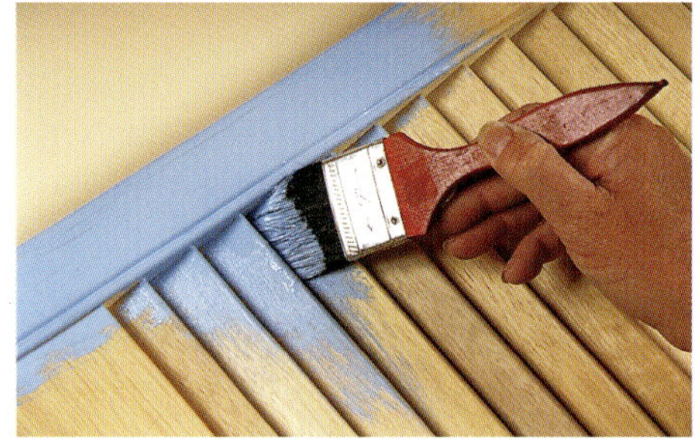

2 (Bottom) With a 2–3 in. (5–8 cm.) basecoat brush apply mid-blue eggshell paint. Dry for 24 hours. Repeat if necessary, including all the areas beneath, on top and in the corners of the slats. When dry, check that no areas have been missed.

Variation 1

Using different and more vibrant colorways in dry brushing can achieve startling results. In this example, the surface has been given a basecoat of vivid turquoise and dry brushed with an apple green. After masking off the top section, it was dry brushed once again, this time using a bright blue.

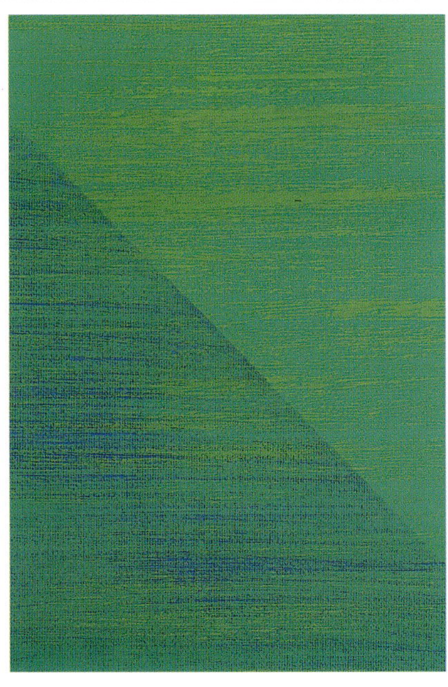

Variation 2

Here, a very dusty, blue green has been carefully over-brushed with a deep cream, creating a serene and elegant look that would enhance any dining room or living room.

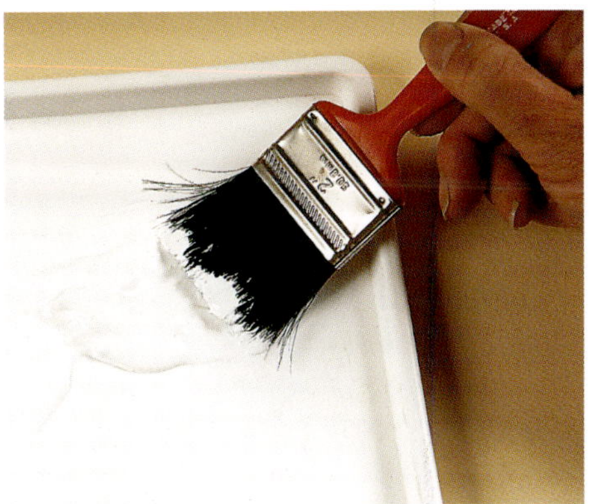

3 Put a little pure white artists' acrylic paint on a clean dish. Using the bristle brush, dip it into the paint making sure that you only pick up a small amount of paint. Dab the brush onto some clean paper towel to remove excess paint leaving the brush as "dry" as possible but still with a workable amount of paint.

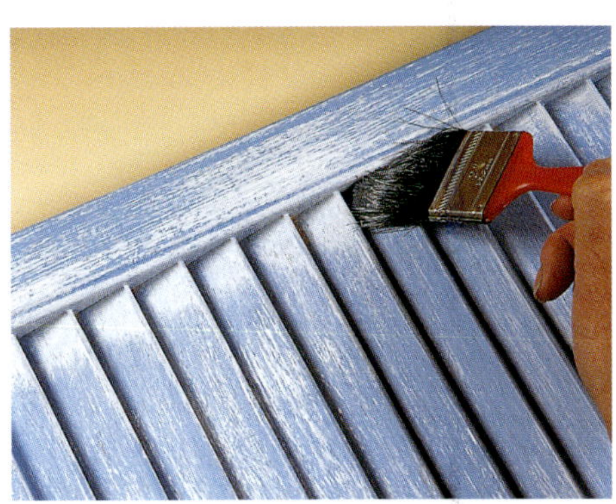

4 Quickly brush the surface of the door, working up and down the sides with quick strokes. Only just touch the surface with the bristles. Keep doing this along the sides until you have the effect you want. Then do the same backward and forward across the slats. Slightly enhance the corners with a further overlay of dry paint. Leave to dry.

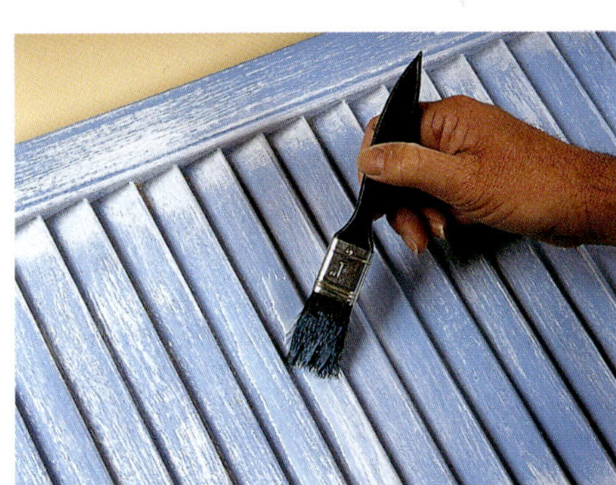

5 Apply two coats of varnish using the varnishing brush. Here we have used a flat acrylic varnish to keep the dusty, soft look, but a satin or gloss varnish may be used if preferred.

6 This ordinary louver door has been given a sun-washed look by the simple technique of dry brushing. The mid-blue over-painted with white has created a "fresh" feel. Finishing with a flat (matte) varnish has left a soft, chalky look like the sunlight effect on seaside boardwalks.

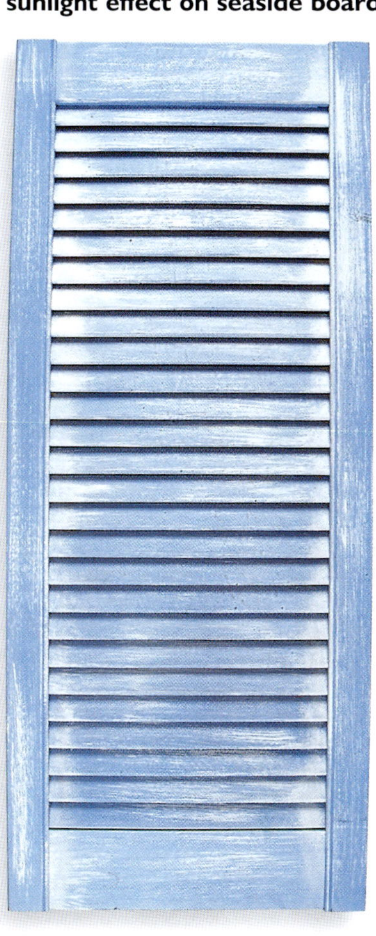

Variation 3

Here you can see how the final effect can so easily be altered by choosing only pastel shades. The basecoat of pink was dry brushed alternately with pale blue, mid-blue and finally turquoise, allowing each color to dry completely before continuing.

Variation 4

A basecoat of dark green, simulated buttermilk paint was applied to the surface of this panel and allowed to dry. Using a clean, dry brush a little gold acrylic paint was gently "dragged" across the surface. This was allowed to dry before lining (see p. 94) with a medium gold, permanent marking pen. The surface was sealed with a coat of spray sealant.

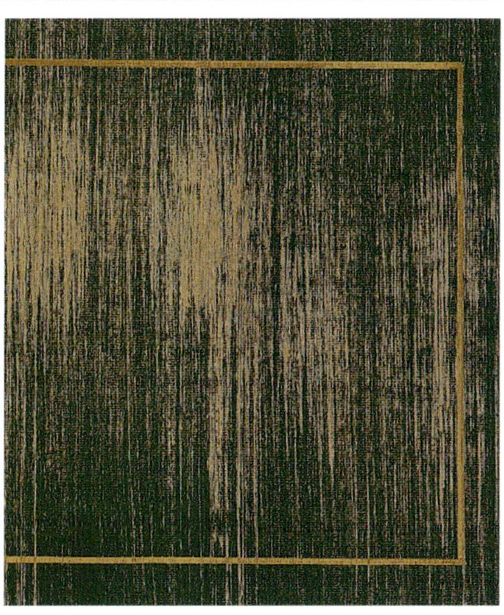

Simple woodgrain

For many years decorative artists have been imitating the look of expensive and exotic woods in paint. Creating these woods is now within the scope of most of us and we can easily achieve either the look of a favorite wood, or a simple woodgrain effect.

Woodgraining, whether to create the look of a specific wood, or a simple woodgrain effect, can be applied to most flat surfaces. It is suitable for use on furniture, moldings, floors, doors and cabinets, as well as decorative items. It is not suitable for carved or molded objects. This technique is not as inexpensive as some, and to achieve a good quality result a little practice is recommended.

Woodgraining works well in both traditional and modern settings. Any color can be used, provided that a woodgrain effect is required rather than the look of real wood. If a realistic wood finish is required, then the chosen colors should reflect this. To achieve good results, practice is advisable. Mistakes are generally due to a badly prepared surface. As the technique shows up surface flaws, start with a smooth finish. If the finish is not to your satisfaction then remove the glaze with a soft, dampened cloth, reapply the glaze and regrain.

You will need:

Tools

• 3 in. (7.5 cm.) bristle basecoat brush • Stippling brush • Fine lining brush • Varnishing brush • Straight edge (ruler) • Heart graining tool (rocker) • Sandpaper or sanding block or pad

Materials

• Store-bought filler • Acrylic glaze • Yellow ocher latex (emulsion) • Pale and dark terracotta semigloss latex (vinyl silk emulsion) • Chalk • Low-tack masking tape • Varnish

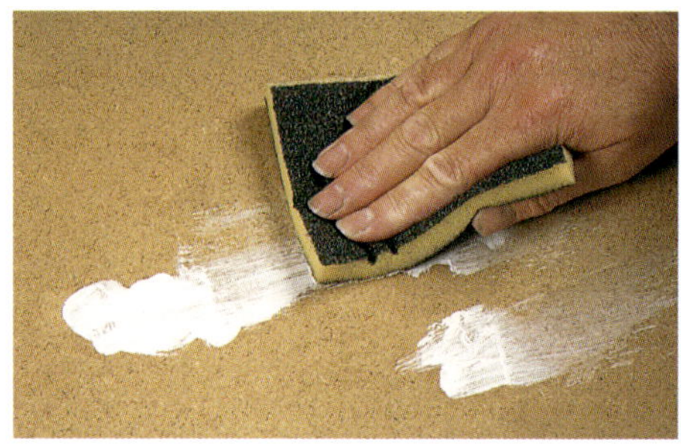

1 Prepare the surface (see *Preparation*, p. 18). Fill in any holes with a store-bought filler. Allow to dry. Sand with a medium-grade sanding pad. Remove dust with a brush and a damp cloth.

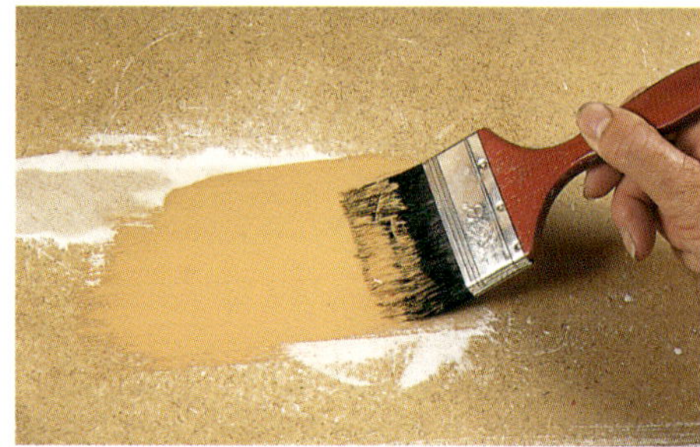

2 Apply a layer of pale terracotta semigloss latex (vinyl silk emulsion) with a 3 in. (7.5 cm.) bristle basecoat brush. Allow to dry. Repeat with a second layer.

Variation 1

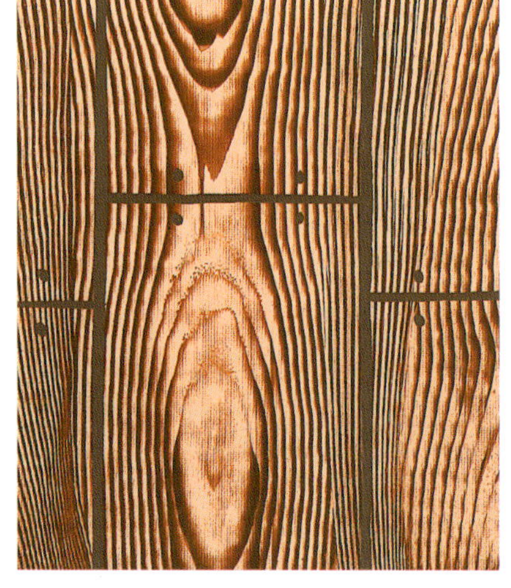

Once mastered, simple woodgraining using a heart graining tool can open up endless possibilities. In this example a traditional red-brown glaze has been used over a basecoat of apricot latex (emulsion) creating an effective grain texture. Some lines in dark brown have been added to simulate tongue-and-groove paneling. For this a fine lining brush was used together with a straight edge (ruler). Nail holes were added to complete the effect.

Variation 2

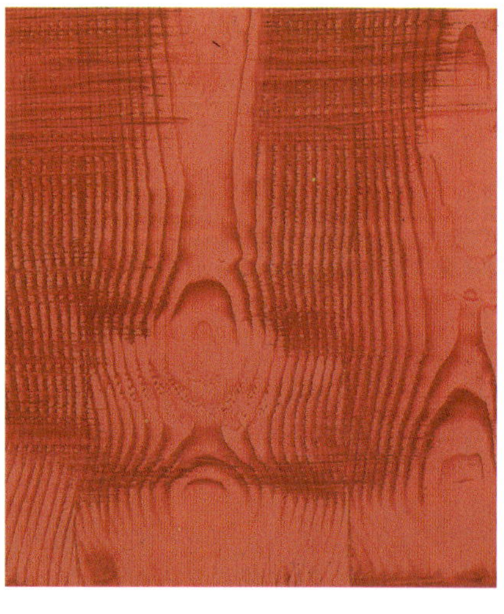

Although you are not limited to using colors of similar hues or shades, the watered silk look is best achieved by choosing colors close together in shade. In this example, after the glaze had gone tacky, instead of using a dragging brush an ordinary 3 in. (7.5 cm.) bristle basecoat brush was dragged across the wood grain creating a more noticeable and solid final effect.

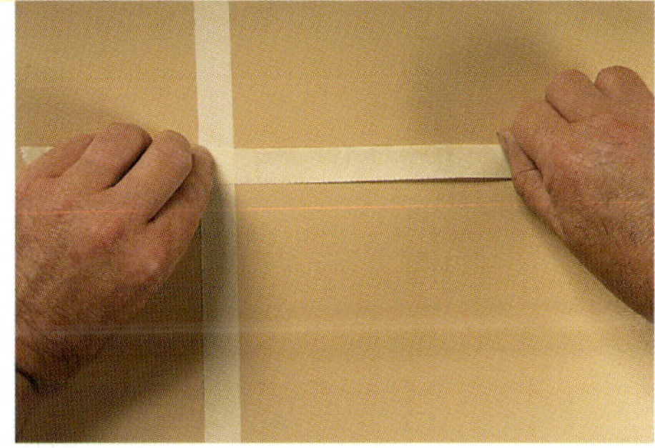

3 Measure and chalk up the panel squares onto the flat surface. Using low-tack tape mask off the outer edges of the panels and gently press the tape into position. Do not press too hard as this may cause the tape to lift the fresh paint when it is removed.

4 Pour some yellow ocher latex (emulsion) into a clean container and add acrylic glazing medium according to manufacturer's instructions. Mix thoroughly and add a little water to make a pouring consistency. Mix enough glaze to cover the entire surface.

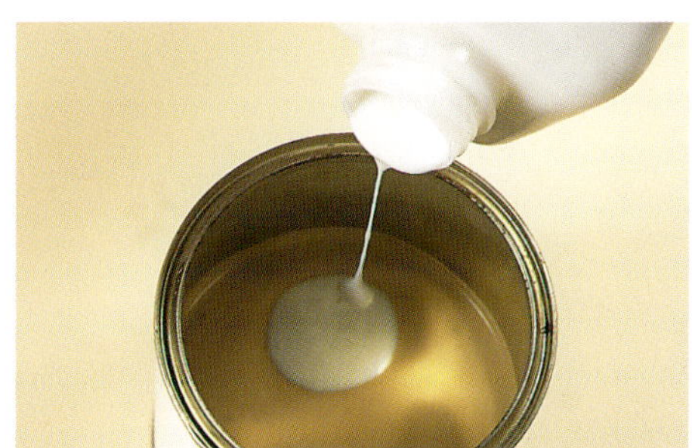

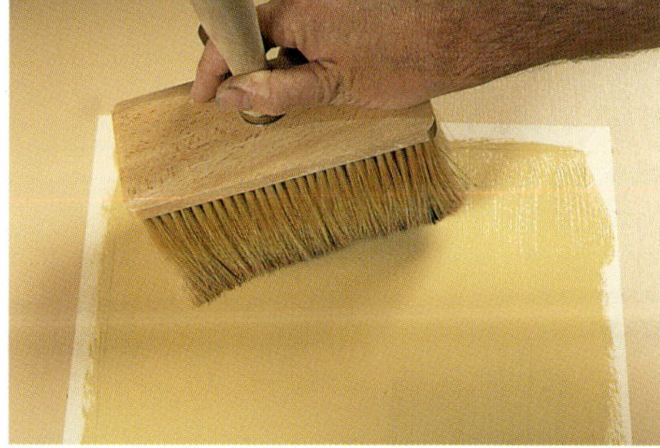

5 Using a 3 in. (7.5 cm.) bristle brush paint the glaze over the surface of the panels within the tape boundaries. Use the stippling brush to stipple out all brushstrokes (see p. 30) and to blend the ocher glaze across the panel surface. Be careful not to paint over the edges.

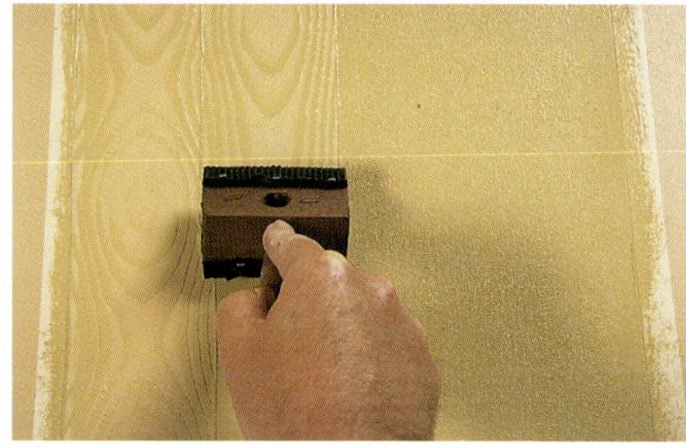

6 Pull the heart graining tool (rocker) through the glaze from top to bottom, carefully rocking it back and forward as you proceed. Remove the excess glaze with a clean, lint-free cloth before starting on the next line. Allow to dry overnight.

7 Remove the tape a little at a time, being careful not to pull away any of the terracotta paint from underneath.

In a clean container mix a little of the dark terracotta with water to a pouring consistency. With the fine swordliner brush and a straight edge outline the panel to the left and top with terracotta. The bottom and right are outlined with dark brown.

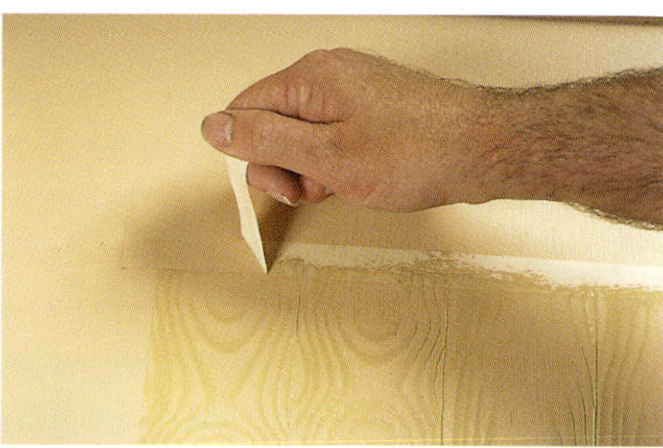

8 The texture of natural wood is admired by most people. Here, on a plain wall, the buff and ocher colors have helped to create a surface that has depth and interest. By combining simple lining and woodgrain techniques (see pp. 94 and 124) the panels have been given an orderly yet casual finish.

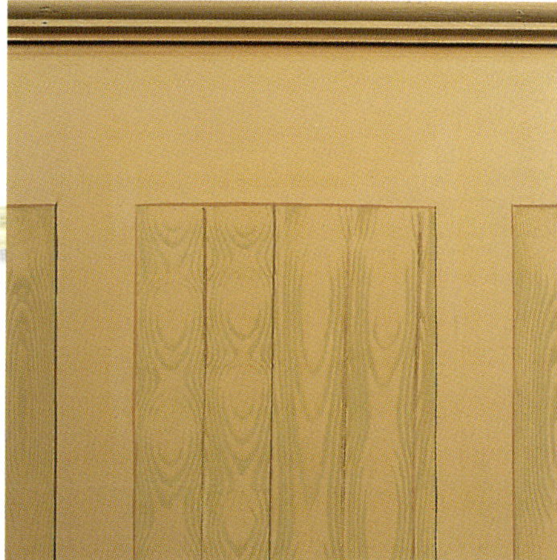

Variation 3

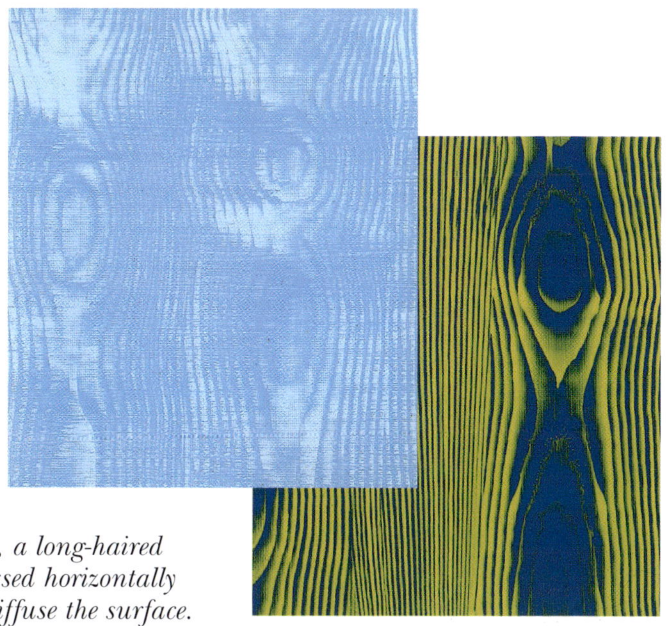

Watered, or moiré silk has been created here. Over a basecoat of pale blue a glaze of mid-blue latex (emulsion) was applied. The heart graining tool was passed through the glaze. When the glaze was slightly tacky after 5–10 minutes (depending upon atmospheric conditions), a long-haired dragging brush was passed horizontally across the graining to diffuse the surface.

Variation 4

By changing colors and using your imagination, fantasy woodgraining can be created to brighten up any setting and yet keep the traditional look of grained wood (left). Here, a bright yellow glaze was applied over a bright blue basecoat and the heart graining tool passed through the glaze.

In context

The three techniques here are characterized by their distinctive tactile look. Used in any colorway and sometimes in conjunction with each other, the result is an individual style that makes a positive statement. Originally both combing and woodgrain were applied to enhance the most simple of boxes and tin trunks, together with smaller decorative items such as shelves and small pieces of furniture. Here they are used in room settings to recreate the basic elements of simple Folk art style.

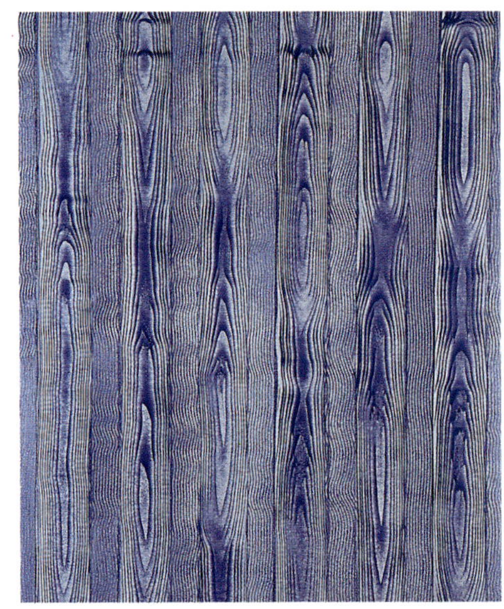

Simple woodgrain

◀ Recreation of tongue-and-groove paneling

The example here shows very clearly the look of bleached and stained tongue-and-groove paneling. The electric blue color works very well to enhance the textural appearance of the technique and also allows plenty of scope for a variety of accessories in many vibrant colorways.

Simple woodgrain

▶ Door panels in a bedroom

Again because of the vibrant and rich nature of the blue color and the use of deep terracotta on the walls and fire surround respectively, the woodgrain panels on the otherwise simple paneled door have created a point of interest that enhances a really attractive bedroom setting—it is simple yet very striking.

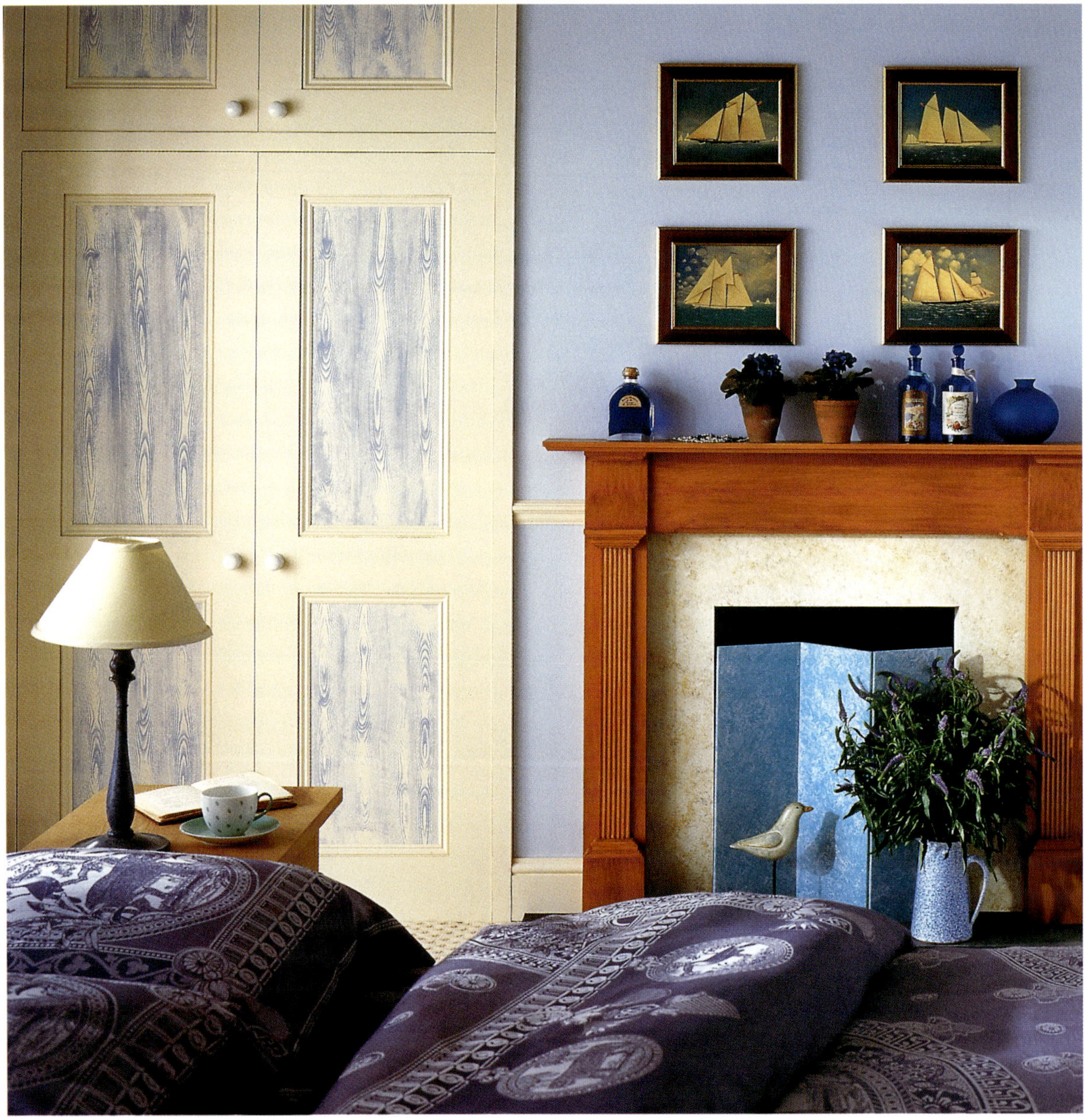

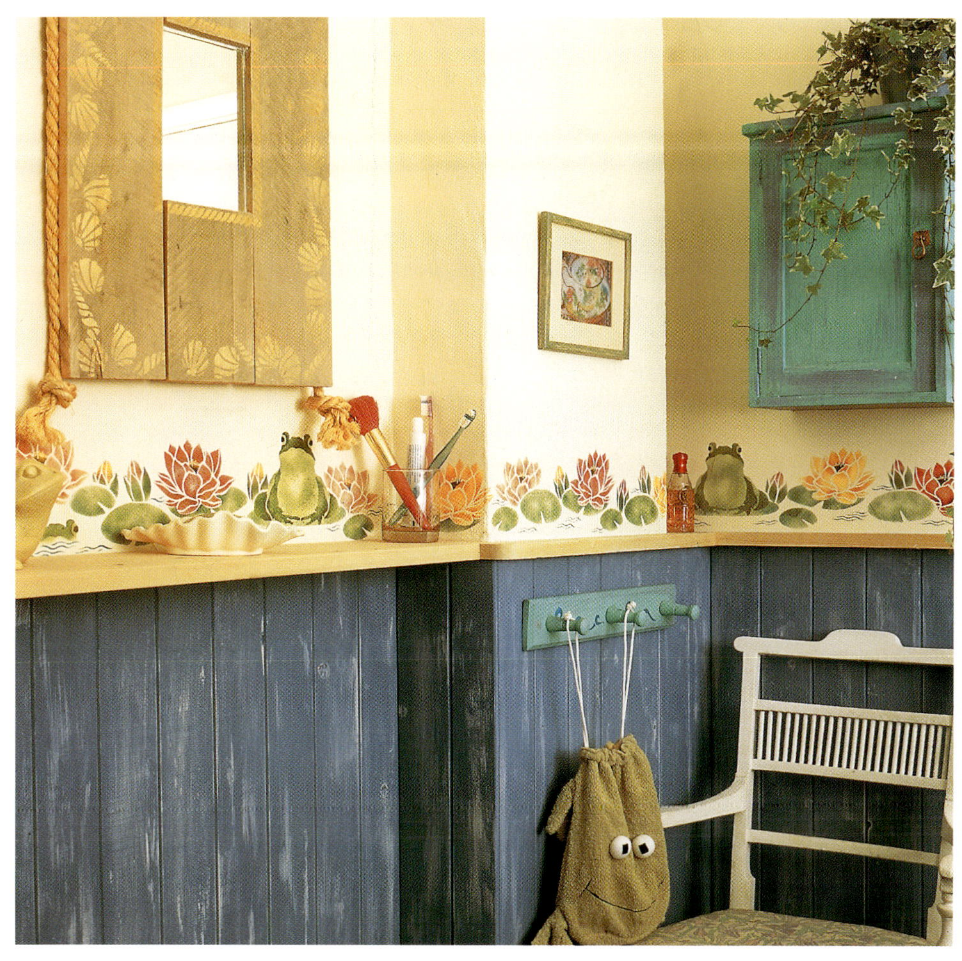

Dry brushing

◀ Tongue-in groove paneled bathroom

The deep Mediterranean blue used as a basecoat for the paneling in this bathroom has been treated to some random dry brushing in white. The result is a very pleasing "watery" effect. It has been enhanced beautifully by the sandy-cream walls and cleverly stenciled border of lilies and frogs. The use of dry brushing again over the blue/green wall cupboard completes the picture of this very attractive aquatic bathroom.

Combing

▶ Walls below dado rail in dining room setting

The beautiful textured detail of combing can been seen to great advantage here on the walls below the dado rail. The "glow" of the Mediterranean look is completed by rag-rolling the walls in a sea coral color and highlighting the look with a Greek key pattern stencil in a simple marbled texture.

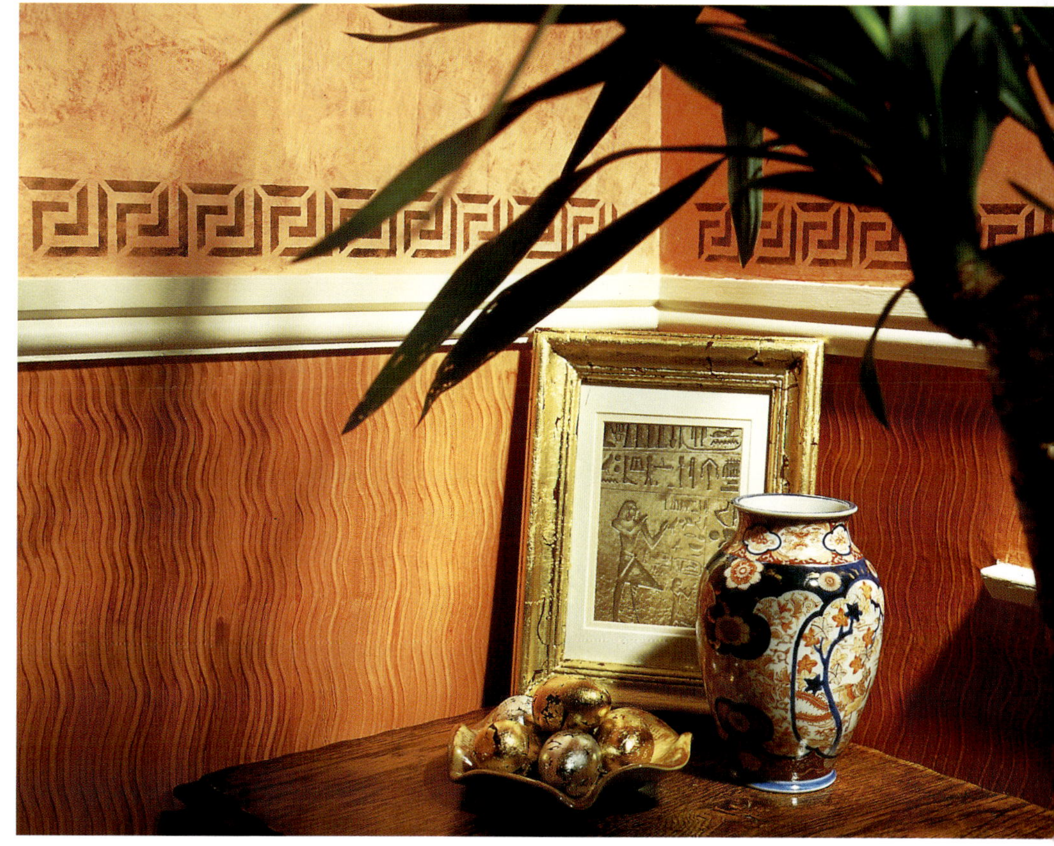

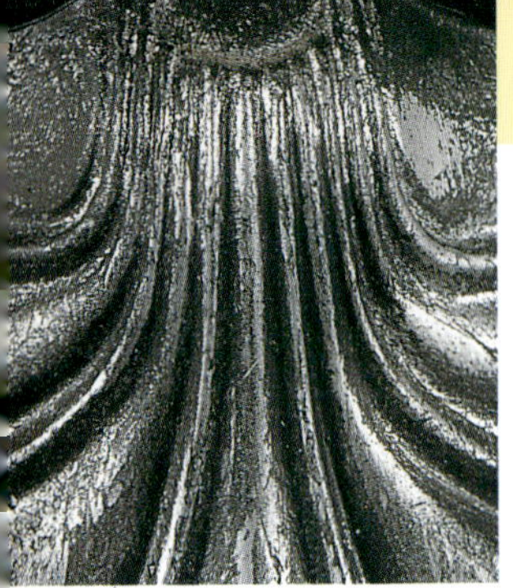

Pewter

Antique candlesticks, serving platters and tankards full of mead and wine come to mind when you think of pewter. This is a very easy effect to create with silver and black paints using the simple techniques of antiquing, aging (see p. 32) and distressing. Pewter, because of its own natural qualities, works well in both period and modern settings, creating a bridge between the old and the new.

A well-executed pewter finish on both doors and cupboard units will create a conversation piece in any setting, although this effect need not be confined to these areas alone. Smaller items such as boxes, tables, lamps and even architectural fittings can all be embellished. For very little expense and with only the minimum of experience you can create the richness of real metal. All of the required materials are readily available at good decorator stores or specialist paint-effect stores.

Preparation is the essence of a quality finish, although the specific preparation will depend on the final effect required. For an old, battered, antique look, for example, small defects in the surface may be left, or even created, using a hammer, nails and a set of keys. If a smooth finish is required, proper sanding and sealing should be carried out (see pp. 18–21).

The pewter effect is very quick to achieve, but do not be tempted to move too quickly, but do follow all the step-by-step instructions carefully. If something does go wrong, remove with a soft cloth and repaint—although remember that flaws in the surface could enhance the natural beauty and add to the authenticity of the finished look.

You will need

Tools

- *2 in. (5cm.) bristle basecoat brush*
- *1 in. (2.5 cm.) bristle brush*
- *Lint-free cloth or kitchen cloth*
- *Good quality 1–2 in. (2.5–5 cm.) varnishing brush*

Materials

- *Silver water-based acrylic paint*
- *Artists' black water-based acrylic paint*
- *Neutral-colored latex (emulsion)*
- *Black latex (emulsion)*
- *Suitable varnish*

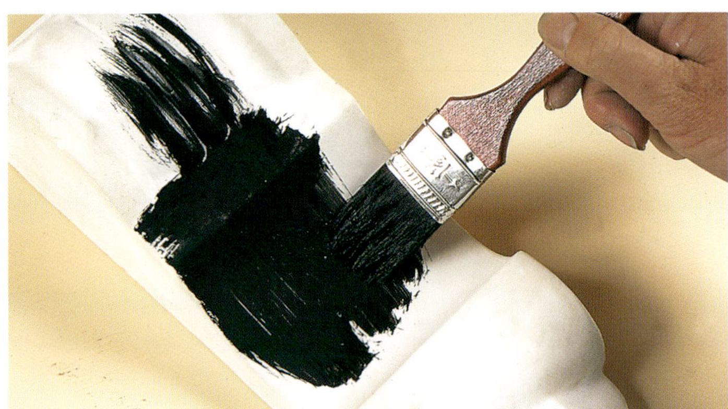

1 Seal the raw plaster surface with neutral diluted emulsion. Let dry. Apply two coats of black latex (emulsion) using a 2 in. (5 cm.) bristle basecoat brush. Let dry.

Variation 1

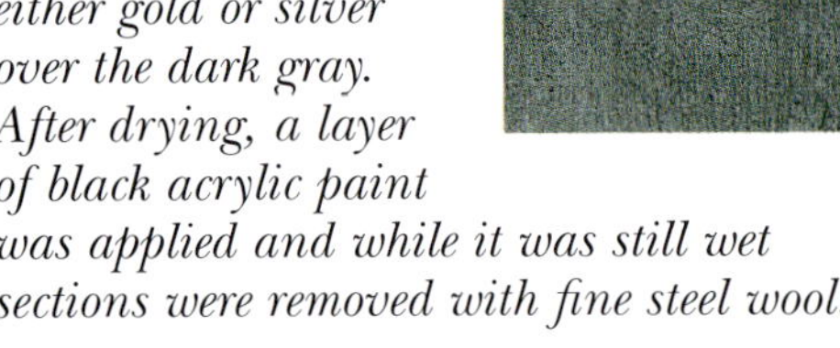

By using some lining effects (see p. 94) over a basecoat of dark gray, two totally different finishes have been created. Each alternate section has been masked off and then painted with either gold or silver over the dark gray. After drying, a layer of black acrylic paint was applied and while it was still wet sections were removed with fine steel wool.

Variation 2

Here, the surface has been painted with a basecoat of buff, allowed to dry, and sprayed randomly with gold and silver. Just before the metallic paint was totally dry the surface was rubbed with some fine steel wool in the same direction as the grain, creating a patchy, and slightly uneven, tarnished look.

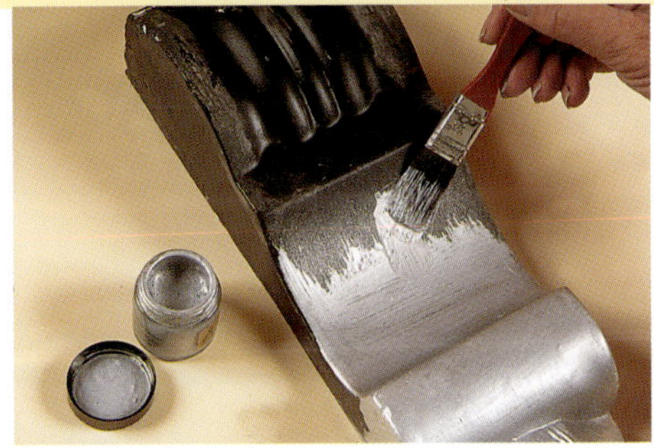

2 **Apply the silver metallic acrylic paint using a 1 in. (2.5 cm.) bristle brush, without too many brushstrokes. Dry. As an alternative to silver acrylic paint, use spray paint available from good decorator or specialist stores and follow manufacturer's instructions.**

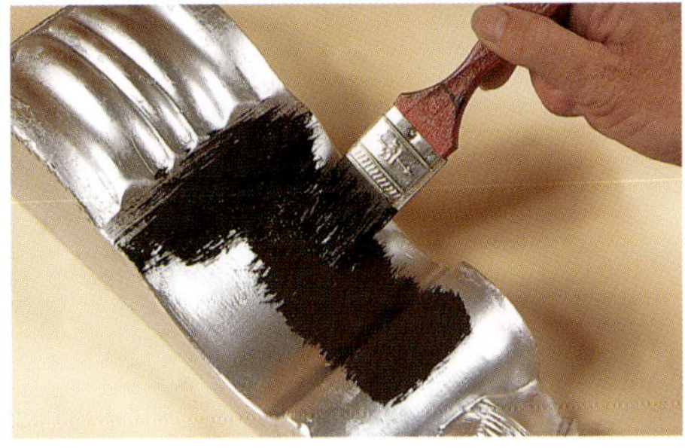

3 **Mix some black, artists' acrylic paint, with a little water to make a creamy consistency. Apply a generous layer over the surface using a bristle brush. You may prefer to use black latex (emulsion) which will work just as well and is possibly less expensive.**

4 **While the black paint is still wet or slightly tacky, remove any excess from the surface with a damp lint-free cloth or a kitchen cloth. For an older and more worn look, rub the black paint into the silver basecoat. For a slightly tarnished look expose less of the silver basecoat. Leave to dry.**

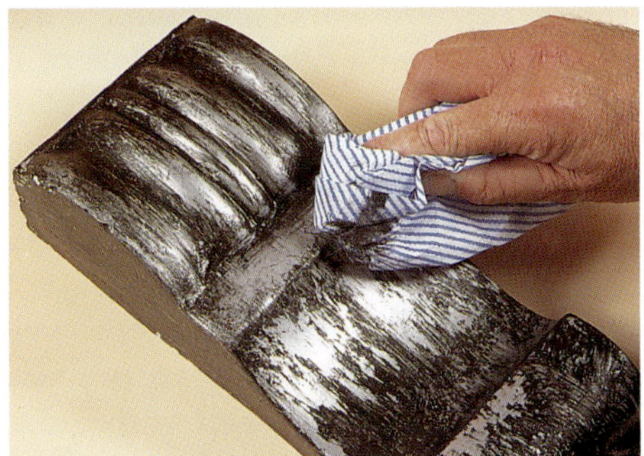

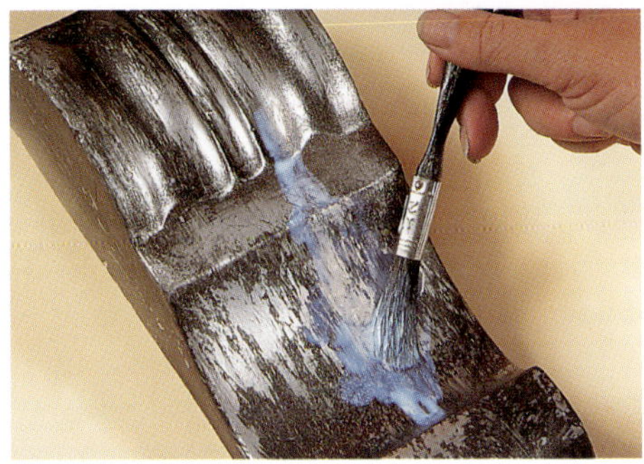

5 **Seal the surface with two coats of flat (matte) acrylic varnish using a varnishing brush.**

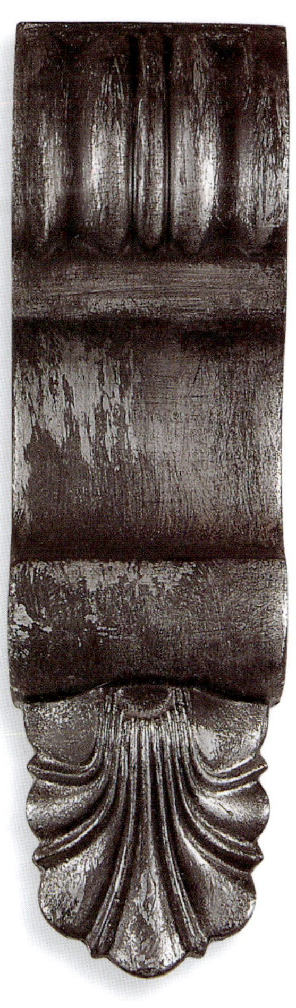

6 **This technique adds brilliance to carved and molded surfaces, such as this corbel, as easily as it does to paneled doors or simple candlesticks. Striking and individual, it can be used to embellish any scheme.**

Variation 3

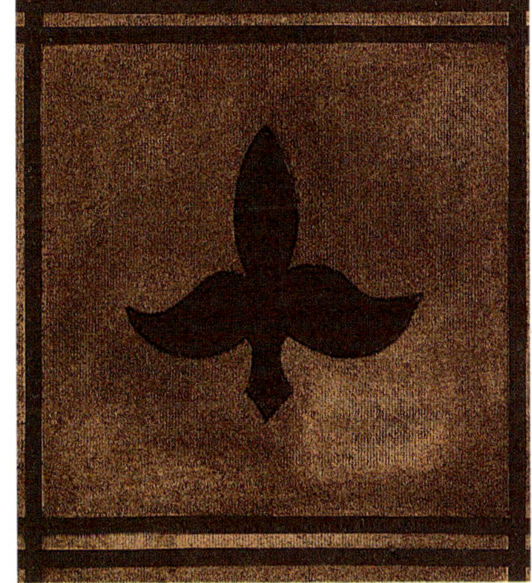

Here, a black, acrylic paint basecoat was applied. When dry, ¼ in. (0.63 cm.) low-tack tape was used to mask off the design area. A positive fleur-de-lys image was fixed to the surface with a little spray adhesive. With a soft cloth, copper wax was applied across the complete panel and buffed to a high sheen. The tape and fleur-de-lys were outlined in black permanent marking pen and the surface sealed with a wax finish.

Variation 4

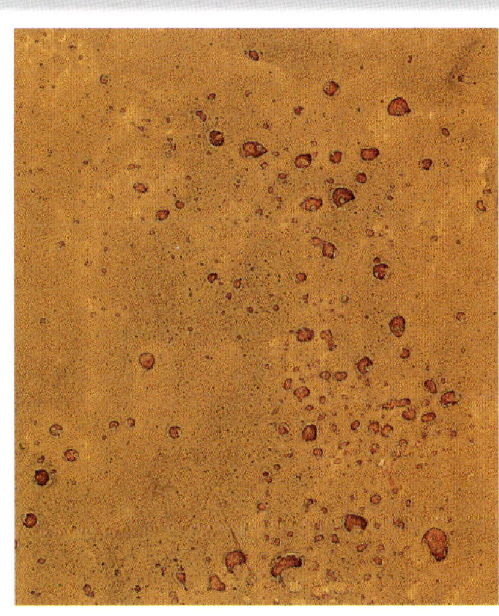

Here, some store-bought "hammerite" paint in gold was stippled (see p. 30) over the panel to create the look of burnished brass. Before the paint had dried, some watered-down acrylic paint in burnt sienna was spattered (see p. 72) onto the surface, using a toothbrush, to create a rusty, pitted look. This was allowed to dry naturally.

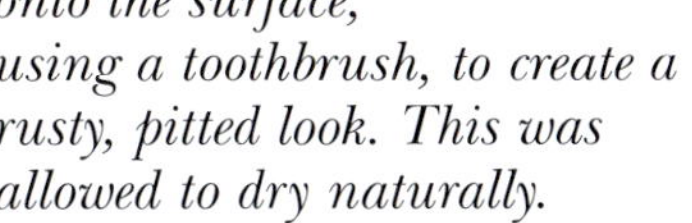

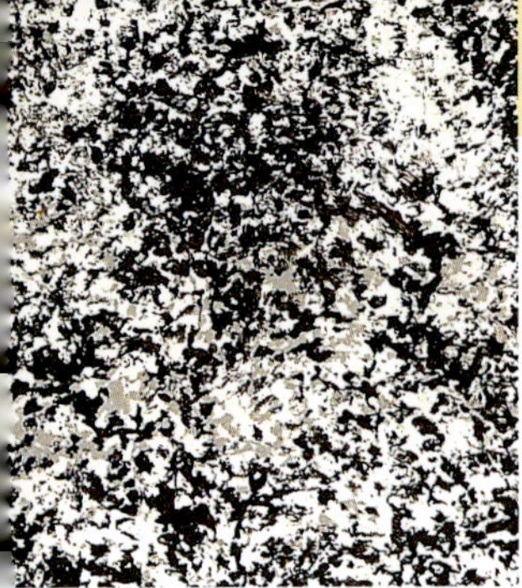

Granite is a stone of solid texture and appearance that can be produced in varying colorways. It is used in large expanses for buildings and floors. Granite is particularly striking used in conjunction with other stone or marbled effects.

Granite

Granite effect is best used in areas that would seem most natural, such as carved fireplace surrounds and mantles, floors and smaller decorative items such as statues, corbels and table tops. It is a reasonably easy effect to achieve once you have mastered the techniques of sponging (see p. 54) and spattering (see p. 72), and works very well in both modern and traditional settings.

Used in a wide range of different colorways, granite effect can add interest to an otherwise very simple and plain setting. The cost of a natural (marine) sponge together with the oil-based paints and glazes can make this technique a little expensive, but the finished result will prove really worthwhile.

If you follow the manufacturer's instructions provided with the products and become familiar with the technique before starting, no real problems should arise. Once again, do not work too quickly. See how the look is building up as you proceed step-by-step to prevent any mistakes. If anything goes wrong, carefully remove the paint with a cloth dampened with mineral spirits (white spirit). Allow the surface to dry and responge, otherwise repaint the area and start again—it is only a coat of paint!

You will need

Tools

• ½–1 in. (1.2–2.5 cm.) bristle brush • 1½–2 in. (3.8–5 cm.) varnishing brush • Paint dishes • Natural (marine) sponge • Rags

Materials

• Shellac (knotting) solution • Pale gray eggshell basecoat • Oil-based undercoat • Black, white, dark gray artists' oil paints • Mineral spirits (white spirit) • Transparent oil glaze • Oil-based gloss varnish

1 Knots in wood produce a resin which can cause discoloration through the paint. After sanding and filling your surface seal any knots with a little shellac (knotting) solution which can be applied with a brush or a soft cloth. Allow to dry. Apply an oil-based undercoat and allow to dry. Apply two coats of the pale gray eggshell basecoat and allow 24 hours to dry.

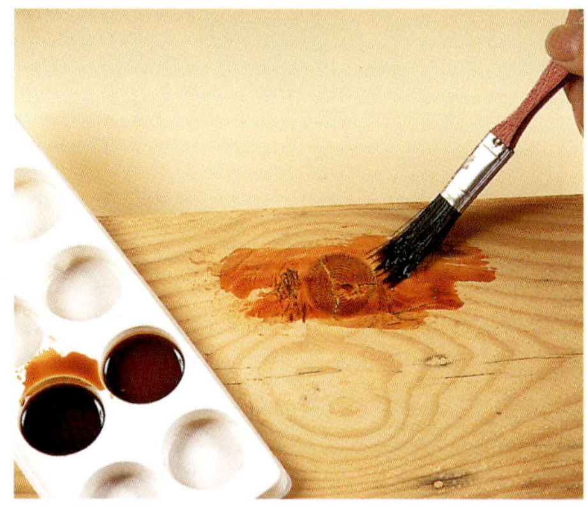

Variation 1

The granite effect can be combined with both lining (see p. 94) and stenciling (see p. 78) to create a dramatic effect. Here a basecoat of black latex (emulsion) was sponged with light and dark gray, followed by turquoise acrylic before being stenciled and the border painted in black and lined in gold.

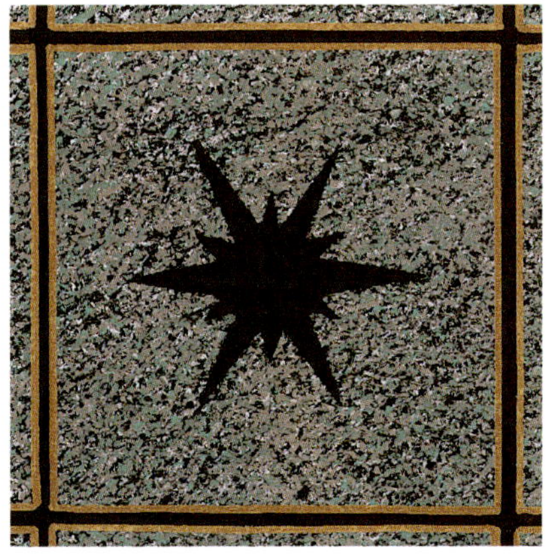

Variation 2

Color is always important and here a very earthy look has been created using a basecoat of saddle brown over-sponged with a layer of terracotta. This was allowed to dry, and then randomly sponged again with beige, adding depth and definition to the surface.

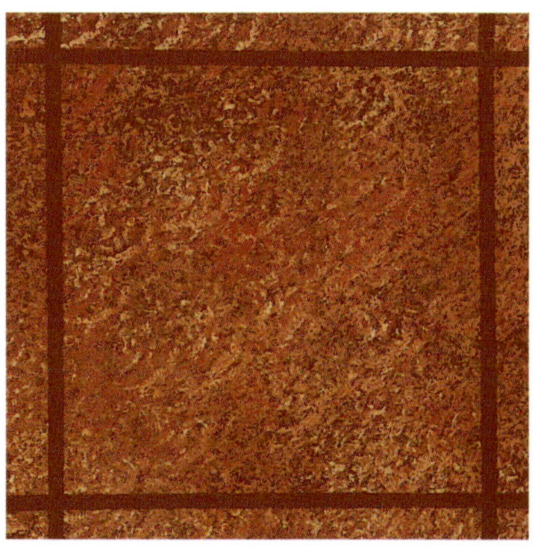

2 Mix up a mid-gray from equal quantities of black and white artists' oil paints. Dilute with a little mineral spirits (white spirit) to make a workable, not too thin, consistency.

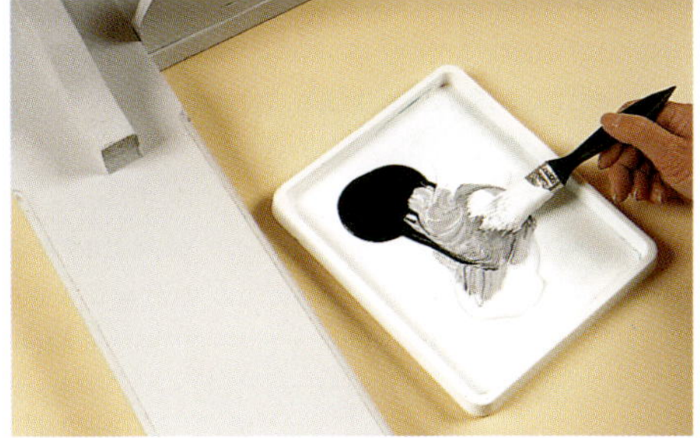

3 Dampen a natural sponge with a little mineral spirits (white spirit) and dip the sponge into the mid-gray paint. Dab onto some clean paper towel or clean paper to remove any excess. Carefully and randomly sponge over the surface.

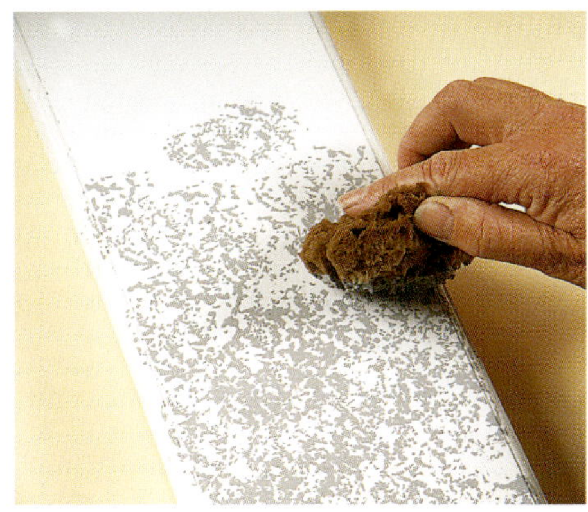

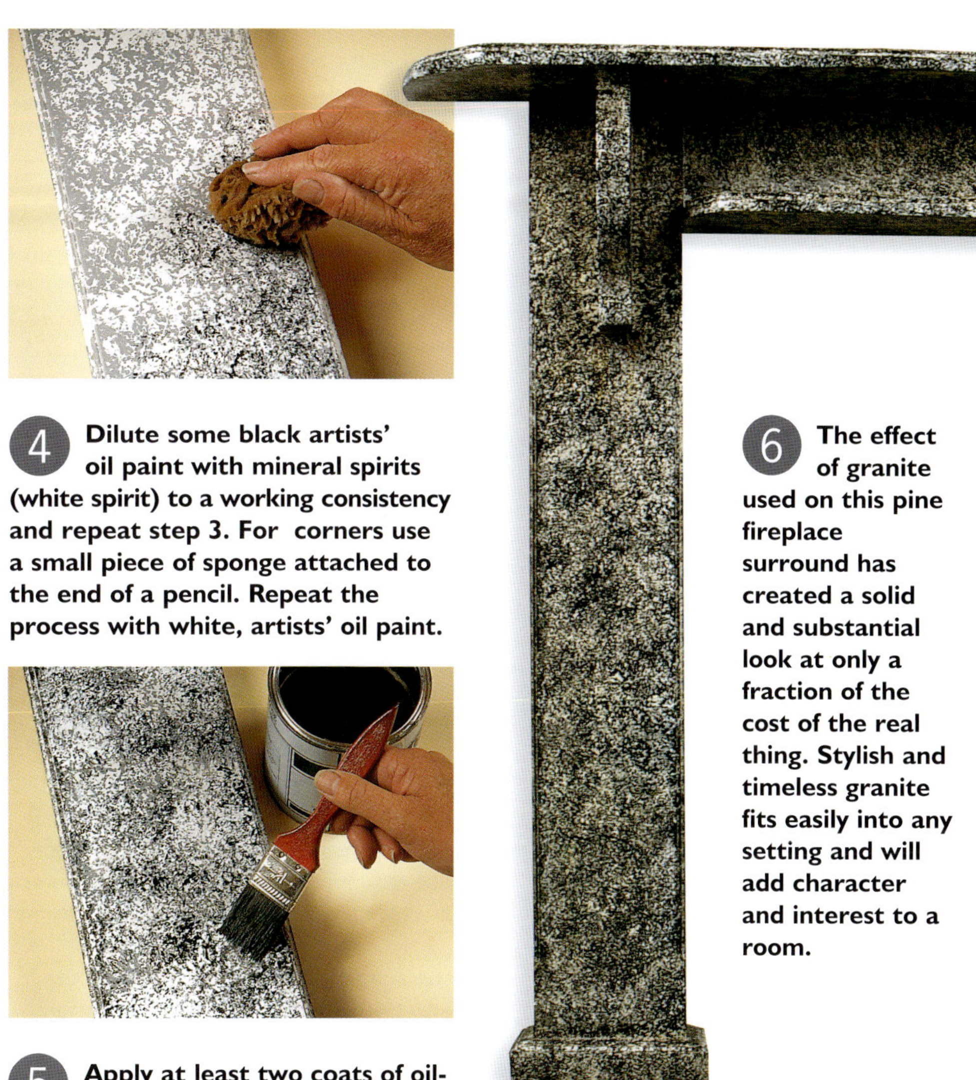

4 Dilute some black artists' oil paint with mineral spirits (white spirit) to a working consistency and repeat step 3. For corners use a small piece of sponge attached to the end of a pencil. Repeat the process with white, artists' oil paint.

5 Apply at least two coats of oil-based gloss varnish allowing adequate drying time between coats.

6 The effect of granite used on this pine fireplace surround has created a solid and substantial look at only a fraction of the cost of the real thing. Stylish and timeless granite fits easily into any setting and will add character and interest to a room.

Variation 3

A very pleasing and quick way to alter the final effect is simply to change the color of the basecoat. Here a pale pink has been used instead of the traditional gray, over-sponged with a layer of pale gray followed by mid-gray, and finally a little black. By masking and lining the edges a credible inlaid effect has been achieved.

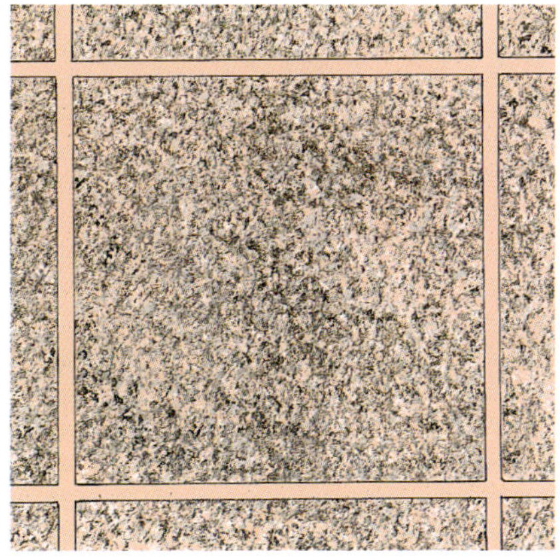

Variation 4

Terrazzo tiling for floors has always been very popular and it is comparatively easy to produce. Over a basecoat of pale green apply different-shaped stencils at random covering the entire surface, using pale gray, dark gray, black and gold. Finally, spatter with black paint using a toothbrush. To complete the illusion a medium gold permanent lining pen and a fine black permanent pen were used to create separate panels.

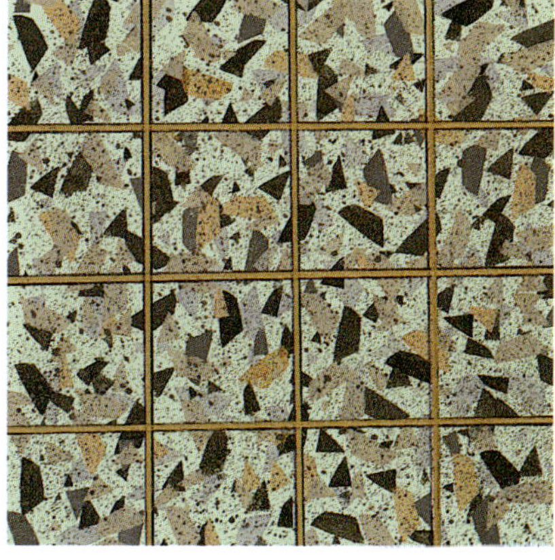

Ragging

Ragging is an extremely versatile technique that has remained popular over the years. It is easy to achieve and yet can create wonderful textures simply by choosing exciting or harmonious colors. It is one of the simplest techniques to master and is very inexpensive to produce. Because of its simplicity, it is possible to achieve stunning results in a comparatively short time.

Both ragging and rag-rolling are ideally suited to any flat surface, whether it be walls and ceilings, or furniture and cupboard units. It is also suitable for paneling and smaller decorative items. The effect works well in conjunction with other paint effects, such as dragging (see p. 62), and is a perfect background for stenciling (see p. 78) or lining (see p. 94).

Carefully chosen colorways can create either the most subtle of finishes or the most vibrant and boldest of fashion statements.

Mistakes should rarely occur when attempting ragging or rag-rolling. The most common pitfall is, as with many paint effects, a tendency to use too much paint on the rags and not to change to a clean rag often enough. Mistakes can also occur if two people attempt to work on the same surface hoping to halve the completion time. Every person has a different "style," and two people should not work together unless one produces the base color and the other the second or top color. If mistakes do happen, immediately and carefully wipe off the surface paint and redo the ragging, otherwise the background should be repainted and the effect repeated. As with any job, do not be tempted to work too quickly, as this is how and when mistakes do happen.

You will need

Tools

• 2 in. (5 cm.) bristle brush • Paint trays or dishes • Plenty of lint-free cloths or a chamois

Materials

• Medium- and fine-grade sandpaper • Mineral spirits (white spirit) • Deep cream eggshell paint • Blue artists' acrylic paint or semigloss latex (vinyl silk emulsion) • Acrylic glaze • Acrylic varnish

1 Sand the surface to a smooth finish using medium and then fine-grade sandpaper. Remove excess dust with a soft brush followed by a damp lint-free cloth. Allow the surface to dry. Apply an undercoat and then a topcoat with a deep cream eggshell paint.

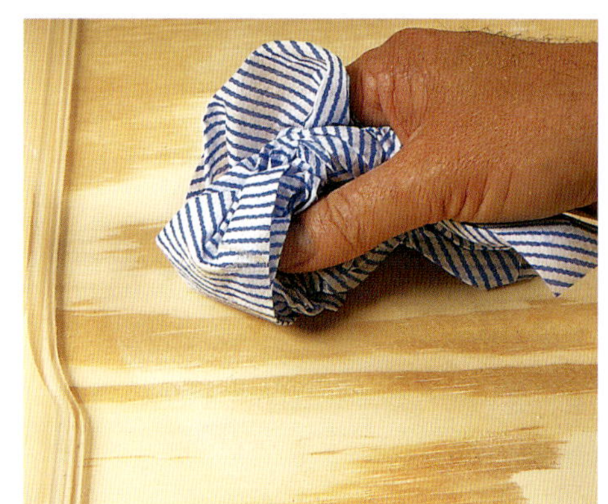

Variation 1

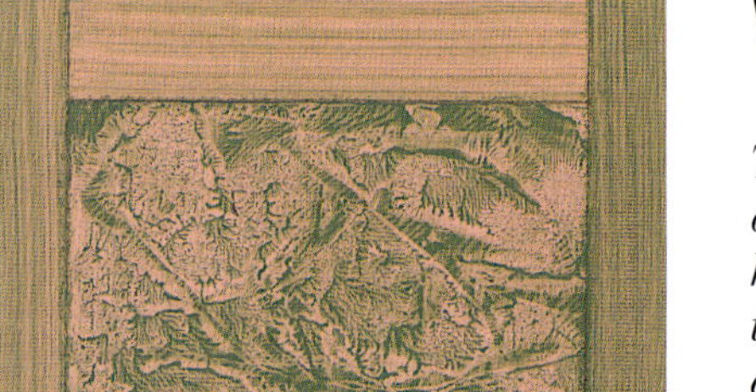

Ragging is a popular effect that has long been used in conjunction with other paint effect techniques, such as, in this case, dragging (see p. 62). Here, over a basecoat of salmon pink, a glaze of mid-green has been ragged and then dragged on the edges with a dragging brush to create a paneled design. The dusty colors have produced a very subdued but elegant result.

Variation 2

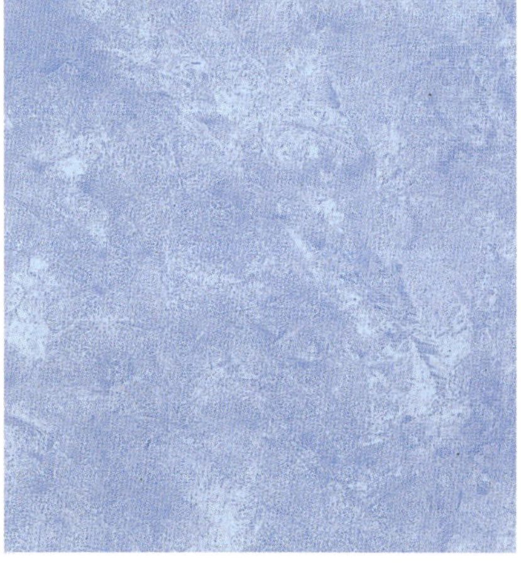

Two very carefully chosen shades of blue have been used here to create a pleasing and relaxing effect. The basecoat of very pale blue was over-painted with a mid-blue glaze, stippled (see p. 30), and then removed by ragging with a clean, dry, lint-free cloth. The resulting texture has added dimension to what could have been a rather flat base.

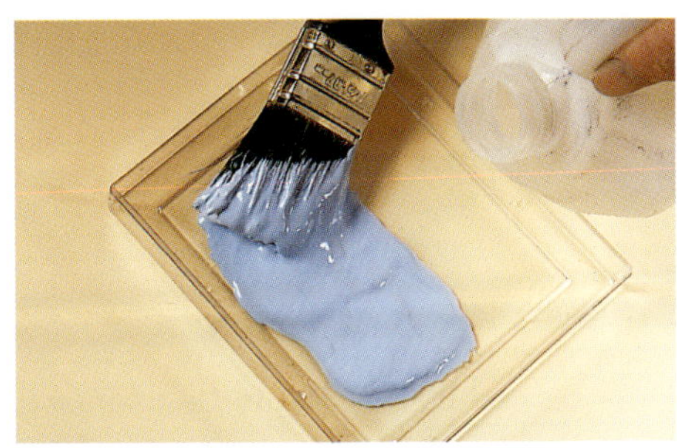

2 Following manufacturer's instructions, mix a glaze of mid-blue, semigloss latex (vinyl silk emulsion) paint with the acrylic glazing medium to a medium flow consistency. (An alternative would be to use a transparent oil glaze tinted with a little eggshell or artists' oil paint in the chosen color).

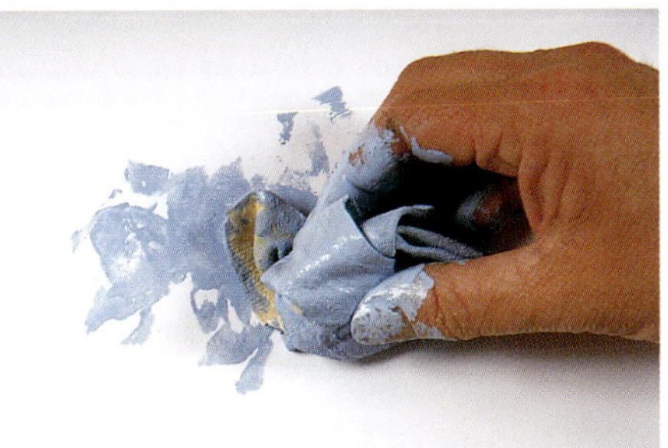

3 Dip your cloth (here I used chamois cloth) into the paint and coat it thoroughly. Remove any excess paint by wiping the cloth on some clean paper. Test the cloth on the paper.

4 Roll the cloth into a loose sausage shape and tuck in all the loose ends. Rag-roll the cloth across the surface in random or irregular strokes, avoiding a "stripy" pattern. Remove any excess splodges. Allow to dry.

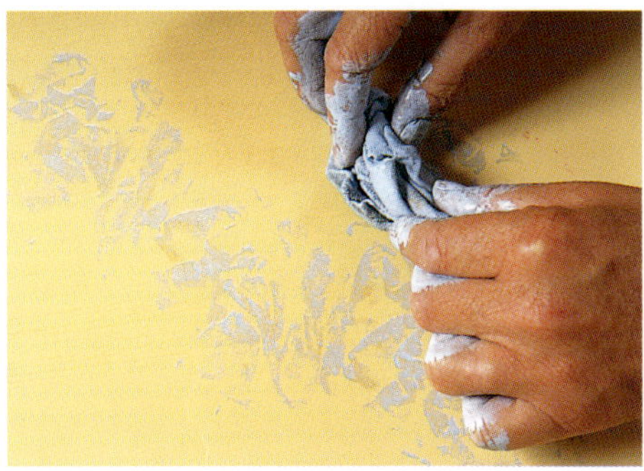

5 Repeat the rag-rolling using a second color. By using two colors any defects in the surface will be hidden, as will any unevenness in the first color. Let dry for 24 hours.

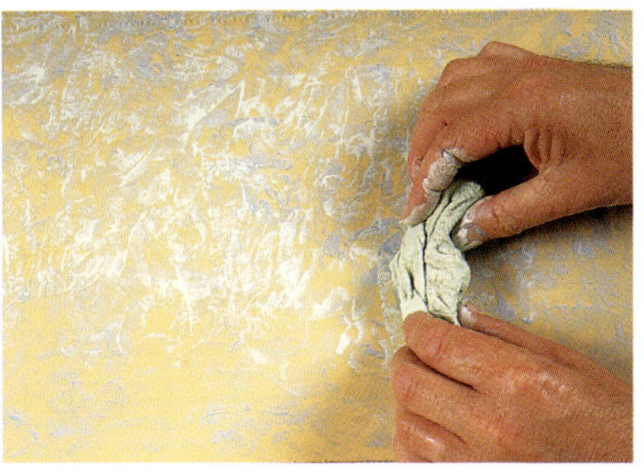

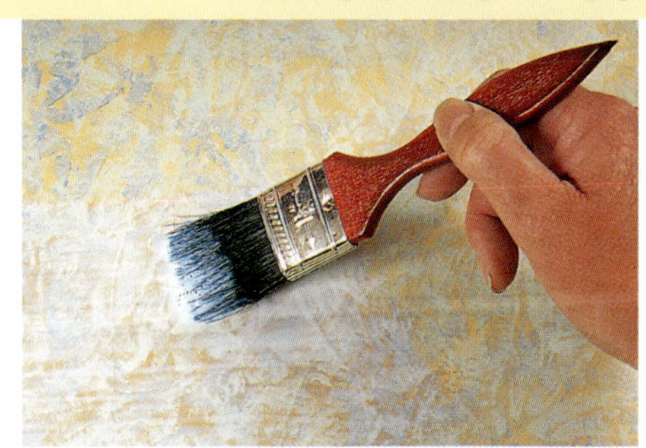

6 If required, apply two coats of acrylic varnish to protect the surface.

7 Complementary colors rag-rolled over each other bring life to these cupboard doors. Ragging is easily done and can give professional results with only a little time and patience.

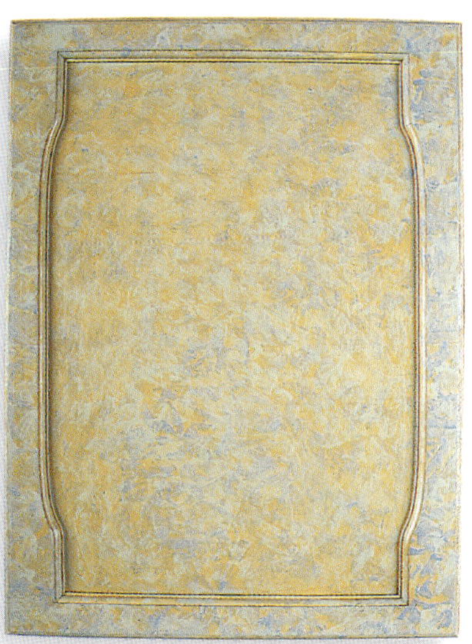

Variation 3

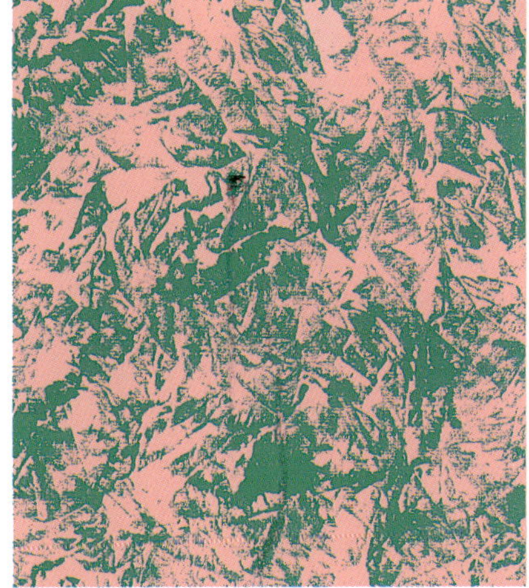

Once again pink and green have been used, but in much bolder shades, creating an entirely different result. The topcoat of green was used undiluted and applied straight onto the basecoat of pink using a chamois cloth, resulting in a very bold pattern with larger flat areas of paint. The "crisper" the cloth, the finer will be the result.

Variation 4

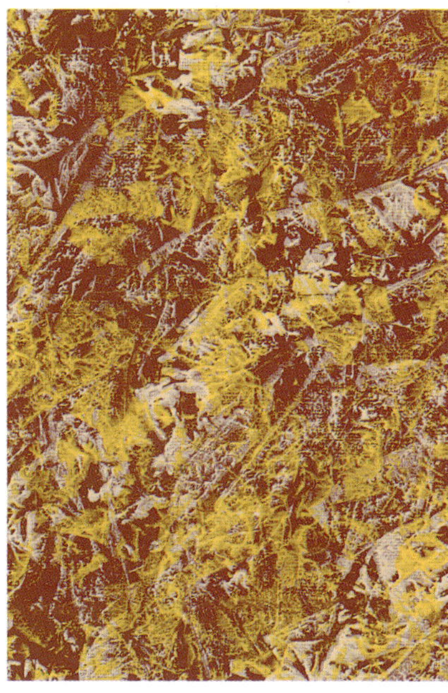

Using two or more colors will tend to even out any chance of noticeable mistakes and also create a vibrant, fun look. Here, over a basecoat of terracotta, a glaze of pale cream has been ragged, followed by a vivid yellow.

Sponging

This inexpensive, simple and basic paint effect is the ideal introduction to the use of decorative paint techniques. The resulting look of the natural (marine) sponge when applied to wet paint has been popular for many years. Sponging can be utilized to produce a wide variety of exciting and creative results from marble (see pp. 132, 136 and 138) and granite (see p. 50) to simple textured finishes of broken color-relief.

You will need

Tools

- *Sponge paint roller or 3–4 in. (7.6–10 cm.) bristle basecoat brush*
- *Paint trays or dishes*
- *Natural (marine) sponge*

Materials

- *Semigloss latex (vinyl silk emulsion) basecoat*
- *Semigloss latex (vinyl silk emulsion) colors for sponging*
- *Varnish if required*
- *Paper (kitchen) towel*

Ideally suited to any flat surface, including walls, ceilings, floors, furniture and fitted units, sponging also works well on small, decorative items such as lampbases, boxes and picture frames. Heavily carved items should be avoided. Although the quality of the surface preparation is always important, sponging tends to cover a multitude of sins and disguises minor flaws and cracks in the surface most effectively, particularly when a combination of one or two colors is involved. Sponging is ideally suited as a base to stenciling (see p. 78).

Good results are quick and easy to achieve with sponging, with only a little practice, so that even the most daunting of rooms can be completed within a day or so. Once you have decided on your choice of colors, it is always advisable to do a sample board. A common mistake is to use colors that, when applied over the top of each other, tend to merge into a rather "muddy" look. It can also be tempting to use too much paint on the sponge, so by practice you will learn to control the amount of paint and eliminate the chance of unsightly "smudges" that will destroy the overall effect.

The creation of too formal a pattern is also a common mistake that can be avoided by constantly turning the sponge during application. If mistakes do occur, you can either remove the offending area immediately with a soft cloth, or allow the sponged area to dry and responge over the top with the base color.

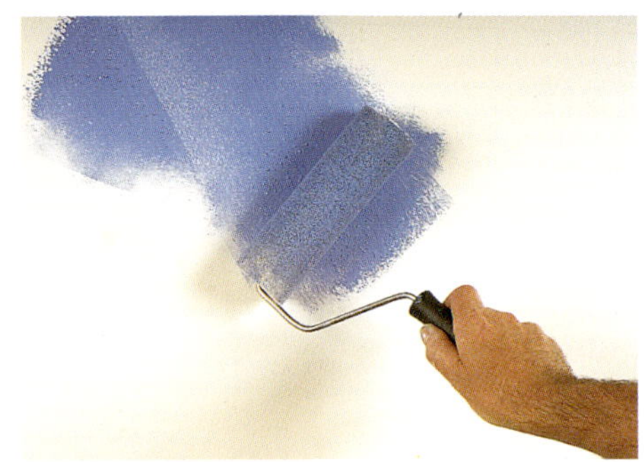

1 Prepare the surface by completing any major repairs. Apply an undercoat. Allow to dry. Apply two basecoats of mid-blue semigloss latex (vinyl silk emulsion) with a sponge paint roller (see p. 23) or a 3–4 in (7.6–10 cm.) bristle basecoat brush. Allow to dry between each coat and before commencing the next step.

Variation 1

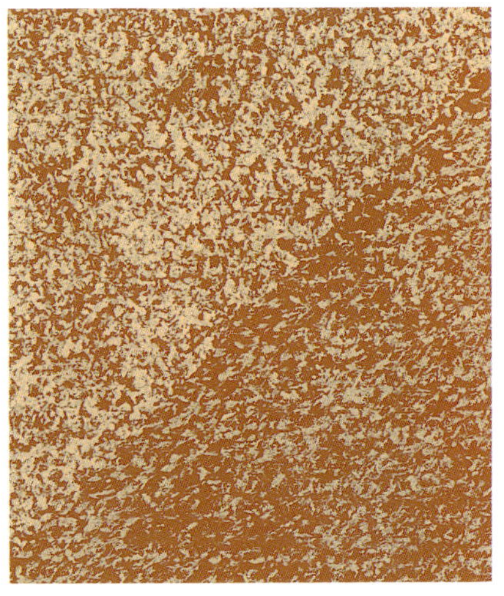

A good quality natural (marine) sponge is necessary to achieve this effect. The basecoat of terracotta was carefully and randomly sponged over with a layer of pale cream. When this had dried the bottom area was masked off and sponged over again with the cream, creating a more even and denser look. This effect is well suited to walls below the chair (dado) rail.

Variation 2

By varying the colorways and using two very vibrant colors, a totally different result can be achieved. Here, emerald green was sponged over a basecoat of mid- but bright blue. The resulting color contrast has created a finish of real depth and movement.

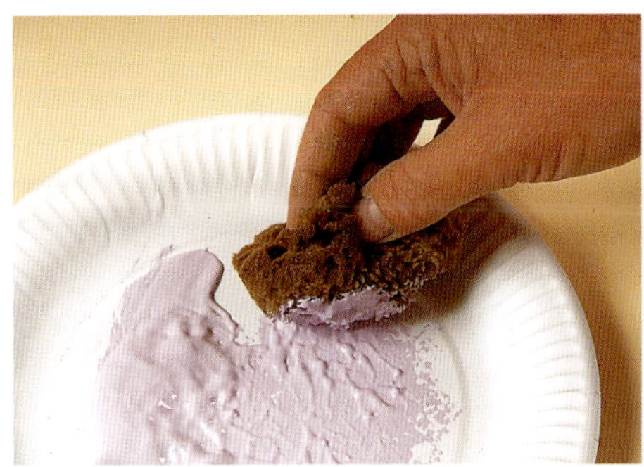

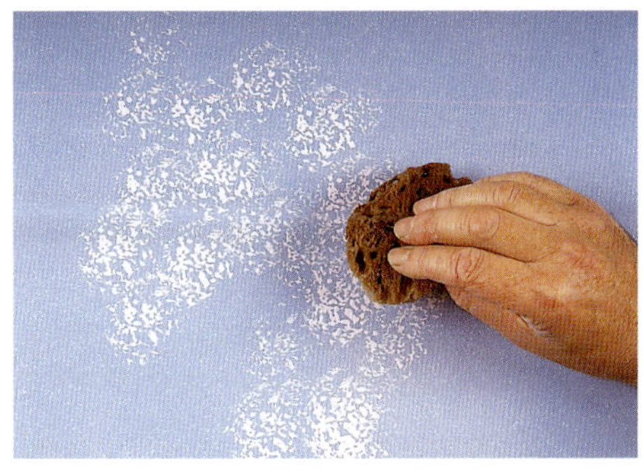

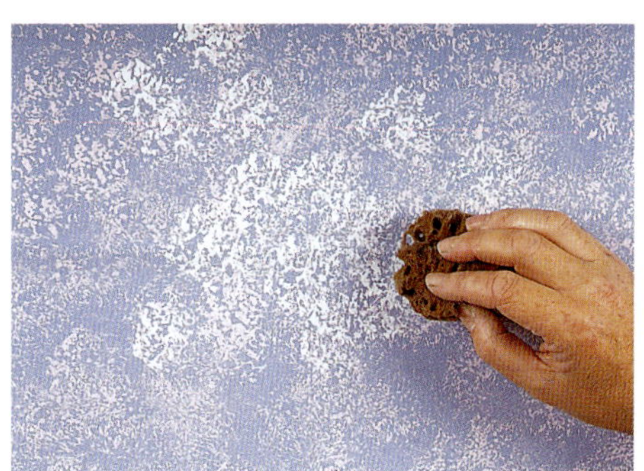

2 **Pour a little lilac semigloss latex paint (vinyl silk emulsion) onto a clean dish (if mixing a certain color, mix enough to complete the job). Dip the sponge into some clean water and squeeze out the excess. Dab the damp sponge into the lilac paint. Do not overfill the sponge, as a little goes a long way. Remove the excess paint from the sponge by dabbing it on the side of the dish or on some clean paper towel.**

3 **Slowly and carefully touch the wall surface with the sponge, being careful not to apply too much pressure (this will cause unsightly splodges). Gently and smoothly remove the sponge and reapply to a fresh area. Gradually turn the sponge as you work to vary the imprint pattern. Reapply a small amount of paint to the sponge, removing excess as necessary. Each loading of the sponge should last for about 8–10 imprints.**

4 **Repeat step 3 using a clean sponge and a semigloss latex (vinyl silk emulsion) in pale green. Sponge the entire surface with the green as before, or, to create a more uneven effect, use the green randomly over the surface. Varnish with a suitable varnish if vulnerable.**

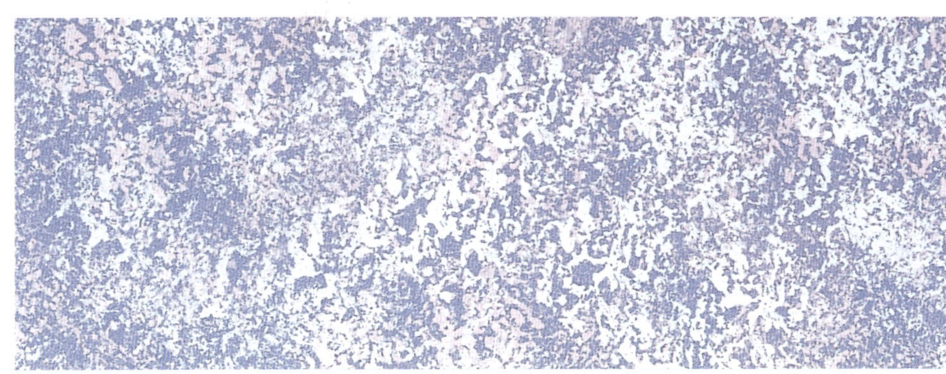

5 **Sponging is a technique that is easily done, and is limited only by your imagination. The qualities of the natural (marine) sponge enhance the two-dimensional surface as well as disguising any flaws that it may have.**

Variation 3

By adding a third color a more controlled diffused effect is achieved, and any surface or sponging technique flaws or unevenness will disappear. With some stenciling (see p. 78), in this case a dolphin, a wonderfully watery effect that would work well in the bathroom has been achieved.

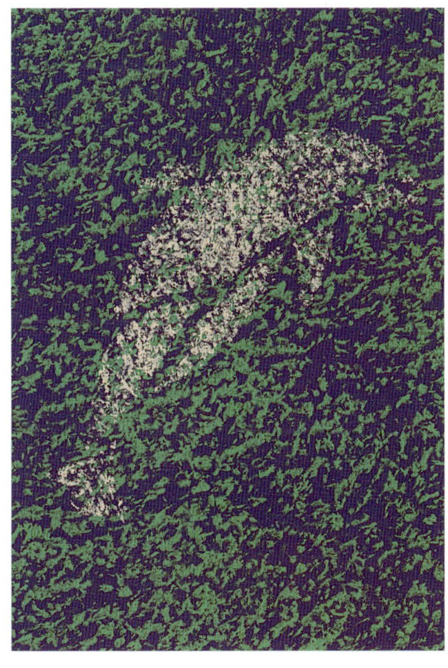

Variation 4

Here, the surface was painted with a basecoat of mid-green, semigloss latex (vinyl silk emulsion) and allowed to dry. Then ¾ in. (1.9 cm.) low-tack tape was used to mask off the design. With a synthetic sponge deep cream and terracotta latex were applied to the surface while each was still wet. When dry, the edges were lined with deep cream using a fine, swordliner brush. The surface was sealed with flat (matte) acrylic varnish.

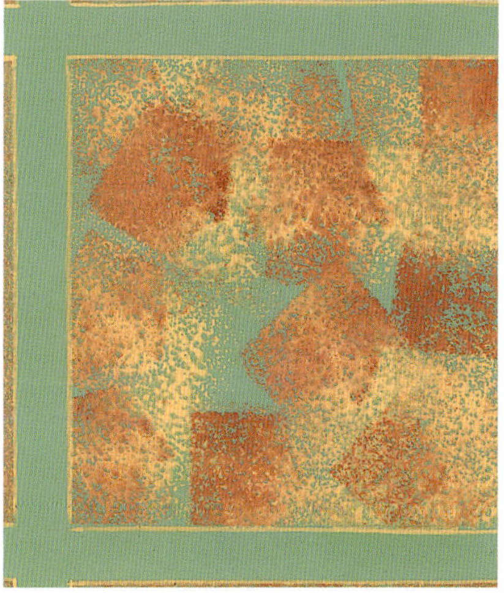

In context

Two of the most popular paint effect techniques are rag rolling and sponging. Apart from being extremely versatile in their own right, they enable exotic effects such as leather and crushed velvet to be created. They are also wonderfully effective when used as backgrounds for other paint techniques such as stenciling, stamping or colored photocopies. In the examples here a spectrum of moods has been created—from the charismatic fun-look to the simple and elegant.

Sponging

▼ Living area

In the example here the living room with its marble fire surround has been subtly sponged in warm tones of cream. As a result the room is now lighter and appears to have increased in size yet at the same time has retained a feeling of absolute cosiness.

Ragging

▶ Wall below dado rail in sitting room

The crispness of the blue in this sitting room has created a feeling of freshness and openness. But by applying the rag rolling technique to below the dado rail, together with the simple woodgrain in the door paneling and on the fire screen, the room has become more cosy and welcoming.

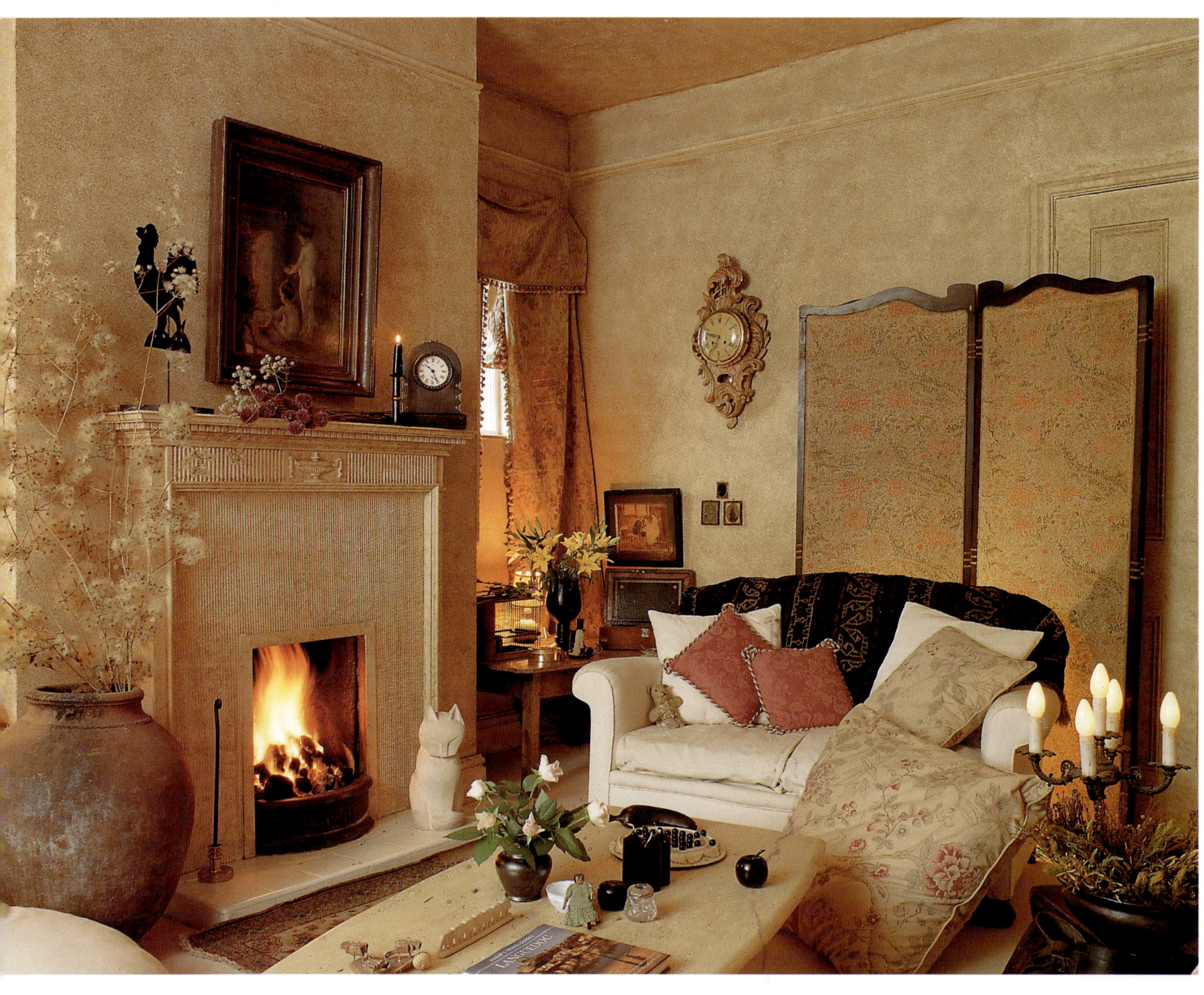

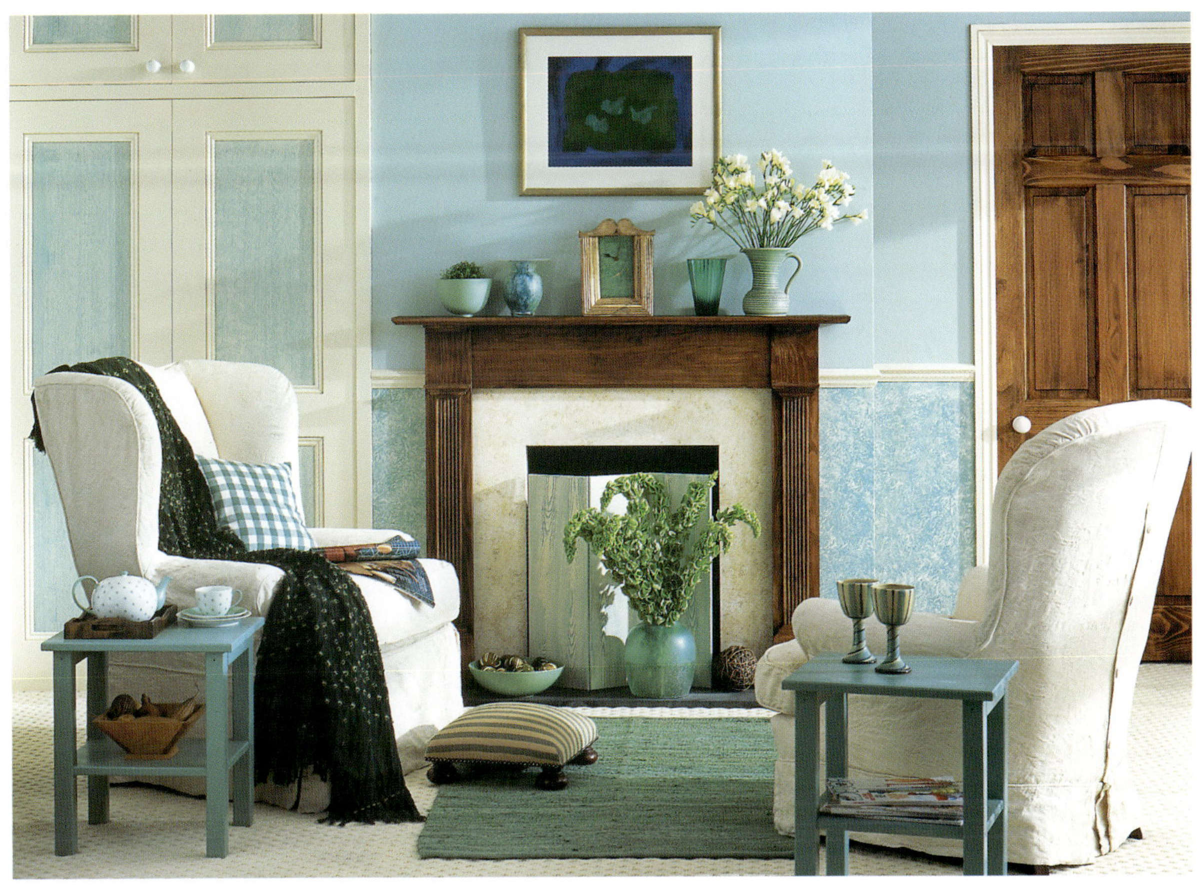

Colored photocopies

▼ The wall of a large open kitchen

Victorian puddings have been temptingly colorwashed and appear to marvellous effect in this kitchen. One can see how cleverly colored photocopies can be used to create looks and schemes that are truly individual and fun.

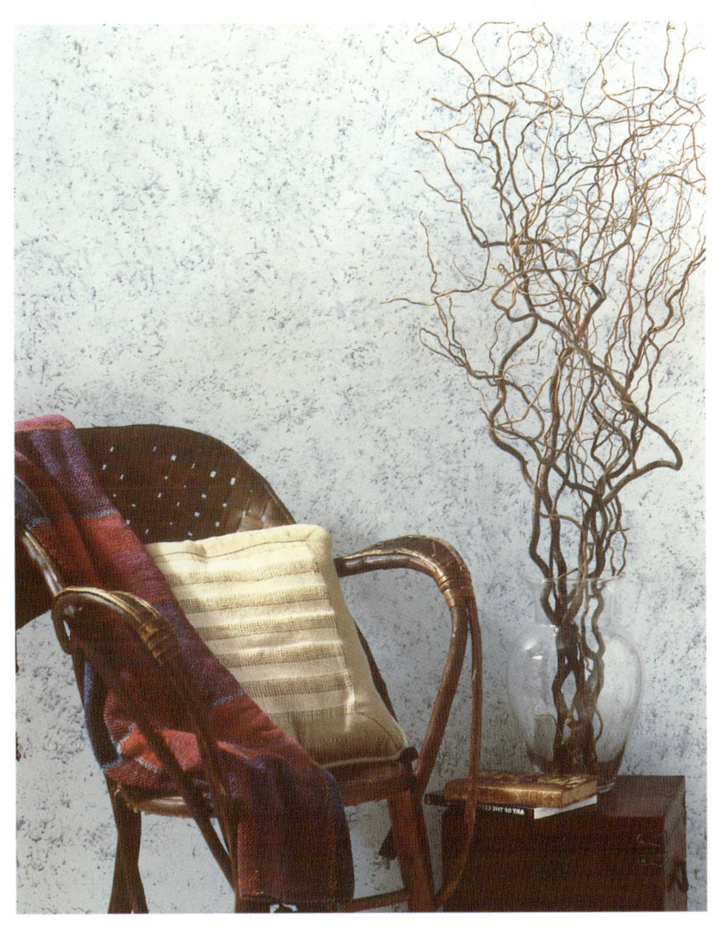

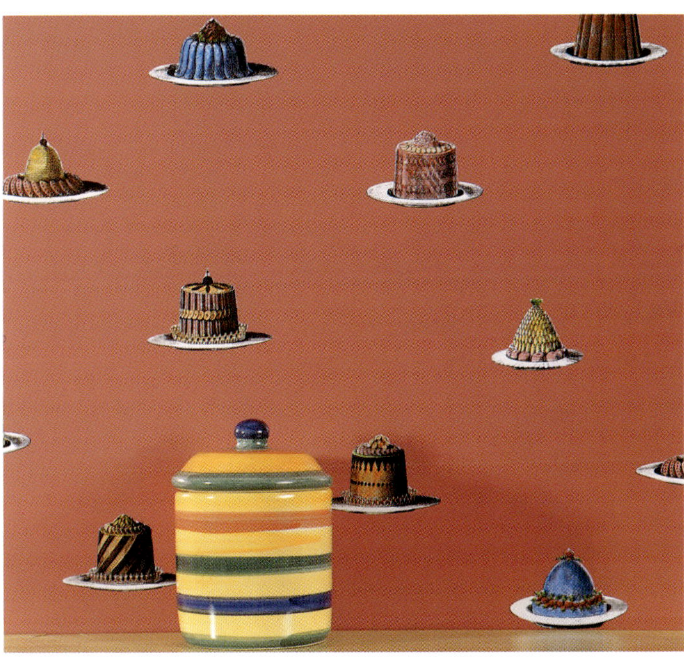

Sponging

◀ In a relaxed informal setting

Sponging, like so many paint effect techniques, is very versatile. Here the extremely open nature of the effect together with the use of both dark and light blues, has successfully created a very tactile look—the large wall areas have been given an additional dimension.

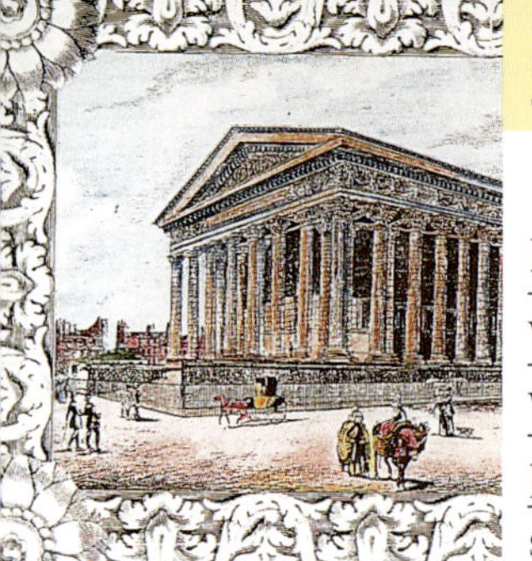

Colored photocopies

Decorating a whole room with colored photocopies or simply placing one or two in strategic positions can be very rewarding, and can produce some highly individual results, particularly if the subject matter has a special meaning to you and your family. The possibilities are endless, and the final results well worth the effort.

For the inexperienced artist, photocopies can be used to create whole scenes and cover large areas, or to add a splash of decoration in a chosen space. Photocopiers can enlarge or reduce images, enabling their use on items ranging from cupboard doors to complete walls. The use of photocopies lends itself to any decorative scheme, whether it is traditional or modern, plain or ornate, and it is very inexpensive and comparatively simple to master.

Careful preparations are important to achieve quality results. Do not rush the job. Think carefully about the placement or positioning of each element in your design. It is a good idea to fix each element into position with some low-tack tape before gluing them, as mistakes are difficult to rectify. Depending on the basecoat, dried photocopies can be quite hard to remove and can mark an absorbent surface. For this reason a basecoat of semigloss latex (vinyl silk emulsion) or eggshell is advised, as this will give you a wipeable surface. When you feel more confident with the technique, it is possible to attempt it on a flat (matte) finish.

You will need

Tools

• Sharp scissors • Fine pointed scissors or craft knife • Cutting mat • Bristle brush • Soft cloth or sponge

Materials

• Photocopies (copyright free) • Colored pencils or watercolor or acrylic paints for coloring • Photocopier size liquid • Spray sealant • Low-tack masking tape • PVA glue or good quality wallpaper paste

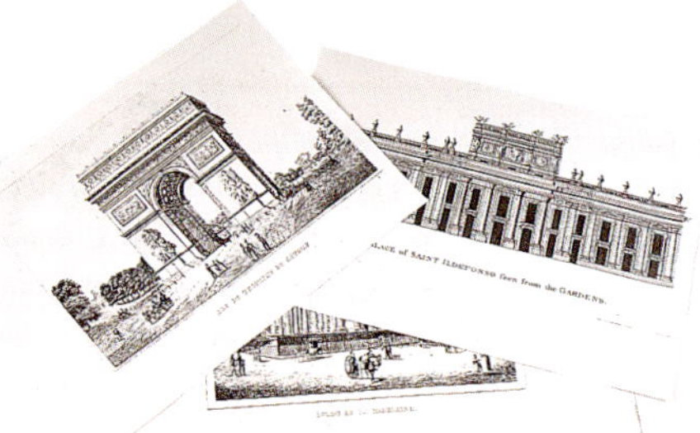

1 **Measure the area to be covered and have the chosen images either reduced or enlarged to the required size. Always have extra copies done in case of mistakes.**

Variation 1

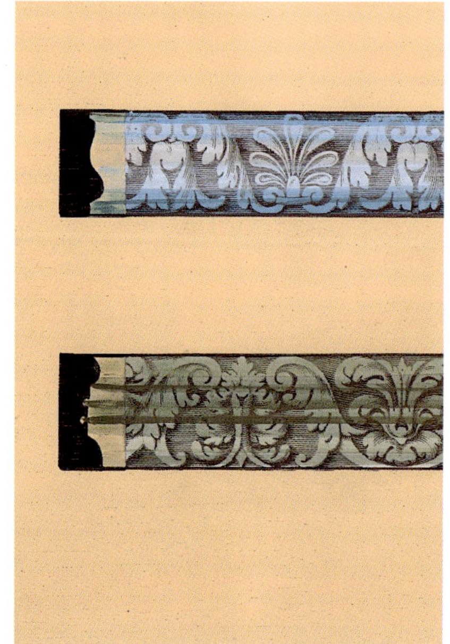

Here, border patterns were applied to the wall, which was painted with cream semigloss latex (emulsion), using PVA adhesive. Blue and green artists' acrylic paints were applied with a lining brush to create a false chair (dado) rail effect. The darker areas are shadow and the lighter are lit areas.

Variation 2

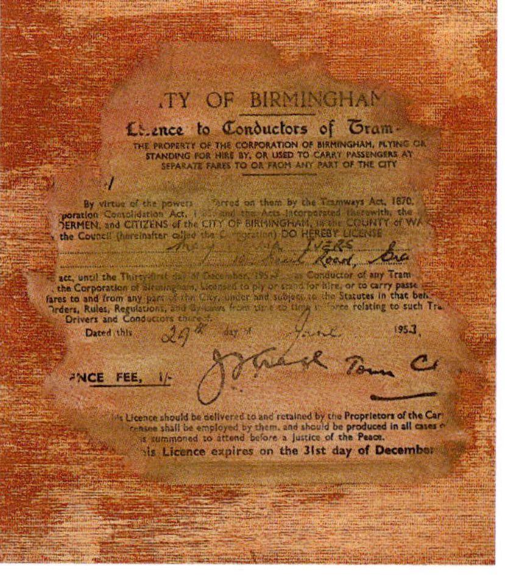

This wall was first painted in a pale cream semigloss latex and left to dry. A wash of terracotta latex (emulsion) was applied and sanded with a scouring pad to create the heavily distressed look (see p. 36). An old streetcar (tram) license was photocopied and applied to the wall with PVA adhesive. The edges were torn off to create the worn look. When dry, washes of green and terracotta acrylic paints were applied.

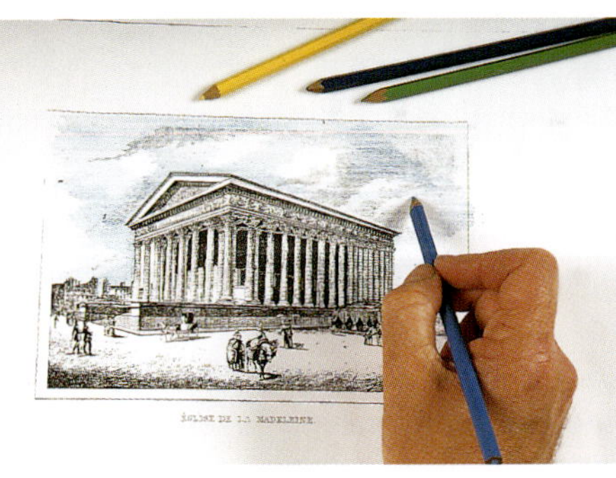

2 Color in the photocopies as required. If you are using watercolor or acrylic paints, apply photocopier size liquid first to strengthen the paper. Use the paint as dry as possible to minimize any mistakes or chance of the paint bleeding. Allow the paint to dry before progressing.

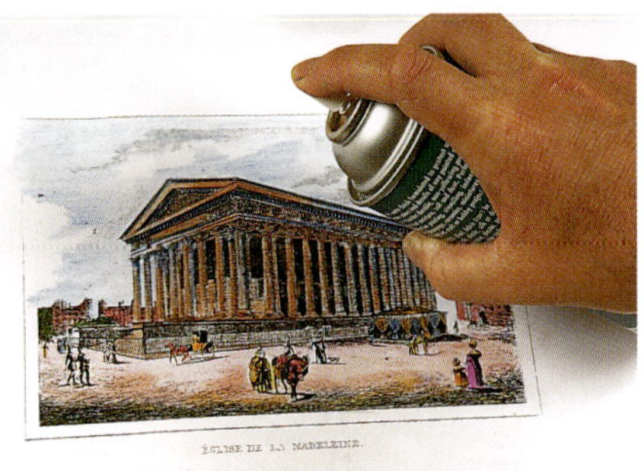

3 When you have completed the coloring, spray the image with at least two thin but thorough coats of sealant.

4 With sharp scissors cut out the image required fairly evenly but not precisely. With a pair of fine pointed scissors or a craft knife and cutting mat, slowly cut around the picture to the required shape. Be careful not to cut through a section that is to be used.

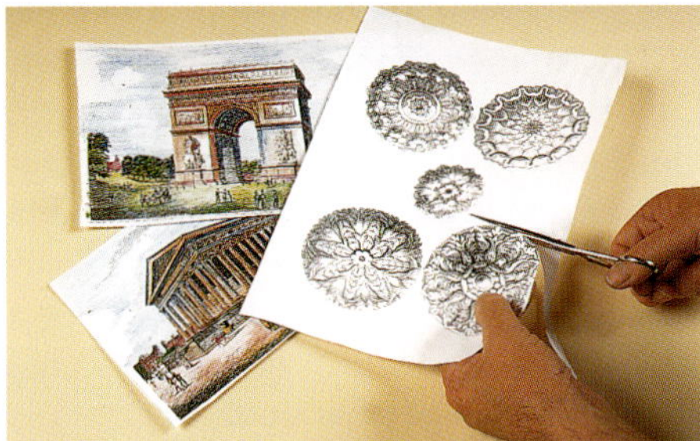

5 Arrange all the pieces of the image in position. Then, with a bristle brush, apply a coat of PVA glue or good-quality wallpaper paste to the reverse side of the image. Always make sure that the glue is applied evenly.

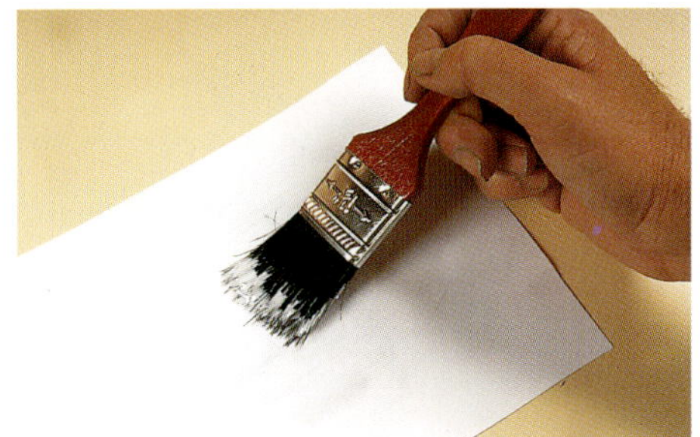

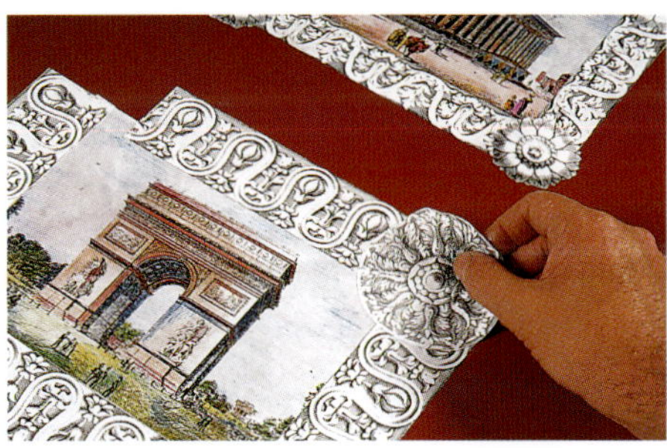

6 Position the image on the surface. With a damp soft cloth or sponge, carefully remove all air bubbles and any excess paste.

7 The use of colored photocopies on the wall here has created a print room effect for very little expense (below). The availability and range of material is endless, and the use of color will add excitement and interest to any wall or setting.

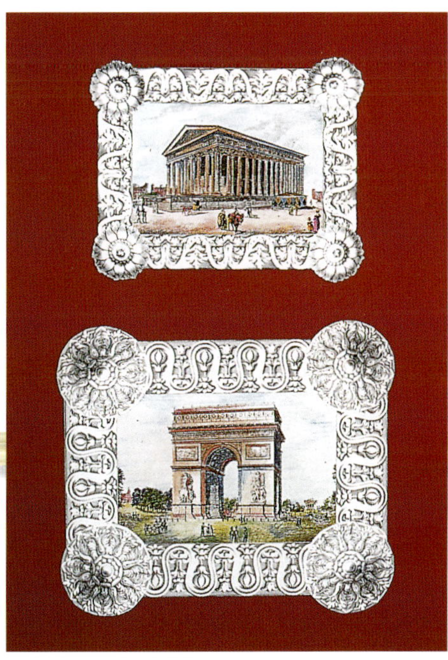

Variation 3

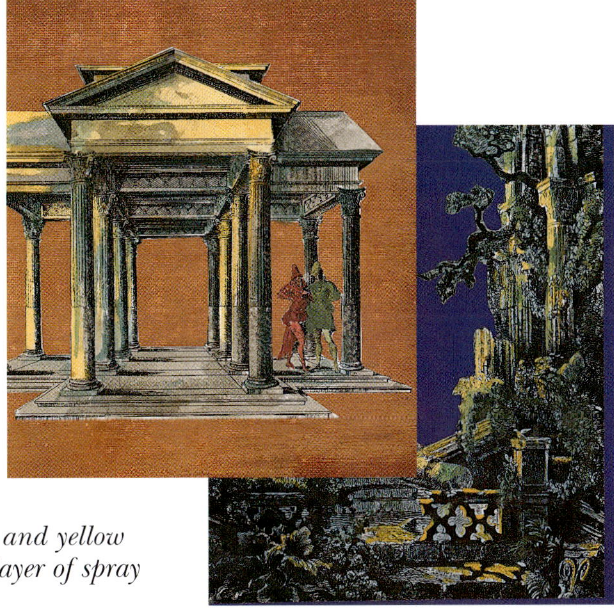

This panel was painted with a deep terracotta latex (emulsion). When dry, this was over-washed with yellow ocher and distressed *(see p. 36)* *with a kitchen scourer. The photocopy was enlarged to the correct size and cut out using a sharp craft knife. The photocopy was applied to the wall with PVA adhesive and colorwashed with blue, gray and yellow acrylic paint. When dry, a layer of spray sealant was applied.*

Variation 4

Here the chosen image (left) was blown up on the photocopier and a compilation of different elements applied to a basecoat of dark blue latex (emulsion) creating the look of a ruined garden at night. Blue and yellow colorwashes were used to highlight the image by simulating moonlight. Finally, the room was stenciled in white acrylic with a little blue to mellow the effect.

Colorwashing

For centuries the technique of layering different colored glazes over a basecoat has been used to create such finishes as rich Chinese lacquer, or to emulate the wonderful mellow look of faded grandeur and simple country. Colorwashing is one of the most versatile of the paint finishes. The effect that colorwashing produces is surprisingly easy to achieve with the minimum of expense and is one that you will, in the end, be truly proud of.

Many areas of the home, such as walls, ceiling rosettes (roses), pilasters and corbels, lend themselves to colorwashing, as do kitchen units, tables and small decorative pieces, including boxes and lampbases. Being such a versatile effect, it works well in its own right as well as with other effects, such as stenciling (see p. 78), stripes (see p. 100) and mosaic (see p. 104).

When choosing a color, the complete palette is open to you, depending on the finished look required. For richness, dark reds and burgundies work well over cream or yellow ocher. For a more subtle effect, yellow ocher over magnolia creates warmth and is very light and airy. For the best results, colorwashing should be done with glazes over a semigloss (silk) finish basecoat. An average room can be very successfully colorwashed in one to two days with the minimum of practice.

By using a sample board, color and technique can be finalized without making mistakes. The most common mistakes are caused by trying to work on too big an area at one time. Approximately 1 sq. yard (1 sq. meter) is the best size area to cover at a time. It is necessary when working on one area to leave a "wet edge" that will merge with the next area while it is still wet. An absorbent basecoat can also cause problems, so follow all the manufacturer's instructions carefully.

You will need

Tools

• *3–4 in. (7.5–10 cm.) soft-bristled brush* • *Synthetic sponge* • *Soft, lint-free cloth* • *2–3 in. (5–7.5 cm.) varnishing brush* • *2–3 in. (5–7.5 cm.) bristle basecoat brush*

Materials

• *Semigloss latex (vinyl silk emulsion) basecoat* • *Acrylic glaze* • *Acrylic varnish for protection*

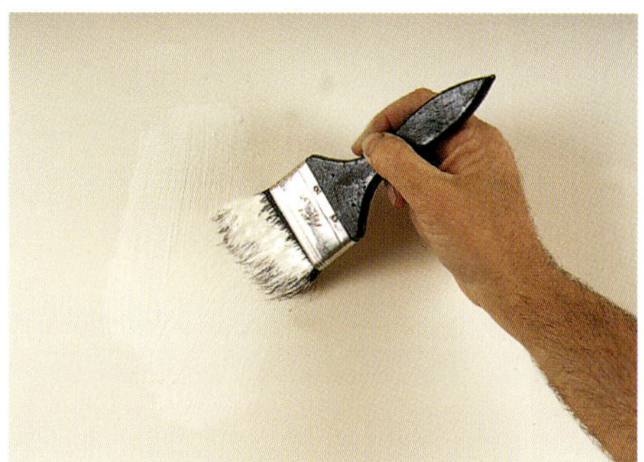

1 **Prepare the surface (see *Preparation*, p. 18). Apply two coats of magnolia semigloss latex (vinyl silk emulsion) using a 3 in. (7.5cm.) bristle basecoat brush. Allow to dry thoroughly between coats and before commencing the next step.**

Variation 1

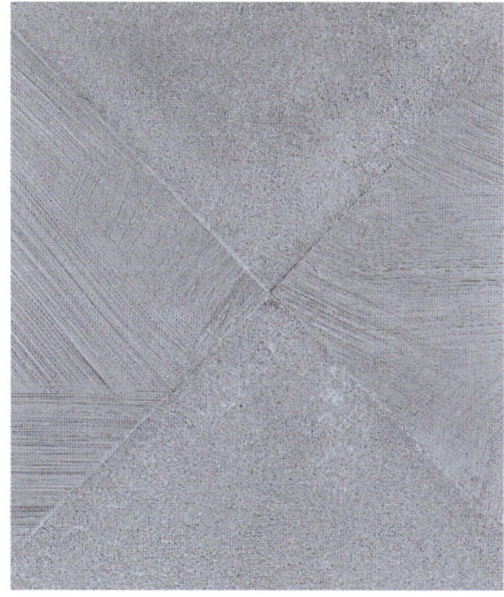

A very effective paneled effect can be achieved by simply masking off one section of the surface at a time with low-tack masking tape, and applying stippling (see p. 30) and colorwashing. Here the chosen glaze color was pale blue used over a basecoat of mid-gray, resulting in a subdued and ethereal look. This would go well in a formal dining or living area.

Variation 2

Brushstrokes are part of the essence of colorwashing and need not be removed. They can create a totally characteristic look, whether it be in a rural or urban setting. Here, the basecoat of lemon yellow has been enhanced by the use of a pale blue glaze, with accentuated brushstrokes.

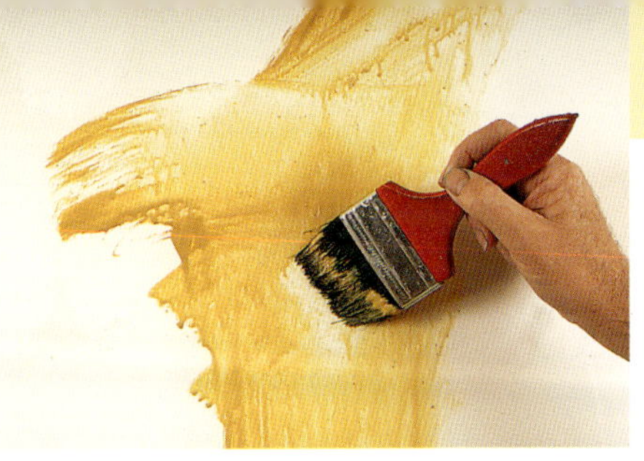

2 **Mix a glaze using yellow ocher semigloss latex (vinyl silk emulsion) or simulated buttermilk paint and acrylic glazing medium, (follow manufacturer's instructions.) Dilute the glaze with water until thin and creamy (about 1 part glaze to 5 parts water). Apply the glaze at random to the surface area, using a 3 in. (7.5 cm.) brush. For large areas apply glaze to a manageable area. Keep a wet edge to the glaze.**

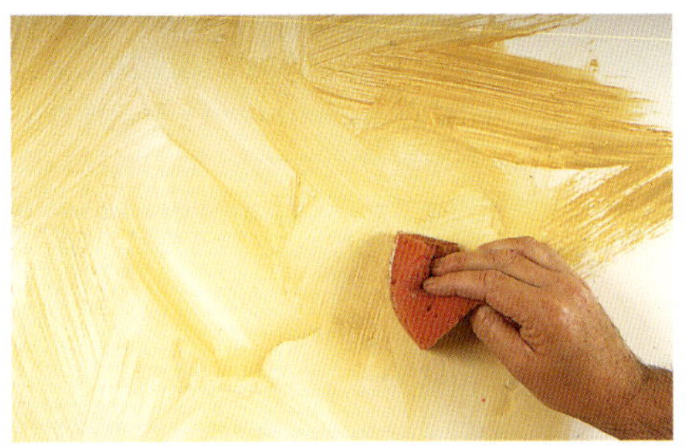

3 **Remove areas of the glaze with a clean, damp sponge, or damp lint-free cloth to create the characteristic patchy look of colorwashing. The more glaze you remove the lighter the final effect will be.**

4 **Brush the surface backward and forward with a clean 4 in. (10 cm.) soft-bristled brush. To remove all brushstrokes use a softening brush (see *Clouding, p.* 86).**

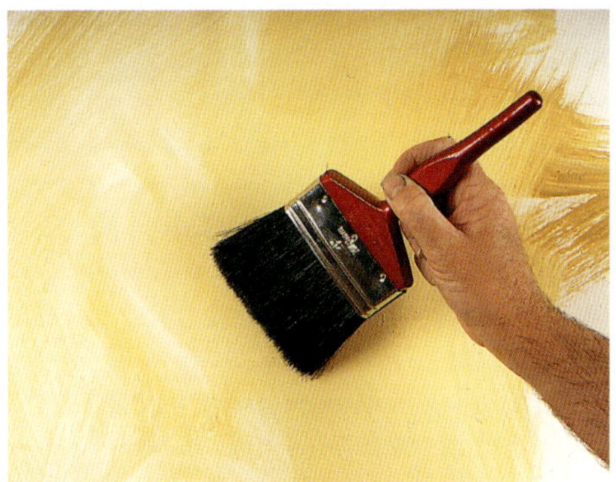

5 **Use a 2–3 in. (5–7.5 cm.) varnishing brush and apply two coats of acrylic varnish. Brush in one direction only to avoid creating brushstrokes. Do not overbrush.**

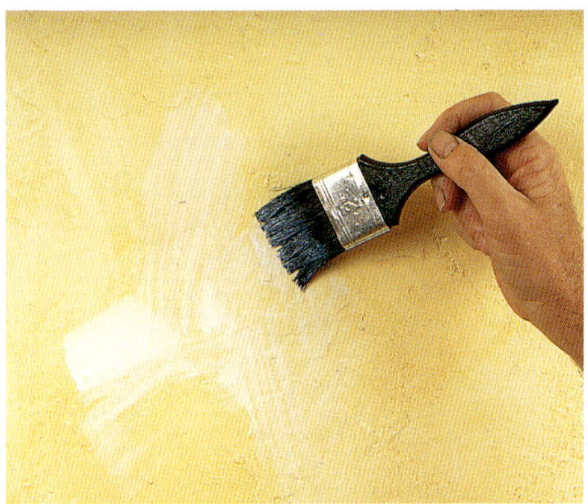

6 **The use of yellow ocher here as a colorwash ensures that the room radiates warmth and vitality. Both soothing and attractive, the effect melts into the background yet still creates a very individual look. A more textured look could be created by leaving many of the brushstrokes showing.**

Variation 3

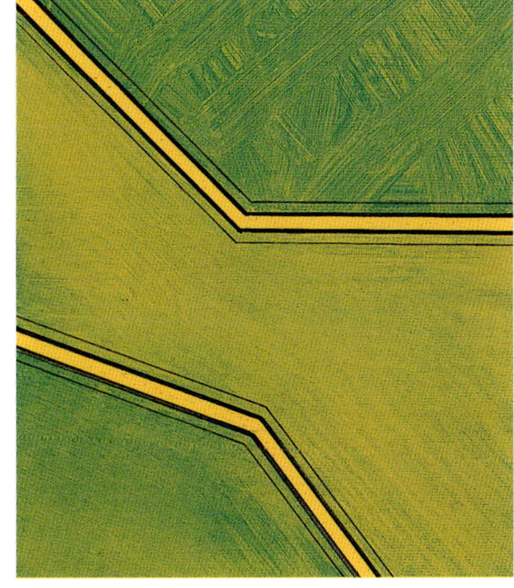

Two layers of bright yellow semigloss latex (vinyl silk emulsion) were applied here, allowing drying time between coats. Then ¼ in. (0.63 cm.) low-tack tape was used to mask off the pattern. A layer of bright green acrylic paint mixed with acrylic glaze was randomly brushed across the surface. The glaze was worked in different ways with a soft 1 in. (2.5 cm.) bristle brush. While drying, the surface was swept with a dry brush to eliminate strokes.

Variation 4

Here, the buff-color basecoat of semigloss latex (vinyl silk emulsion) was colorwashed with a very pale yellow ocher latex (emulsion), mixed with a little acrylic glazing medium. The brushstrokes were left and the glaze applied more heavily around the edges. When dry (24 hours) another glaze of dusty rose was applied using crisscross brushstrokes.

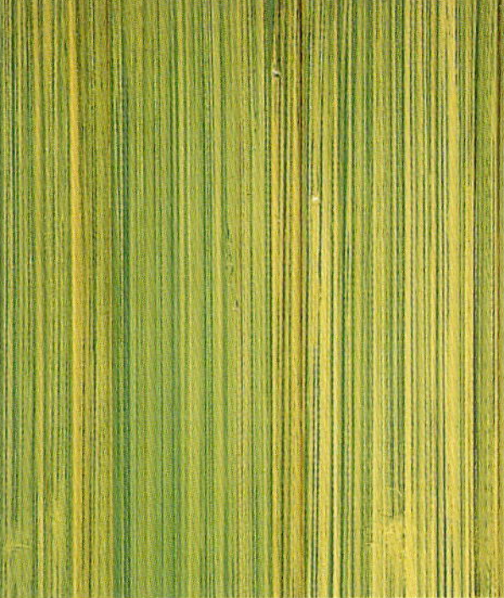

Dragging

Dragging is possibly one of the most elegant and luxurious of all the paint finishes. It can be used to create a wide range of effects and moods simply by dragging a brush through the glaze. The final effect can be subtle or bold, and is limited only by your imagination. Dragging will enhance any room or scheme.

Dragging is best suited to well-prepared flat surfaces, as it is a technique that will show flaws in the base. For the beginner it is best to attempt small items such as boxes, cupboards and chair (dado) rails rather than to attempt walls immediately. The effect works well in conjunction with rag rolling (see p. 52), and is an ideal background for stenciling (see p. 78) and lining (see p. 94).

Your choice of color depends on the color scheme required. For a subtle, elegant look choose two subdued colors, such as dark cream over pale cream. For a bold look use contrasting colors that are strong and vibrant, such as apple green and bright blue, and yellow and orange.

Dragging is inexpensive but it does take practice, so a sample board is a good idea. Most mistakes are caused by appyling too much pressure on the brush when dragging it through the glaze or by using too much glaze. Both problems can be overcome with practice. Any build-up of glaze on the panels of units or doors can be removed by using a dry brush to lift the glaze.

If you are attempting dragging on a large area such as a wall, where you have to use a ladder, try not to remove the brush from the wall as you work from top to bottom but work your way down the ladder keeping the brush at an even pressure. If you do have to remove the brush, carefully go over the overlap with a clean brush and try to vary the position of the overlap on each attempt.

You will need

Tools

• *White or pink undercoat* • *2–3 in. (5–7.5 cm.) bristle basecoat brush* • *½ in. (1.2 cm.) bristle brush* • *2 in. (5 cm.) glazing brush* • *Dragging brush* • *Stippling brush* • *Fine-grade sandpaper*

Materials

• *Eggshell paint* • *Transparent oil glaze* • *Mineral spirits (white spirit)* • *Flat (matte) oil-based varnish*

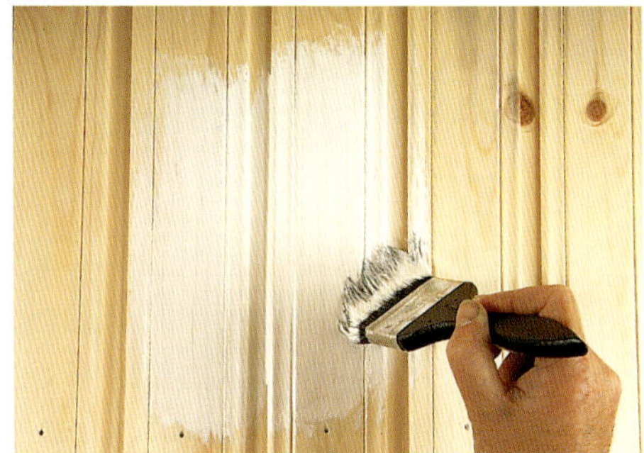

1 **Prepare the surface (see *Preparation*, p. 18). Apply a layer of undercoat. Allow to dry. Sand with a fine-grade sandpaper and remove all the dust. Dragging will show up any imperfections in the surface and therefore it does require really good preparation.**

Variation 1

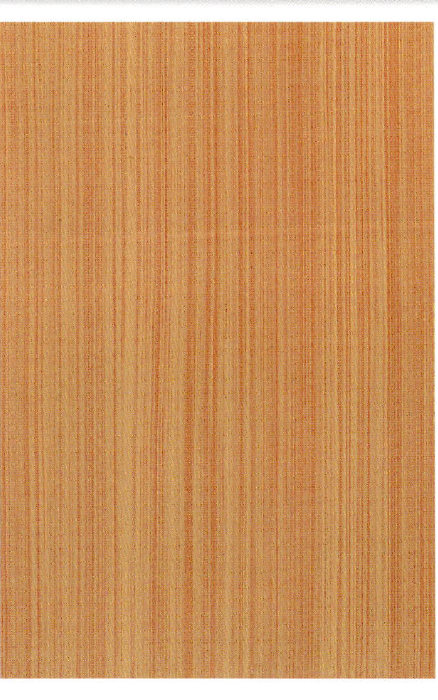

Dragging is traditionally a very elegant effect, although by varying the colorways it can become quite bold and striking. For our sample swatch, we have used a deep apricot basecoat, applied a buff-colored glaze over the top and carefully pulled the long-haired dragging brush through the glaze.

Variation 2

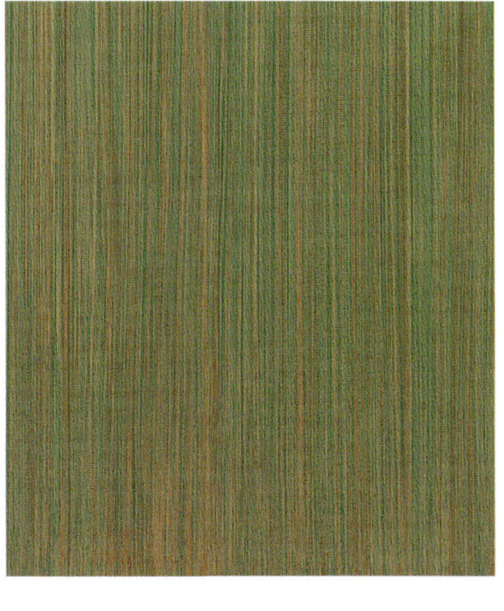

By mixing or layering different colored glazes over the top of each other, the depth and texture of the paint effect can be altered. In this example, a mid-green glaze has been added over the top of the swatch sample in Variation 1. The whole character of this finish has been changed by the addition of one simple color. By combining these two effects above and below a chair (dado) rail, a pleasing background scheme can be achieved.

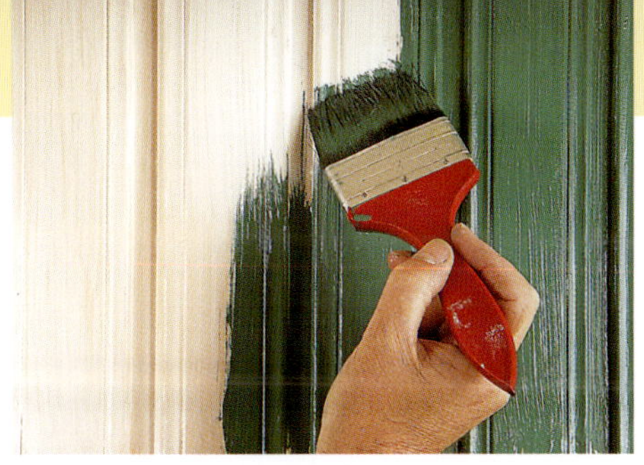

2 With a bristle basecoat brush apply a basecoat of teal blue eggshell paint. Allow to dry. Apply a second coat making sure that any recesses and joints (joins) in the paneling are completely covered. Allow to dry.

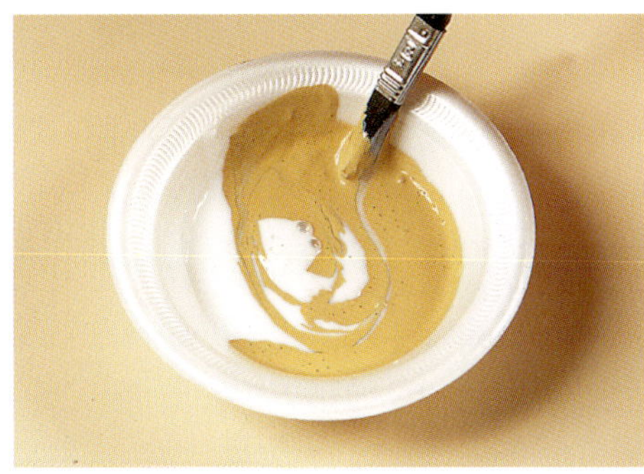

3 Mix a glaze from yellow ocher eggshell paint and some transparent oil glaze, following manufacturer's instructions. With a little mineral spirits (white spirit), thin if necessary to a heavy cream consistency. For a more transparent look dilute the glaze more, being careful not to make the glaze so thin that it will run.

4 With a 2–3 in. (5–7.5 cm.) glazing brush apply the glaze as evenly as possible across the surface, with strokes from top to bottom if dragging vertically. If dragging a large surface, work on an area that you can easily manage.

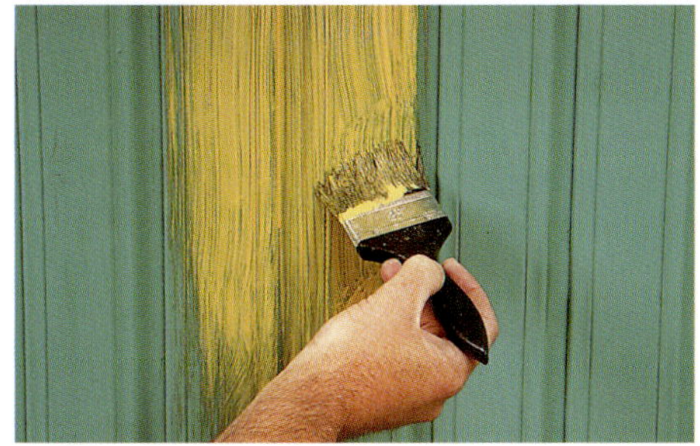

5 Use a good quality stippling brush to stipple or "pounce" out the brushstrokes in the glaze (see *Stippling*, p. 30). Make sure that all recessed areas are stippled and that any excess glaze is removed to avoid runs or drips.

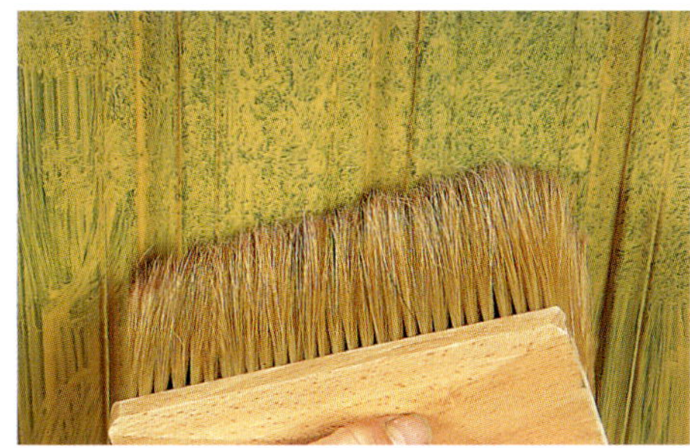

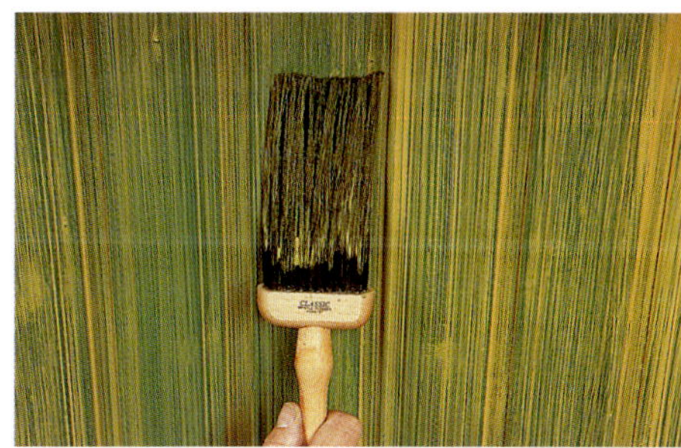

6 Pull a dragging brush through the wet glaze at an angle of 45 degrees, working from top to bottom. Any glaze build-up at the top or bottom should be removed with a dab from a clean, dry bristle brush and the excess wiped away with clean paper towel before continuing. Wipe the dragging brush clean after each stroke.

7 Dragging is one of the most elegant paint techniques (below). Here our colorways have enhanced the traditional "feel" of the tongue-and-groove bar area, lifting the bar and adding a light and warm vitality to the room.

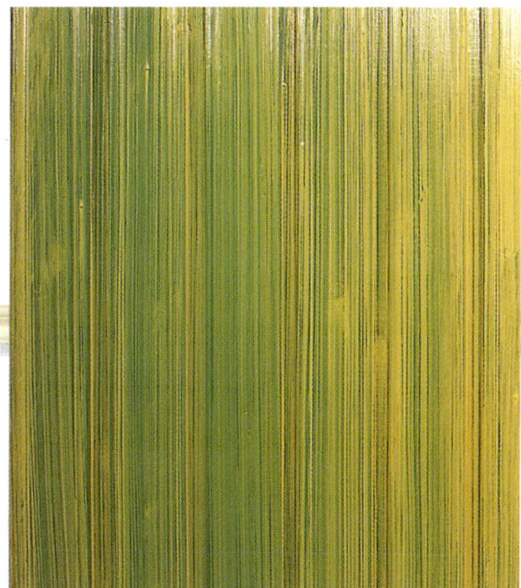

Variation 3

Most decorative paint effects work well together and none more so than ragging (see p. 52) and dragging, which complement each other perfectly. In this example a very pale blue glaze was used over a basecoat of mid-blue. Remember always when you are combining effects to allow each stage to dry thoroughly before attempting the next stage.

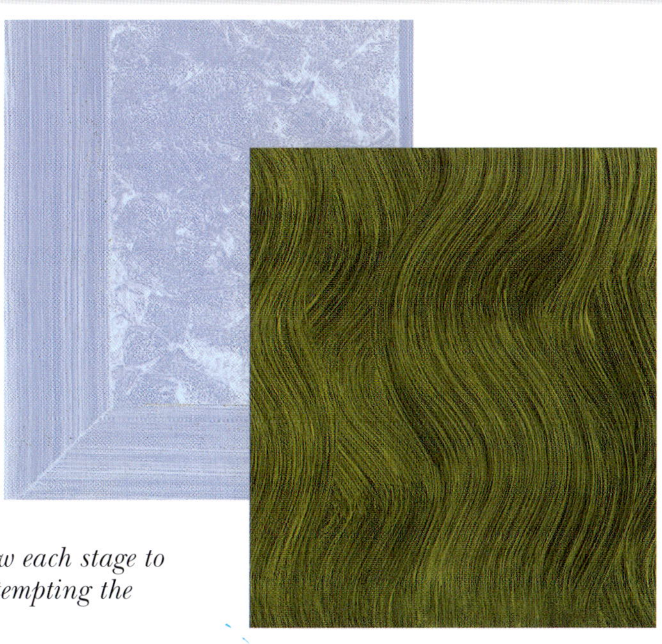

Variation 4

Many optical fantasies can be created using wavy lines. The possibilities are endless but should be carefully thought about first. The sample here was done on a black basecoat. A brilliant yellow glaze was applied and then dragged using a long-haired brush pulled in wavy motions across the surface (left).

In context

Colorwashing and dragging are broken paint effects that can create very diverse results—from the sophisticated to the casual and from the very elegant to the most simple of country looks. They can also create a finish that will suit the most fastidious of people but are effects that can, with practice, be successfully carried out by almost anyone.

Dragging

▶ Country kitchen

Our gallery photograph here shows very clearly how two effects can be successfully combined into one. The walls were first colorwashed with warm terracotta and then "dragged" with a cloth in parallel lines through the glaze. This has created a very attractive example and one that will suit most country kitchens.

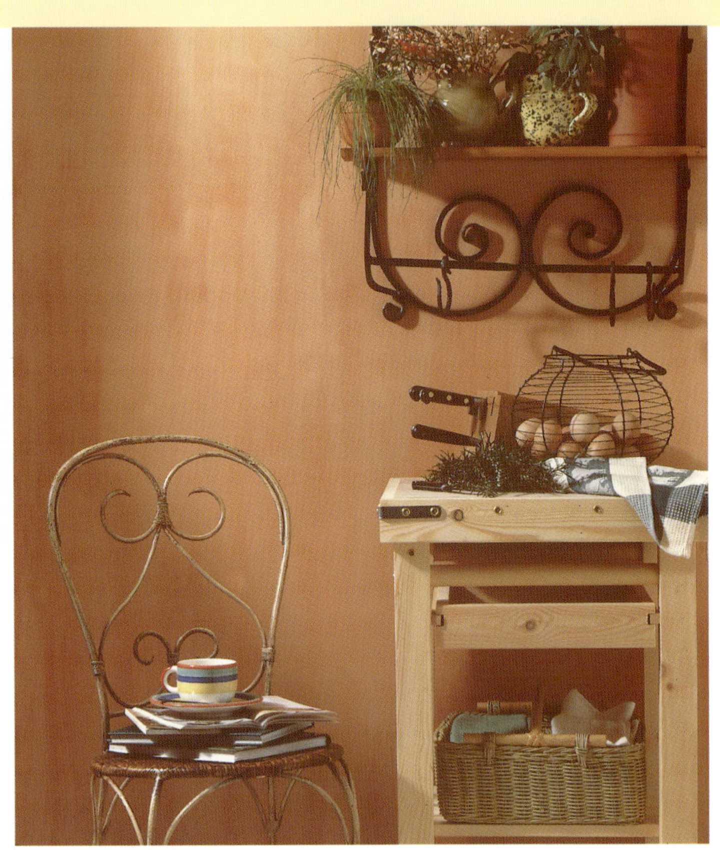

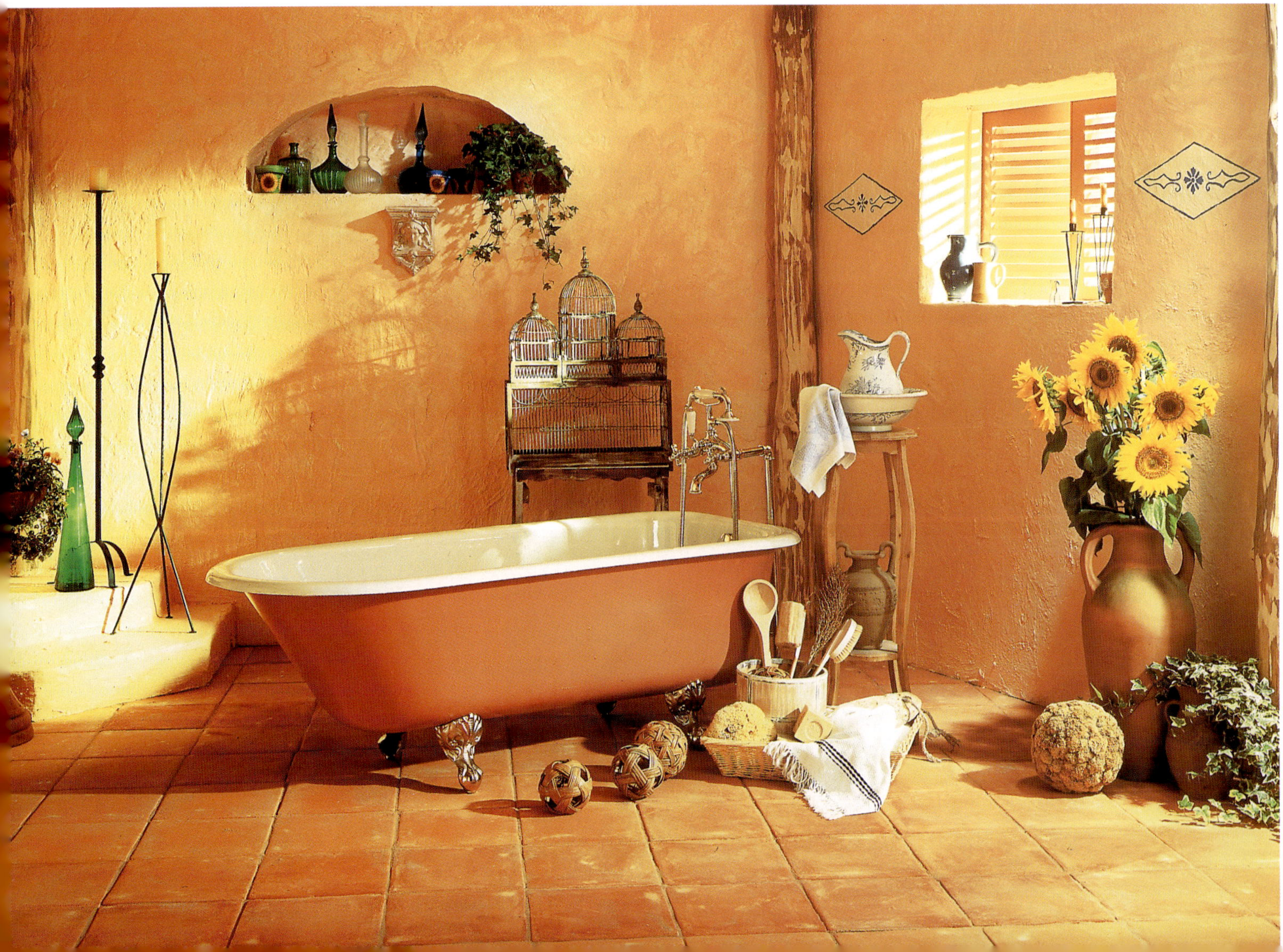

Dragging

▶ Elegant sitting room

The crispness of the blue dragged walls, together with the distressing of the surrounding moldings of the bookcases and window recesses, help to highlight the display of beautiful blue and white porcelain in this sitting room. This decorative scheme is brought together with the shades of blue-striped fabric covering the sofas.

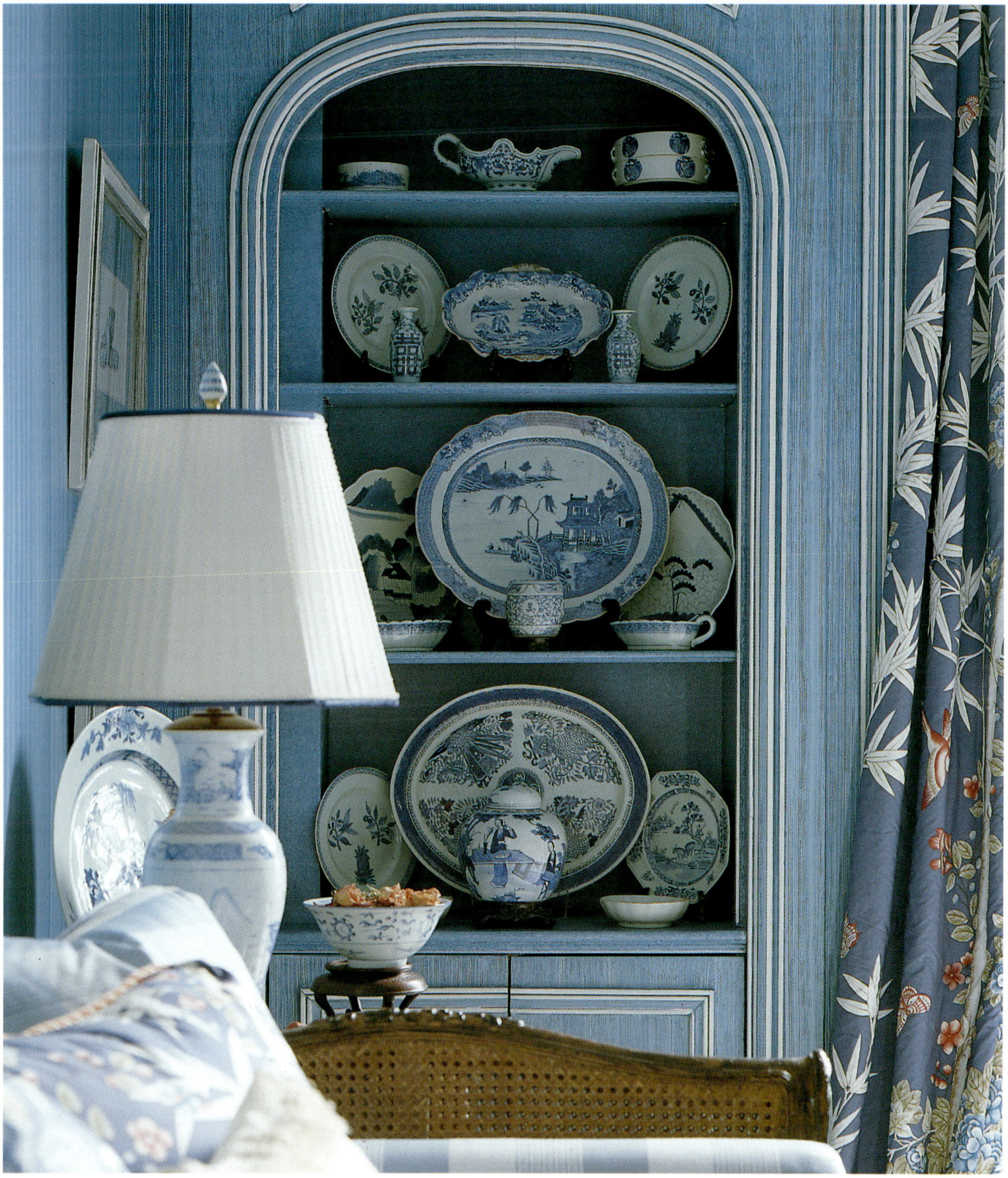

Colorwashing

◀ Bathroom with rough plastered walls

This terracotta and ocher colorwashed bathroom looks warmly inviting, relaxing and spacious. The scheme is very effectively complemented by the terracotta quarry tiles and simple, but imaginative accessories. The result definitely has the feel of the Mediterranean about it.

Colorwashing

◀ Sample panel

Brushstrokes have been left to create texture. Over a basecoat of dark blue two glazes have been applied, the first of deep purple and the second, once dry, a glaze of lilac.

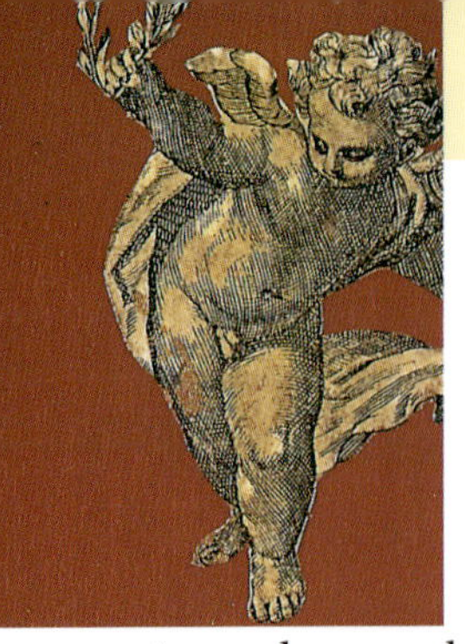

Découpage

Découpage, or the art of applying paper cut-outs to a surface, is an extremely popular decorative technique that can transform everyday objects into works of art. Finding ideas for découpage from magazines, calendars and other sources is as much fun as applying the technique itself. Découpage is a relaxing technique that will give highly individual results that can be enjoyed for years to come.

Découpage can be applied to any flat surface and is ideally suited to walls, cupboards, paneling, ceilings and floors, as well as fireplace surrounds, mantles and boxes. A well thought out, prepared and placed attempt at découpage will give any object or room a new lease of life. Découpage has an added advantage of producing highly individual results at a very low cost. The basic materials are paper cut-out pictures from such sources as magazines, calendars and catalogs.

Découpage works well in both traditional and modern decors, especially with other effects such as crackleure (see p. 96), colorwashing (see p. 60) and ragging (see p. 52).

Make sure the surface is properly prepared, as all flaws will show. Cut out and position the various elements of the design carefully to ensure the result you want. If mistakes occur, remove the picture and replace with care.

You will need

Tools

• *Scissors or sharp craft knife* • *Sandpaper* • *PVA glue or wallpaper paste* • *Soft cloths* • *2 in. (5 cm.) varnishing brush*

Materials

• *Source material (such as scraps or prints)* • *Spray sealant* • *White or pink oil-based undercoat* • *Yellow ocher artists' oil paint* • *Burgundy eggshell paint* • *Varnish*

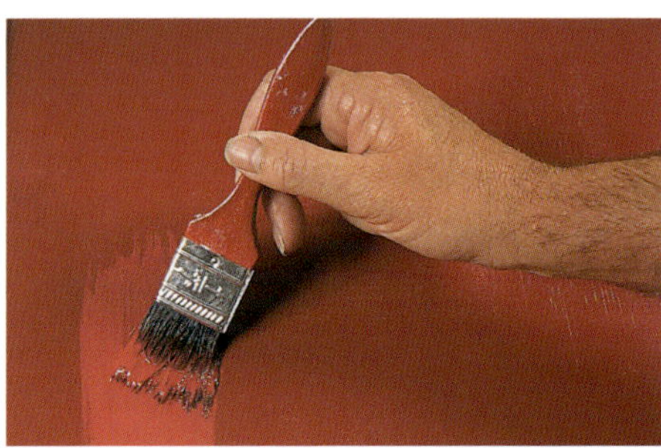

1 Prepare the surface (see *Preparation* p. 18). Apply the undercoat and allow to dry overnight. Apply two coats of burgundy eggshell using the laying off technique (see p. 24).

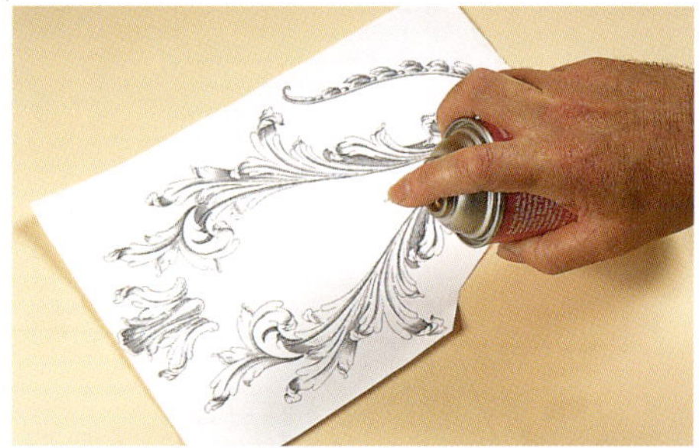

2 Spray your selected photocopies with a coat of sealant, following the manufacturer's instructions. This will strengthen the print, allowing for easier cutting and gluing at later stages.

Variation 1

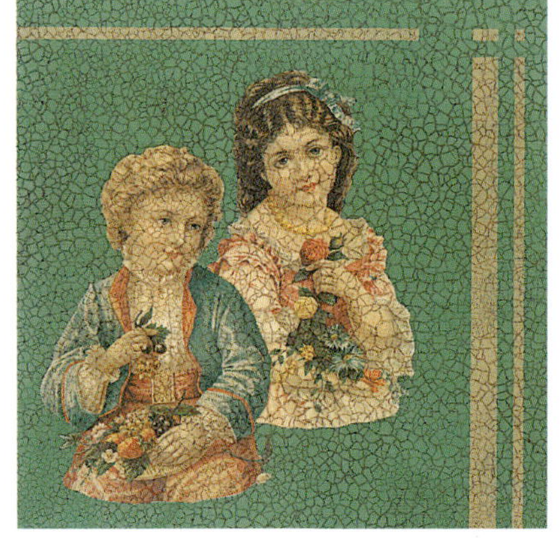

For centuries découpage has been a popular pastime, and it has developed into an art form. Here a Victorian theme has been created using scraps bought over the counter and then applied to a mid-green background. To add authenticity to the look, low-tack masking tape was used to create lines in cream (see p. 94), and finally crackleure was used (see p. 96). The cracks were highlighted with raw umber oil paint.

Variation 2

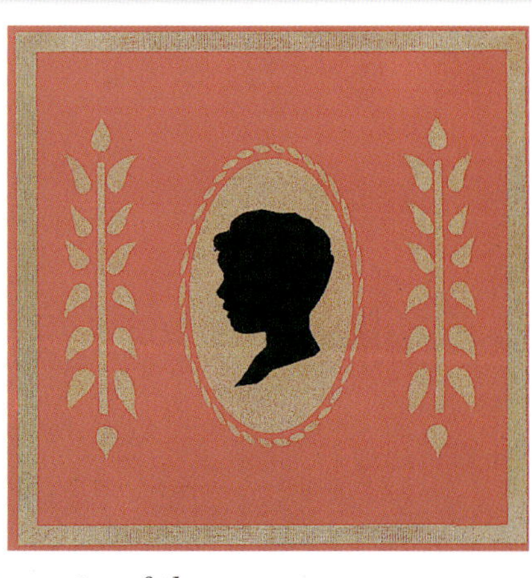

This elegant look was achieved using a basecoat of dusty, rose pink in conjunction with stenciling (see p. 78) and lining (see p. 94) using gilt acrylic paint. The silhouette was cut from a photocopy (see p. 58) and finally applied to the center of the frame using the découpage method.

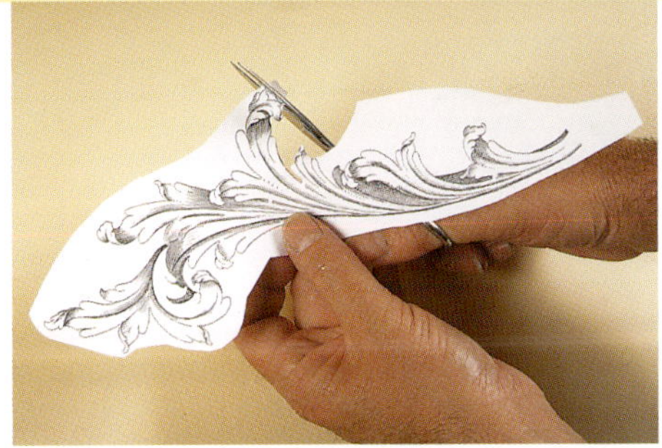

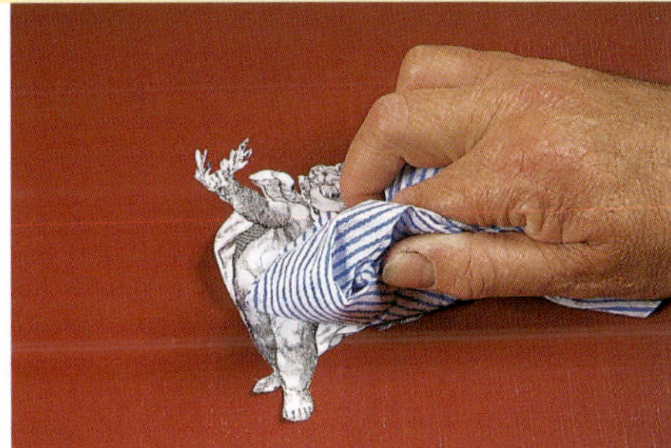

3 **Allow to dry for a few minutes and then roughly cut round the image. Using fine scissors or a craft knife, carefully cut out the details.**

4 **Experiment with different arrangements of the images until you achieve what you want. Do this on a sample area or on the cupboard panel carefully using a little blu-tack to fix the image in place. Do not press too hard as this will crease the image.**

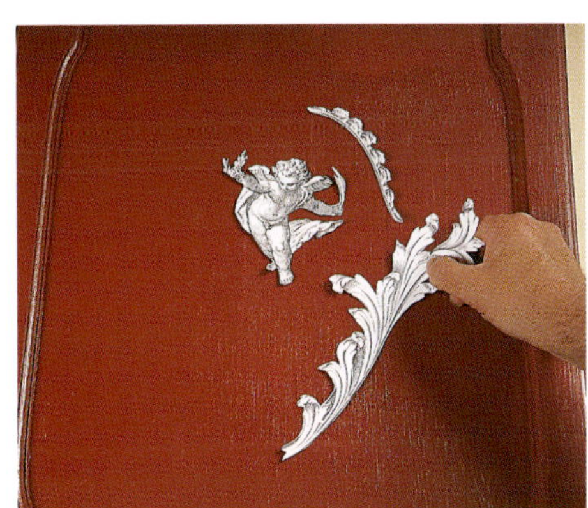

5 **When you have finalized the arrangement apply some PVA adhesive or good-quality wallpaper paste to the back side of each cut-out, and put some paste on the door panel. Slowly position the cut-out on the surface and remove all air bubbles by wiping a damp cloth over the cut-out and smoothing toward the edge. Wipe away excess glue.**

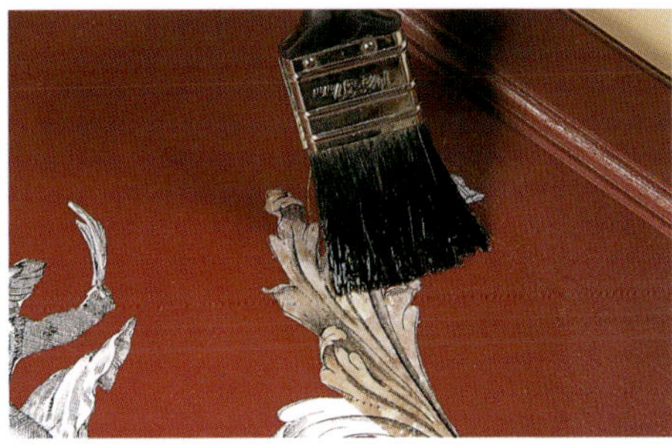

6 **When dry, apply at least 3 to 4 coats of a suitable varnish. Here we have chosen an oil-based gloss varnish tinted with just a hint of yellow ocher in the first coat only. Allow to dry between coats.**

7 **The enormous amount of source material available means that découpage can vary from the simple and casual through to the exotic and opulent. The door here in rich burgundy and gold, with cherubs and acanthus leaves antiqued to remove the new crispness, creates a feeling of real romanticism.**

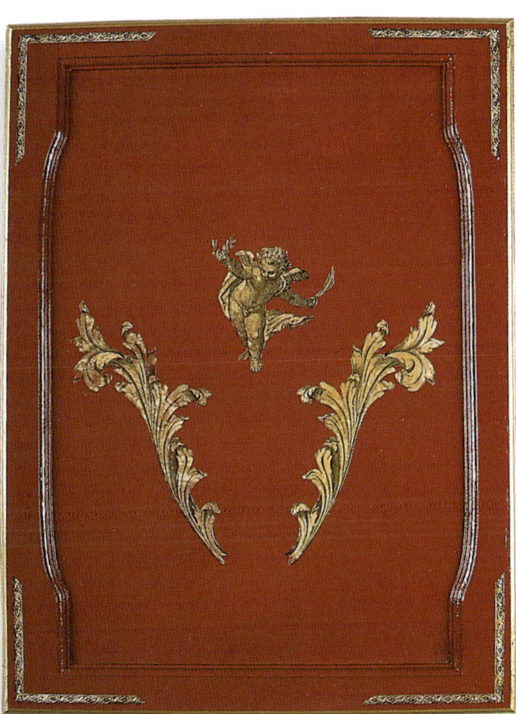

Variation 3

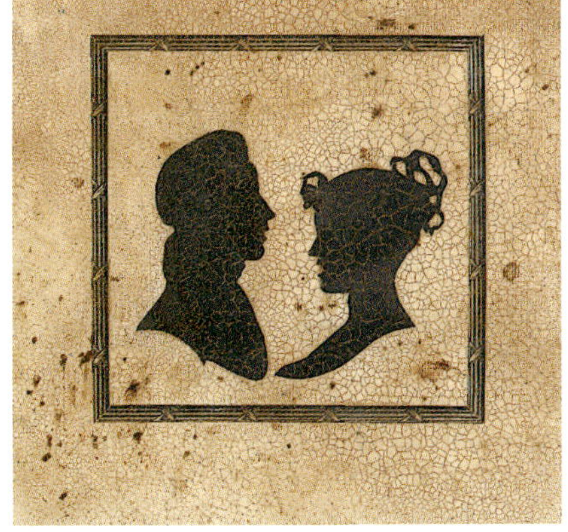

Once again, a photocopy of silhouettes and a traditional border design were carefully découpaged over the basecoat of off-white. The aged parchment effect was achieved by dabbing some strong coffee over the surface and adding a few solid coffee grounds. After allowing this to dry, the surface was then crackleured (see p. 96) and finally antique-brown furniture polish was rubbed into the exposed cracks.

Variation 4

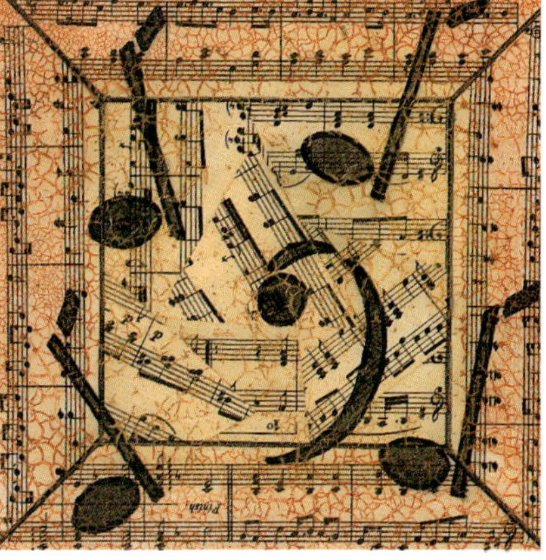

Sheet music was applied here in such a way as to create a paneled look. This was allowed to dry, then lined with a black permanent marking pen, and music notes stenciled (see p. 78) with black acrylic paint. The whole panel was allowed to dry overnight before applying the crackleure varnish following the manufacturer's instructions. The resulting web of cracks was highlighted with yellow ocher and crimson artists' oil paint.

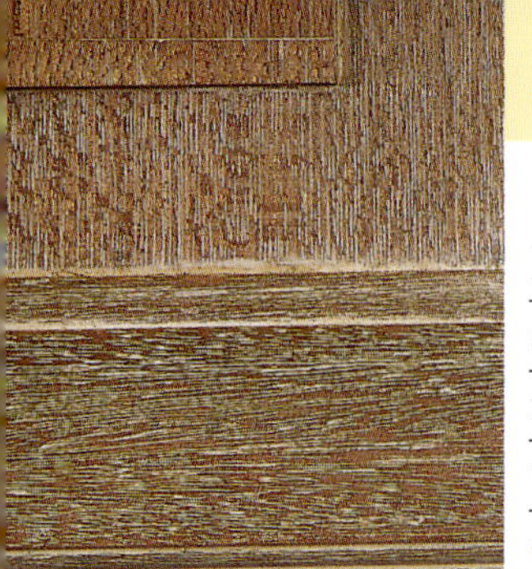

Liming creates a soft, mellow finish that allows the natural look of the woodgrain to show through. The effect is reminiscent of seaside boardwalks and sun-bleached wood.

Liming

Achieving good-quality results when liming can be a little time consuming as the surface has to be correctly prepared. All traces of varnish and paint should be removed from the surface with a stripper, following the manufacturer's instructions, before opening up the grain with a wire brush. A final sand with fine-grade steel wool and a wipe down with a damp cloth, and you are ready to proceed.

Because of the nature of liming, the ideal surface is wood with an open grain. For this reason window frames, baseboards (skirting boards), and so on, are all ideal for liming, as are wooden units, tables and countertops. It is an inexpensive technique, and is reasonably quick once the initial preparation has been completed. The materials are readily available in good decorator stores and specialist shops, although you can make your own liming wax .

A common mistake is the grain not being sufficiently open to enable enough wax to be absorbed to highlight the effect. To overcome this, reuse the wire brush to open up the grain a little more, and then reapply the wax. If the look is not what you want, the wax can be removed by cleaning with steel wool and mineral spirits (white spirit), and you can then simply begin the process again. To help avoid this, experiment on a small area, possibly underneath or on the back of the surface.

You will need

Tools

• Metal or wire brush • Gloves • Coarse and fine steel wool • Soft, lint-free cloths • Soft brush

Materials

• Varnish or paint stripper • Liming wax • Mahogany wood stain • Clear furniture wax • Protective gloves

1 Sand the surface and remove all traces of dust with a soft brush and a damp cloth. Stain the surface with a dark woodstain. Here we have used mahogany applied with a soft, lint-free cloth. Allow to dry overnight.

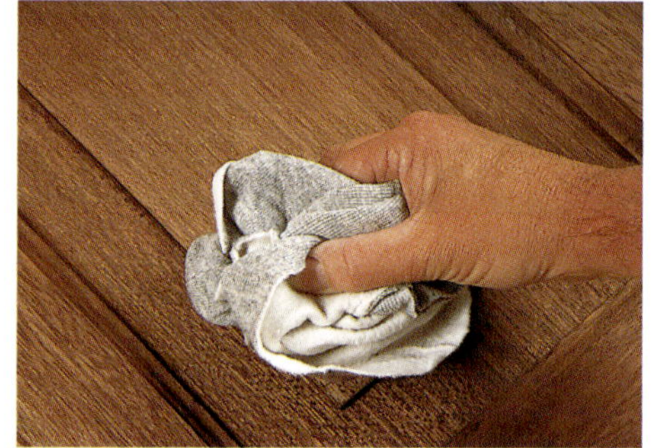

Variation 1

Liming is best done on real wood as the success of the effect depends on opening and highlighting the grain of the natural wood with wax, most commonly white. In this painted variation a white glaze has been painted over a dark brown basecoat. The glaze was then "flogged" with a long-haired dragging brush, working from the bottom up and "flicking" the bristles.

Variation 2

Here a white glaze has been painted over a basecoat of vivid purple, allowed to go slightly tacky, and then fine-grade steel wool passed across the surface, following the grain at all times. This creates a very passable version of simulated liming.

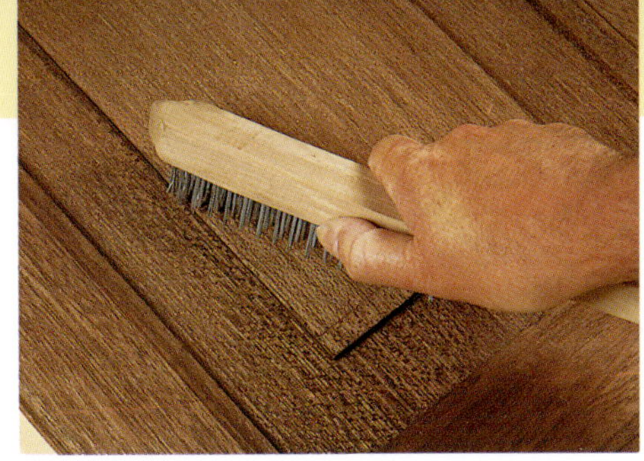

2 Slowly and gently, but firmly, pull a stiff wire brush along the natural grain of the wood removing parts of the softwood and "opening up" the grain. Continue over the entire surface, including the edges and raised panels, and also work across the outer framework of the door panel. Remove excess dust.

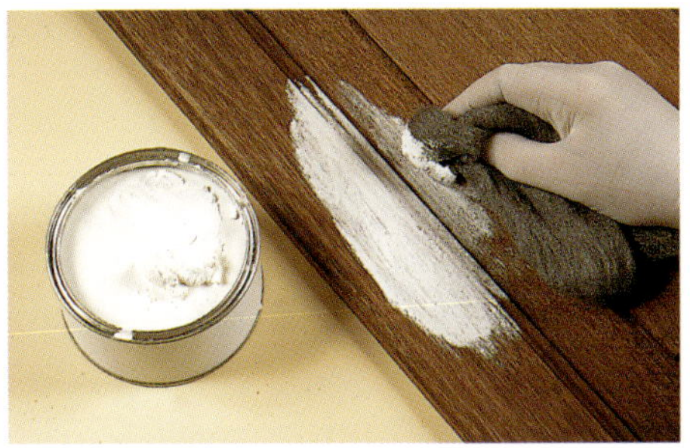

3 Wearing gloves, apply a generous layer of white liming wax with some fine steel wool (0000 grade) into the entire surface, making sure that all awkward corners and recesses are covered. Work in the same direction as the grain ensuring that the wax penetrates the grain. Allow to dry.

4 Still wearing gloves, apply clear furniture wax with fine steel wool. Work along the grain and remove excess white liming wax. Change steel wool regularly to avoid clogging. Work until the desired effect is achieved. Allow to dry.

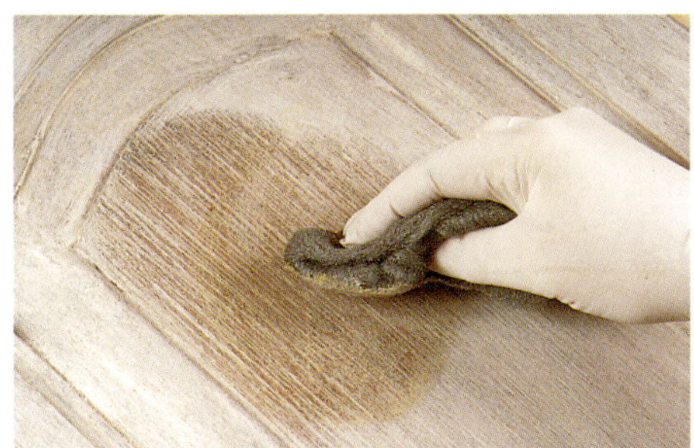

5 Using a soft cloth, apply a generous coat of clear furniture wax, working into the corners and along the grain. Remove any excess wax with a clean, soft, lint-free cloth. Allow to dry. Finally, buff with a clean, soft cloth to a soft sheen.

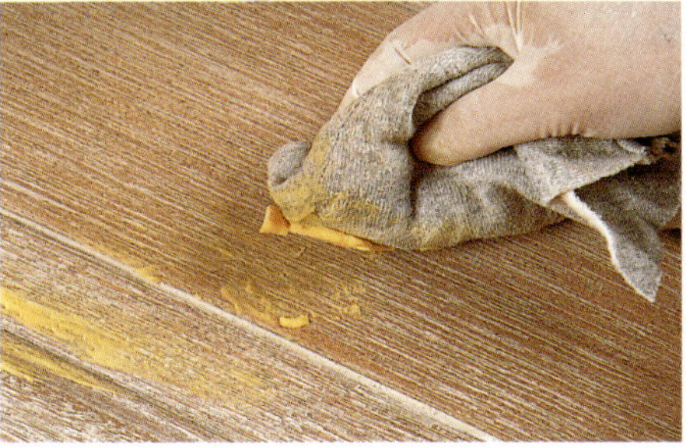

6 The effect of liming shows up the grain in what would otherwise be a rather ordinary, flat surface. The paneled doors here have been revitalized by the use of traditional, white liming wax, but any tinted colored wax could be used to customize the look to suit the decor. A little hard work achieves a very stylish finish.

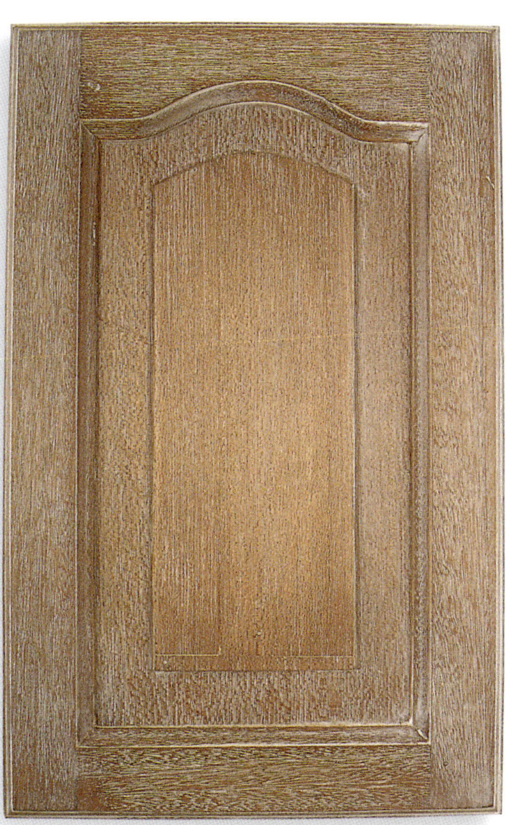

Variation 3

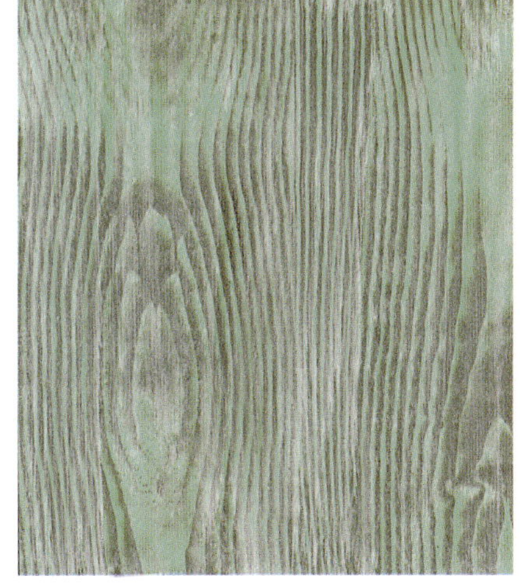

An acrylic glaze made from 1 part mid-green latex (emulsion) to 3 parts acrylic glazing medium was applied over a mid-gray latex basecoat. The woodgrain effect was achieved by passing a heart graining tool (rocker) through the glaze. When dry, diluted white latex (1 part paint to 6 parts water) was brushed across the surface. Finally, a protective coat of flat (matte) acrylic varnish was applied.

Variation 4

Here, a mid-green acrylic glaze (1 part latex [emulsion] paint to 4 parts glaze) was applied over a yellow ocher basecoat of semigloss latex (vinyl silk emulsion). This was then combed across the surface with a wide-toothed, metal comb and left to dry. After sanding of the surface to distress the colors (see p. 36), a weak wash of white latex (emulsion) —1 part paint to 6 parts water — was brushed over the surface.

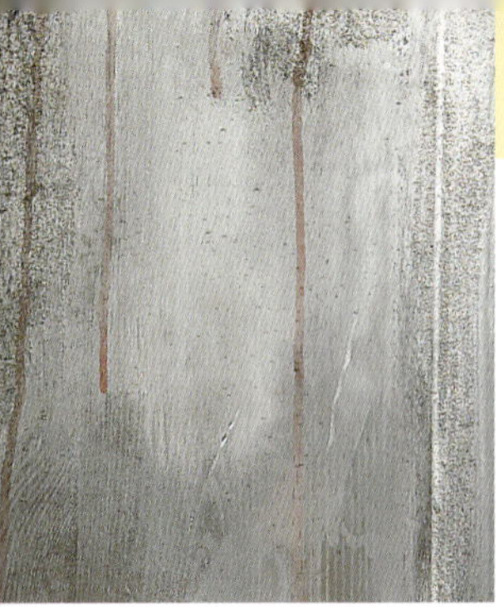

Painted iron

The finish of metal, whether it looks new or looks as if it has had many years' exposure to the elements, can be used to excellent effect around the home. It can be employed to create a myriad of effects of a very individual nature. A metal paint finish can give the impression of increasing the size of a room, or it can reflect available light in a very mellow or theatrical way.

The look of painted iron can be used to great effect on doors, paneling and baseboards (skirting boards), as well as fireplace surrounds, frames and decorative items. It is suited to both period and modern settings.

The effect of painted iron is inexpensive to achieve, and with a little practice and an eye for detail plain surfaces can become a focal point in any setting. Follow the instructions of both the manufacturer and our step-by-step guide for good results. The metal technique covers flaws in the surface, so that any problem that may arise can be improved by the finished effect.

Any metallic color may be chosen as a basecoat to create various effects and colorways, and to draw together a chosen color scheme. Bold colors can be used to create a sumptuous look for an elegant and stylish formal setting, while copper creates a more subdued but equally splendid finish. Used with lining (see p. 94) and stenciling (see p. 78), very distinct finishes can be achieved.

You will need

Tools

• 2–3 in. (5–7.5 cm.) bristle basecoat brush • Paint dish • ¼ in. (0.63 mm.) bristle Fitch (flat) brush • A bunch of keys • Soft lint-free cloth

Materials

• PVA glue • Silver sand • Silver metallic paint • Raw umber and black acrylic paint • Flat (matte) or satin oil-based varnish • Rust colored latex (emulsion)

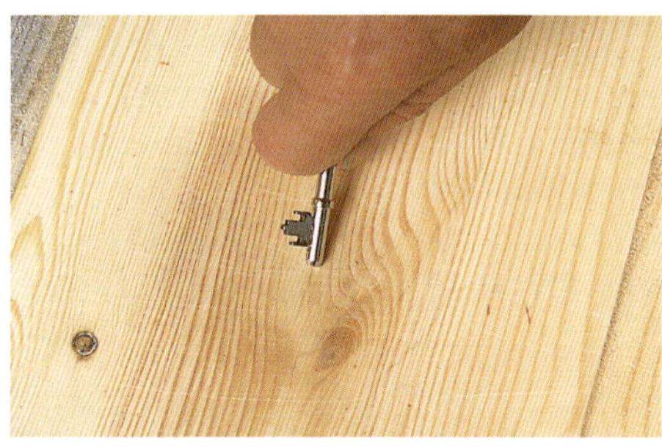

1 With a bunch of keys, a screwdriver, or any suitable metal object, score and mark the surface at random. Be careful not to overdo this, as too much can spoil the final effect.

2 On areas where natural oxidation would occur evenly apply a generous layer of PVA glue using a bristle brush. Sprinkle sand over the surface of the wet glue. Let dry and dust off any loose sand.

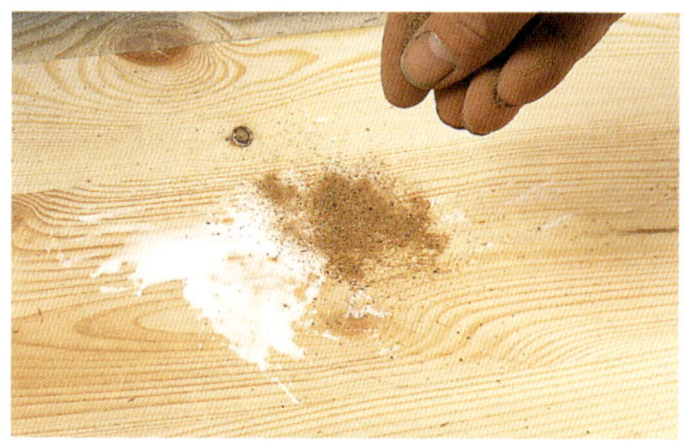

Variation 1

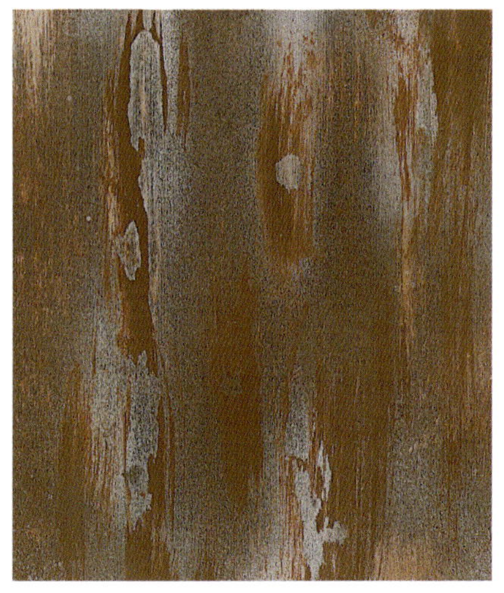

Creating effects such as painted iron and rusty metal can be challenging and very gratifying. The basecoat in this example was painted with silver spray paint and allowed to dry. Some furniture wax was then applied to the surface (see p. 25). A deep, rusty brown layer of glaze was then applied over the whole area and, once dry, removed with fine sandpaper.

Variation 2

Once again the surface was sprayed with two coats of silver spray paint and left to dry. A layer of PVA wood glue was then randomly stippled across the basecoat and, because of the metallic nature of the silver paint, was allowed to separate, creating puddles. Silver sand was then applied and the whole effect left to dry. A muddy, brown glaze was then washed across the completed panel.

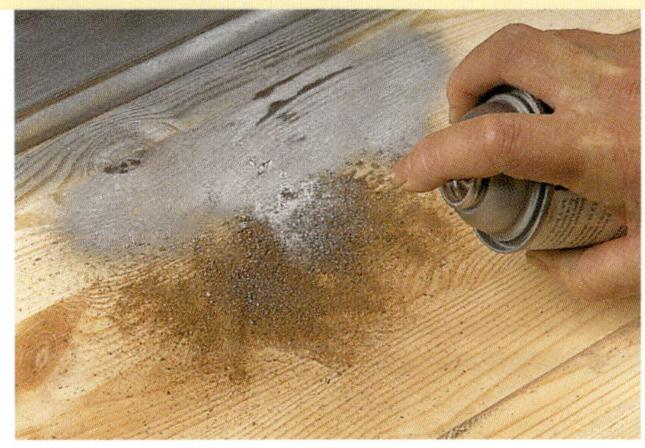

3 Spray the surface with two or three thin coats of silver metallic spray paint following the manufacturer's instructions. Allow to dry between coats. To vary the color of the silver, use silver acrylic paint or chrome spray with the silver metallic spray. Allow to dry.

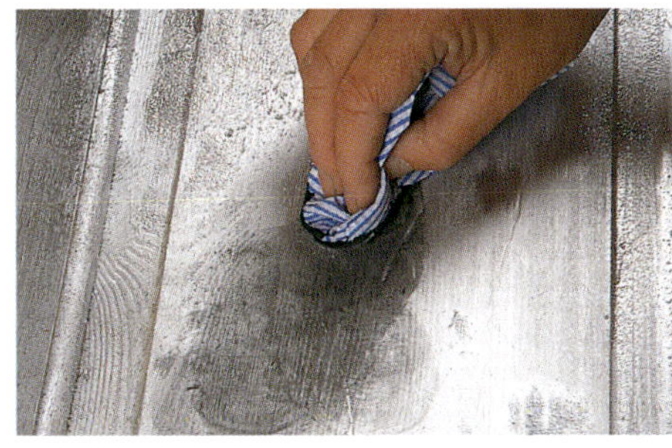

4 In a clean dish mix a little black artists' acrylic paint with raw umber. Add water to get a pouring consistency. With a soft, lint-free cloth apply the paint to the metallic surface. Work it into the grain to form a tarnished effect, leaving some untarnished areas.

5 Dilute a little rust colored latex (emulsion) or artists' acrylic paint with water to achieve a light cream consistency. With a Fitch brush, dribble it down the surface in natural rust areas. Just before the dribbles dry you could carefully wipe them with a soft cloth to remove any still wet paint but leave a textured sharp edge.

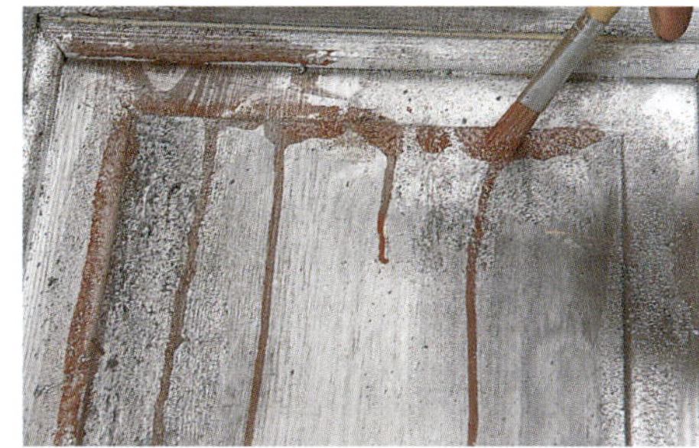

6 Apply a layer of sealant or varnish if required, following the manufacturer's instructions. Use a satin varnish to achieve a slightly polished metallic finish.

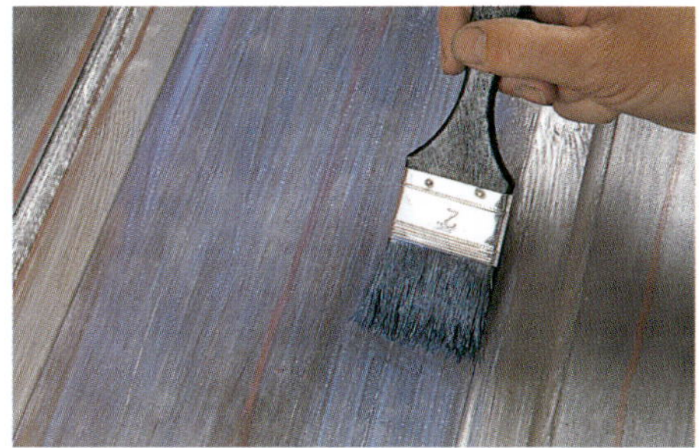

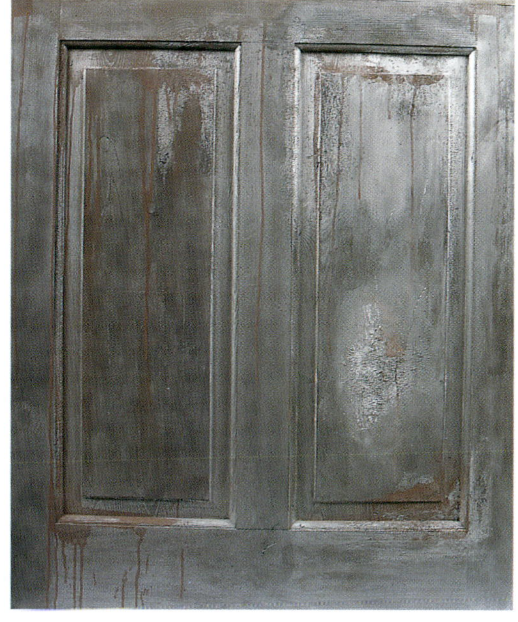

7 The painted iron effect on this door creates a positive and forthright effect. The use of silver accentuates the moldings reflecting movement and yet, at the same time, retaining a sense of solidness. This is a technique that makes a very strong design statement.

Variation 3

Here, we carried out all the steps in Variation 2, including applying the final muddy, brown glaze. After this had been left to dry for at least 24 hours, a second glaze of black was applied over the brown, and carefully worked into the grain. The top surface was then lightly grazed with fine sandpaper to achieve a more tarnished look.

Variation 4

The surface of this panel was sprayed with gold paint, and once dry the panels marked off with low-tack masking tape, working each of the two opposite panels at one time. They were then coated with oil-based varnish tinted with a little brown artists' oil paint. A little phthalo green artists' oil was used to highlight the edges. The central panel was lined with a gold permanent marking pen and sealed with a spray sealant.

Spattering

Spattering is great fun to do and can produce some unusual results. By layering carefully chosen colors, wonderfully random effects can be achieved, which will add individuality to any project. The use of spattering, whether on its own, or in conjunction with other techniques such as marble (see p. 132, 136 and 138), granite (see p. 50) and lapis lazuli (see p. 74), will add texture and interest to an otherwise plain and flat surface.

Spattering is a technique that allows your imagination to run riot as far as color choice is concerned. Bold color will create a vibrant setting whereas subtle color can look very sophisticated and stylish.

It is a paint effect that is ideally suited to furniture, table tops and paneling, and it also looks very good on small objects such as lampbases, picture and mirror frames and bowls. Larger areas can be a problem because spattering creates a very variable effect. However, as you gain in confidence and experience, this can be overcome.

Spattering is inexpensive to achieve as the humble toothbrush can be substituted for the stiff-bristled decorator brush and will do just as good a job.

Problems may arise in obtaining evenness of color, especially over large areas. But this can be overcome by lots of practice. Ideally the paint should be a thick-cream consistency, allowing "flow" and thereby eliminating unsightly blobs and splodges. A non-absorbent basecoat enables any of these blemishes to be quickly wiped off with a soft cloth and carefully reapplied.

You will need

Tools

- *2–3 in. (5–7.5 cm.) bristle basecoat brush* • *Paint dishes* • *Stiff-bristled Fitch brush or toothbrush for spattering*

Materials

- *Gray undercoat* • *Non-absorbent basecoat of chosen color in semigloss latex (vinyl silk emulsion)*
- *Semigloss latex (vinyl silk emulsion) in chosen spattering colors*
- *Newspaper for protection*
- *Varnish for protection (optional)*

1 Prepare the surface (see *Preparing plasterwork*, p. 21). Make sure the surface is dry. Apply the undercoat with the bristle basecoat brush. Allow to dry.

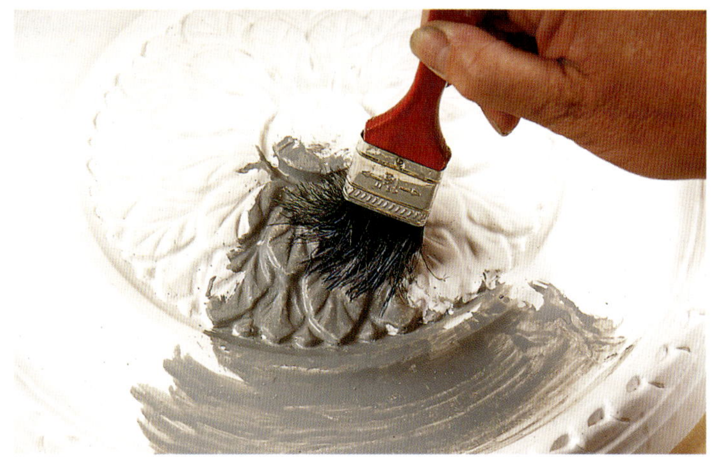

Variation 1

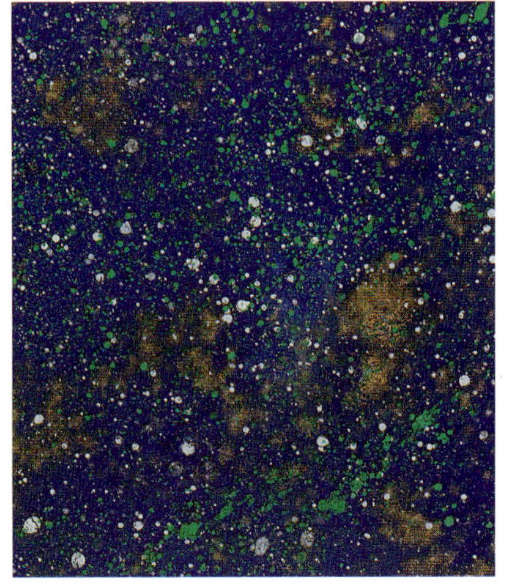

For this example an oil glaze of deep blue has been stippled (see p. 30) over a basecoat of yellow ocher, and the surface carefully spattered with mineral spirits (white spirit) to separate the glaze. After drying, acrylic paint was spattered on with a toothbrush, using white followed by emerald green, to create a three-dimensional look.

Variation 2

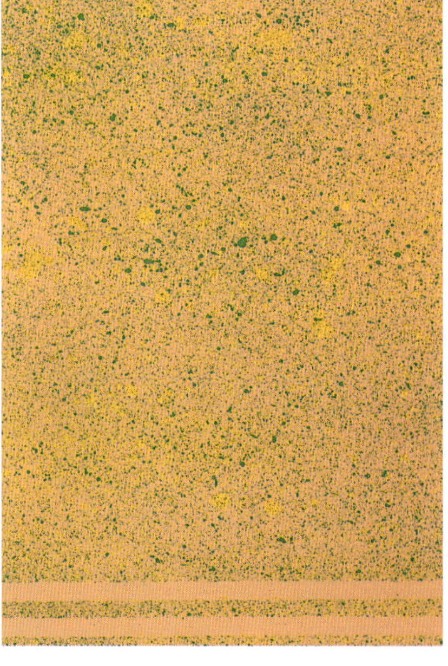

By varying the colorways and the intensity of the spattering, more subdued results can be created. Here, a stiff-bristled, Fitch brush was loaded with bright yellow paint and gently tapped with a stick over a basecoat of deep peach. This was followed with a spattering of emerald green paint.

2 **Paint the surface with the pale blue basecoat using the bristle basecoat brush. Make sure the paint covers any awkward areas and that there is no paint build-up in the recessed areas.**

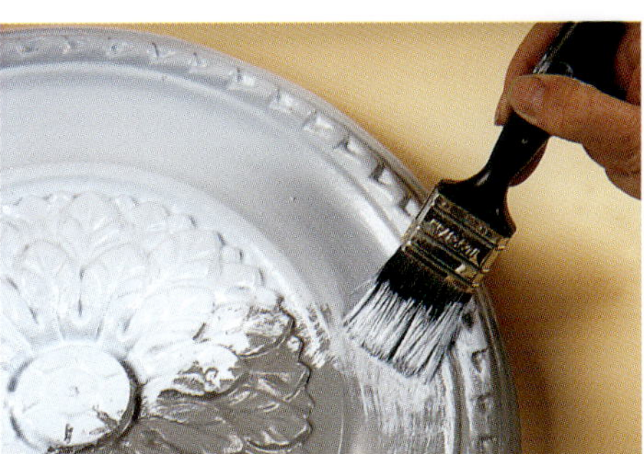

3 **In a clean dish mix the mid-blue paint with water until it is a pouring consistency. Using a toothbrush, spatter the surface with an even spray of the mid-blue paint. Allow this to dry.**

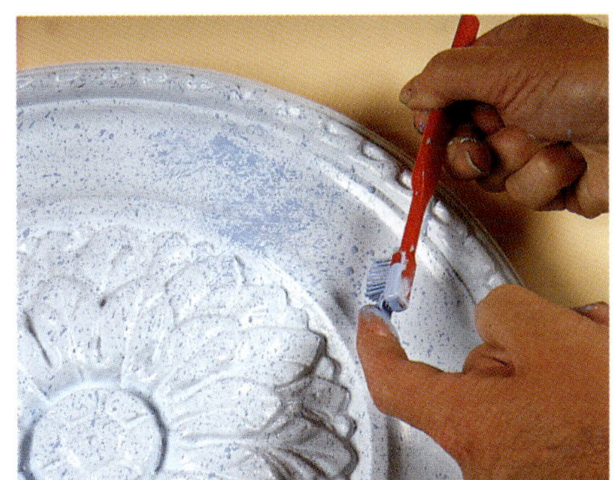

4 **Dilute the deep blue paint with water until it is a pouring consistency. Once again, spatter the surface evenly using a toothbrush.**

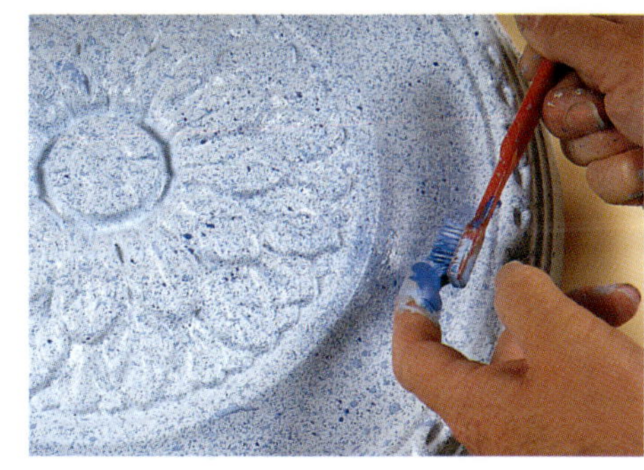

5 **The choice of three shades of blue to spatter the surface of this ceiling rosette (rose) has created a defined yet subdued finish that is full of depth. The effect of spattering is spontaneous and relies entirely upon your own personal taste—opening up endless possibilities for both design and color.**

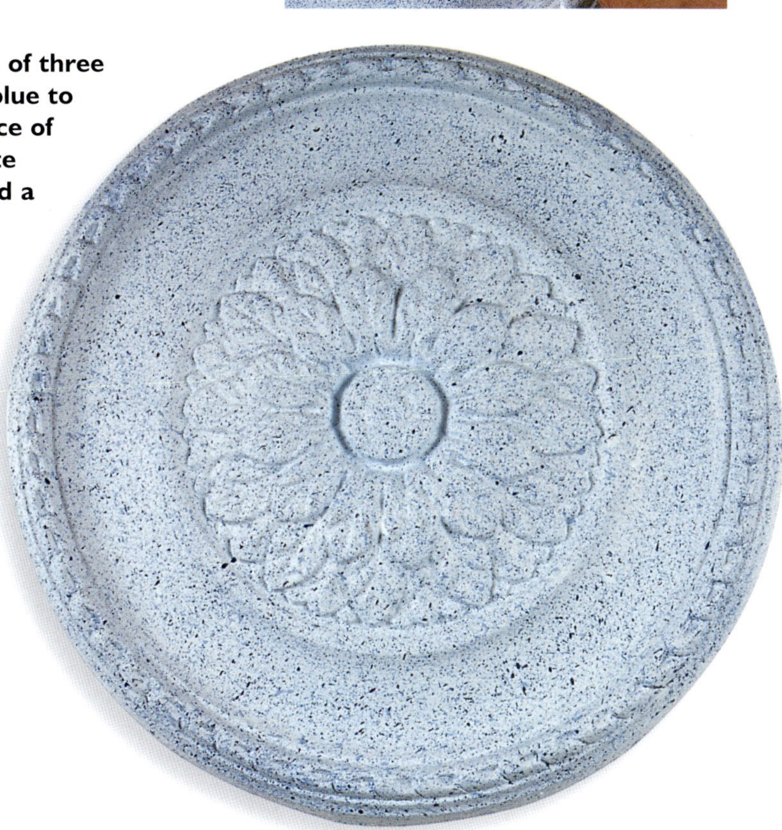

Variation 3

Using a diffuser available from good art supply stores, the basecoat of deep pink has been more evenly spattered with mid-green, allowed to dry, and then, extremely carefully, spattered again using a pale cream. By choosing colors similar in shade, elegant results can be achieved with the diffuser. However, the diffuser creates a more controlled and less random effect.

Variation 4

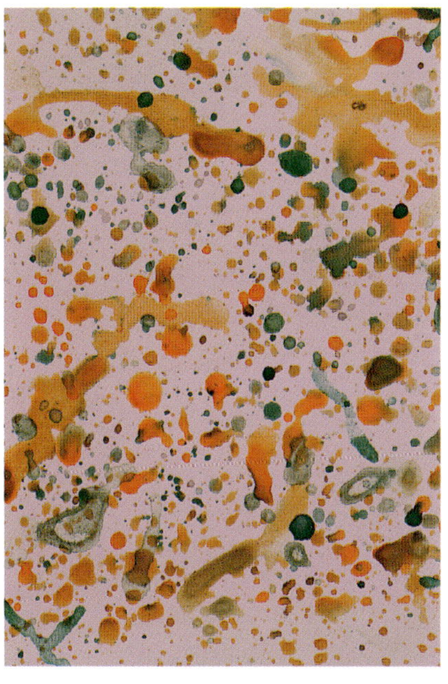

In this alternative, brightly colored wood stains and a hairdryer have been used. The basecoat of lilac was heavily spattered with the orange, green and yellow wood dyes, and quickly dried off using a hairdryer. These dyes are very thin and should only be used on a horizontal surface.

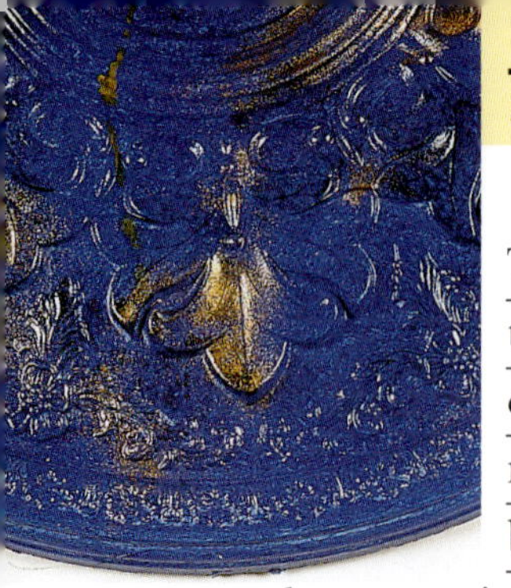

The beauty of this vibrant and expensive blue mineral has often been imitated over the centuries. Its depth of color and glints of fool's gold can be used to create effects that will enhance any decorative scheme.

Lapis lazuli

Lapis lazuli is a very expensive precious mineral, and today is used in very small quantities. So when it is imitated as a decorative paint effect, it is best to limit it to smaller, decorative items, such as picture frames, boxes and lampbases, although it can be used on paneling and cupboard doors. Careful placement is essential for such a visually striking paint effect. If you are not careful, the effect can easily dominate rather than add to what can otherwise be a well-balanced and striking period or modern setting.

This is quite an expensive finish to create due to the initial expense, but when averaged out over several different projects the cost is not so prohibitive, and all the materials will last if cared for. Do not substitute cheaper versions for good brushes and materials as this will reflect in the finished result.

Like any paint effect that is copying the "real thing," to avoid mistakes look at pictures of lapis lazuli before starting and get a feel for its construction and look. Lapis lazuli works well when used as an inlay with effects such as marbling (see p. 132) and when combined with gilt lining (see p. 94). Mistakes should not happen if you follow instructions, but if a mistake does happen remove the ground or basecoat with a soft cloth and mineral spirits (white spirit) and reapply that area. Using oil-based products allows a reasonable working time before they dry, enabling easy and quick removal if necessary. If the paint has dried, then sand the finish, reapply the same basecoat and start again.

You will need

Tools

• 2–3in. (5–7.5 cm.) bristle basecoat brush • Good quality 2 in. (5 cm.) varnishing brush • Small natural (marine) sponges • Fine artists' brush for veining • Fine bristle brush

Materials

• Mid-blue basecoat of semigloss latex (vinyl silk emulsion) Artists' tube oils in French ultramarine, Prussian blue and yellow ocher • Transparent oil glaze or gilp • Mineral spirits (white spirit) • Gold-colored bronzing powder • Acrylic varnish (optional)

1 Prepare the surface (see *Preparation*, p. 18). All holes or cracks should be filled and sanded to a fine smooth finish. Make sure that the plaster is completely dry. Apply an undercoat of diluted semigloss latex (vinyl silk emulsion) with a 2–3 in. (5–7.5 cm.) bristle basecoat brush. Allow to dry.

Variation 1

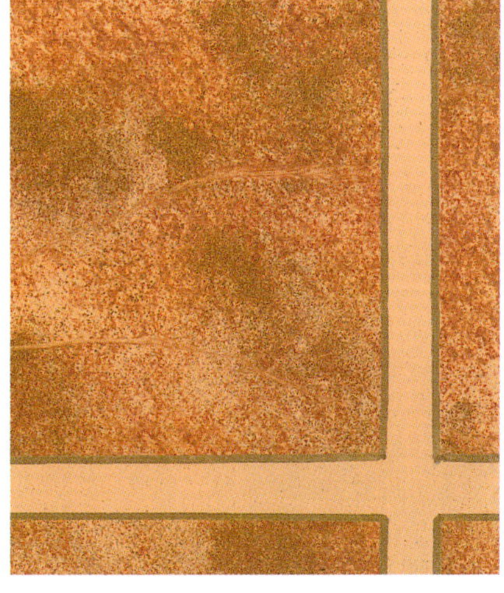

In this variation, after masking off the basecoat of apricot, a glaze of terracotta was sponged on fairly randomly. This was quickly followed by veining with a soft, fine, artists' lining brush while the glaze was still wet. Gilt powder was then dropped carefully onto the wet glaze, and again the effect carefully softened. The lines were produced with a medium gold permanent marking pen and a straight edge (ruler).

Variation 2

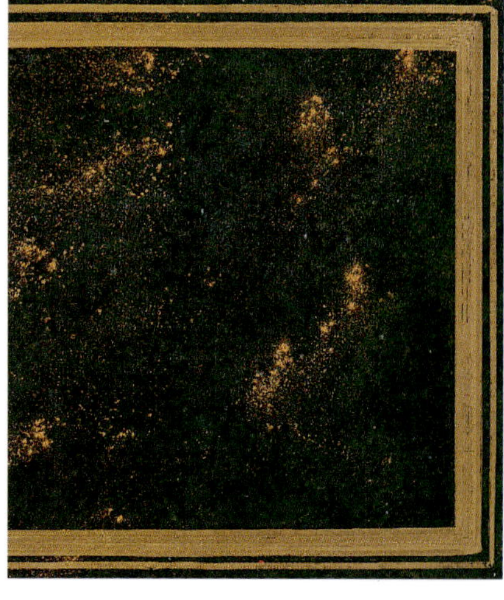

Yellow ocher and French ultramarine artists' oil paint, diluted with a little mineral spirits (white spirit), was sponged over a background of two coats of black eggshell. While still wet, bronzing powder in deep gold was dropped onto the surface with a soft, dry artists' watercolor brush. The panel was then lined (see p. 94) with a gold permanent marking pen. It was sealed with spray sealant before a coat of oil varnish was applied.

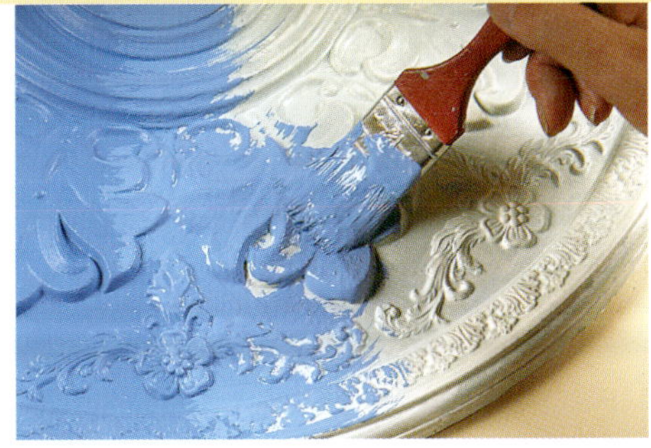

2 Using a 2 in. (5 cm.) bristle basecoat brush, apply a coat of mid-blue semigloss latex, stippling (see p. 30) the paint into any awkward areas. Allow to dry and apply a second coat making sure that you have not missed any recessed areas. Dry overnight.

3 Using either some gilp (see recipe p. 15) or some transparent oil glaze, mix a little artists' oil paint in French ultramarine to a smooth paste. In a separate container do the same with a little Prussian blue artists' oil paint. Do not over thin.

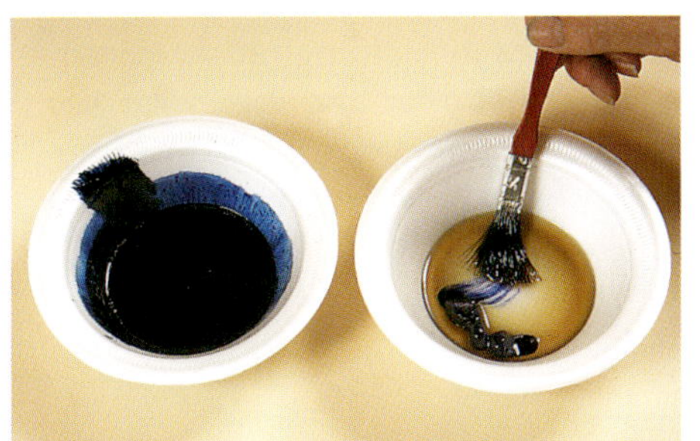

4 Using a natural sponge, cover the surface at random with the French ultramarine glaze, allowing only minute amounts of the basecoat to show through. Vary the intensity of the sponging to create depth of color and be sure to cover all recessed areas.

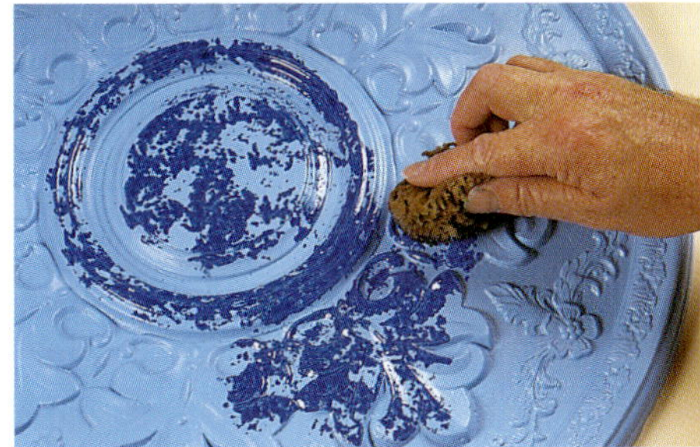

5 While this is still wet, use a clean natural sponge and repeat step 4 using the Prussian blue glaze. Blend as you work. Do not over sponge. Reapply highlights of ultramarine blue with a clean sponge but do not merge the colors.

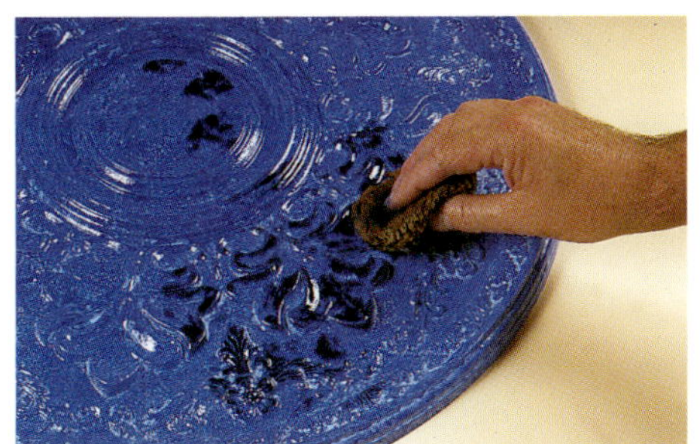

6 Mix some yellow ocher paint with mineral spirits (white spirit) and dribble over the surface sparingly using a fine bristle brush. Apply some veins of gold or bronzing powder using a fine artists' brush. Add highlights by dusting lightly with the bronzing powder. Do not overdo the veining. Allow to dry. Apply acrylic varnish if required.

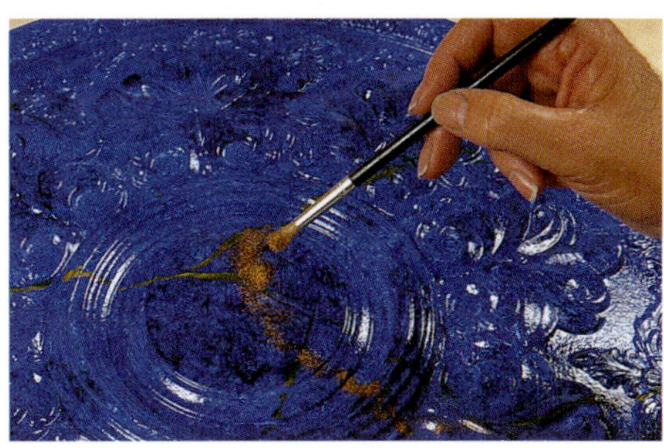

7 Rich, opulent and truly luxurious describes this ceiling rosette (rose), which has been made to look like lapis lazuli.

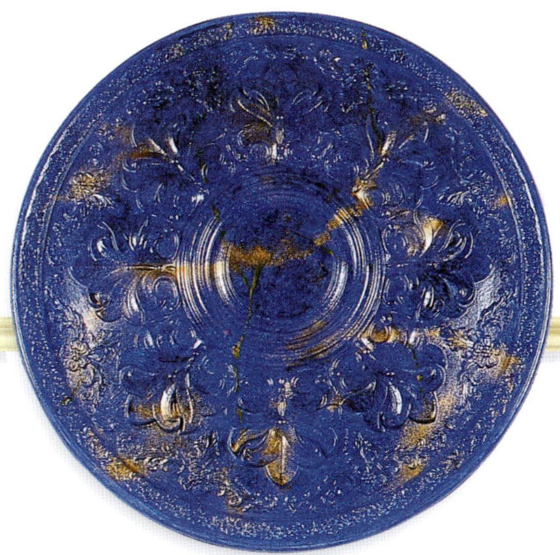

Variation 3

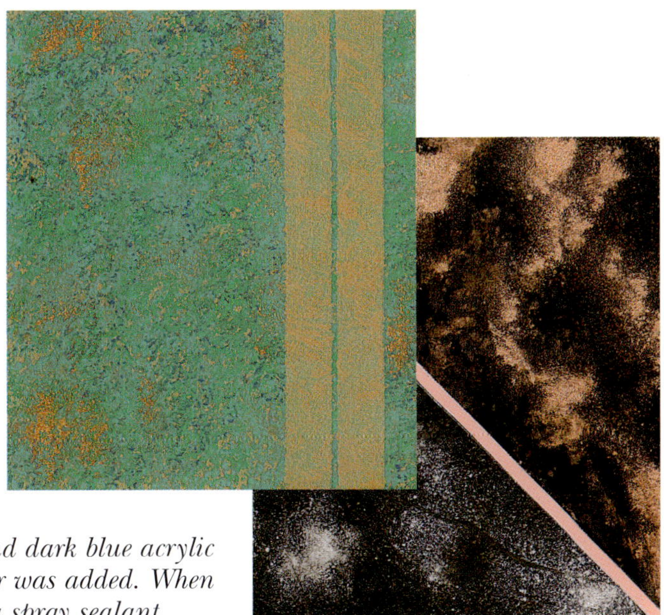

This panel was first painted with mid-green semigloss latex (vinyl silk emulsion) before the frottage technique using acrylic glaze and gold acrylic paint. When dry, a stripe was applied using low-tack tape. While slightly wet, the surface was sponged with green, turquoise and dark blue acrylic paints. Bronzing powder was added. When dry, it was sealed with a spray sealant.

Variation 4

The rich and attractive finish of lapis lazuli has been regularly copied, but the technique can be applied to almost any colorway. Here, a black oil glaze was painted over a pink basecoat. As the glaze was drying the surface was powdered with copper and aluminum powder, using a soft brush.

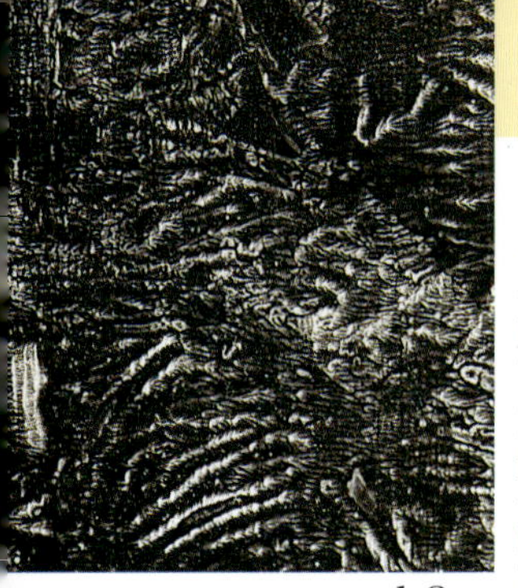

Slate

Slate, when it is used to highlight an architectural feature such as floors, roof tiles or a carved fireplace surround, provides great depth and definition due to its stratified effect. Variations in color and dimension make slate an interesting material to work with. The finished effect of this special technique can make a plain surface both interesting and highly individual.

As with any simulation of stone or marble (see p. 132), slate is best used in situations where it would occur naturally, such as carved fireplace surrounds, counter and table tops and small boxes. When used in larger areas such as floors, it is best used with a marble finish or something similar to create a paneled effect. Reminiscent of country kitchen floors or paving stones, the slate technique is fairly easy to perfect requiring only a little practice with a glaze manipulation and frottage (see p. 28). It is also very inexpensive to complete.

It is best suited to the traditional slate-gray colors for realistic results, but you need not be limited by this. The technique does lend itself to being used in an imaginative way to fit in well with most traditional or modern settings. It looks particularly good when used in kitchens, greenhouses (conservatories) and bathrooms as a floor treatment.

The chance of making a mistake is minimal, but if a mistake does happen then you should simply rework the glaze and continue.

You will need

Tools

• 2in. (5 cm.) bristle basecoat brush • 2 in. (5 cm.) glaze application brush • 2 in. (5 cm.) varnishing brush • Sanding block • Plenty of newspaper

Materials

• Store-bought filler • Mid-gray eggshell basecoat • Artists' oil color, black and white • Transparent oil glaze • Mineral spirits (white spirit) • Suitable varnish

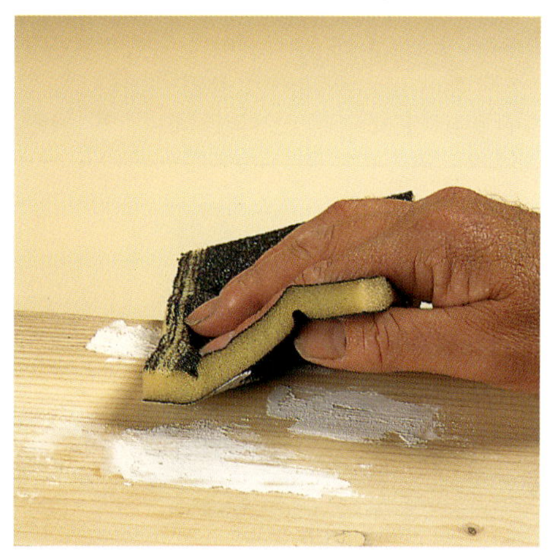

1 Fill any holes or cracks with a store-bought filler, using a spatula or knife blade. Allow to dry overnight. Sand to a smooth finish using medium- and then fine- grade sandpaper or sanding block. Remove all traces of filler and dust with a soft brush and a damp cloth. Apply an undercoat and allow to dry.

Variation 1

Here, two coats of dark gray, semigloss latex (vinyl silk emulsion) were applied and allowed to dry. The basecoat was stippled with PVA glue before some fine sand and grit were applied. This was left to dry overnight. A glaze (1 part dirty-cream paint to 3 parts acrylic glaze) was applied across the surface randomly, brushed and left to dry. The flat (matte) finish creates the effect of weather-beaten stone.

Variation 2

Two coats of black eggshell were applied to this panel and allowed to dry. Using a simple gilding technique (see p. 134), gold size (water-based) was stenciled onto the surface and then Dutch metal leaf was applied. When this was dry, a coat of gloss oil varnish tinted with a little viridian artists' oil paint was added, allowed to dry, and then followed by two more coats of clear gloss oil varnish.

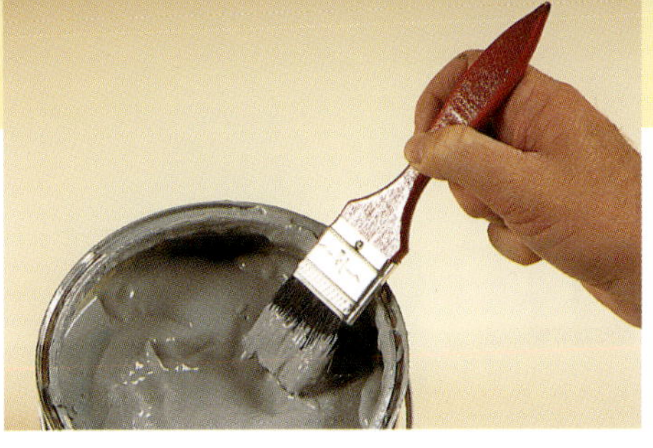

2 Load the bristle basecoat brush with mid-gray eggshell paint. Do not overload the brush—the paint should come about two-thirds of the way up the brush. Apply two layers of basecoat, allowing the paint to dry between coats.

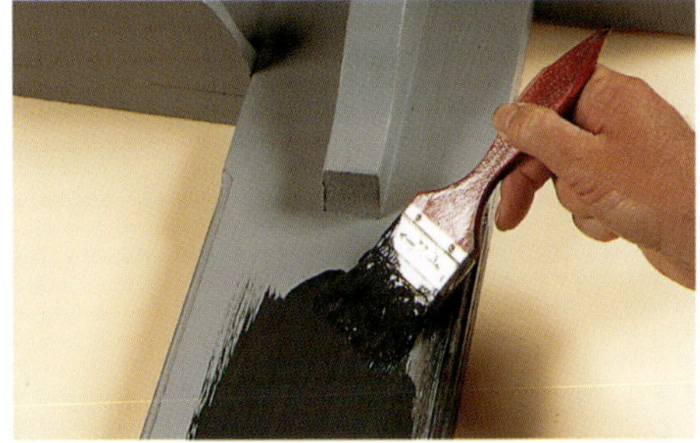

3 Mix up a glaze, following the manufacturer's instructions, from transparent oil glaze and black artists' oil paint. Dilute with a little mineral spirits (white spirit) to half and half consistency. Make sure that the glaze and paint are completely blended (see *Finishing and protecting* p. 24). Apply a layer of glaze, working on a small area at a time and keeping a wet edge. Stipple out the brushstrokes (see p. 30).

4 Lay a sheet of newspaper over the surface and roughly smooth down. The final effect will be enhanced by any folds or creases and they need not be removed. Overlap the areas slightly to avoid any broken lines.

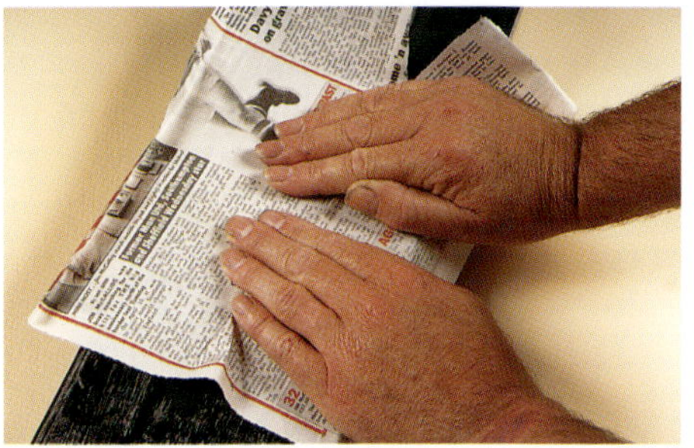

5 Remove the newspaper and discard immediately, making sure wet paint or glaze does not mark other furniture or areas. Immediately apply a fresh glaze to the next area and repeat steps 4–5. Allow the entire surface to dry. Seal the surface with an appropriate varnish.

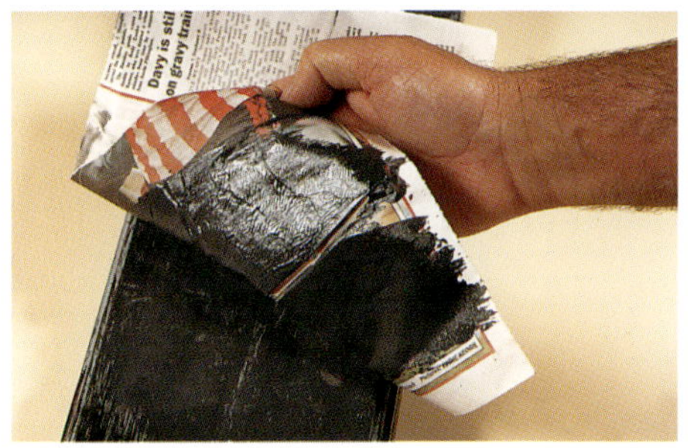

6 The finish of highly polished stone, whether it be granite, marble or slate, adds a feeling of luxury to any decor. Here the humble fireplace surround, now resembling slate, would fit into the most stylish of settings. The final effect has achieved a look that is solid and decorative.

Variation 3

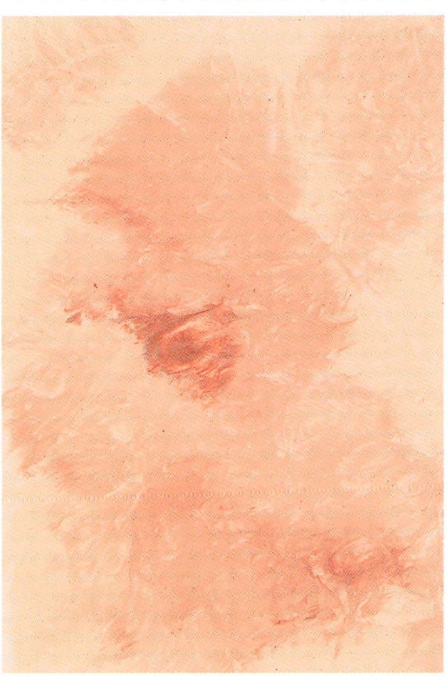

Here, over a basecoat of apricot latex (emulsion), two glazes were applied at the same time. The first was a pale pink and the second a deep dusty pink (1 part latex [emulsion] to 3 parts acrylic glaze). The technique of frottage (see p. 28) was then applied. When dry, a coat of satin acrylic varnish was added.

Variation 4

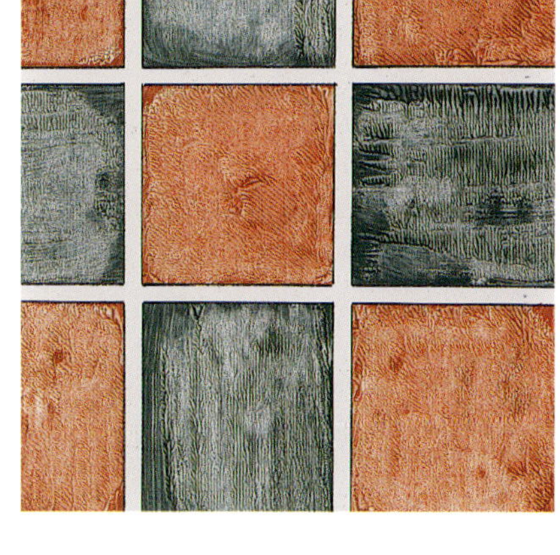

A pale gray basecoat of eggshell was applied to this floor panel and allowed to dry. Using ¼ in. (0.63 cm.) low-tack tape, a tile pattern was created. Two glazes were mixed (3 parts glaze to 1 part terracotta and 1 part slate-blue artists' oil paint.) Each colored panel was painted and the frottage technique (see p. 28) applied. The tape was removed and the floor allowed to dry. Finally, three coats of flat (matte) oil varnish were applied.

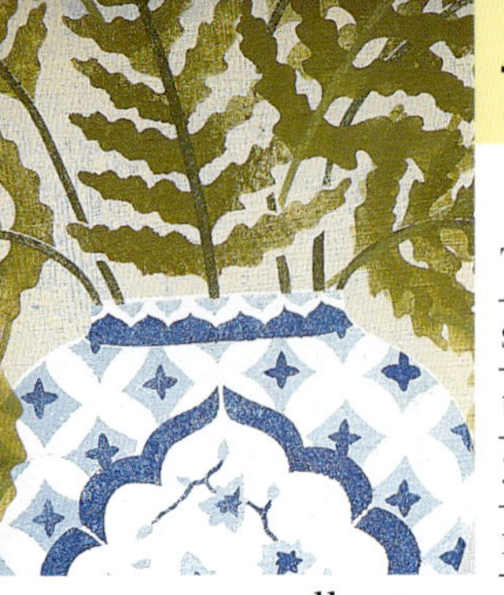

Stenciling

The art of stenciling can be traced back some 3000 years or more, and is still an excellent way of creating a coordinated decorative scheme in one room or throughout the home. By designing your own stencil, you can introduce an element that adds a personal touch to a room or piece of furniture.

Small items such as lampbases and shades, frames and boxes, can all be beautifully and simply decorated by the use of a stencil. With ingenuity, walls, floors, cupboards and fitted kitchens can be transformed for little expense.

It is possible to stencil with most paints, but I recommend the use of proper stencil paints, which are available in a wide range of colors. These are quick drying and if used correctly avoid the common problem of "bleeding," paint seeping under the stencil. Accidental mistakes within the pattern, such as stenciling a bit you don't want, can be either incorporated into the design or removed by wiping off with a soft cloth. If this is not possible, begin again.

There are no hard and fast rules for stenciling, which is a technique that lets you use your imagination to create interesting and special effects. After a little practice, you will find that you can change a room in a few hours with one simple stencil. The key to good stenciling is patience. Also, do not use too much paint and use only good-quality soft-bristled stencil brushes. There are no substitutes if you want a good-quality finish.

The versatility of stenciling allows you to create schemes and ideas from nothing, whether in a period or modern setting. It works well over a background of almost any other paint effect, particularly rag-rolling (see p. 52) and colorwashing (see p. 60).

You will need

Tools

• *Low-tack masking tape or spray adhesive* • *Chalk* • *½ in. (1.3 cm.) bristle stencil brush* • *2–3 in. (5–7.5 cm.) bristle basecoat brush* • *½–1 in. (1.3–2.5 cm.) bristle stencil brush* • *2–3 in. (5–7.5 cm.) varnishing brush* • *Stencil*

Materials

• *Stencil or acrylic paints* • *Acrylic glaze* • *Suitable varnish* • *Paper (kitchen) towel*

1 Prepare the surface (see *Preparation*, p. 18). Then apply a basecoat. Allow to dry. Colorwash the surface as required (see *Colorwashing*, p. 60). Allow to dry.

Variation 1

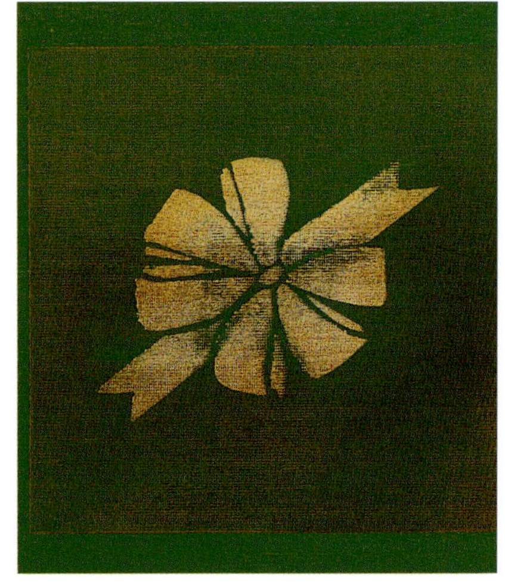

Stenciling can be used in many ways. Here, the bow was stenciled in off-white over a basecoat of dark green. The stencil was allowed to dry completely and was then distressed (see p. 36) using wax tinted with raw umber powder pigment and some fine steel wool (grade 0000). The extent of the distressing is a matter of personal choice, but can be left slightly faded or can be very worn indeed.

Variation 2

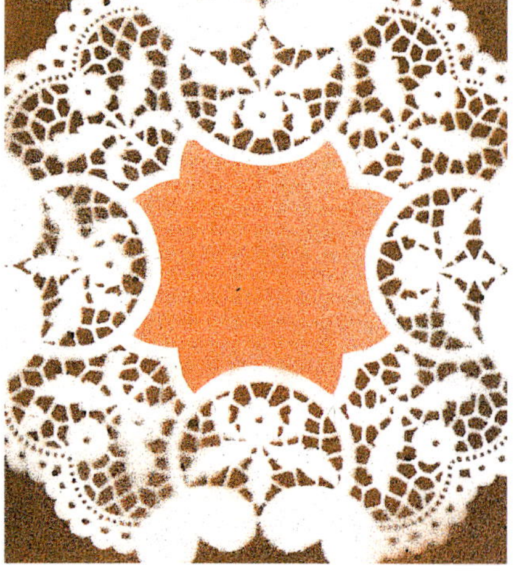

Stencils can be made in many ways and from the most unlikely things. Here a doily was placed over an off-white basecoat and a tan spray paint was used to create the pattern. It was then sprayed again using a dark brown color. By cutting out the center of the doily and respraying with the tan spray, a more multi-dimensional effect has been created.

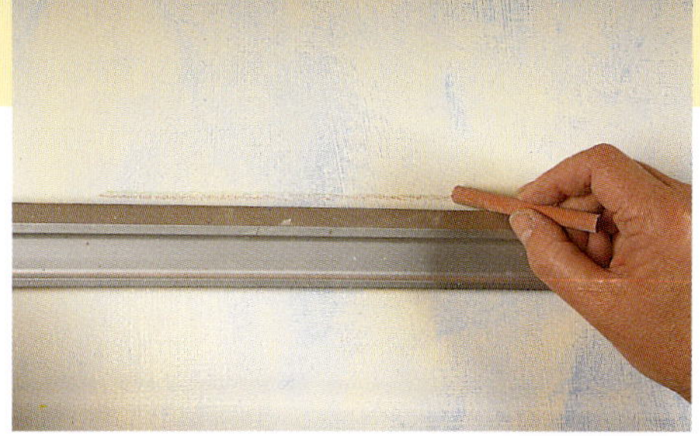

2 **Use a tape and chalk to center and level your pattern onto the surface. If the pattern is repeated, measure and chalk each section. If necessary use a plumb line for verticals.**

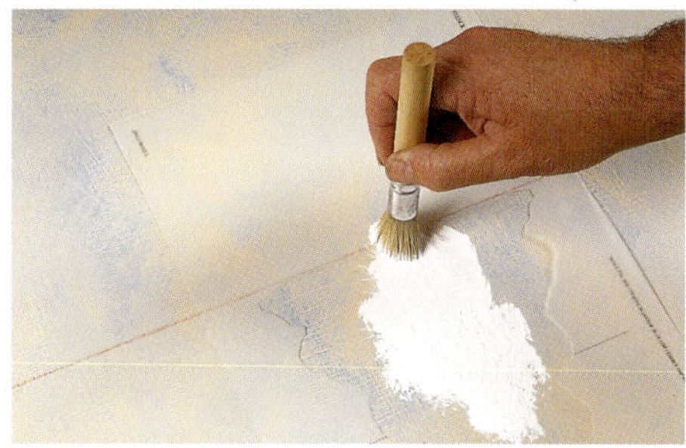

3 **Apply a little spray adhesive to the reverse of the stencil template and dry for a few seconds before placing the stencil in position. Pour some acrylic paint into a dish. Dip the stencil brush into the paint. Remove excess paint on a paper towel. The paint on the brush should be as dry as possible. What looks like very little paint is probably more than enough. Stipple or "pounce" the brush onto your surface (see *Stippling*, p. 30) through the stencil.**

4 **Apply a little spray adhesive onto the reverse of your second stencil and position it following the registration marks. Use a clean, dry brush to apply the second color following the instructions in step 3.**

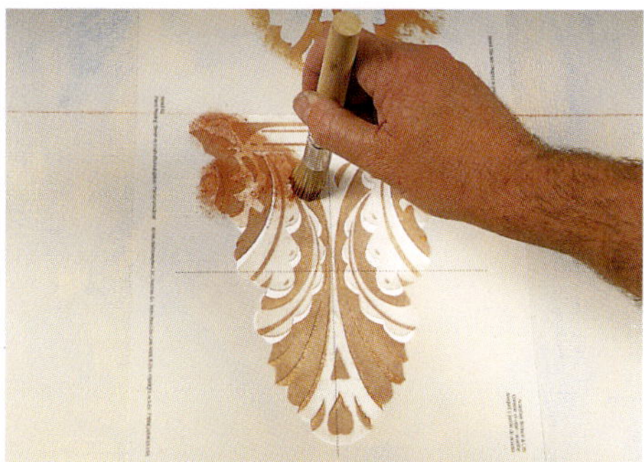

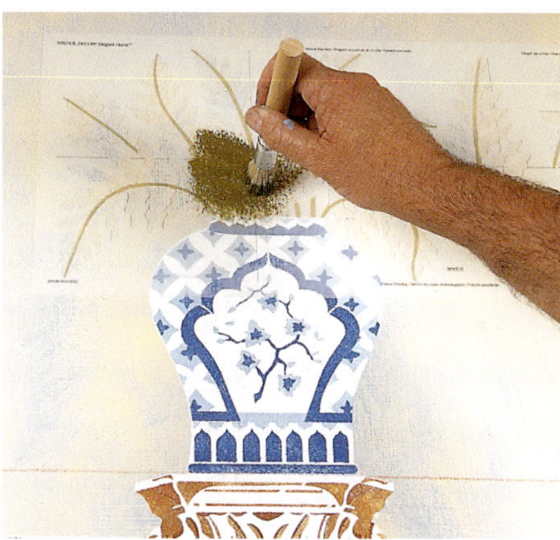

5 **Follow step 3 to add all the pattern shapes to complete the picture.**

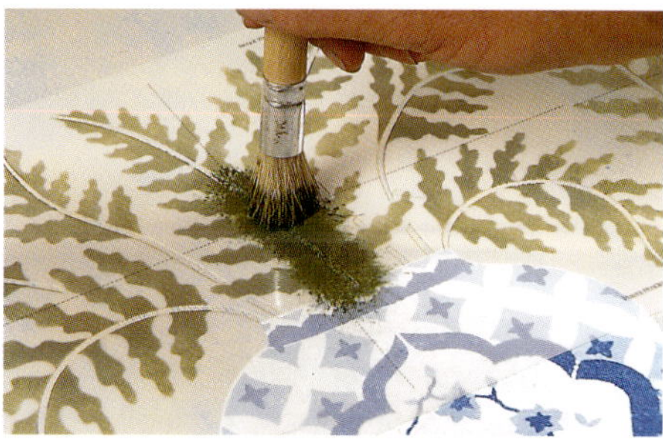

6 **Use overlays or second and third layers of stencils to create a three dimensional effect. Here we are adding a central stalk to the spray of fern leaves.**

7 **The beauty of stenciling is that you can create pictures without being an artist. Simple or elaborate effects can be achieved by layering and combining different paint finish techniques. Here a *trompe l'oeil* effect has been created using a bought stencil which could be beyond most people's ability to paint by hand. Varnish for protection.**

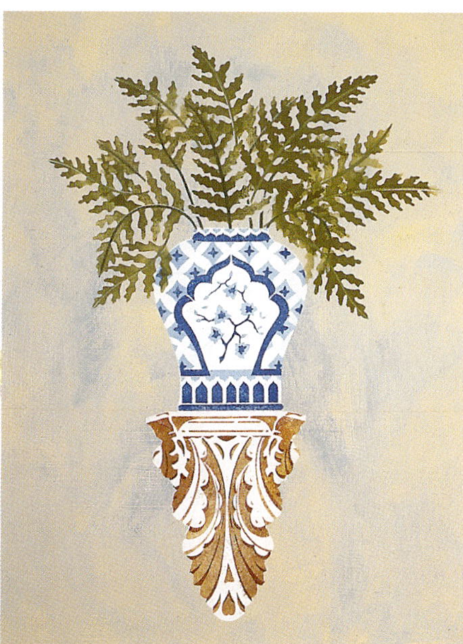

Variation 3

To achieve an effect such as this (left), the basecoat of teal blue was masked off and the solid, cut-out section of an elephant stencil fixed to the base with a little spray adhesive. Then, using a diffuser, a layer of deep rose pink was sprayed and allowed to dry, before repeating using a pale cream.

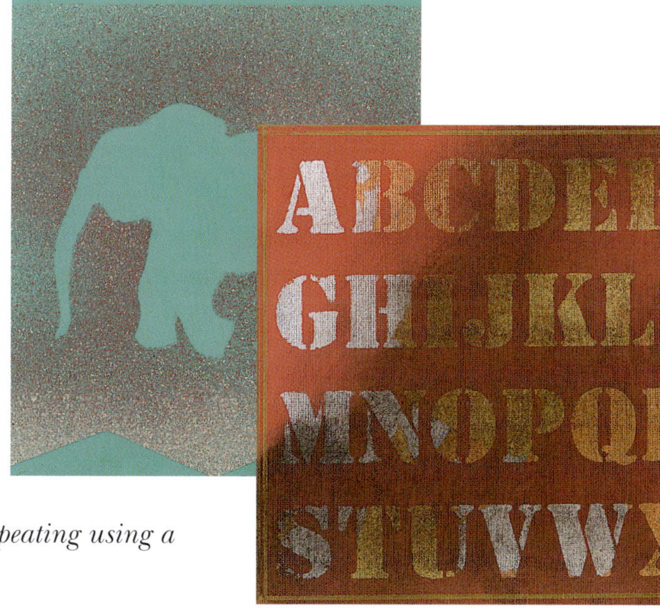

Variation 4

Here, some gold size (see p. 78) is stenciled over a basecoat of dark dusty pink. This was allowed to go tacky before applying copper, gold and silver leaf to the stenciled surface. After brushing away the excess, the surface was finished off by antiquing (see p. 32) with antique-brown furniture wax.

In context

The examples here show three very different, yet simple ways of using the decorative paint and paper effects of stenciling, découpage and spattering. Paint effects do not have to be either very complicated or very time consuming—sometimes the simplest ideas and techniques are just as pleasing and satisfying as those that involve many hours of painstaking work.

Spattering

▶ Panel for a bathroom

Here a tactile patina creates depth and interest. Our example uses three different, but related, earthy colors; terracotta, peach and lemon. A turquoise base-coat highlights the technique yet is not too over-powering.

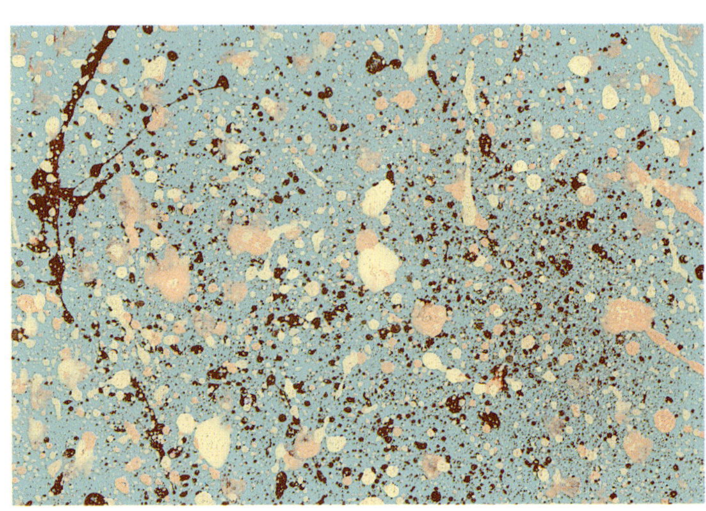

Découpage

◀ Sitting room wall

The mellow tones of dusky pink colorwashed walls have been accentuated by the use of a wonderfully full acanthus leaf garland, discreetly tinted in shades of yellow ocher. Both colors draw on the rich tones of the highly-polished wooden fire surround.

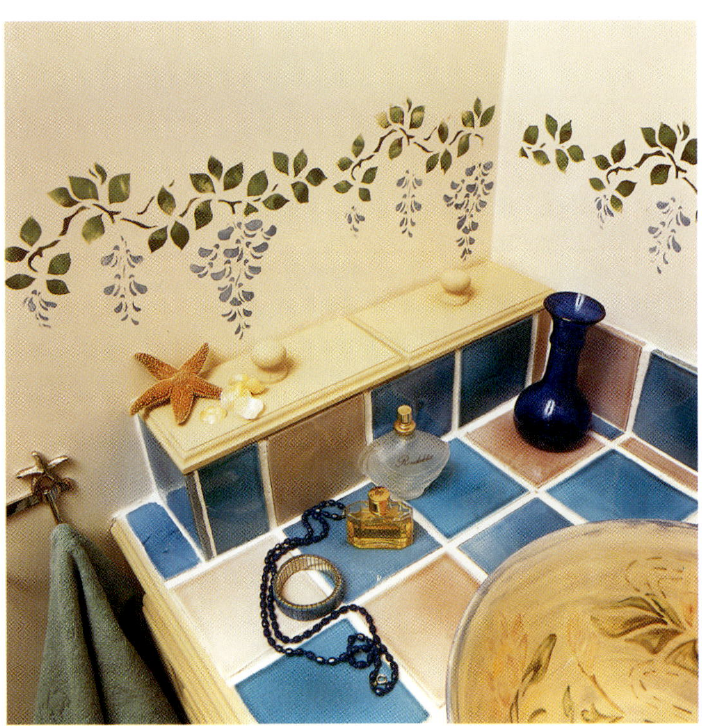

Stenciling

▲ Tiled bathroom

A simple wisteria stencil has added fluidity and interest to this simple, tiled bathroom. The varying shades of blue in both the flowers and the tiles seem to emphasize the subtlety of the colorwashed wall behind, blending to create a very relaxing ambience.

Stenciling

▶ Themed sitting room

The use of several stencils in traditional Native American designs, combined with a simple stylized cactus have successfully created a "themed" room setting. The buff colorwashed walls reflect perfectly the earthy warmth of these traditional colors.

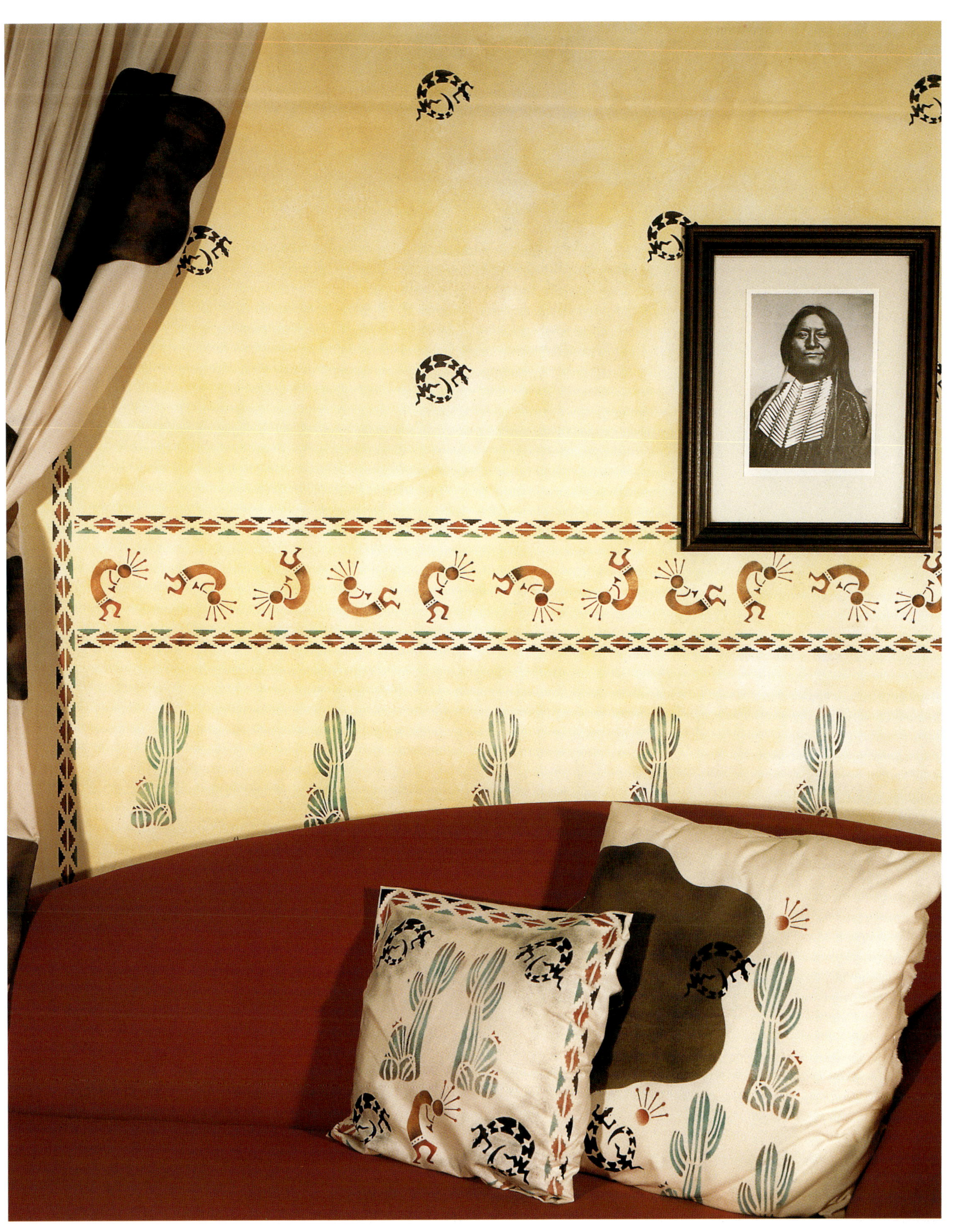

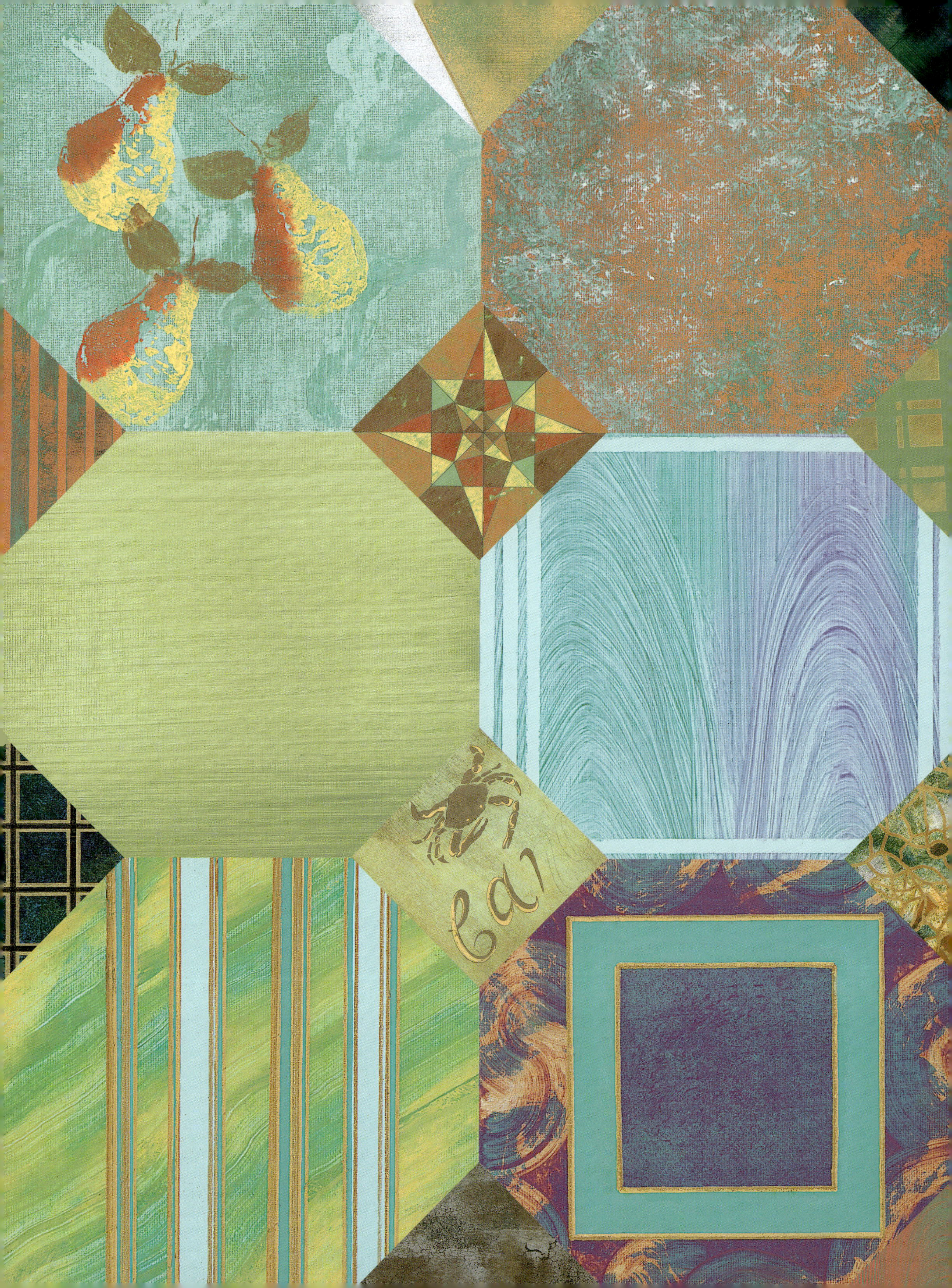

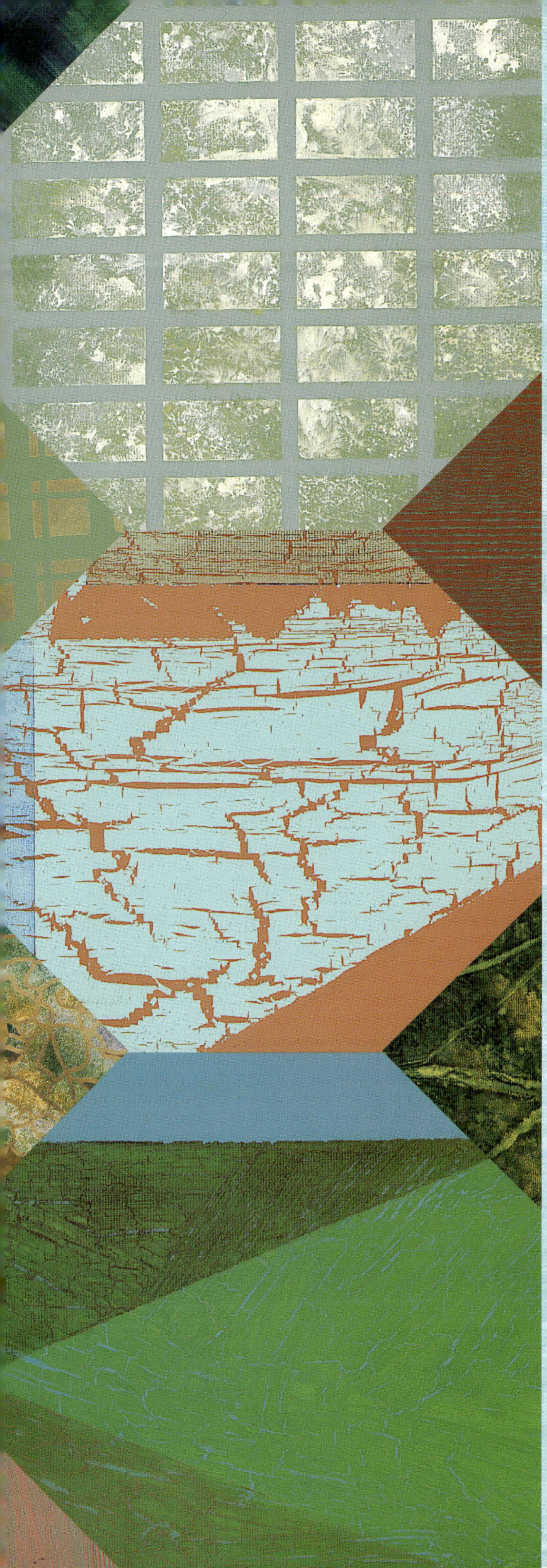

The Advanced Techniques

Do not be put off by the word advanced, the techniques here are well within the reach of anyone who understands the effect and how to achieve it. We have included in this section techniques that need just a little more practice or take time to produce. Some may need patience and understanding as well as a basic knowledge but they are within the capabilities of most of us. Marbling and the simulation of exotic woods and semi-precious stones, once confined only to the professionals, can now be achieved by the experienced amateur. Always follow and ensure that you understand the step-by-step instructions and study the pictures carefully, and soon you too will be creating fantastic finishes.

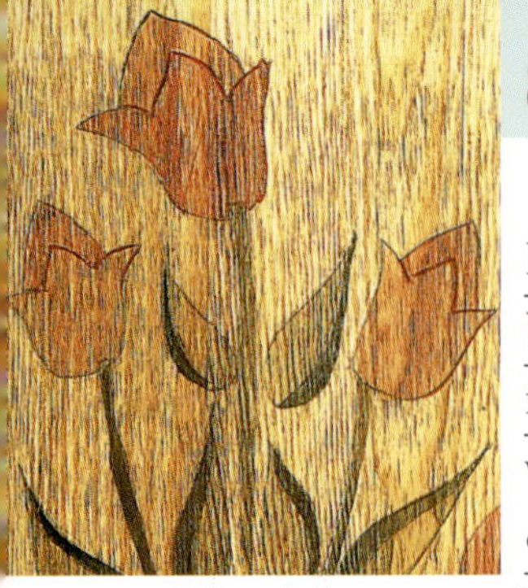

Woodstain inlay

Expensive, beautifully inlaid furniture is now within the reach of any decorator. Wood dyes or colorwashes can be used to create credible marquetry and parquetry designs worthy of any artist. For centuries the skills of marquetry craftsmen have been the envy of many, but now you can, with a little practice, emulate wonderful and intricate designs.

Fireplace surrounds, door panels and cupboards are perfect for this treatment, as are smaller objects such as table tops, boxes, and picture and mirror frames. But the effect is not recommended for carved surfaces. It fits in well with both traditional and modern settings, and colors are limited only by your own choice.

Inexpensive to achieve yet superbly creative, marquetry adds individuality and style to any room. With patience and a good eye, even an inexperienced painter can achieve satisfactory results. The golden rule is not to rush, because any mistakes with wood dye are impossible to remove without extensive resanding, as the dyes penetrate the wood and stain it to a greater depth than a simple coat of paint.

Good-quality wood dyes or paints are the best to use because home-made glazes can go streaky. Following all manufacturer's instructions will help to eliminate any errors that may arise.

You will need

Tools

- *Sharp pencil* • *Craft knife*
- *Paint dishes* • *Fine artists' watercolor brush* • *pencil*
- *Fine black permanent liner pen*

Materials

- *Pattern for tracing* • *Tracing paper*
- *Stencil paints or artists' acrylic paints in chosen colors or wood dyes*
- *Sandpaper* • *Spray sealant*
- *Furniture wax*

1 Prepare the surface by filling all holes and sanding with a fine-grade sandpaper to achieve a smooth surface. Remove all traces of dust with a damp cloth.

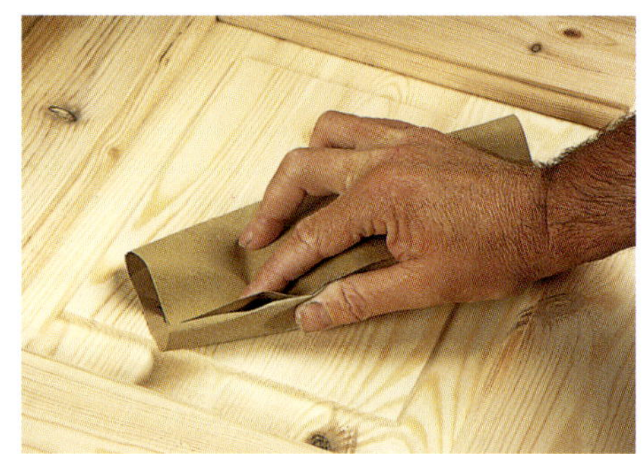

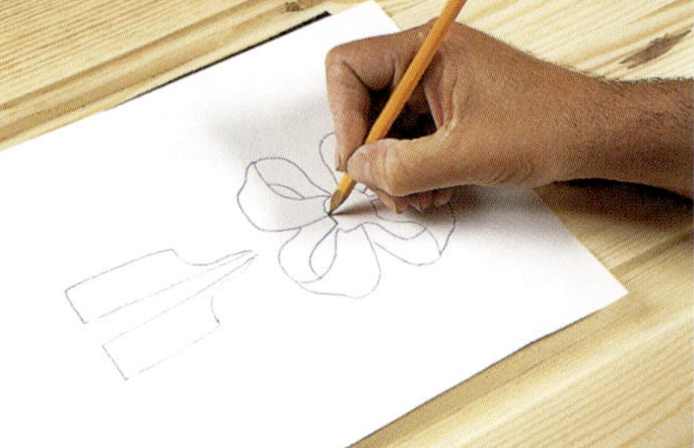

2 Measure your surface area and use a photocopier to adjust the size of the design. Trace design onto surface with a pencil (see *Tracing*, *p.* 88)—ensure image is centered and the outline clear and complete.

Variation 1

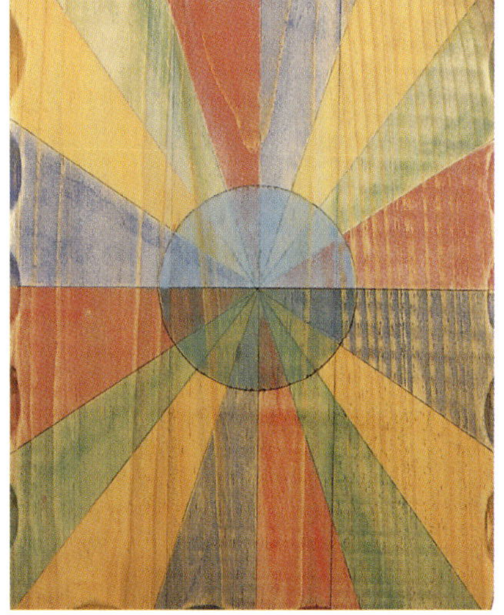

The very nature of some woods and their natural grain make them better suited to staining than painting. Here the beautifully developed graining has been accentuated by the use of four colors that work well together: yellow, green, red and blue. Water-based wood dyes were used and sealed with a coat of antique pine furniture wax.

Variation 2

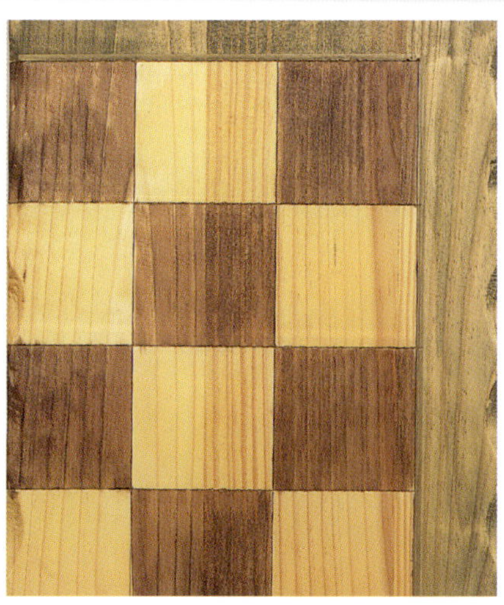

Here, simple geometric patterns have been cut into the wood in 2 in. (5 cm.) squares leaving a 1½ in. (3.8 cm.) border. Water-based wood dyes in yellow pine, moss green and red mahogany were used to create a checkerboard (chequerboard) effect. A finish of this sort would suit a pine floor in either a greenhouse (conservatory) or a kitchen.

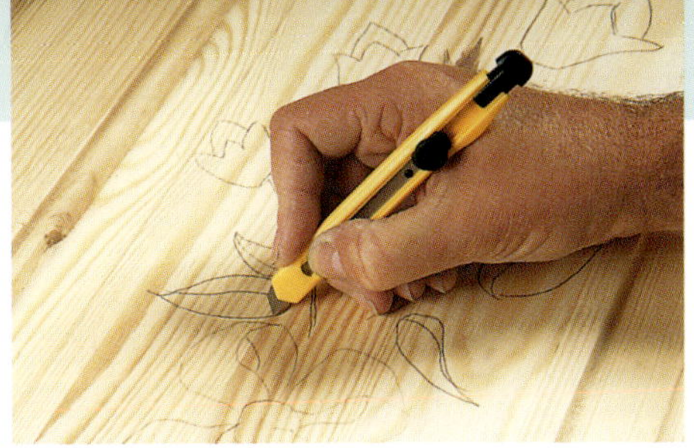

3 With a sharp craft knife or scalpel slowly and carefully score around all the edges of the traced image. Work slowly to avoid the chance of slipping and be extremely careful when cutting over existing knots in the wood. Very slightly overcut at each corner.

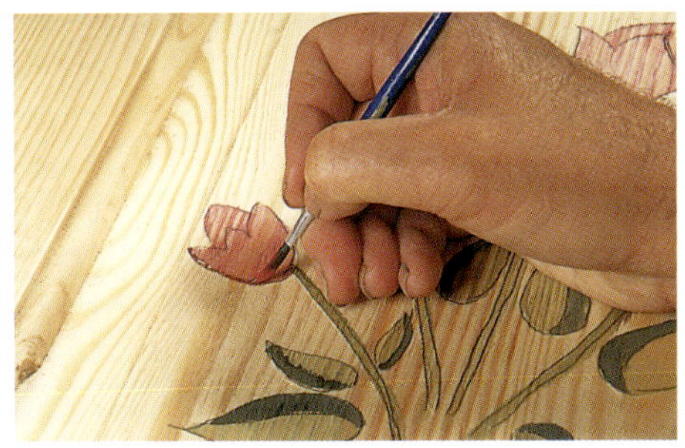

4 Prepare paints on separate dishes by diluting stencil paints or artists' acrylic with water to a thin consistency (about 1 part paint to 8 parts water). Store-bought colored wood dyes are also readily available. With a fine artists' watercolor brush, paint or stain each part of the design with your chosen color. Complete one color and dry before the next. Dry for 24 hours.

5 If required, outline each part of the design with a fine black permanent liner pen. Allow to dry. Apply two or three thin layers of spray sealant across the painted image surface. Allow to dry between layers.

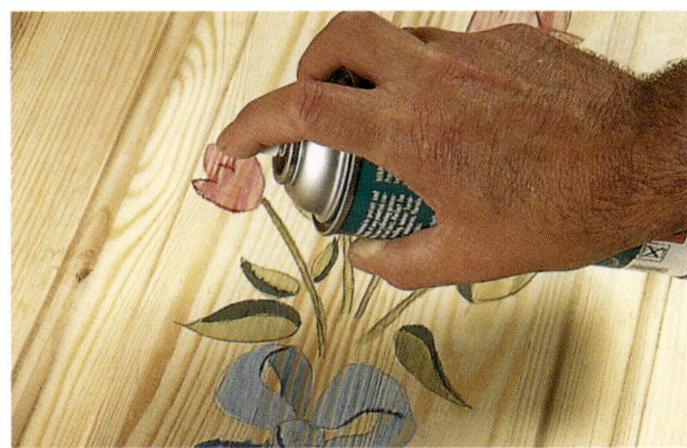

6 Apply either antique brown furniture wax or a clear wax tinted with a powder color of your choice (see p. 14) across the entire surface with a soft, lint-free cloth. Make sure that all streaks are evened out. Allow to dry. Buff to a soft sheen.

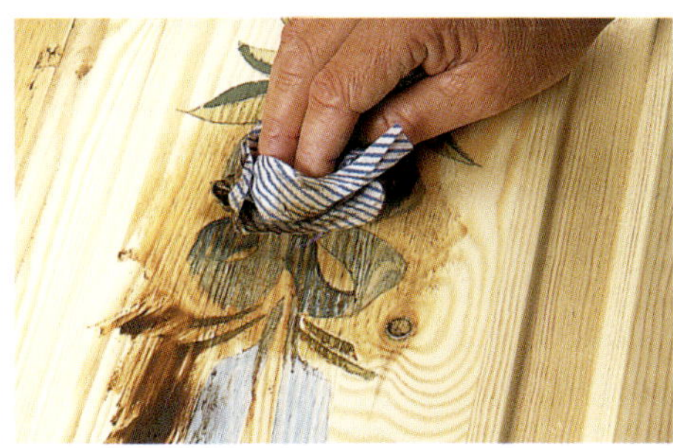

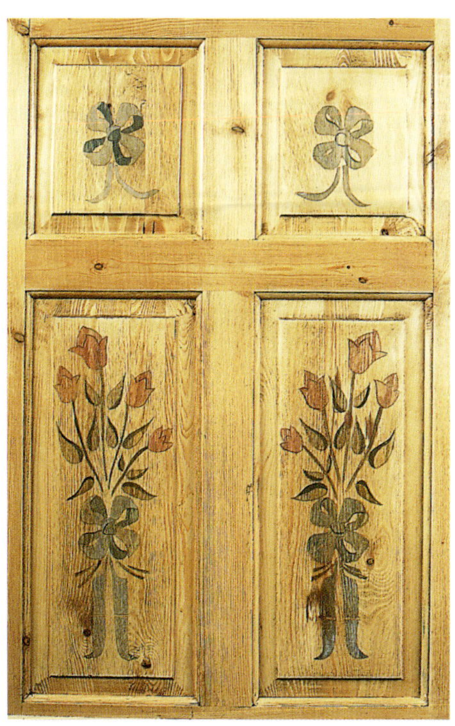

7 The beauty of this effect is that it allows the wooden, paneled doors to merge into the surroundings, yet we can still admire the natural woodgrain beneath. Wonderfully intricate patterns or simple, geometric designs can cover the surface without obscuring its natural depth. This effect produces an end result that would be very expensive and extremely time-consuming to create in reality.

Variation 3

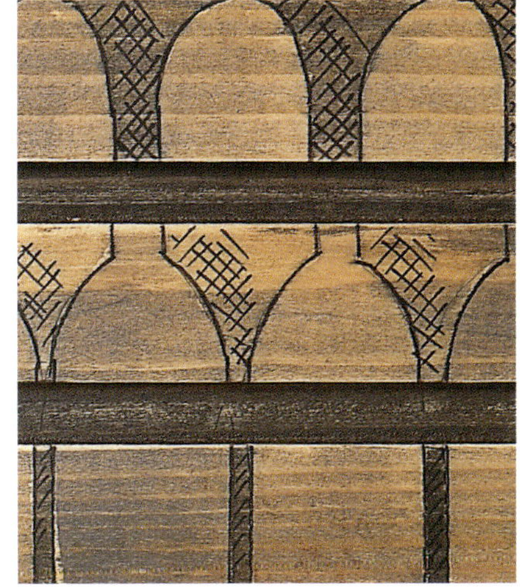

A simple architectural pattern was drawn onto this piece of pine baseboard (skirting board) in pencil. The lines were then scored with a craft knife. Black and gray acrylic paint was diluted and applied to the relevant section. When dry, the pattern was highlighted with a fine black permanent marking pen. A spray sealant was applied and then a coat of flat (matte) oil varnish.

Variation 4

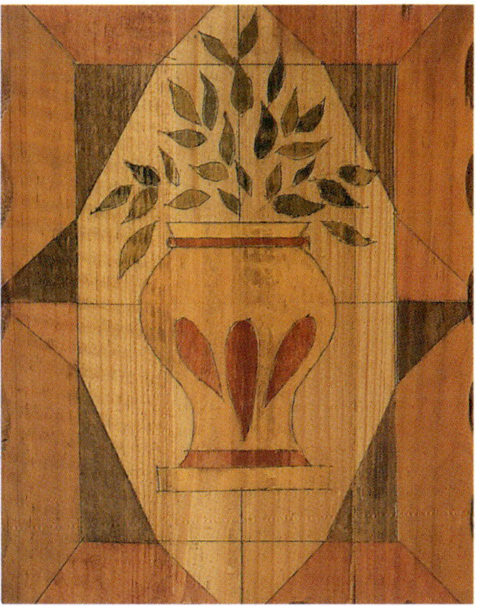

After sanding this pine panel to remove blemishes and excess varnish, the pattern was drawn on using a sharp pencil. The pattern was then scored along each line with a sharp craft knife. With diluted artists' acrylic paint (1 part paint to 8 parts water) each section was painted with a fine artists' brush. After drying, the surface was lightly sanded and a coat of antique pine furniture wax applied.

Clouding

The beautiful, ethereal effect of clouding will add a little bit of magic to any room. When created well, it can give depth and dimension to the most average of settings.

Clouding is a more difficult finish to achieve successfully. Practice in the use of glazes, and the blending of wet edges, is necessary to create an evenly "clouded" surface, free of the brush marks and the slightly harsher edges that characterize colorwashing (see p. 60). Practice on sample boards until you are confident enough to try the real thing.

Clouding works well on any smooth surface, such as walls and ceilings, and some furniture and cupboards. Remember that the technique of clouding will show up any imperfections in the surface, so thorough surface preparation (see p. 18) is essential. Experiment with a variety of colors. Color choice can be subtle and elegant by choosing very close shades such as yellow ocher on deep cream, or bold and wild by using bright and vivid colors such as apple green on magnolia.

Clouding is very inexpensive to achieve, the only real cost will be good-quality brushes, which should not be replaced with inferior ones. A successful finish relies on the final, very smooth manipulation of the glazes, which can only be correctly achieved with the best brushes and a very soft, lint-free cloth. Clouding is an ideal background for stenciling (see p. 78) and découpage (see p. 66), and also works well with other effects such as dragging (see p. 62) and rag-rolling (see p. 52) and even *trompe l'oeil* (see p. 79).

You will need

Tools

- *2–4 in. (5–10 cm.) soft-bristled colorwash brush*
- *3–4 in. (7.5–10 cm.) bristle basecoat brush*
- *Badger softening brush or dusting brush*
- *¾ in. (1.9 cm.) low-tack masking tape*
- *Soft, lint-free cloth*
- *Synthetic (cellulose) sponge (optional)*
- *Varnishing brush*

Materials

- *Semigloss latex (vinyl silk emulsion) basecoat*
- *Acrylic glazing medium*
- *Mid-blue latex (emulsion) for tinting glaze*
- *Flat (matte) acrylic varnish for protection (optional)*

1 Prepare the surface (see *Preparation*, p. 18). If the surface you are painting has an area that you do not want to touch, as with the chair (dado) rail on this wall, use low-tack masking tape to protect the area. Place the edge of the tape as flush as possible against the rail.

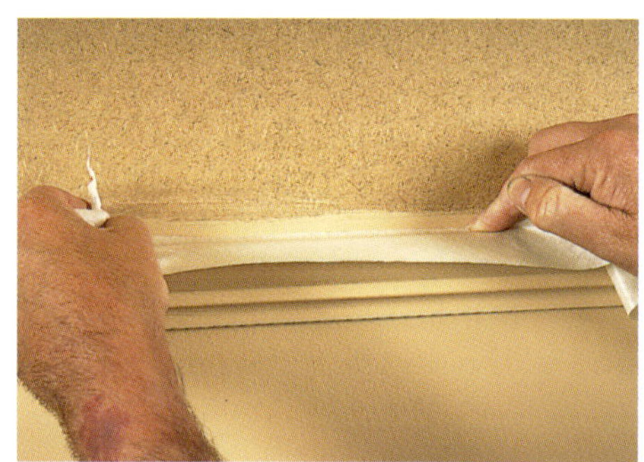

Variation 1

Close to colorwashing, clouding is a slightly more advanced technique needing a little more experience in the manipulation of the glazes. In our first variation two shades of purple have been chosen using artists' acrylic and semigloss latex (vinyl silk emulsion.) The basecoat of mauve was first applied and allowed to dry before applying the acrylic glaze of deep purple. The colors create a soft and pleasing effect.

Variation 2

Our second variation has created a very elegant effect because of the color and the means of glaze manipulation. An apricot acrylic glaze was applied over a basecoat of buff semigloss latex. The brushstrokes were softened, and sections of the glaze removed with a natural sponge using the negative sponging technique.

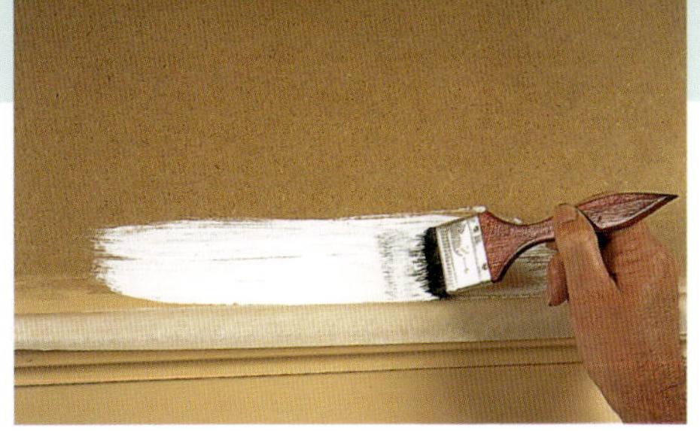

2 Apply an undercoat using the bristle brush. Press up tightly along the full length of the chair rail and follow by either using a roller or a 3–4 in. (7.5–10 cm.) basecoat brush. Allow to dry. Apply at least two layers of basecoat, allowing drying time between each coat. We have used white semigloss latex (emulsion).

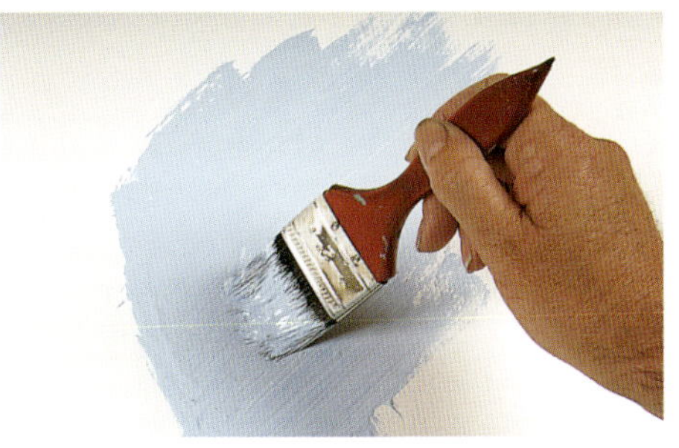

3 Mix mid-blue latex (emulsion) with acrylic glazing medium, 1 part paint to 6 parts glaze. Stir well and dilute with water until it is like light cream. Mix enough to cover the surface. Use color washing brush to apply glaze to the basecoat and keep a wet edge (see p. 15). Vary direction to help blending. Use a clean brush to spread evenly.

4 With a soft, lint-free cloth or a synthetic (cellulose) sponge remove random areas of the glaze to create patchy white and blue shapes. Work as quickly as possible, as the working time of the glaze is about 15 to 20 minutes. Make sure you keep a wet edge.

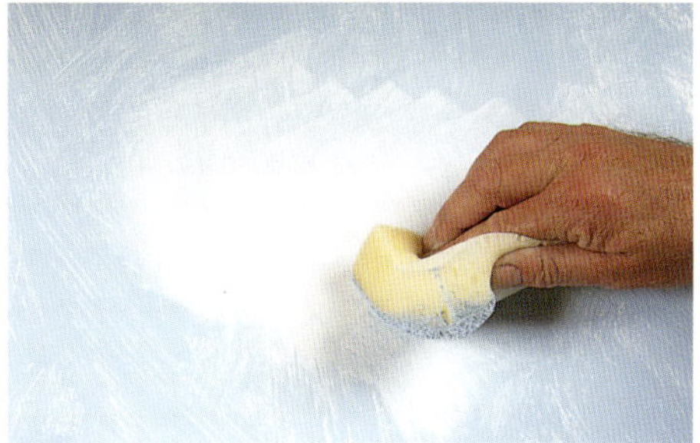

5 When the surface is blended to your liking, soften out the brushstrokes using a badger softening brush (or a dusting brush). Work quickly, otherwise the effect will dry with darker, patchy edges.

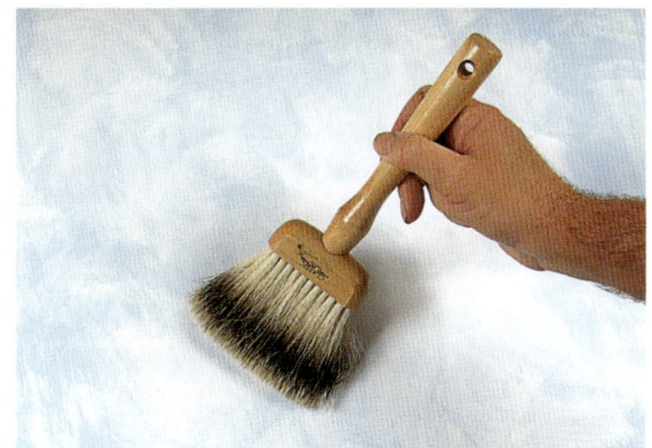

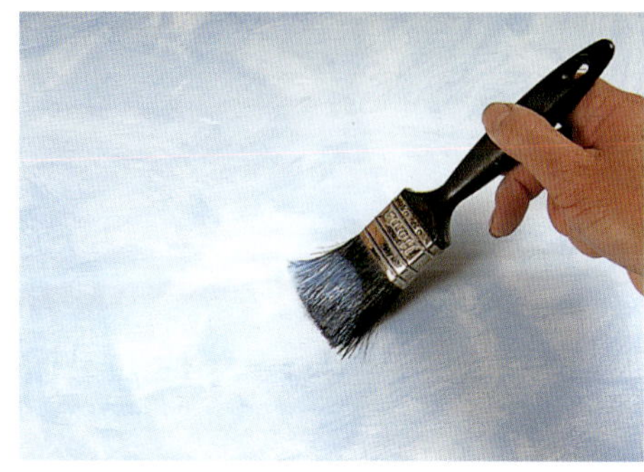

6 Apply a coat of flat (matte) acrylic non-yellowing varnish with a varnishing brush.

7 Here our walls have been given an ethereal finish by choosing natural colors which evoke hazy, azure skies. Blues, often thought of as cold colors, can be warm and relaxing. Clouding is an effect that is easy to live with and adaptable for any room or decorative scheme, opening up rather than closing in space.

Variation 3

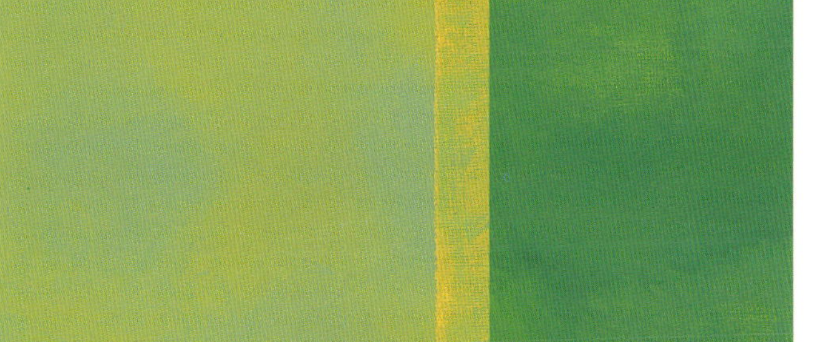

By changing the colorways again a totally different dimension has been achieved. The effect here is bright and airy. A basecoat of mid-green and a glaze of vivid yellow have been combined, the central section masked off and pure yellow paint applied to the edge with a soft cloth, creating a window or frame to enhance the subtlety of the clouding.

Variation 4

In this example a glaze of turquoise semigloss latex (vinyl silk emulsion) was applied over a lime-green basecoat of simulated buttermilk paint (left). The absorbency of the basecoat here has resulted in a patchy effect that is more casual in nature than the refined effect you get with a non-absorbent surface.

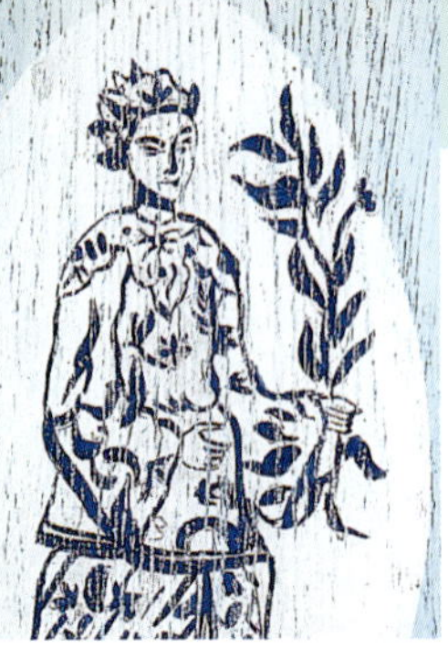

Tracing

The varied shades of a blue-and-white background can create an extremely striking and exquisite visual effect. Delft tiles have often been used as centerpieces in cupboard doors, box lids and table tops. Decorative plates and dishes have been displayed on shelves in kitchens and dining rooms, and hung on walls in living rooms. With a little ingenuity, you can create the look of blue-and-white china in your own home.

You will need

Tools

• Sizes 1–3 artist ox hair brushes • 2–3 in. (5–7.5 cm.) bristle basecoat brush • Fine watercolor brush • ½ in. (1.3 cm.) stencil brush • Low-tack masking tape • Acetate for oval stencil • Sharp pencil • Carbon and tracing papers • Sharp scissors

Materials

• Source material (pictures, etc.) • Artists' acrylic colors in white and navy • Eggshell paint in white and navy • Spray adhesive

Tracing fits in very well with both modern and period settings and can be used on plates and tiles as well as on intricate picture frames. It can be used to create a border around photocopies (see p. 58), and works well over a rag-rolled background (see p. 52) and sponged (see p. 54) or colorwashed backgrounds (see p. 60). Although I have chosen to create a blue-and-white effect, any color combination may be chosen, depending on the mood and style of the required finished effect.

Work slowly and follow all the instructions carefully; this will reduce the chances of mistakes. If mistakes do occur, wipe them off immediately or repaint the background and start again. The possibility of creating whole scenes is, with a little foresight and planning, well within the reach of the basic decorator.

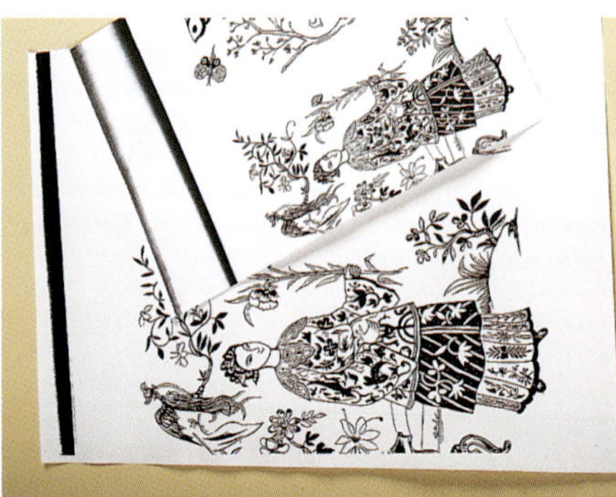

1 Measure the area to be covered by your image and have the chosen images either reduced or enlarged to the required size on a photocopier.

2 Distress the surface (see p. 36). Here the surface was painted in navy blue eggshell, left to dry and a layer of white eggshell applied. It was then heavily distressed with a medium- then a fine-grade sandpaper to let the paint and natural wood to show through.

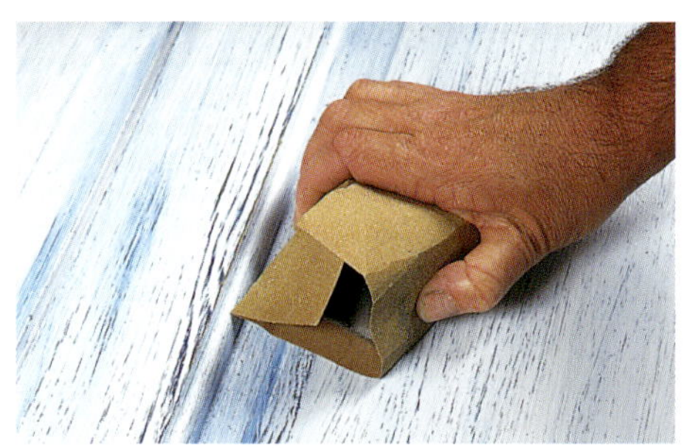

Variation 1

This surface was given a coat of pale pink latex (emulsion) and then colorwashed with dark pink latex and a yellow ocher acrylic glaze. The design was traced into position and the relevant section painted using acrylic paint and fine brushes. The tracing was half left to create depth and interest.

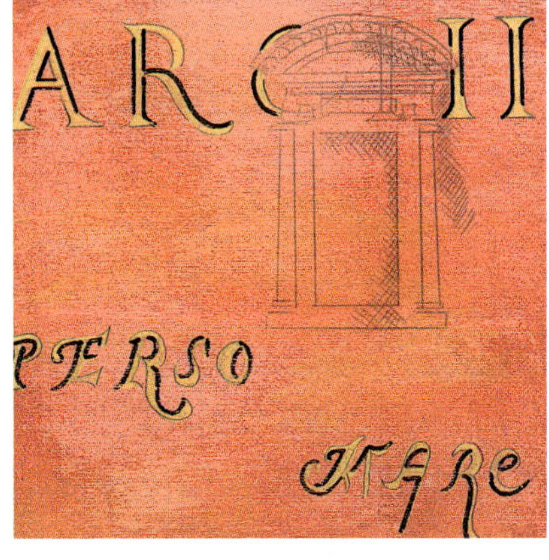

Variation 2

Here, the mid-green basecoat of semigloss latex (vinyl silk emulsion) was wiped over with a glaze of olive green (1 part paint to 3 parts glaze), followed by a yellow ocher glaze. When dry the design was traced into position. With a fine artists' brush the sections were painted olive green. When dry the surface was over-painted with yellow ocher to highlight certain sections.

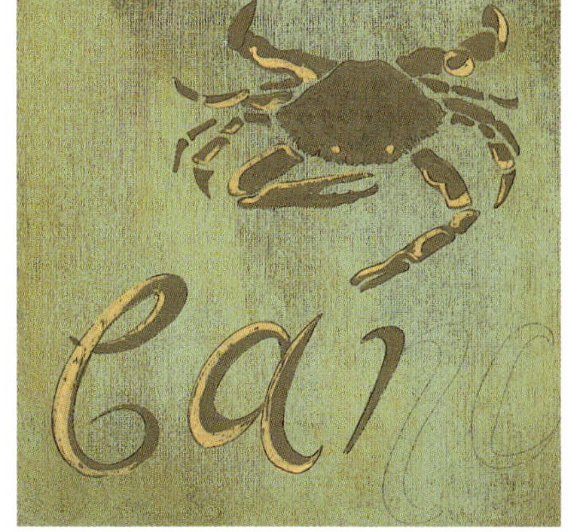

3 **Measure area where tracing is to be positioned. On stenciling card or acetate draw an oval shape with a permanent marker pen and cut out with scissors. This will be used as background to the tracing. Measure tracing to ensure it will fit.**

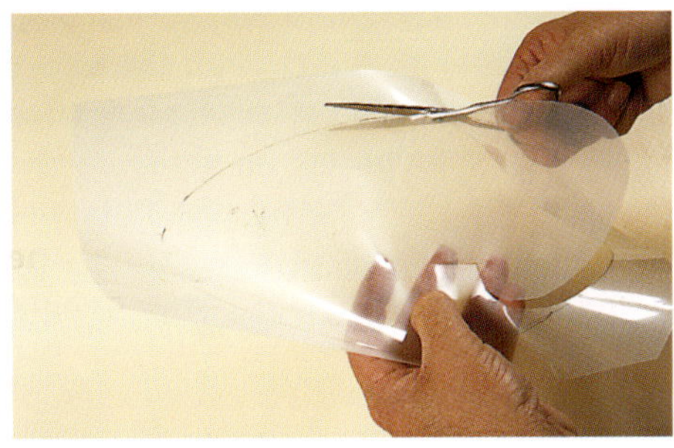

4 **Apply a little spray adhesive to the back of the stenciling card or acetate and place it in position. Using the stencil brush and some artists' white acrylic or white stencil paint, stencil the oval onto the door panel (see *Stenciling*, p 78). Allow to dry.**

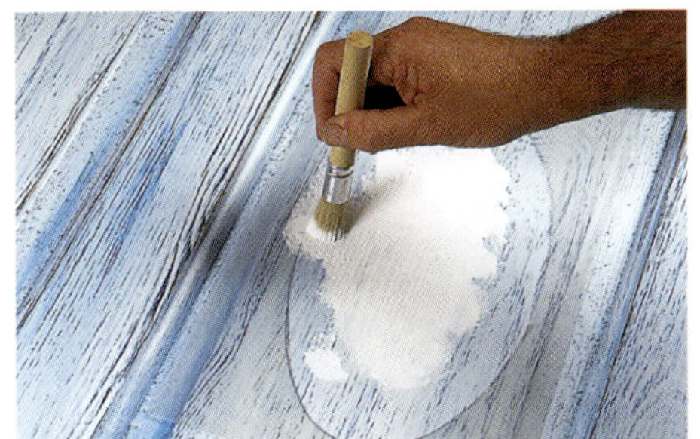

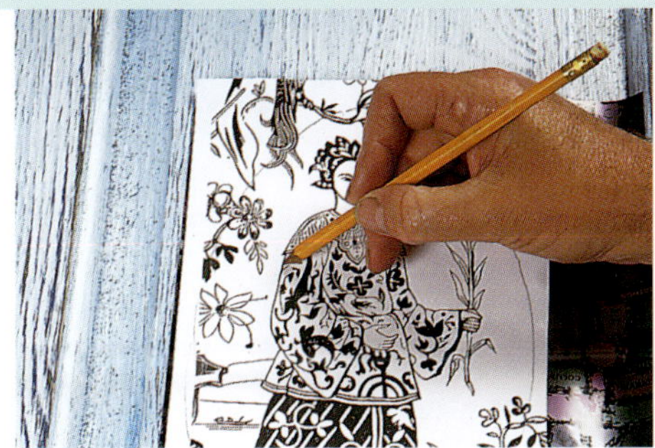

5 **Fix a suitably sized piece of carbon or tracing paper with a little tape to the back of your tracing, ink side facing out. Carefully place the tracing and the carbon paper in position over your stenciled panel. With a sharp pencil methodically and slowly trace around the image to be transferred. Check intermittently that nothing has slipped and that the lines are clear and correct.**

7 **The blue-and-white colors of Delft china have been used here to create an oriental theme for this door paneling. Because the image is traced, high-quality results can be expected. Aged and distressed the image becomes more romantic and illusory, reliving the charms of bygone eras.**

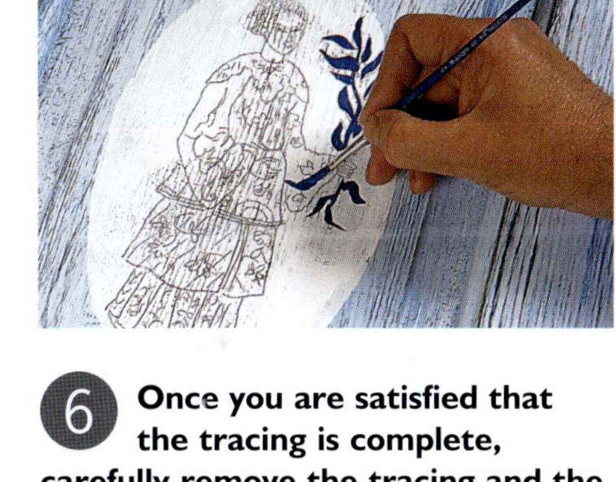

6 **Once you are satisfied that the tracing is complete, carefully remove the tracing and the carbon paper. Pour some navy blue artists' acrylic paint into a clean container. Add a little water to achieve a smooth, heavy cream consistency. With a fine artists' ox hair brush, slowly paint in all the traced areas. Allow to dry. Apply a layer of wax or varnish for protection if required.**

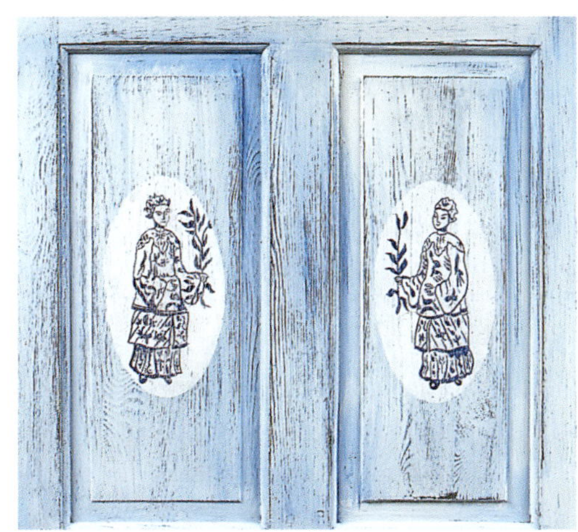

Variation 3

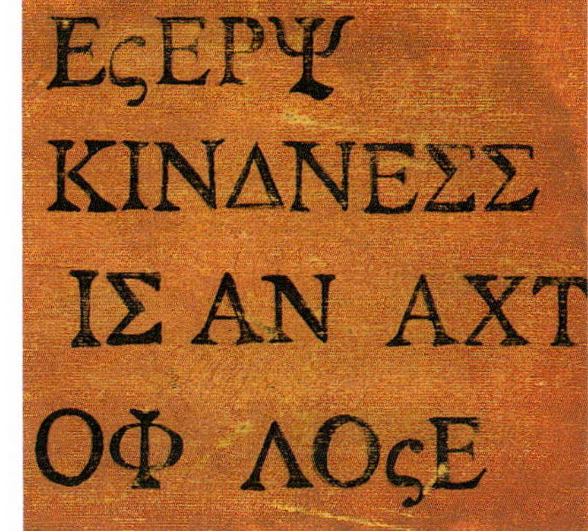

Here, a coat of deep terracotta latex (emulsion) was applied over the basecoat of bright yellow latex. When dry, the surface was sanded quite heavily with fine-grade sandpaper and a kitchen scouring pad to create a distressed effect. The design was traced onto the surface with a sharp pencil and tracing paper, and the symbols filled in with black acrylic paint. When dry, the whole surface was rubbed with a scouring pad.

Variation 4

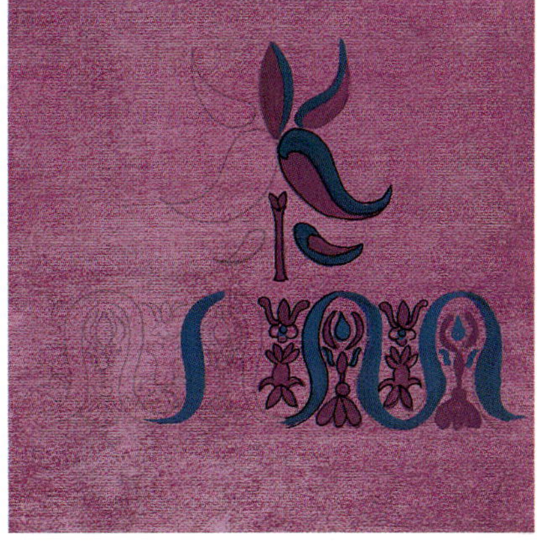

This surface was painted with a coat of mauve semigloss latex (vinyl silk emulsion) and allowed to dry before being wiped with a glaze (1 part paint to 3 parts acrylic glaze) of bright purple. The stylized flower design was drawn up and then traced onto the panel and over-painted in purple and bright blue acrylic paint. The tracing has been left to show how the effect is actually achieved.

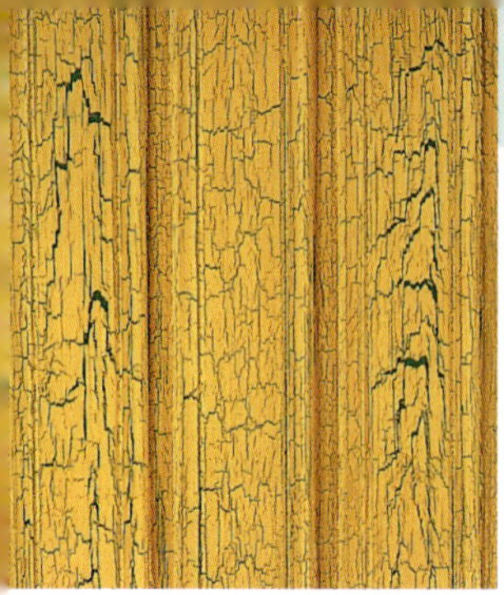

The weather affects nearly everything in one way or another, and nothing more so than painted exterior woodwork. Using crackleglaze you can create the wonderfully tactile effect of cracked paint in your own home.

Crackleglaze

Crackleglaze is an effect ideally suited to all sorts of woodwork from decorative items such as lampbases and boxes, to chests-of-drawers and architectural features such as doors, baseboards (skirting boards) and window frames. You may wish to apply crackleglaze to walls, but remember that although the effect is very pleasing, it can look a little overwhelming when used on large areas that would not normally be prone to flaky and weathered paint.

It is an inexpensive technique to achieve because your outlay for tools and materials is minimal. However, the finished surface is most vulnerable and needs a protective varnish which should be applied with the best quality varnishing brush you can afford.

Because of the nature of this finish you can experiment with a wide range of color combinations. By experimenting on sample boards, mistakes can be avoided. The technique works very well with colorwashed walls (see p. 60) to give an overall look of faded grandeur or a simple rustic country look.

The crackleglaze medium is available in good decorator stores but it does take a little practice. All manufacturer's instructions should be strictly adhered to. The most common pitfall is to over-brush the topcoat, causing a break up of the cracked effect. If repainting is needed, allow the topcoat to dry then carefully paint in any areas previously missed. Otherwise remove the whole surface by washing with water, allow the surface to dry and begin again.

You will need

Tools

• *A good 2–3 in. (5–7.5 cm.) bristle decorator's brush* • *3–4 in. (7.5–10 cm.) decorator's brush* • *A quality 2–3 in. (5–7.5 cm.) varnishing brush*

Materials

• *Basecoat color* • *Topcoat color* • *Crackleglaze medium (appropriate paint should be chosen according to manufacturer's instructions)* • *Appropriate varnish*

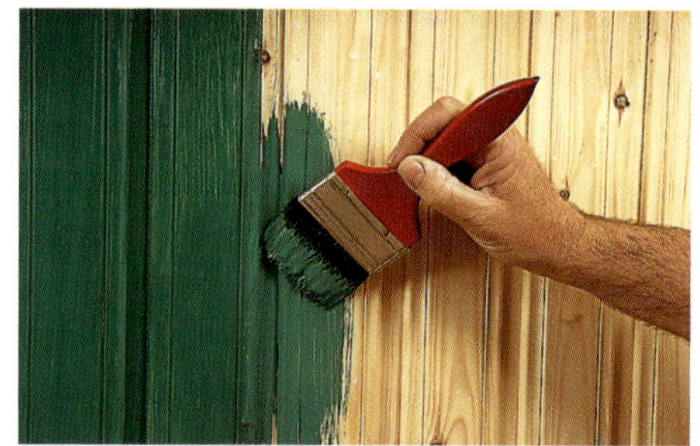

1 **Fill all holes and sand to a reasonably smooth surface. Remove all dust with a damp cloth. Apply two basecoats of peacock blue simulated buttermilk. Latex (emulsion) may be used but do check with the manufacturers' instructions of the crackleglaze being used. Allow to dry overnight.**

Variation 1

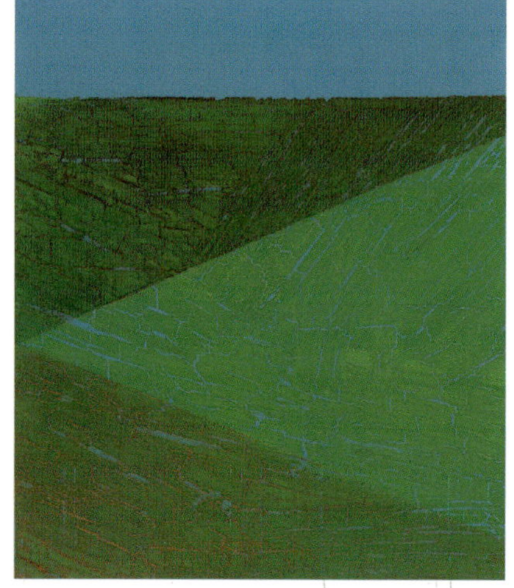

Crackleglaze is an exciting effect to try but it can be a little temperamental. For this variation apple green has been applied over the crackle medium, which has a basecoat of medium blue. The final effect was finished with clear wax tinted with raw umber (top), and clear wax tinted with yellow ocher powder color. The central section has just been waxed.

Variation 2

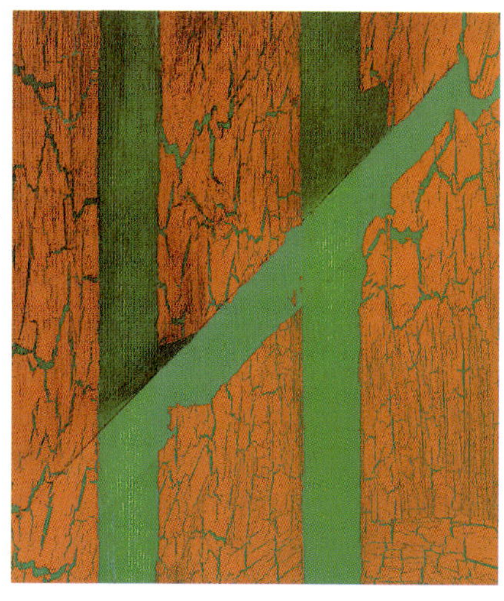

A striped effect has been incorporated here by using vertical strips of low-tack masking tape over a ground of bright green. The crackleglaze was applied over the entire surface and allowed to dry, before applying a bright orange paint with quick, vertical strokes. Finally, the top section was waxed with burnt umber powder tinted wax, and clear wax used for the bottom section.

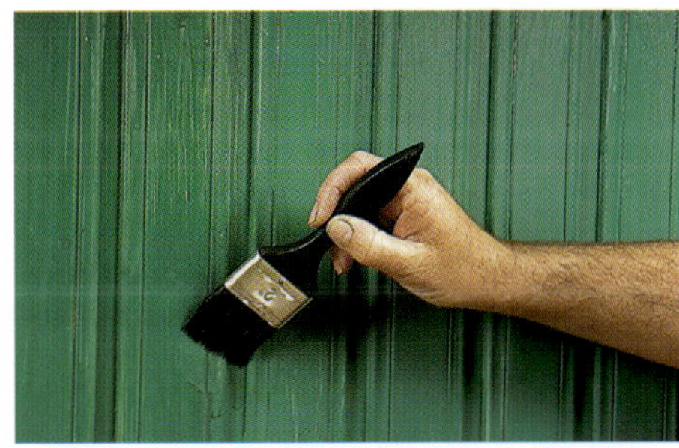

2 Apply a generous layer of the crackleglaze medium with a 2 in. (5 cm.) bristle brush, avoiding unsightly runs. Ensure the joint (join) between each panel in the tongue-and-groove is covered. Allow to dry.

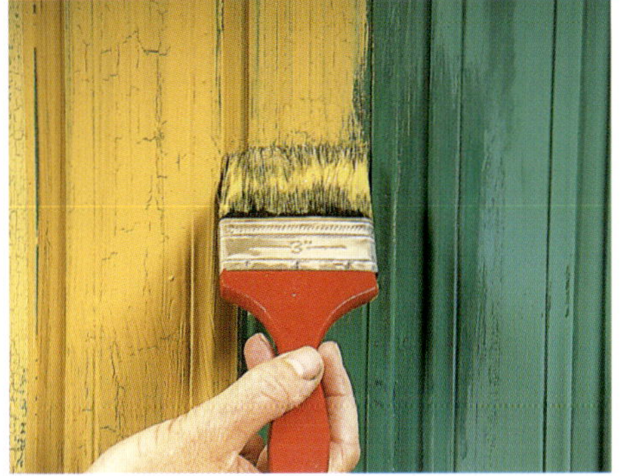

3 Apply a layer of yellow ocher simulated buttermilk paint with a 3 in. (7.5 cm.) bristle basecoat brush. Paint vertically with the ridges of the paneling. Make sure that the paint gets into the grooves. Do not over-brush.

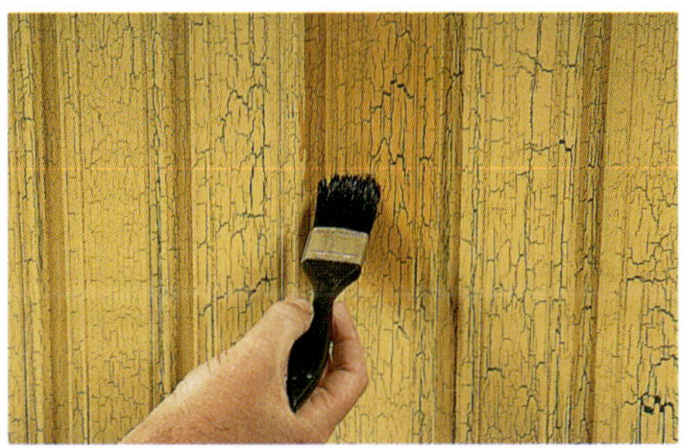

4 Apply at least two coats of varnish to protect the surface. If you have chosen a hard finish, varnish with at least two coats of an oil-based varnish. Acrylic varnish may be used but be careful not to over-brush and start the cracking reaction again. Furniture wax may also be used.

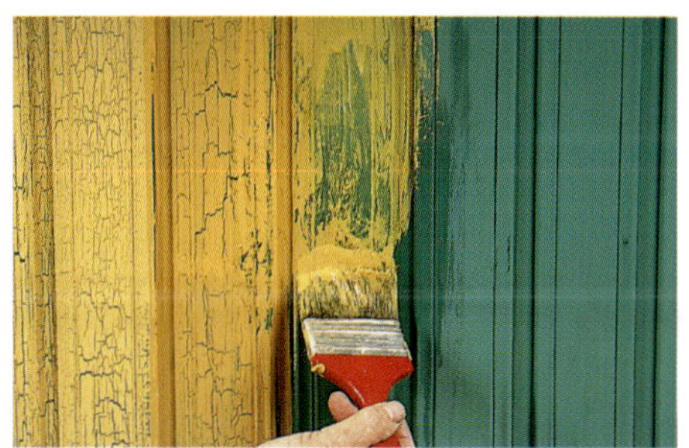

5 If over-brushing happens, the glazing medium and paint tend to mix into very unsightly patches. The surface becomes sticky and unmanageable and can only be repaired by sanding. Completely remove the surface and start again.

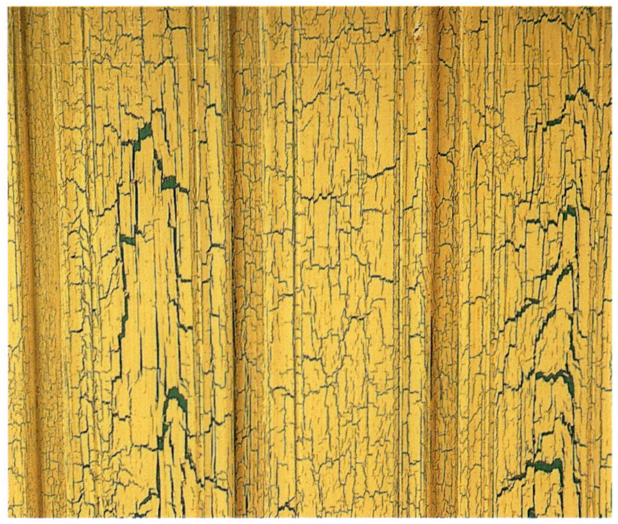

6 The tongue-and-groove paneling used here is brought to life by the use of warm ocher over peacock blue-green, two colors that work very well with each other. The crackled effect accentuates the surface, creating an individual look that is easy to live with and which is also particularly eye-catching.

Variation 3

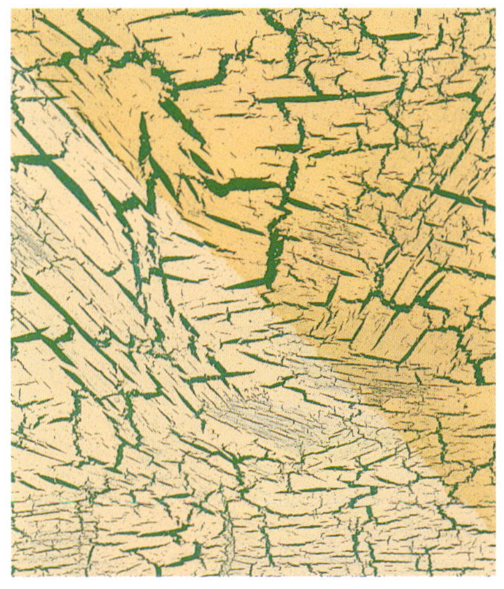

Choosing two different colors will accentuate flaking paint cracks. Here, a crackleglaze medium was applied over a basecoat of apple green, which had been allowed to dry. When the medium had also dried, a layer of pale cream paint was applied in very random, quick brushstrokes. The darker section was antiqued with an oil-based exterior varnish.

Variation 4

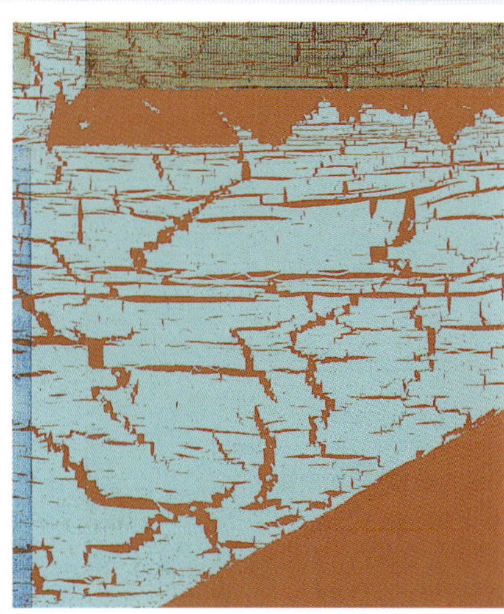

Here the sample has a basecoat of terracotta over which a topcoat of turquoise has been applied to create a quite stunning effect. The top section was antiqued with brown umber tinted wax, and the left section with bright blue tinted wax.

In context

This gallery section shows examples of three more very different techniques, namely woodgrain stain inlay, clouding and crackleglaze. Each one creates a very different look and has been applied in contrasting settings to bring to life walls, floors and ceilings. Built-in fitments can also be given a complete face lift to complement any new scheme.

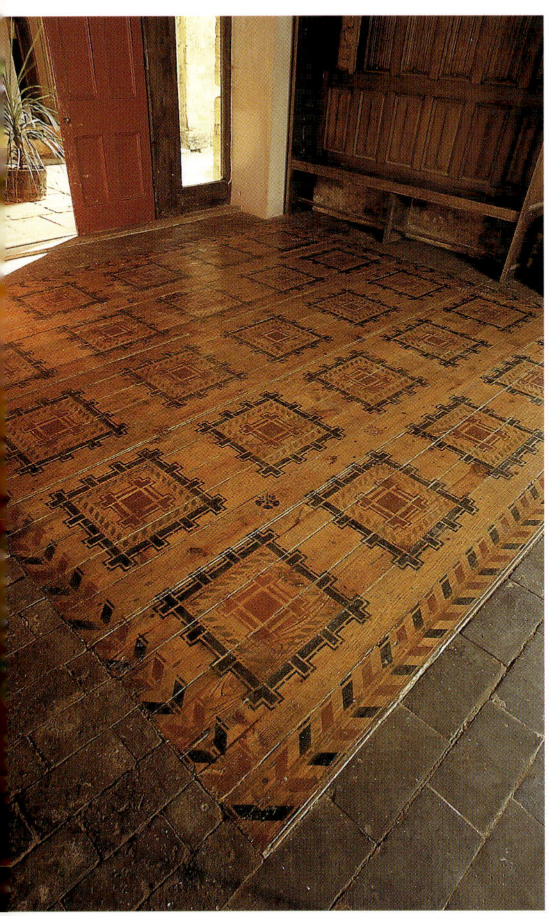

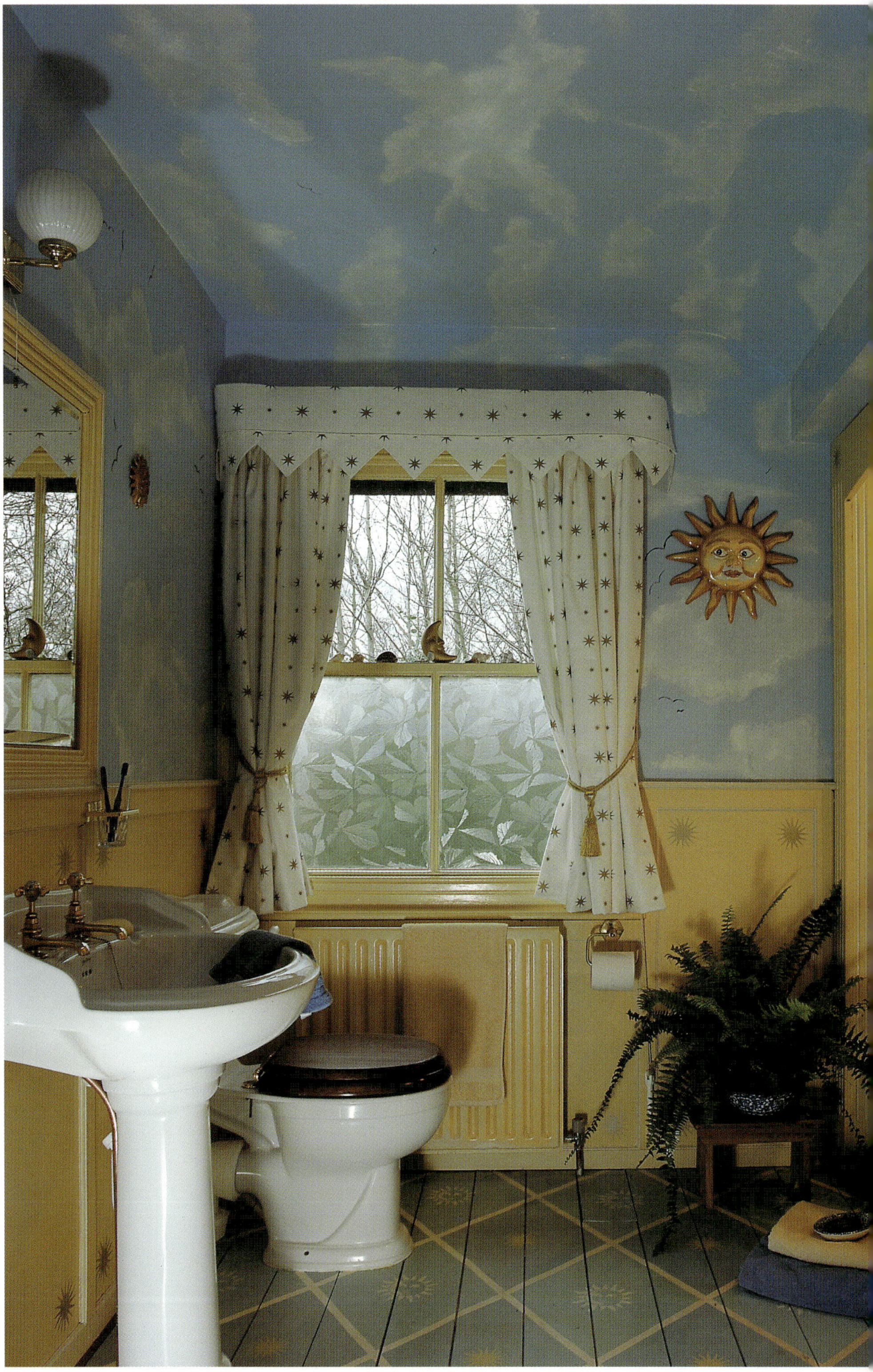

Woodgrain inlay

▲ Floor panel

The simple solidity of this flagstone tiled floor has been lifted by the addition of a floor panel created by using wooden floorboards painted with stain to create the appearance of woodstain inlay.

Clouding

▲ Paneled bathroom

This striking example of clouding on the walls and ceiling of this beautifully accessorized bathroom, has been completed by the use of warm ocher stippled and stenciled panels below the dado rail and around the bath. The colorwashed, stenciled and lined floor helps to create a feeling of "floating on air."

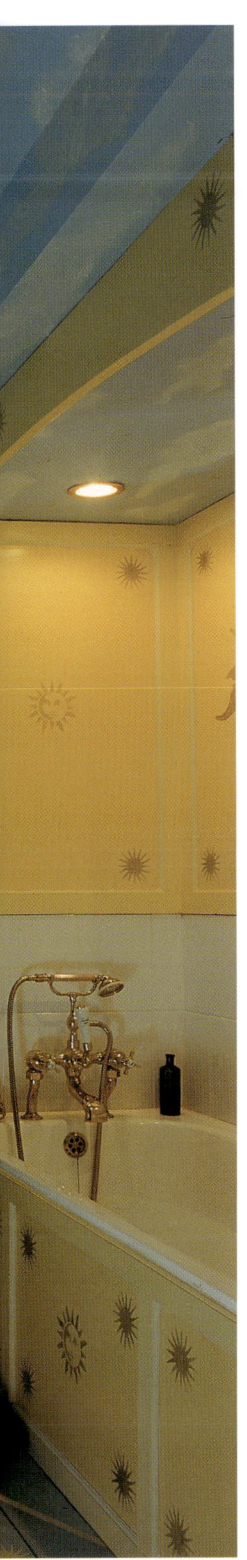

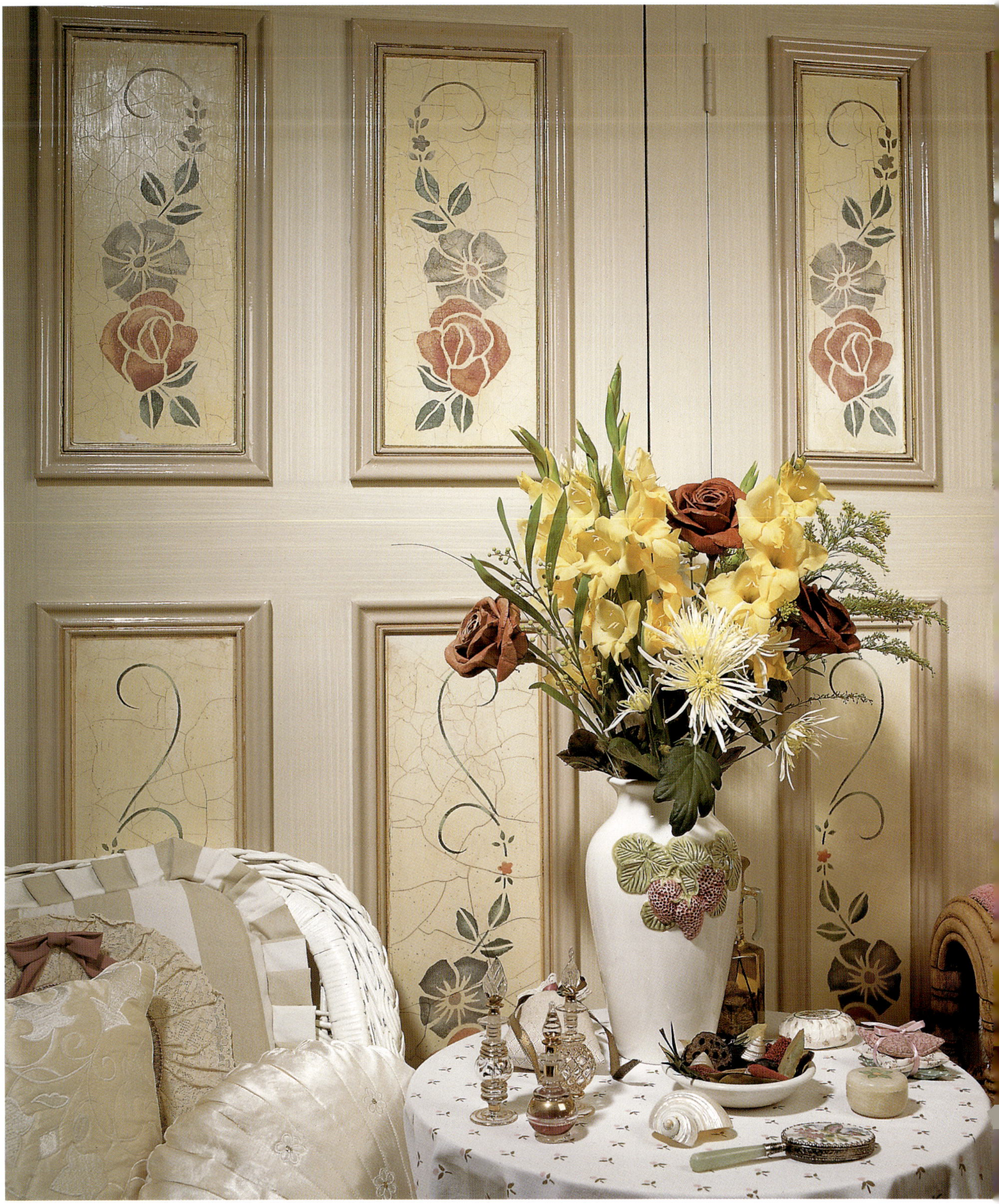

Crackleglaze

▲ Wall paneling and doors in an elegant living room

These very beautiful panels have been created by subtle dragging in pale mushroom/gray over a white ground around the panels. The panels themselves have been highlighted with stenciling over a pale green background creating an opulent inlaid effect. The scheme has been complemented by crackleglaze in the panels giving them the effect of gentle aging elegance.

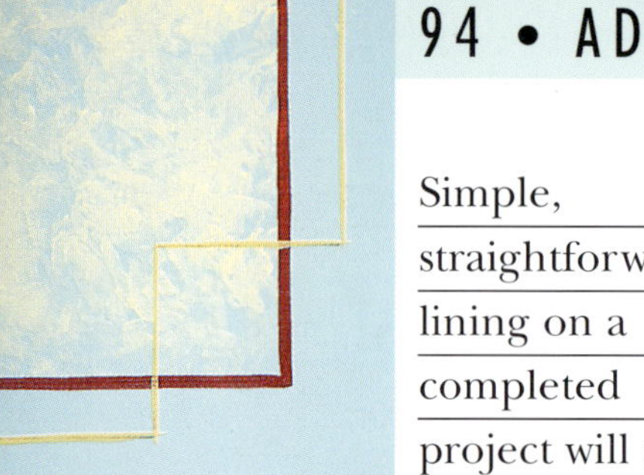

Simple, straightforward lining on a completed project will add a touch of elegance and style. When used carefully, depth and dimension can be added, creating much sought after but simple *trompe l'oeil* (see p. 79) effects.

Lining

As a border on cupboards, paneling, table tops, doors and fitted units, lining will complete the final effect. It is also very effective on smaller flat surfaces such as boxes and picture frames. Lining can be used in any colorway and is suited to both modern and traditional decorative schemes.

Good-quality lining brushes are essential for a quality finish. Lining brushes are moderately expensive but if well cared for will give many years of use.

Mistakes are generally caused by the lack of a steady hand—this can be improved with practice and care during application. Another fault is using paint that is too thick. The consistency of the paint should be similar to that of heavy cream, for flow and control. Using an absorbent basecoat such as flat latex (vinyl matte emulsion) makes it impossible to remove mistakes, so the ideal basecoat is a non-absorbent paint such as semigloss latex (vinyl silk emulsion) or eggshell. To correct mistakes on flat (matte) paint repaint and start again.

You will need

Tools

• *Swordliner brush* • *¼ in. (0.63 cm.) lining brush* • *Ruler or straight edge* • *2–3 in. (5–7.5 cm.) bristle basecoat brush* • *¾ in. (1.9 cm.) low-tack masking tape* • *Rag for rag-rolling* • *Sharp pencil* • *Paint dishes*

Materials

• *Crimson and yellow ocher acrylic paints* • *Turquoise eggshell paint* • *Transparent oil glaze* • *Cream artists' oil paint* • *Mineral spirits (white spirit)*

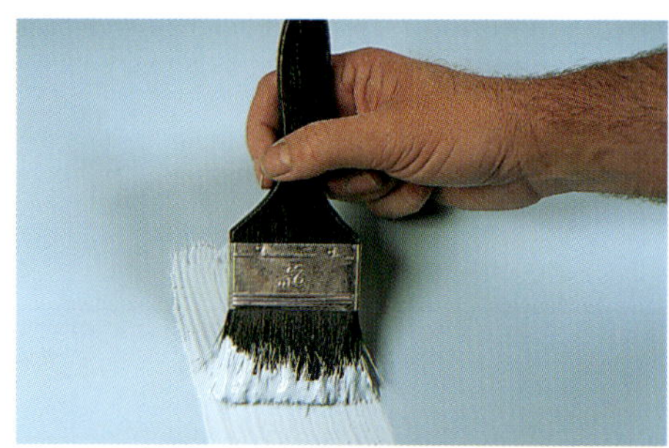

1 Prepare the surface (see *Preparation*, p. 18). Apply undercoat. Dry. With a bristle brush apply a coat of turquoise eggshell paint. Allow to dry. Repeat with a second coat. Allow to dry.

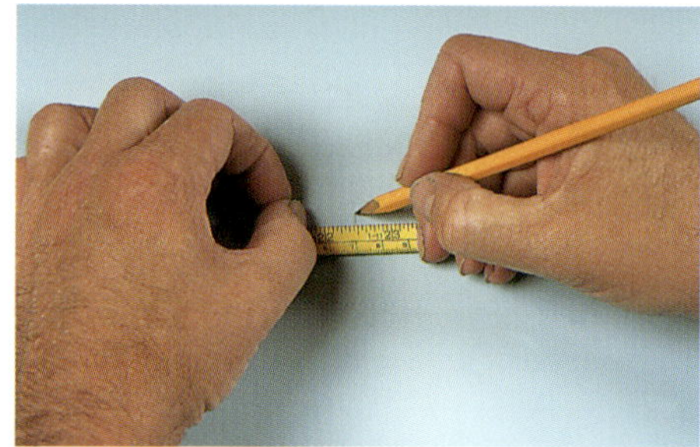

2 With a ruler and a pencil measure 4 in. (10 cm.) in from the edges round the panel (vary the measurements as you feel necessary). With pencil and a straight edge, mark edges of the inner panel.

Variation 1

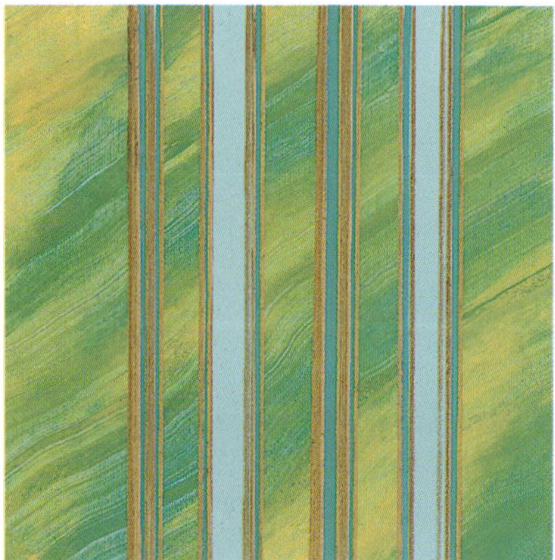

Here, on a basecoat of pale turquoise semigloss latex (vinyl silk emulsion), low-tack tape ½–¾ in. (1.3–1.9 cm.) was used to mask off the striped areas. Separate acrylic glazes of yellow ocher and pale blue were applied to

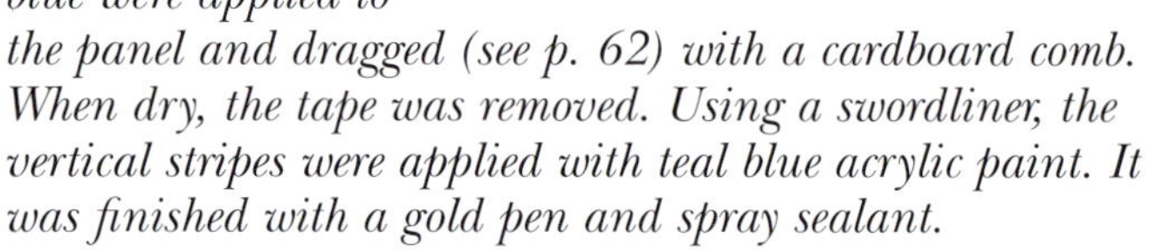

the panel and dragged (see p. 62) with a cardboard comb. When dry, the tape was removed. Using a swordliner, the vertical stripes were applied with teal blue acrylic paint. It was finished with a gold pen and spray sealant.

Variation 2

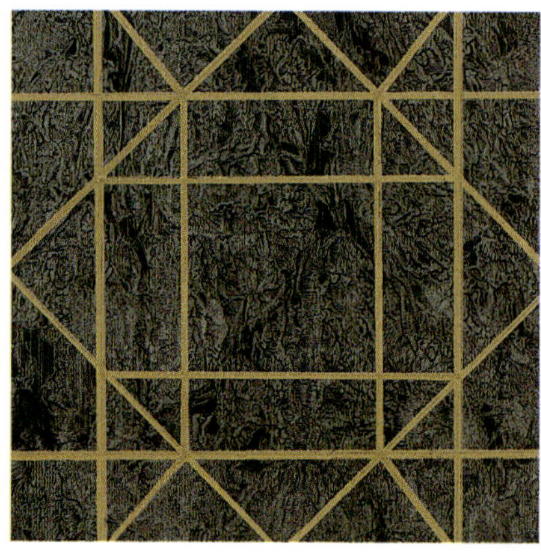

Two coats of mid-gray (1 part white to 1 part black) eggshell were applied to this panel and allowed to dry. Ivory and black artists' oil paints were mixed with transparent oil glaze and applied to the surface. The frottage technique (see p. 28) was applied. When dry, the pattern was measured, marked off with chalk and lined with a gold permanent marking pen. It was sealed with sealant and two coats of oil-based varnish were added.

3 Apply low tack tape around the outside edge of the pencil marks. Press it down gently to avoid any bleeding of paint underneath. Do not over-press as this may cause it to lift or peel the basecoat paint off when removed.

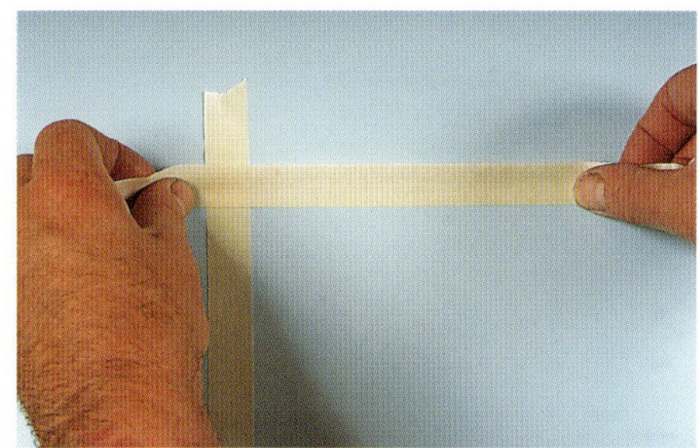

4 Mix some oil-based glaze with a little pale cream artists' oil paint. Mix in some mineral spirits (white spirit) to achieve a heavy cream consistency. Follow the step-by-step instructions for rag-rolling (see p. 52) and rag-roll the central panel. Allow to dry overnight.

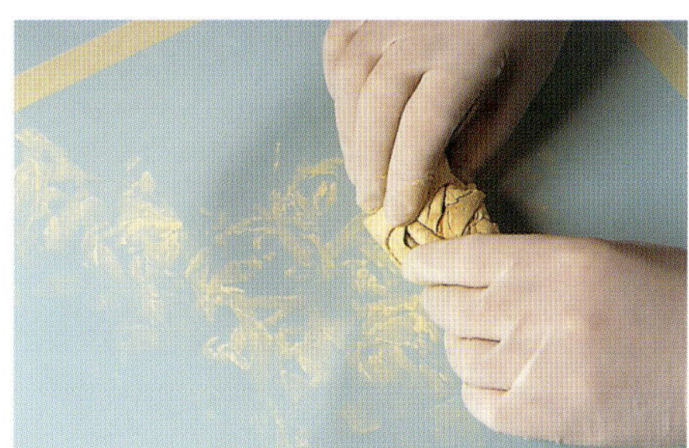

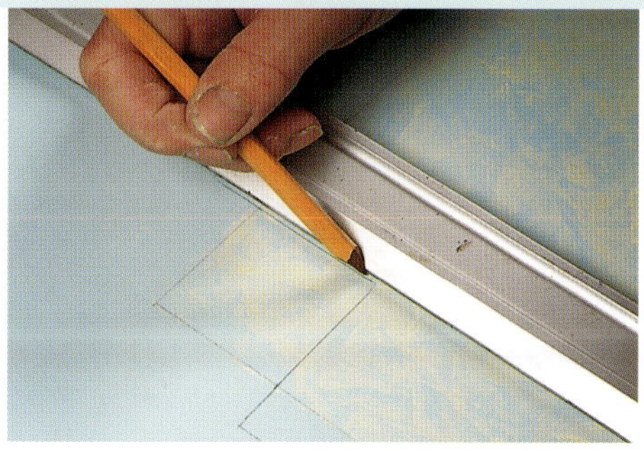

5 Carefully remove the tape and with a straight edge and a sharp pencil measure and outline the panel in your chosen pattern. Measure each section carefully and make sure not to overdraw the design—light pencil or chalk marks are sufficient.

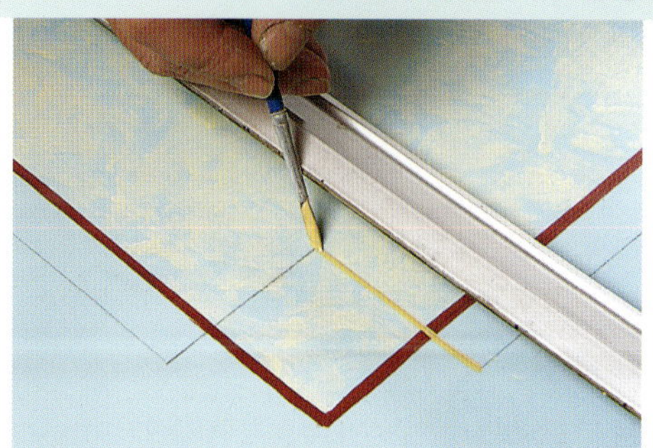

6 In separate dishes pour some artists' acrylic paints in yellow ocher and crimson. Mix with water to get a pouring consistency. With a swordliner brush and a straight edge, apply paint along the drawn guidelines in one clean stroke. Reload the brush as necessary. When using the straight edge keep it at an angle off the panel to stop any paint from bleeding under the edge.

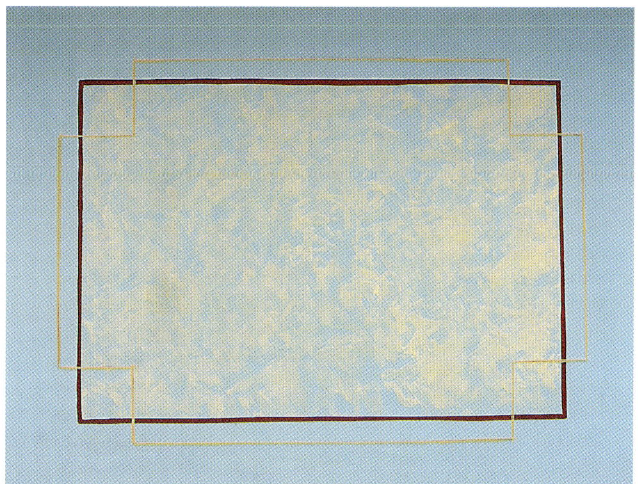

7 Simple textured panels can be given a further dimension with lining. This panel has been given a new lease of life by adding a border in complementary colors. Lining adds interest to any surface in any decor.

Variation 3

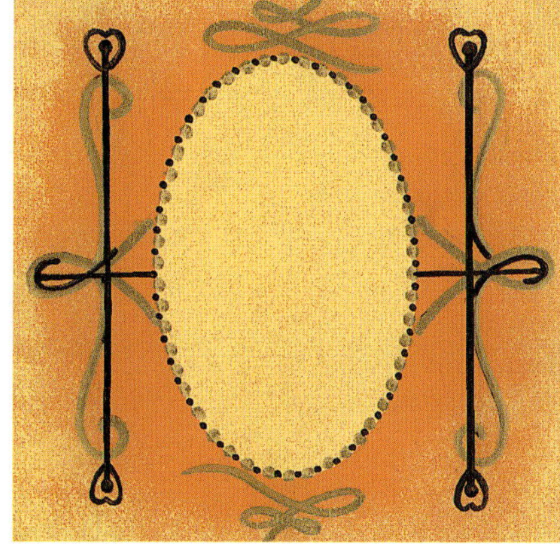

This panel was painted with a burnt orange semigloss latex (vinyl silk emulsion) and allowed to dry. An oval was cut out of stencil card and placed in position. Lemon acrylic paint was applied to the center oval. After removing the stencil, the edges were stippled (see p. 30) with lemon. The panel was completed by lining with a ruler and gold and black medium marking pens, and sealing with a spray sealant.

Variation 4

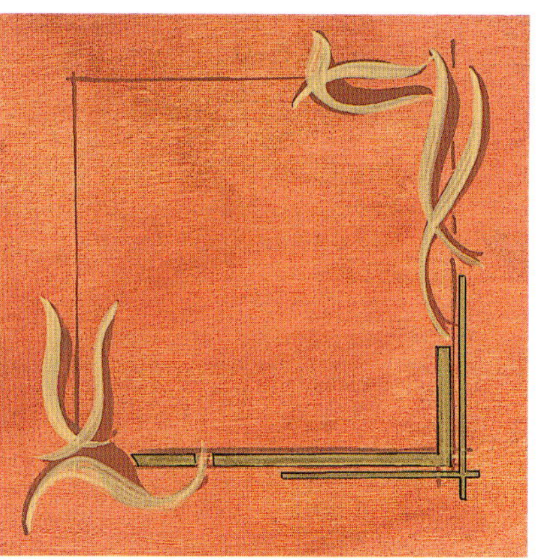

Here, a deep, dusty pink latex (emulsion) diluted with a little water was colorwashed (see p. 60) over a basecoat of buff semigloss latex (vinyl silk emulsion). The surface was then "wiped" with a lint-free cloth. With a pencil, the basic design was drawn in and the narrow lines filled in with a ruler and dusty pink acrylic paint. With a medium swordliner the leaf shapes were painted on, dried and over-painted in cream. The gold permanent pen was used last.

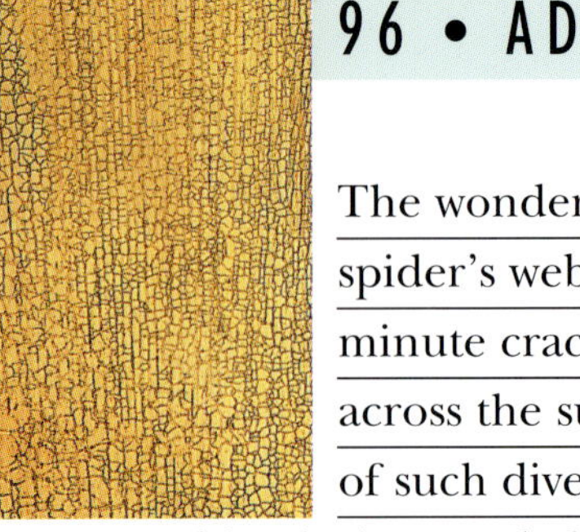

The wonderful spider's web of minute cracks across the surface of such diverse items as old paintings and china can be created in your own home literally overnight. Crackleure gives the look of age in a beautifully soft and mellow way.

Crackleure

The charm of crackleure finish is that it looks wonderful when applied to almost any small surface, such as small pieces of furniture, picture frames, wastepaper bins and lampbases. If applied with careful thought, architectural features such as chair (dado) rails, doors and ceiling rosettes (roses) can also look very attractive with a crackleure finish. This technique also works well with other finishes, such as stenciling (see p. 78) and découpage (see p. 66).

This is a moderately expensive technique to start, but the varnishes will go a long way, and if used for a number of projects the cost becomes far more moderate. Crackleure varnishes are available at good decorator stores and specialist paint effect shops, but gold size (see p. 94) and gum arabic can be substituted, and these are also available from good art stores.

When attempting crackleure, manufacturer's instructions should be adhered to. Always use a sample board, as practice is necessary. The final finish can depend on the condition of and type of basecoat, atmospheric conditions, thickness of the varnishes and the method of application. If something goes wrong, carefully remove the top, water-based varnish with a damp cloth, allow the surface to dry, and redo the basecoat and topcoat. Do not be deterred by the intricacy of this technique, as the final results are well worth the effort.

You will need

Tools

• 2 in. (5 cm.) bristle basecoat brush • 1 in. (2.5 cm.) bristle basecoat brush • Soft, lint-free cloths

Materials

• Basecoat of latex (emulsion) • Crackleure (2 parts) • Raw umber oil paint (artists' tube) • Oil-based varnish for protection

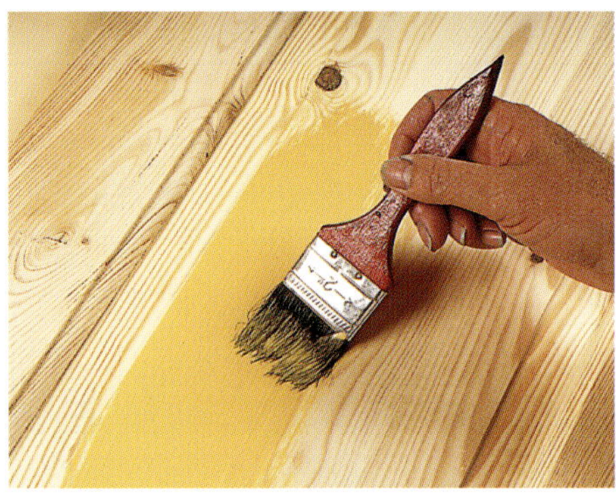

1 Sand all rough areas. Remove dust with a brush followed by a damp cloth. Using a 2 in. (5 cm.) bristle basecoat brush apply two coats of pale ocher latex (emulsion). Allow drying time between coats. Here we did not apply an undercoat as the door was internal and required an old, aged final effect which would show the grain and knots of the natural wood.

Variation 1

Crackleure can be temperamental as the final finish depends on many conditions; but experimentation can be fun. In our first variation a metallic copper base was applied to the surface. When touch dry, the crackle basecoat was applied, then the topcoat applied as per manufacturer's instructions. Due to the dampness of the basecoat the whole effect becomes "cloudy" as it dries. A wax finish accentuates the copper in the cracks.

Variation 2

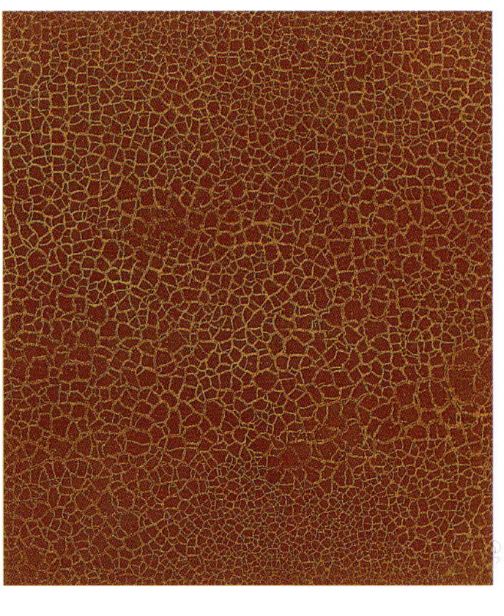

By varying the colorways, a real antique leather effect can be created. The basecoat of crimson semigloss latex (vinyl silk emulsion) was applied to the surface and allowed to dry. The crackleure technique was then applied, and finally the cracks that had formed with the aid of a hairdryer were highlighted with gilding cream, leaving a very impressive and rich finish.

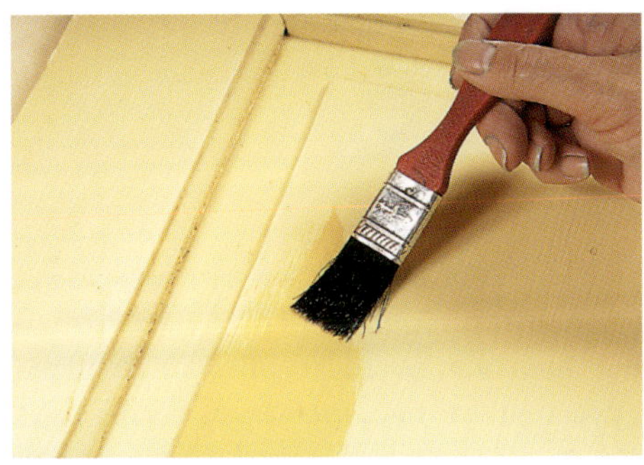

2 **Using a 1 in. (2.5 cm.) bristle basecoat brush apply the first coat of the crackleure varnish following manufacturer's instructions. Make sure that the panels are evenly and completely coated.**

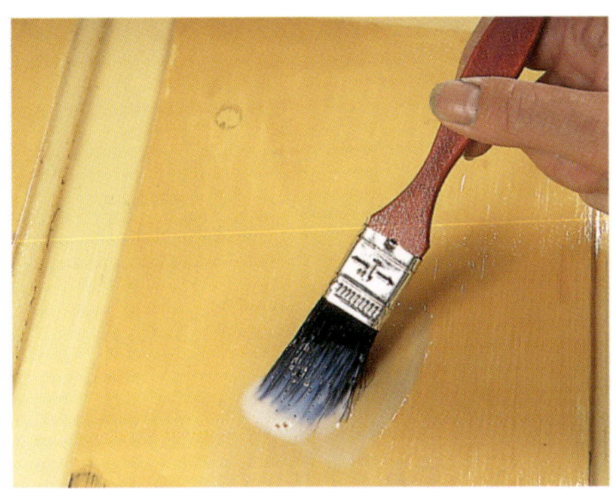

3 **When the varnish is touch dry, apply the water-based topcoat quickly and randomly using a clean 1 in. (2.5 cm.) bristle brush. Allow to dry.**

4 **Once the two varnishes have worked against each other and a fine web of cracks has formed on the surface, rub in some artists' oil paint in raw umber using a soft, lint-free cloth. Rub the oil paint evenly into and across the panel.**

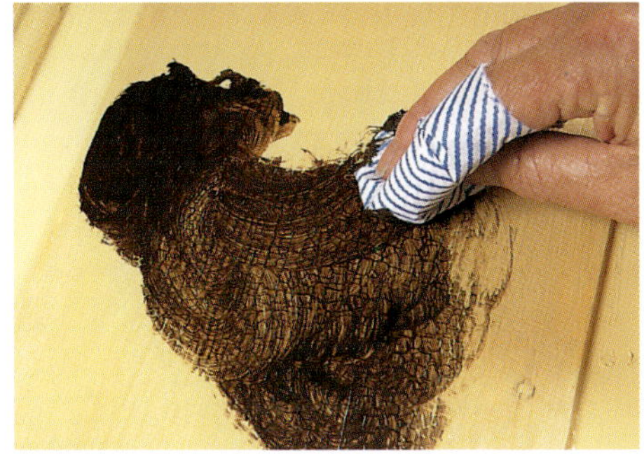

5 **Remove excess oil paint with a clean, lint-free cloth. Replace the cloth as necessary. Keep working on the surface with clean cloths until the desired intensity of color is achieved. Seal with oil-based varnish.**

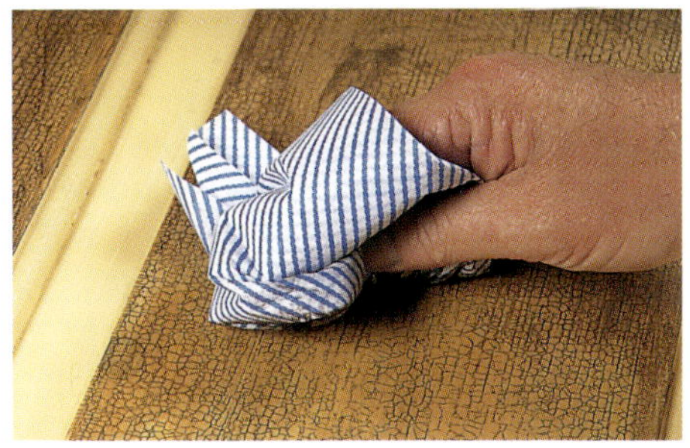

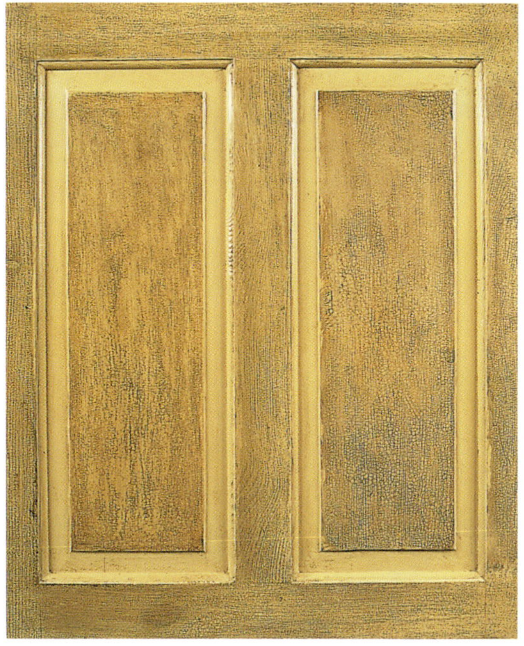

6 **Crackleure creates an individual and interesting surface that is subtle and attractive. Although the effect works well when used with other techniques, such as stenciling and découpage, the panels here have enough surface depth to sustain interest.**

Variation 3

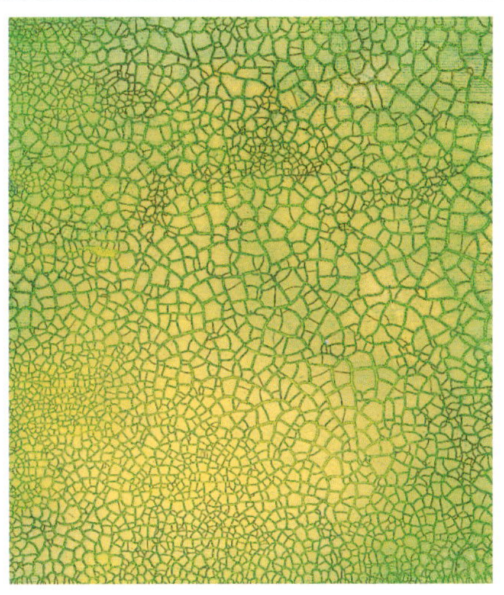

Once again color variation has proved that the same technique can give varied results. Here, the basecoat of vivid yellow was treated with the crackleure effect and the final layer dried in the sunlight. Then, apple-green oil paint was used to accentuate the cracks. Not all the apple-green paint was removed from the surface, achieving an uneven, aged look.

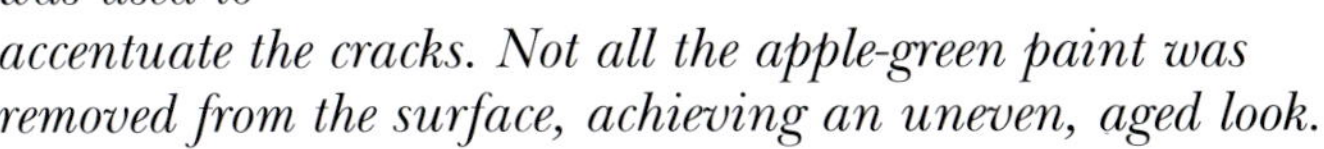

Variation 4

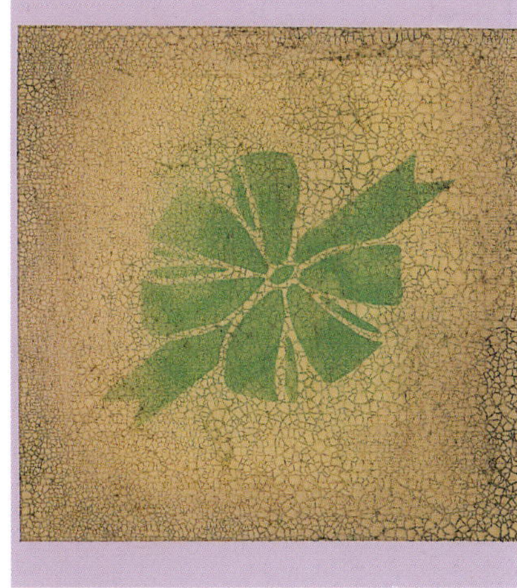

Combining the crackleure effect with stenciling *(see p. 78)* *has always been a favorite for antiquing. In this example, a basecoat of mauve was over-stenciled with a lime-green bow. The edges of our panel were masked with ¾ in. (1.9 cm.) low-tack masking tape before applying the crackleure varnish. The cracks were accentuated with burnt umber oil paint, and then some areas were highlighted with apple-green oil paint.*

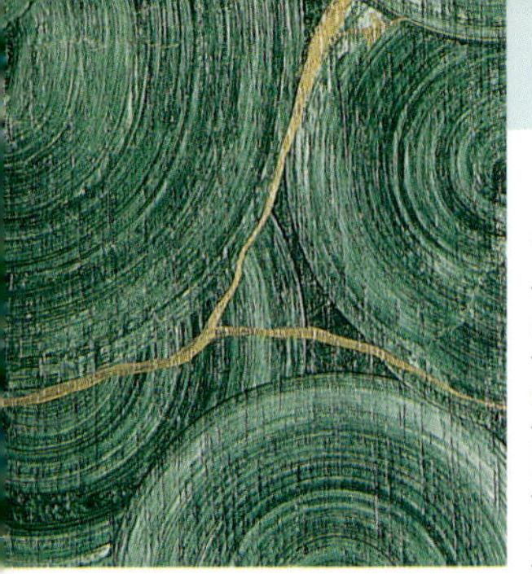

The rich and expensive look of real malachite has been simulated in paint for centuries and produces the most vibrant decorative effect. Striking and very individual, ordinary objects can be given a transformation that will be the envy of all of your friends.

Malachite

Malachite effect needs practice in manipulating and using a cardboard comb and glaze. An infinite variety of patterns can be achieved with malachite, so each item will have an individual finish. It is best suited to smaller decorative items such as boxes, lampbases, corbels, picture frames, borders, table tops and cupboard doors. If used as an inlay (see p. 128) on walls and floors, it will enhance any room in a traditional or modern setting.

Malachite should be done with the best quality brushes. Natural colors such as ultramarine, turquoise and viridian should be used, but added lining (see p. 94) and stenciling (see p. 78) in shades of gold will produce a beautiful final product.

Any mistakes made when using the comb will enhance the finish, but may be wiped off carefully with a cloth dampened with mineral spirits (white spirit), and then the glaze reapplied and recombed.

You will need

Tools

• *Card for combing* • *Craft knife* • *Paint dish* • *Glazing brush* • *2–3 in. (5–7.5 cm.) basecoat bristle brush* • *Fine artists' brush* • *Soft, lint-free cloths*

Materials

• *Turquoise-green eggshell basecoat* • *Artists' oils in French ultramarine, yellow ocher and viridian* • *Gold acrylic paint* • *Transparent oil glaze or gilp* • *Fine grade sandpaper* • *Mineral spirits (white spirit)* • *Suitable varnish*

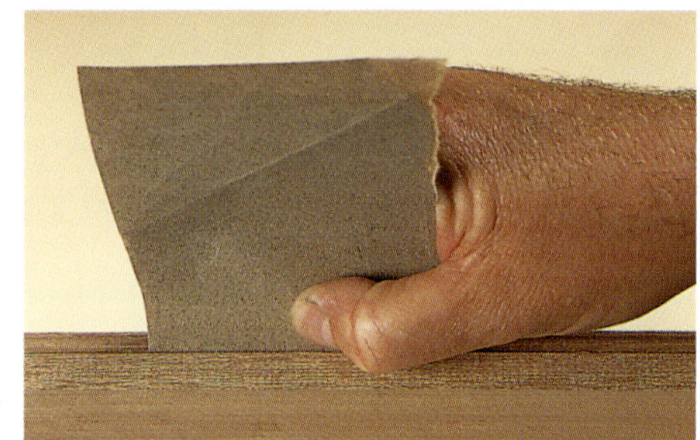

1 Prepare the surface (see *Preparation*, p. 18). Fill holes with filler. Sand using medium- and fine-grade sandpaper. Sand edges and paneled areas. Fold sandpaper to access corners and edges. Seal with undercoat and dry.

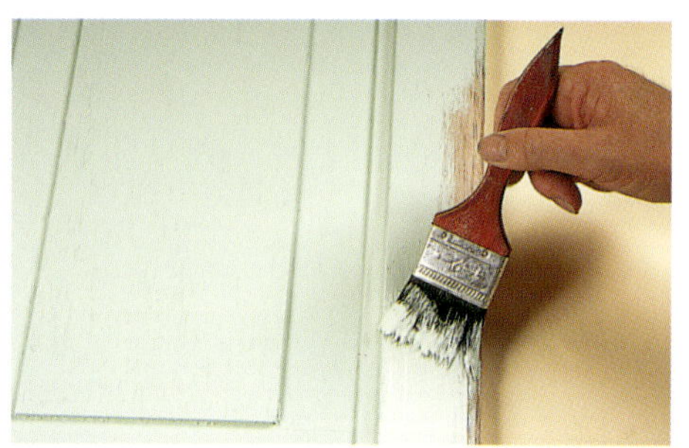

2 Using the bristle basecoat brush apply two coats of turquoise-green eggshell. Allow at least 24 hours drying time between each coat. Carefully resand the surface to a smooth finish using fine sandpaper. Remove all dust.

Variation 1

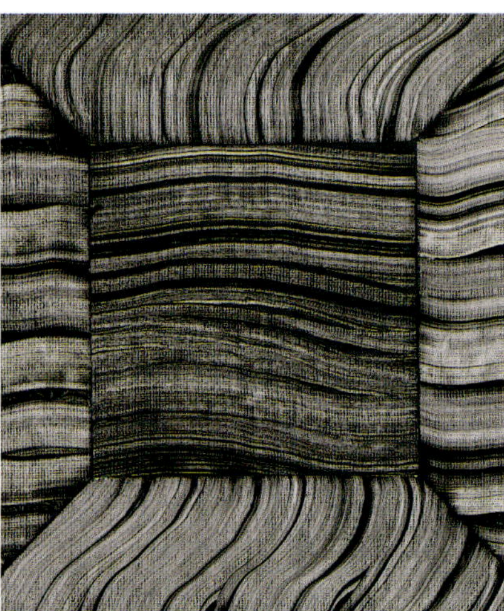

Here, two coats of white eggshell were applied to the surface, each section masked off separately over a period of three days, and a glaze of artists' black oil paint and transparent oil glaze applied. A cardboard comb was dragged through the glaze and the surface allowed to dry. Finally, a coat of oil-based gloss varnish was added for protection.

Variation 2

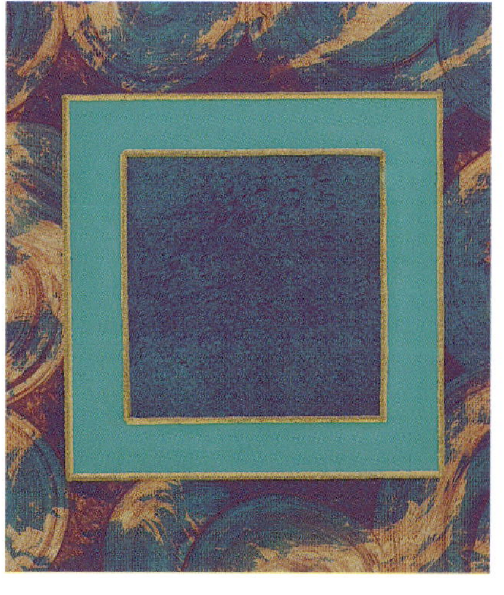

In this rather striking example a basecoat of peacock blue was masked off with the central square using ¾ in. (1.9 cm.) low-tack masking tape. The outside edge was gilded randomly with gold acrylic paint before a glaze of rich purple was grained in the malachite tradition over the top. The central panel was stippled with purple glaze and, once dry, the masking tape was removed and the edges lined with a permanent gold marker.

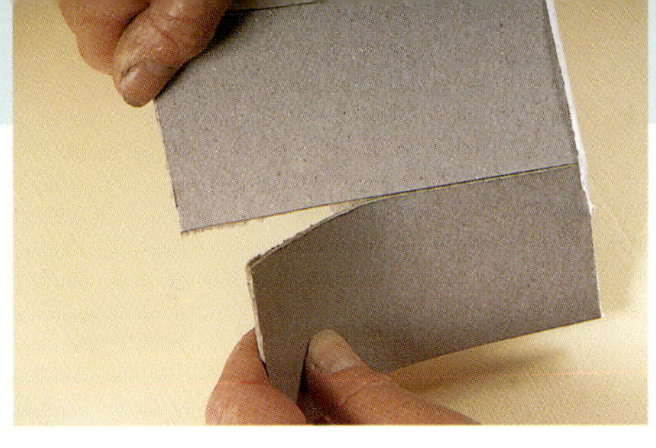

3 Score some pieces of thick (6-ply) card with a craft knife and tear off several strips. The torn uneven edge will be used to create the characteristic graining of malachite and each "comb" may vary, so it is ideal to make up 5 or 6 at a time of different widths.

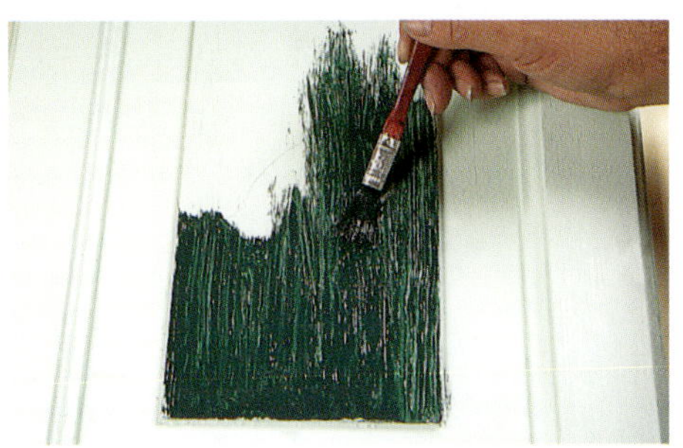

4 In a clean dish mix artists' oil paints in viridian and French ultramarine with a yellow ocher and a little gilp (p. 15) to a double cream consistency. Ensure that oil colors are well mixed to avoid streaks. Using the glazing brush, apply the mixed glaze to the panel. If glaze gets on unwanted areas remove immediately with a soft cloth and a little mineral spirits (white spirit).

5 While the glaze is still wet, dab the surface with a soft, lint-free cloth, as evenly as possible. Use clean cloths as necessary.

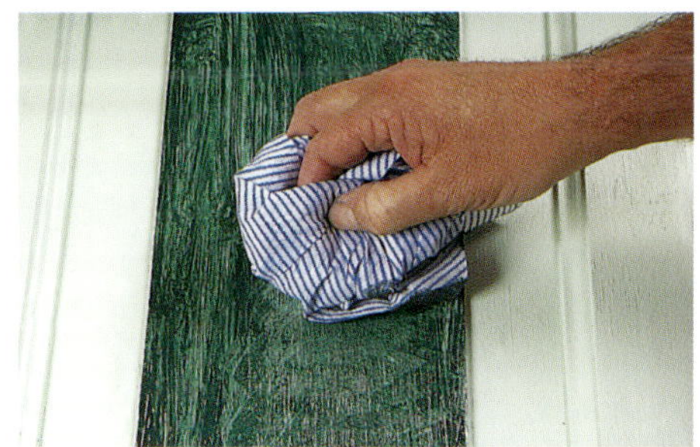

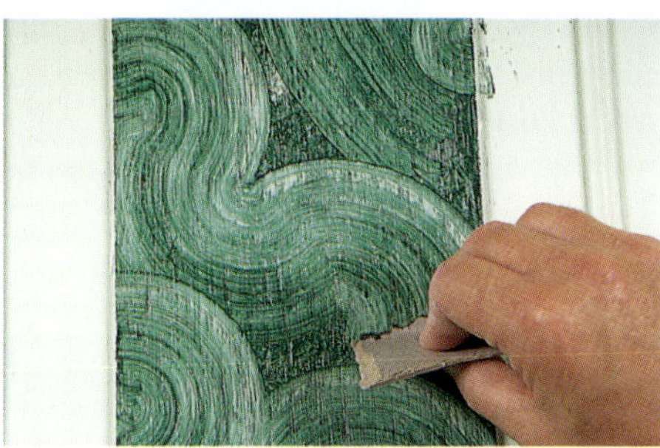

6 Carefully and slowly draw the card comb through the glaze in both wavy and semi-circular patterns. After each use gently wipe the excess glaze from the comb with a clean cloth. Continue across the surface. If the comb becomes too soft, replace it with a new one. Allow to dry.

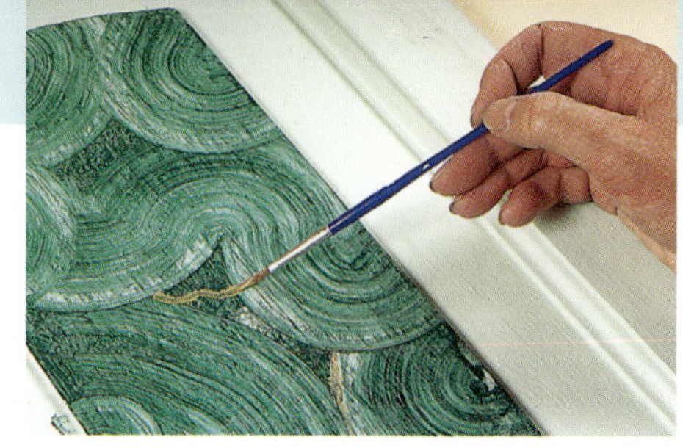

7 With a fine artists' brush and gold acrylic paint, carefully and systematically apply gold veins between the "swirls" of the malachite grain. Be very careful not to overdo the effect. Apply a coat of varnish.

8 The textural nature of malachite creates endless patterns of movement and vitality on any surface (below). Rich and exotic, the intense green combined with gold, and the characteristic grain, will enhance any decor.

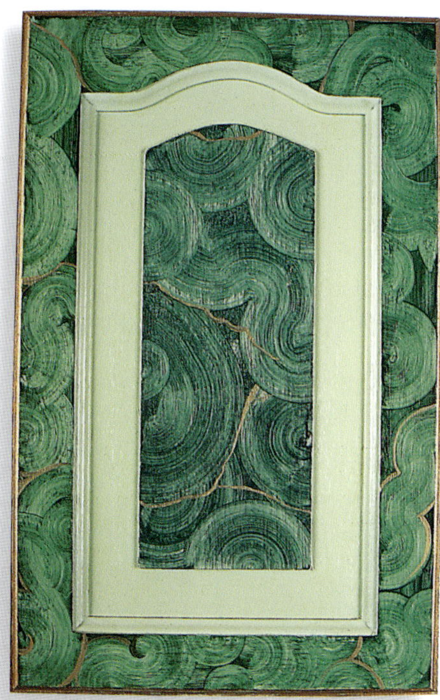

Variation 3

Malachite is a truly luxurious looking stone effect, even when other colorways are applied. Here, the basecoat of black has been covered with a glaze of acrylic gold paint, and dabbed with copper powder. The complete area was stippled, and a cardboard comb was used to create that characteristic malachite graining.

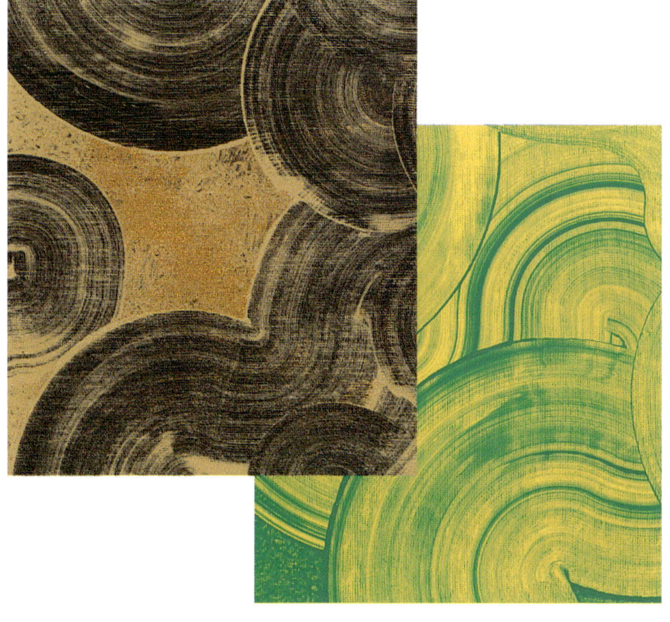

Variation 4

The traditional malachite graining is one of the most eye-catching effects as the colorway here shows (left). The emerald-green glaze was applied and stippled over a basecoat of bright yellow latex (vinyl silk emulsion) before being given the cardboard comb malachite treatment quickly and evenly.

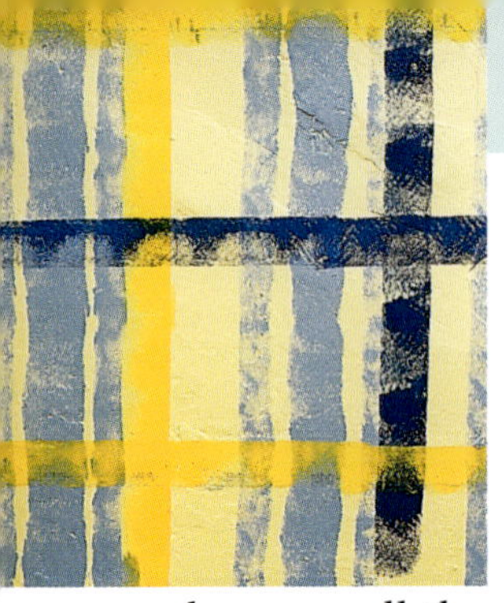

Stripes

Rich plaids or Regency stripes, gingham checks, wavy lines or symmetrical chevrons all these and many other patterns can be created to enhance any room. Of all paint finishes, striping is one that can really make a bold and personal statement. The fresh look of ginghams in blue, greens, and yellows would work well in a kitchen or living room, while in a child's room a fantasy decor can be created.

You will need

Tools

• *2–3 in. (5–7.5 cm.) bristle basecoat brush* • *Chalk* • *Plumb line (or weighted string)* • *Cellulose sponge roller 8–10 in. (20–25 cm.)* • *String* • *Sharp scissors or craft knife* • *Low-tack stencil tape* • *Paint tray* • *Newspaper* • *2 in. (5 cm.) sponge rollers* • *Straight edge (ruler)*

Materials

• *Semigloss latex (vinyl silk emulsion) basecoat* • *Contrasting paint for stripes* • *Varnish (optional)*

Striping is very inexpensive and is suited to most surfaces and any room in the house. The selection of colorways is limitless and can be chosen to complement an existing decor or to create a completely new feel to a room.

Stripes can be created on a background of sponging (see p. 54) or rag-rolling (see p. 52). This technique is ideal for walls, ceilings, furniture, cupboards and floors, and the surface need not be absolutely perfect. All that is required is a little practice using the roller and paint, and away you go!

If any mistakes are made, then because of the semigloss latex (vinyl silk emulsion) basecoat they can be wiped off quickly and reapplied. Also, by following a chalked plumb line, all stripes can be easily applied straight if required. Do not try to work one color stripe over another too quickly; allow each to dry before continuing. As with many paint effects, if you do make mistakes, whether they be color or effect, the damage can be repaired by applying another basecoat of paint.

1 **Prepare the surface (see *Preparation*, p. 18). Apply an undercoat. Allow to dry. Apply two top coats of pale lemon semigloss latex (vinyl silk emulsion). Allow to dry between coats. Measure and chalk in the vertical lines using a plumb line. Note which lines will be of which color. Allow for your chosen spacing plus the width of the roller. Repeat across the entire surface.**

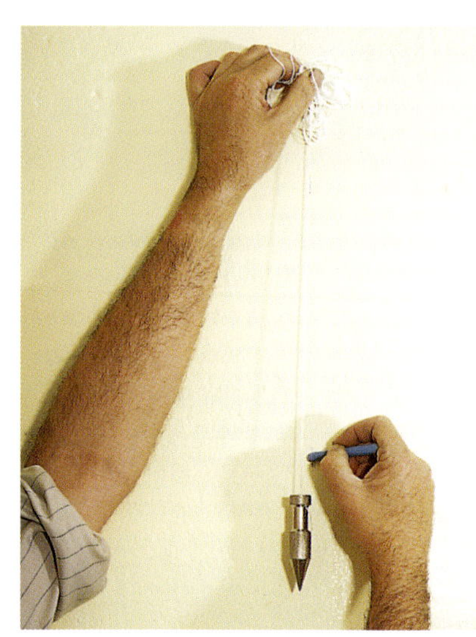

Variation 1

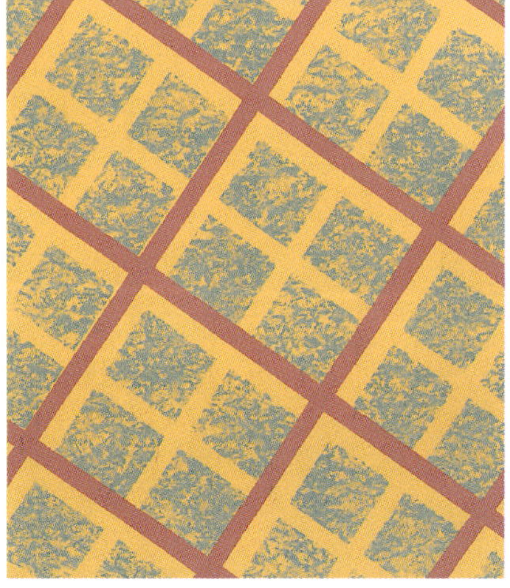

The effect of plaid or tartan has been created here using low-tack masking tape over a basecoat of yellow ocher after first measuring and marking the position of the tape. The entire surface was then sponged with a mid-blue paint and allowed to dry before removing the tape. The finished effect was created by lining the surface with the dusty pink acrylic (see p. 94).

Variation 2

Here, 1 in. (2.5 cm.) and ¼ in. (0.63 cm.) stripes were measured and marked with chalk and low-tack masking tape over a basecoat of apricot. The wide and narrow stripe was then rag-rolled (see p. 52) in mid-blue and the medium stripe painted in solid lemon. When the paint was dry, the tape was removed and the striping process repeated by adding the gold lines in gilt wax.

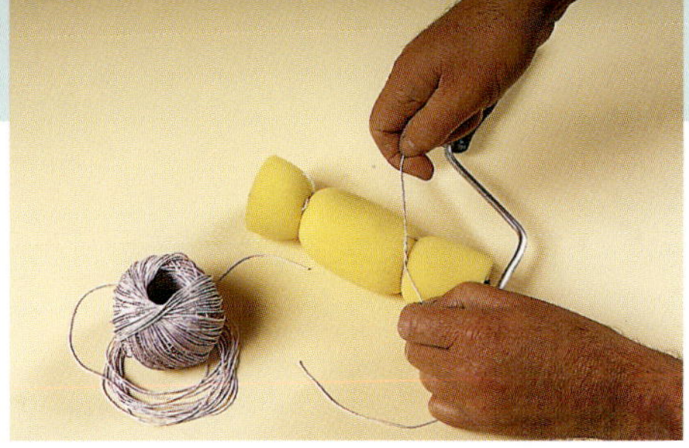

2 Tie the pieces of string around a 10 in. (25 cm.) cellulose sponge roller. Vary the distance between each piece of string to create a random striped pattern. Remove excess pieces of string with sharp scissors or a craft knife without cutting the sponge.

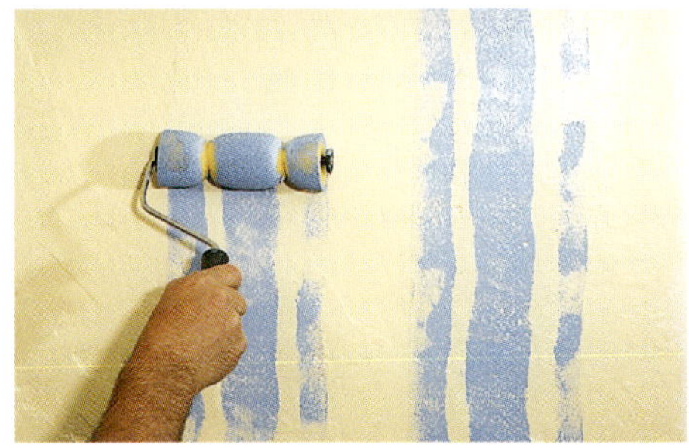

3 Use low-tack tape to seal off any areas around the space to be painted. Pour a little mid-blue, semigloss latex (vinyl silk emulsion) into a paint tray. Dip the roller in the paint. Remove excess paint on clean newspaper. Working from the bottom up, quickly and evenly apply paint following the chalk lines across the surface. Reload the roller as and when necessary. Allow to dry.

4 With a 2 in. (5 cm.) sponge roller, apply some dark blue semigloss latex (vinyl silk emulsion) as in step 3. Repeat the pattern across the surface as required. Let dry. Repeat, but this time using a clean 2 in. (5 cm.) roller and some bright yellow latex (emulsion). Dry.

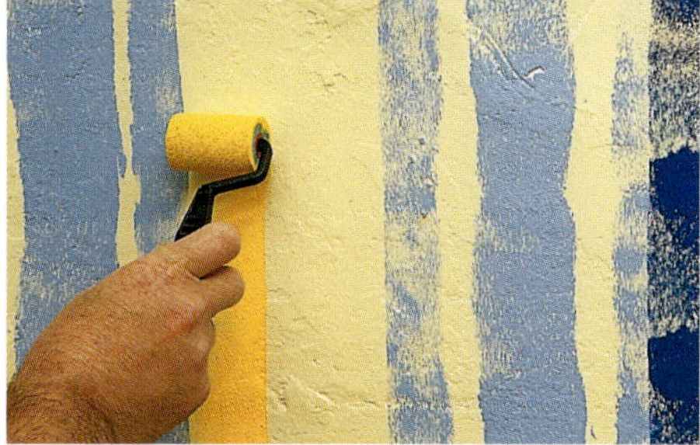

5 Measure and mark the horizontal lines. Using a straight edge (ruler), chalk in all the horizontal lines. Note which lines will be of which color. Ensure that all measurements are correct and that the horizontal lines are level.

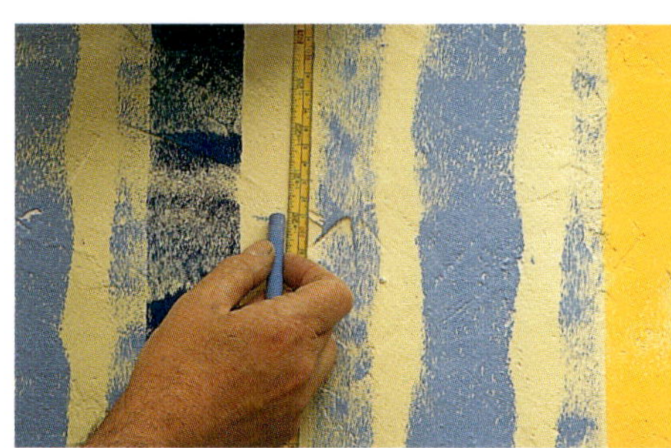

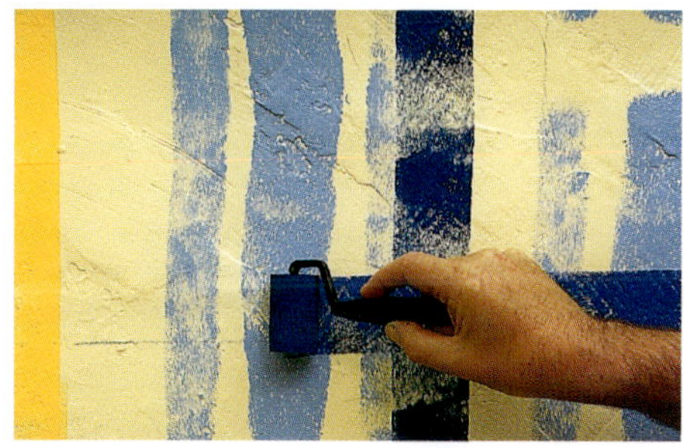

6 With a 2 in. (5 cm.) cellulose sponge roller carefully paint along the horizontal chalk lines. Repeat as necessary and allow to dry. Apply the yellow paint following the same instructions. Allow to dry. Apply suitable varnish for protection if required.

7 The colors chosen here have created a fresh and striking look suitable for a modern interior (below). By varying colorways and types of stripe, the look can be elegant and suited to a formal decor.

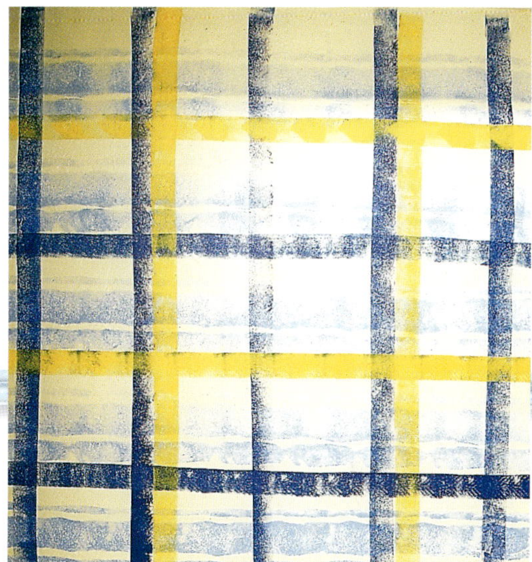

Variation 3

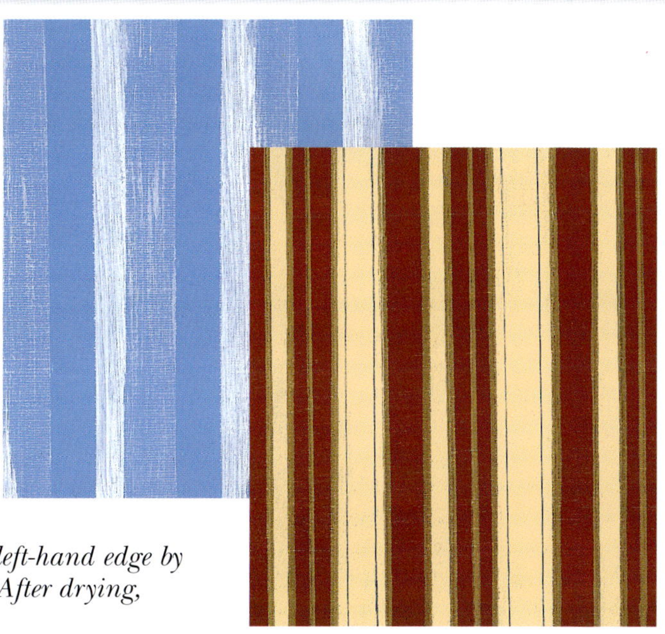

A very fresh and pleasing look has been created here using white over a basecoat of medium blue. The stripes were measured and masked off with ¾ in. (1.9 cm.) low-tack masking tape and the entire surface dry-brushed with the white latex (emulsion). As the paint dried, it was "intensified" at the left-hand edge by constant over-brushing. After drying, the tape was removed.

Variation 4

Stripes can look very simple, but by using the same taping technique a more formal Regency look (left) can be created. A basecoat of crimson was left to dry then taped with ¾ in. (1.9 cm.) low-tack tape. The cream was painted over the whole surface and left to dry. The gold and black stripes were added using a fine black permanent pen, and a medium gold permanent pen with a straight edge (ruler).

In context

The crisp edges and the strong definition of the effects used in these gallery examples serve to complete each of the designers schemes. The three painting effects of lining, malachite and stripes have been used to give height and solidity to otherwise rather plain areas. The results are extremely chic, and also create totally different moods, from the utmost simplicity to one of severe and stylish elegance.

Lining

▶ Simple door in entrance hall

By using the two colors of cream and blue, together with a little raw umber, the shading of this very plain door has been lifted by the use of simple lining in the four panels. The proportions are perfect and the colorwashed walls have completed the effect by drawing the focus of attention into the overall ambience in a very subtle way.

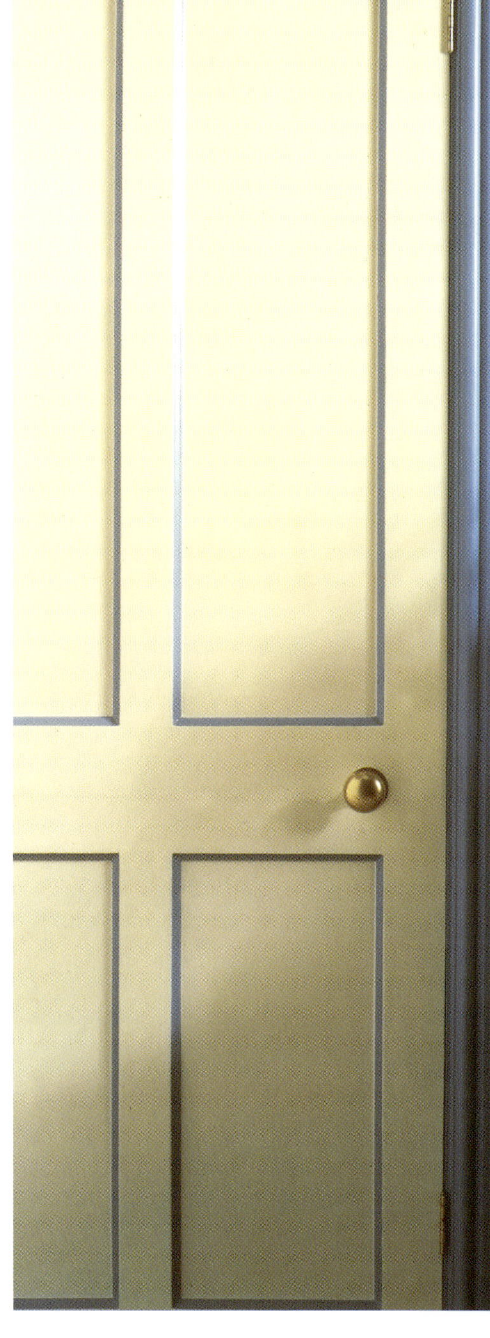

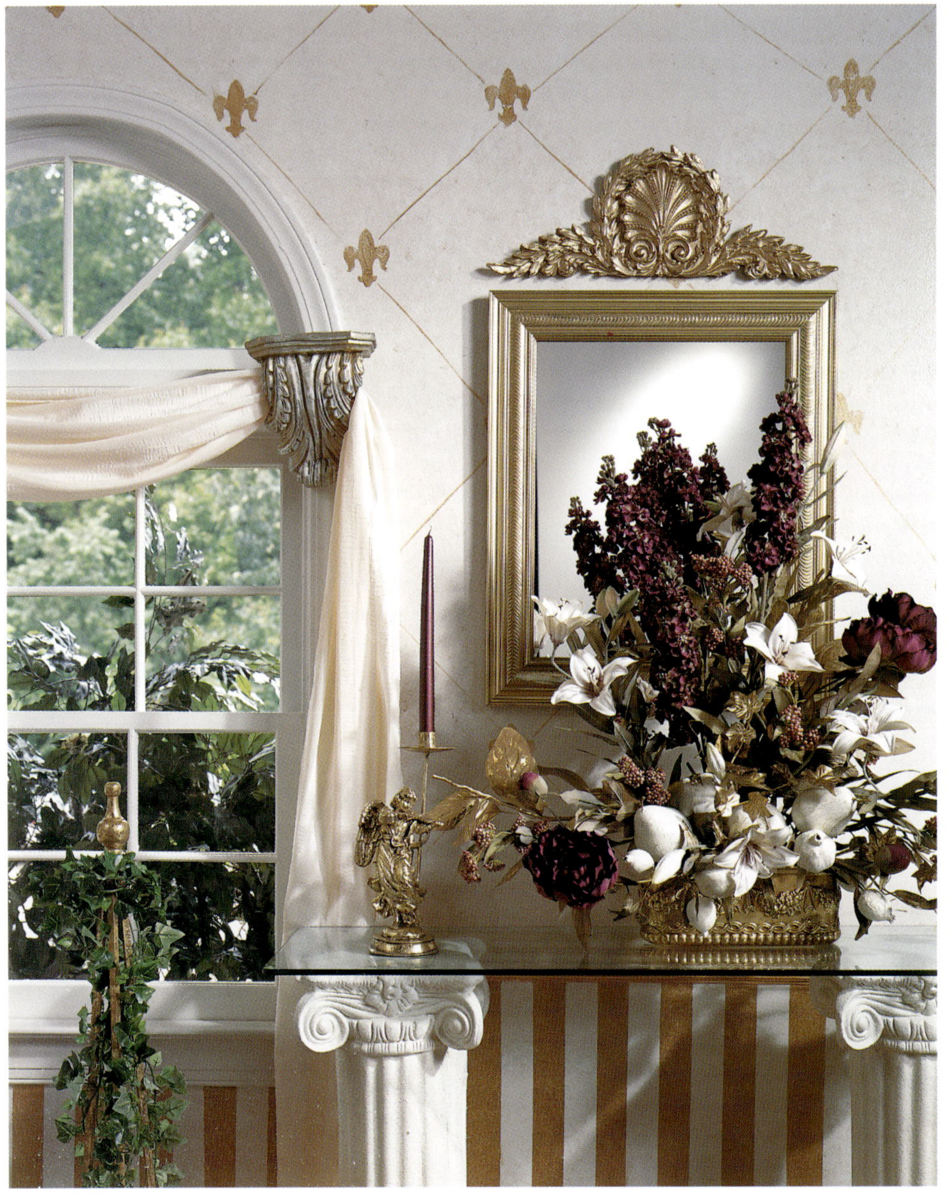

Lining

◀ Elegant drawing room

The use of very simple gold lining, together with fleur-de-lys stamping on the wall has made this entire room much more formally attractive. Light sponging on the wall has added both interest and depth, and the hand-painted stripes below the dado rail accentuate the elegant proportions of the room setting.

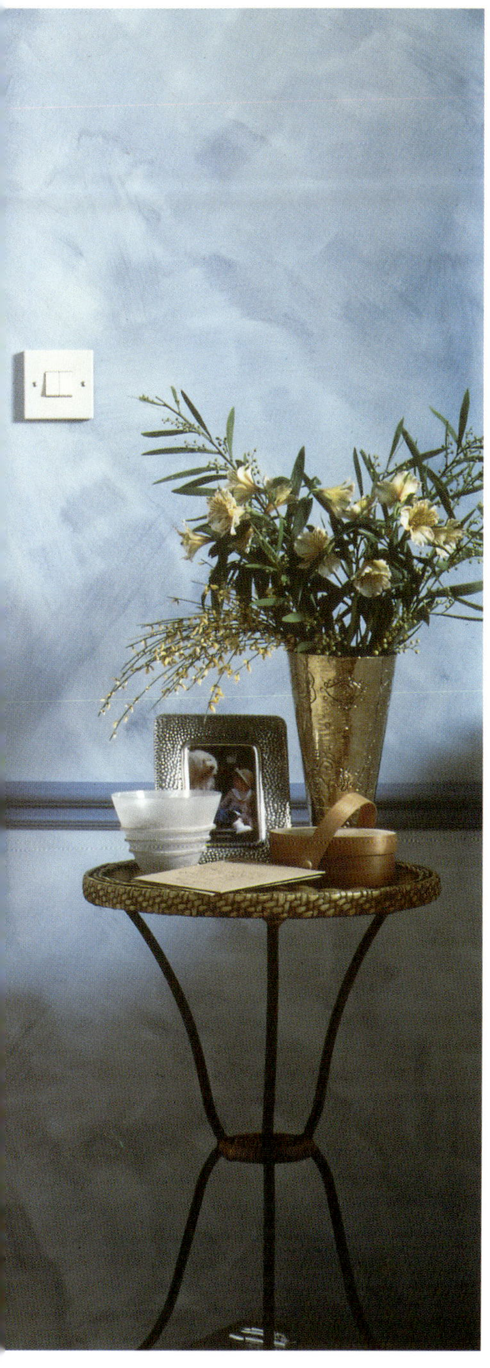

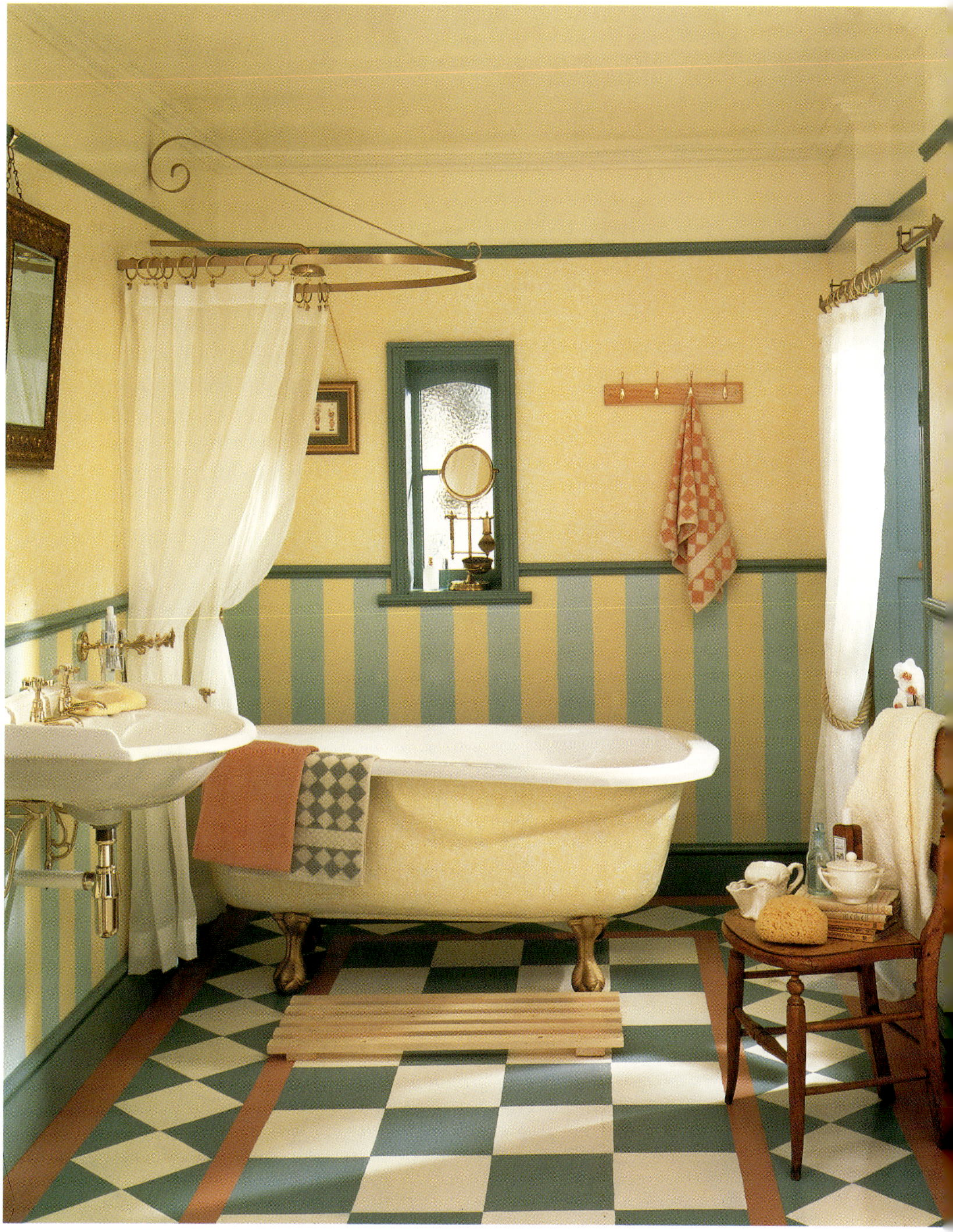

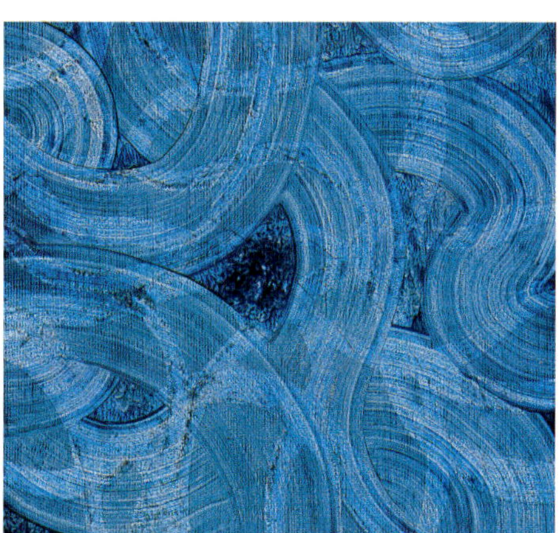

Malachite

◀ Panel for cupboard doors

Although the true malachite colors are blue and green, our gallery example shows a very simple yet striking combination of blue over silver that creates a shimmering depth on an otherwise flat surface area.

Stripes

▲ Bathroom

This beautifully coordinated and roomy bathroom has been given extra height by adding vertical stripes to the wall below the dado rail. Rag rolled walls and an extremely attractive painted floor add a little more to the feeling of luxury.

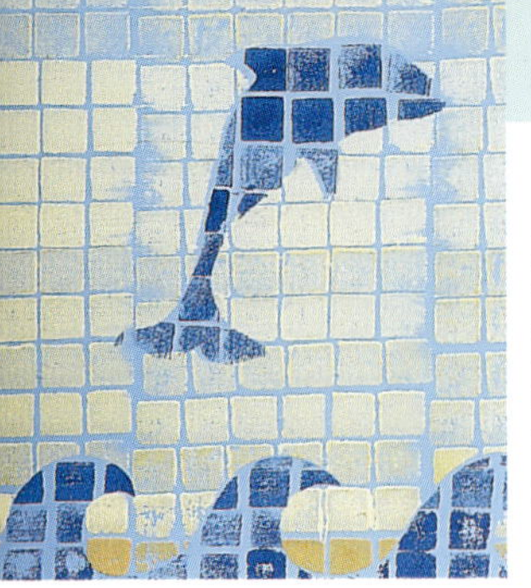

Mosaic

Many beautiful and intricate mosaics have been discovered among the ruins of ancient cities in countries such as India, Italy and Greece. They are very expensive to produce from the semi-precious stones, marble and glass that were originally used, but now it is possible to achieve the same effect using paint.

Creating exotic and individual decorative schemes in mosaic effects is, with practice, within reach of most decorators. The effect is ideal for kitchens and bathrooms, where it can be applied to walls, furniture and floors. Countertops and tables also look very good when decorated in this way.

Mosaic is an inexpensive technique and allows for an imaginative use of color. It can look quite beautiful in period and modern settings, and mixes well with old and new accessories. It is best to employ this technique where mosaic could possibly be used in reality, although this is, of course, a personal choice.

As most of the equipment is improvised, a little artistic ability is an advantage. Do not work too quickly, prepare properly and sketch the finished piece first. Mistakes will probably be as a result of the misplacement of stencils, or too much paint, and can be removed with a damp cloth or painted out.

You will need

Tools

• *2–3 in. (5–7.5 cm.) bristle basecoat brush* • *½ in. (1.3 cm.) bristle brush* • *Permanent marker pen* • *Stencil card (oiled manila card)* • *Chalk* • *Craft knife* • *Foam-backed carpet or kitchen cloth* • *Straight edge (ruler)* • *Sharp scissors* • *Wood block (for fixing carpet squares)*

Materials

• *Semigloss latex (vinyl silk emulsion)* • *Appropriate varnish* • *Waterproof PVA glue* • *Spray adhesive* • *Permanent marker pen* • *Pale cream and navy latex (emulsion)*

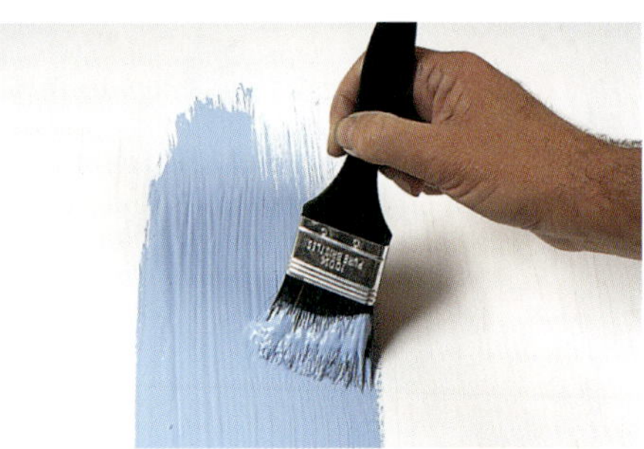

1 Prepare the surface (see *Preparation*, p. 18). Apply an undercoat. Dry. With a 2–3 in (5–7.5 cm) bristle brush apply two coats of pale blue semigloss latex (vinyl silk emulsion). Dry between coats before starting the next step.

2 With a permanent marker pen draw your design onto a sheet of stencil card (oiled manila board). With a sharp craft knife, cut out the design. Keep the cut-out shapes and the piece of card.

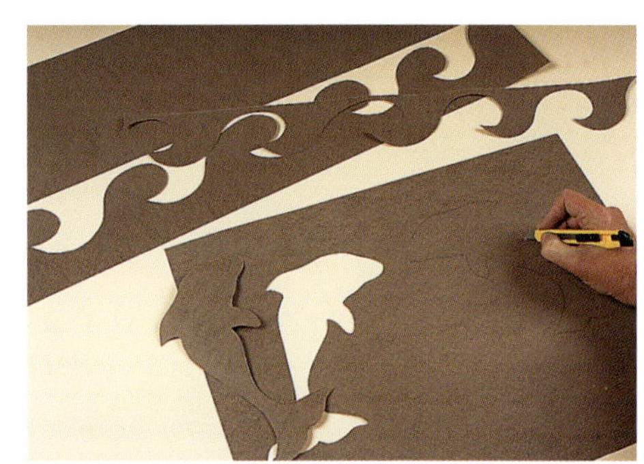

Variation 1

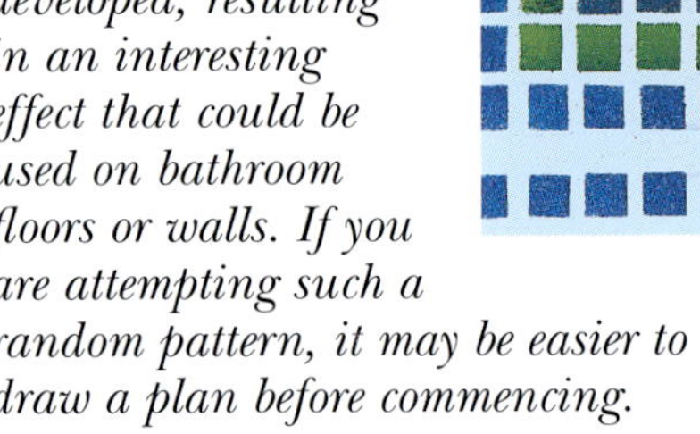

Producing a mosaic finish from paints is fun and quite straightforward. Here, the spacing and colorways were chosen as the design developed, resulting in an interesting effect that could be used on bathroom floors or walls. If you are attempting such a random pattern, it may be easier to draw a plan before commencing.

Variation 2

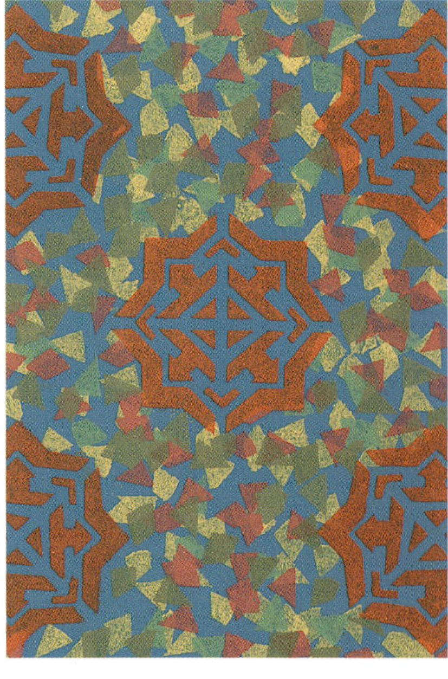

This stencil was applied over a background of two coats of cornflower blue semigloss latex (vinyl silk emulsion). The stencil was made from a quilting pattern and small triangles cut from stencil card. The stencil was painted with orange, lemon, olive green, dark pink and mid-green stencil paints.

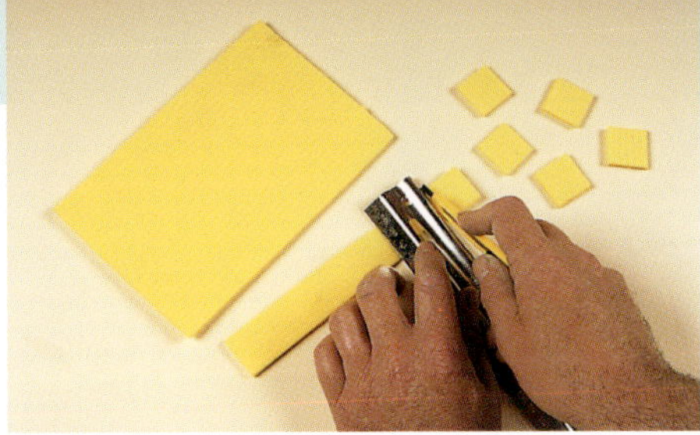

3 **Cut out 1 in. (2.5 cm.) squares of foam kitchen cloth, or foam-backed carpet or squares of cut-out carpet (see *Stamping*, p. 108) using a craft knife and a metal straight edge (ruler) or some sharp scissors.**

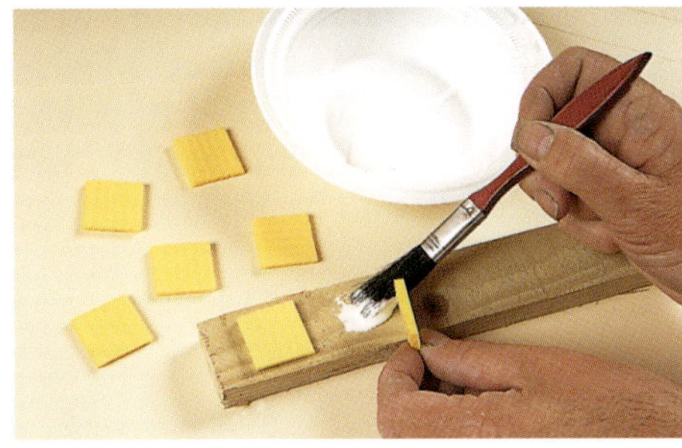

4 **Cut some lengths of wood (here we have used ready available 2 x 1 in. [5 x 2.5 cm.] planed softwood) into 2 in. (5 cm.), 4 in. (10 cm.) and 8 in. (20 cm.) lengths. With a ½ in. (1.3 cm.) bristle brush and some PVA glue place the squares of foam along the length of the pieces of wood. Space the foam pieces evenly. Ideally you should produce a single pad stamp, a double pad stamp, and a six pad stamp.**

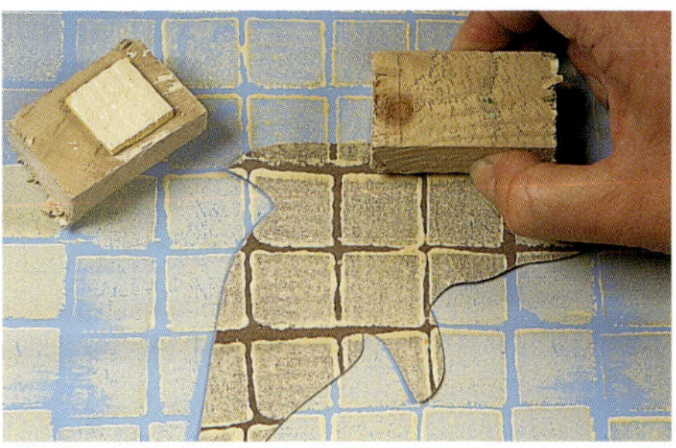

5 **Apply a little spray adhesive to the back of the cut-out stencils and place in position. Apply some pale cream latex (emulsion) to the squares using the block you find easiest to control (see *Stamping*, p. 108). Press the pads across the entire surface, background and stencils. To create stripes, change the paint color. Allow to dry.**

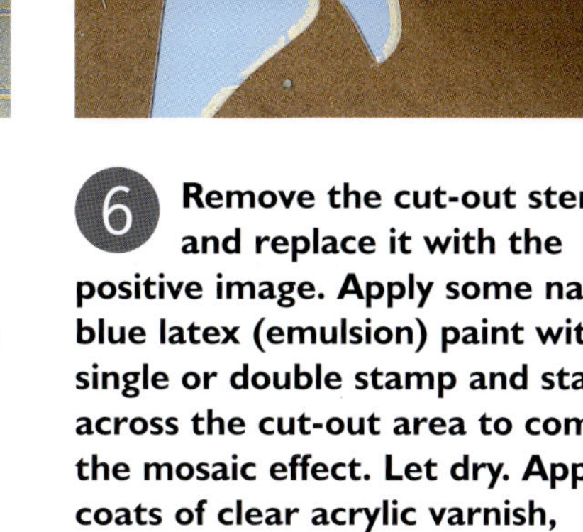

6 **Remove the cut-out stencil and replace it with the positive image. Apply some navy blue latex (emulsion) paint with the single or double stamp and stamp across the cut-out area to complete the mosaic effect. Let dry. Apply two coats of clear acrylic varnish, waterproof and non-yellowing.**

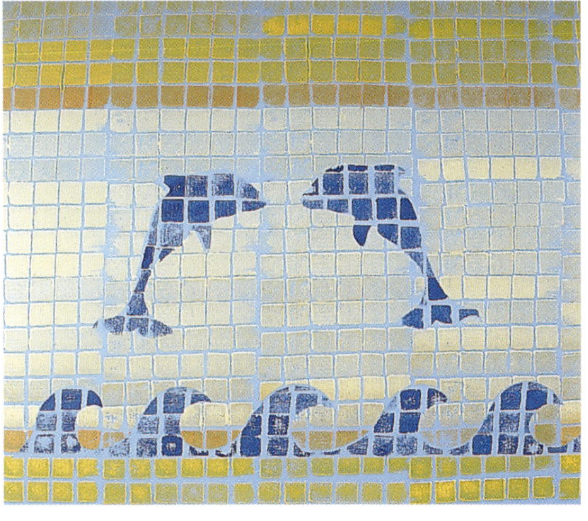

7 **The colors and wonders of the ocean have been recreated here in a timeless, traditional and interesting way. The mosaic effect adds that little bit of extra magic to this bathroom wall. Fun and challenging to do, this technique can be applied to any surface, and with a little patience superb professional results can be achieved.**

Variation 3

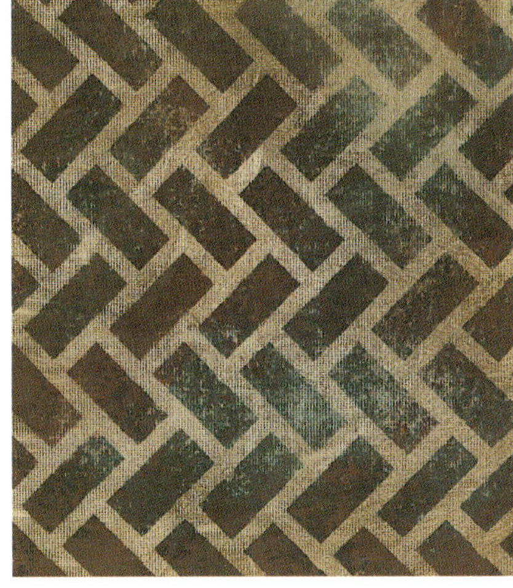

Low-tack tape was stuck down in lines at 90 degree angles to create the look of old brick paths. A coat of pale cream latex (emulsion) was used. Artists' acrylic paint in terracotta and mid-blue was sponged over (see p. 54) separately but while still wet. When dry, the tape was removed and the surface colorwashed in moss-green acrylic paint. This was left to dry and then sanded. Two coats of flat (matte) acrylic varnish were applied.

Variation 4

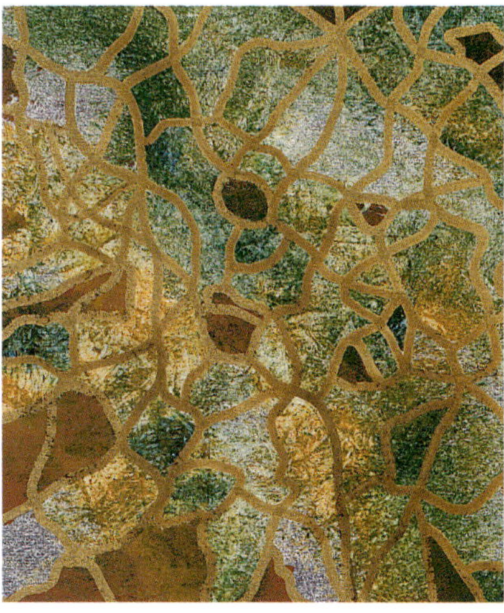

Here, random patches of aluminum leaf (see p. 134) have been applied over a deep terracotta eggshell basecoat. Next, yellow ocher and French ultramarine blue artists' oil paint, mixed with a little transparent oil glaze, was stippled (see p. 30) onto the surface and allowed to dry. The crazy paving effect was drawn in with a medium gold, permanent marking pen and sealed with spray sealant.

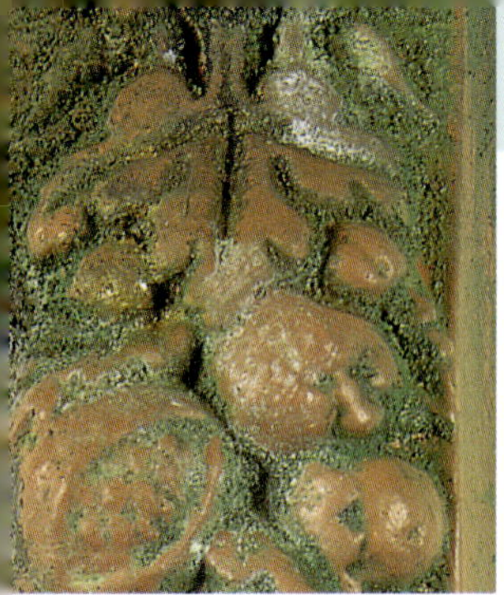

The results of many years' exposure to the elements can lend age to natural terracotta, giving it a beauty that conjures up visions of tiled floors in country kitchens, or the beauty and timelessness of some historic homes.

Aged terracotta

Terracotta is well suited to small decorative and architectural accessories such as corbels, ceiling rosettes (roses), lampbases, picture frames and boxes, and can also be applied to larger areas such as floors. It will work better in kitchens, bathrooms, greenhouses (conservatories) and family rooms rather than the more formal sitting-rooms or bedrooms.

A professional result is moderately inexpensive to achieve and requires only practice in glaze manipulation. To avoid mistakes, keep to the accepted colors and follow all the manufacturer's instructions for the materials used. Oil glazes have an extended working time of about 30 minutes, and can be wiped off with a cloth and mineral spirits (white spirit) and the glaze reapplied if mistakes happen. However, mistakes would probably enhance the aged appearance, and may not need to be removed. The chances are they will end up looking good!

You will need

Tools

• 1 in. (2.5 cm.) bristle basecoat brush • Clean plate • Lint-free cloth or paper (kitchen) towel • ½–1 in. (1.2–2.5 cm.) bristle stippling brush

Materials

• Basecoat in pale terracotta eggshell • Cream semigloss latex (vinyl silk emulsion) • Transparent oil glaze • Artists' oils in viridian and yellow ocher • Silver sand or sawdust • Mineral spirits (white spirit)

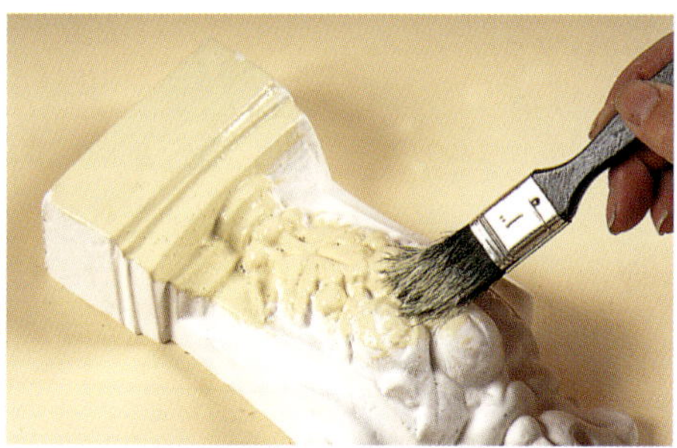

1 Make sure the plaster is dry. Seal the surface with diluted semigloss latex (vinyl silk emulsion) diluted to a light cream consistency. Allow to dry. Any chips or flaws in the surface of the plaster will enhance the final appearance.

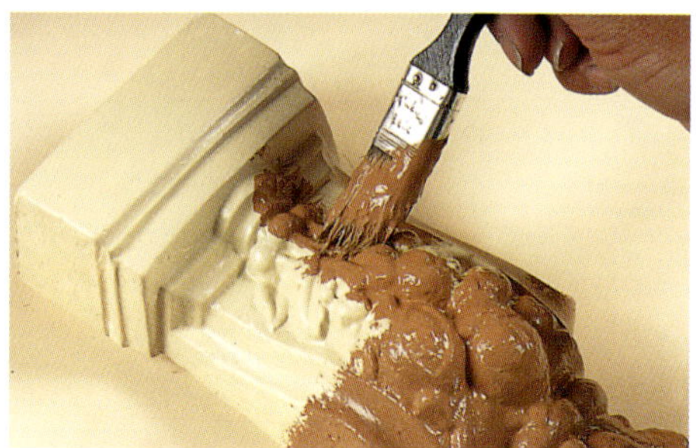

2 Using a 1 in. (2.5 cm.) bristle basecoat brush apply two coats of pale terracotta eggshell to the surface. Dry between coats. Some of the basecoat can show through if desired, to give a variation in the final surface color.

Variation 1

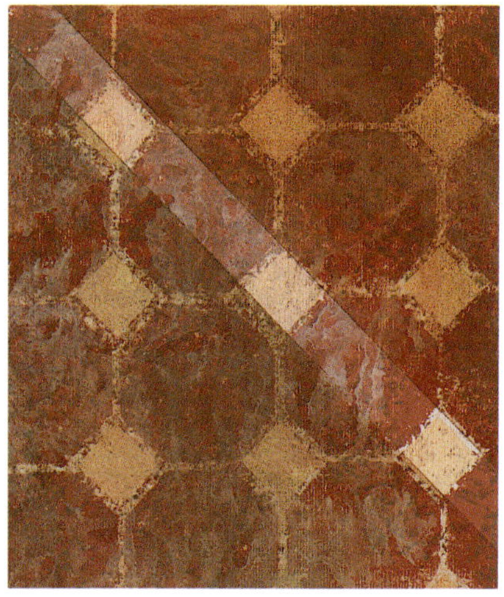

Stenciling (see p. 78), colorwashing (see p. 60) and antiquing (see p. 32) have been combined to create this quarry-tile effect floor. Over the basecoat of cream were stenciled the "octagonal" tiles in dark terracotta, which were "filled in" with a smaller square stencil using cream acrylic paint. Once dry, colorwashing glazes of white and olive green were added. It was finished by waxing with clear wax tinted with burnt umber powder color.

Variation 2

The surface here was originally bright orange semigloss latex (vinyl silk emulsion). Over this was colorwashed (see p. 60) a glaze of moss-green. As the paint was drying the surface was wiped with a soft, lint-free cloth. After the surface had dried it was lightly spattered (see p. 72) with moss-green paint followed by a light spattering of black acrylic paint.

3 On a clean plate, mix some transparent oil glaze with some artists' viridian oil paint tinted with a little yellow ocher. You may need to add a little mineral spirits (white spirit) to make a creamy consistency. Add a little sand or sawdust to the mixture to create texture.

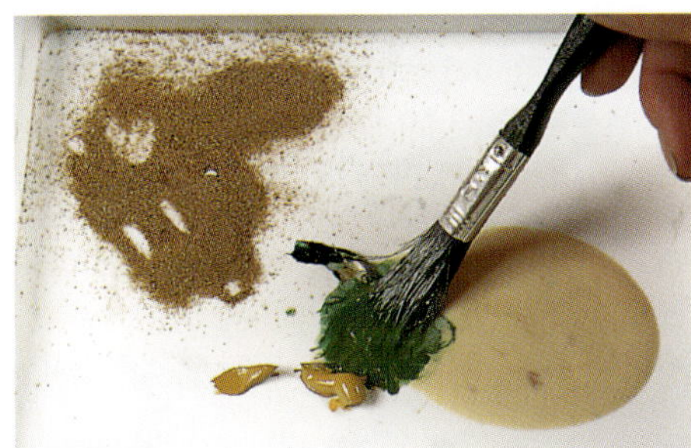

4 Using a ½–1 in. (1.3–2.5 cm.) bristle brush, stipple the glaze over the surface ensuring that it totally covers all the awkward areas (see p. 30).

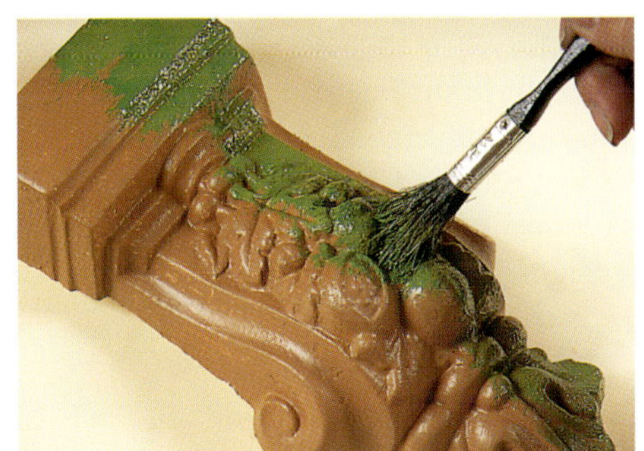

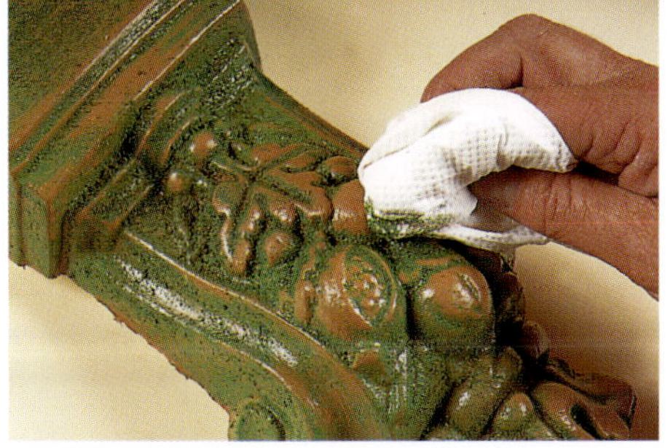

5 Allow the glaze to become tacky (this should take about 5 to 10 minutes) then wipe the surface with a clean, lint-free cloth or paper towel. Replace the cloth or towel often as you remove excess glaze. Keep the build-up of glaze in the carved areas and highlight the raised areas. Dry.

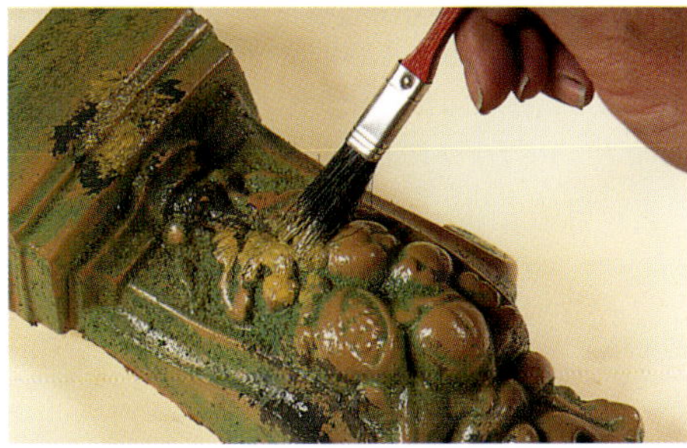

6 Mix a little yellow ocher with some mineral spirits (white spirit) and brush lightly into any recessed areas using a ½ in. (1.3 cm.) bristle brush. Be careful not to overdo it as the entire look can be destroyed by overworking the colors.

7 This very simple plaster corbel has been given a finish that once could only have been achieved from years of exposure to the effects of rain and sun. Moldings, cupboard doors, floors and walls can all be given this aged romantic feel quickly and effectively.

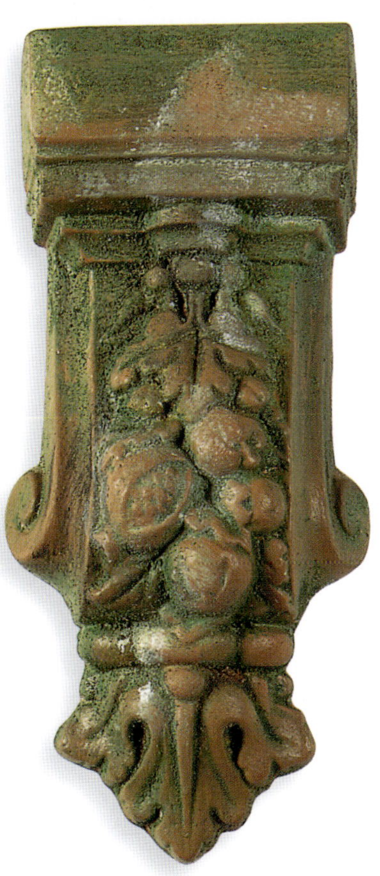

Variation 3

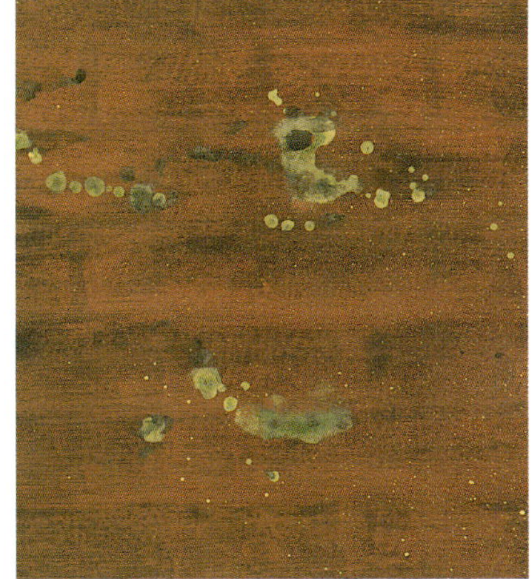

This surface was painted with cream semigloss latex and left to dry. A cellulose sponge was cut into a brick shape, covered in PVA glue and applied in a wall pattern. When dry, terracotta latex was applied and left to dry. Olive green acrylic paint was then sponged over the surface. When dry, a cream and a green acrylic paint were diluted and spattered (see p. 72) onto the surface. After drying it was sealed with flat varnish.

Variation 4

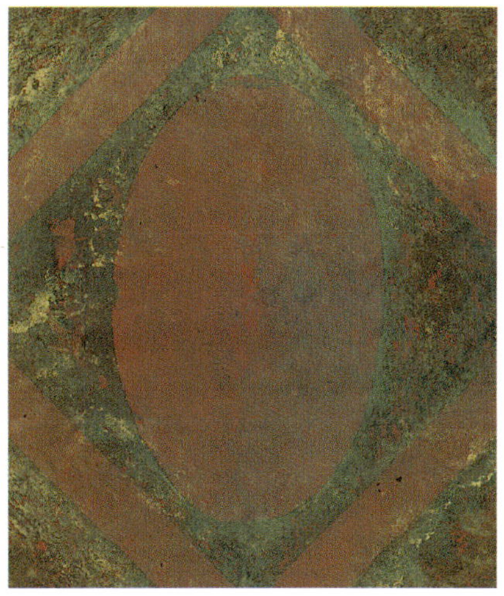

Two coats of deep terracotta semigloss latex (vinyl silk emulsion) were applied and left to dry. The panel was masked with low-tack tape, and an oval cut from stencil card was positioned with spray adhesive. Crackleglaze was applied and left to go tacky before deep moss-green and deep cream latex were sponged (see p. 54) onto the surface. The tape was removed before applying a sponging of the pure color. When dry, it was varnished.

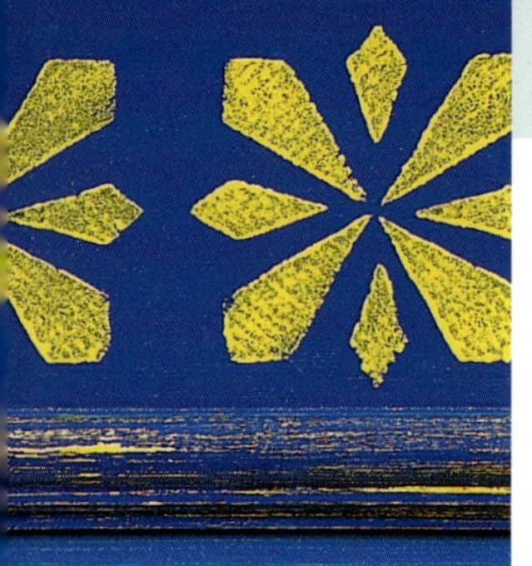

Stamping, as an effect, can produce a wide range of eye-catching results, and when used in conjunction with a technique such as colorwashing (see p. 60), it can create a relaxing and peaceful interior. Because you make your own designs, you can be as imaginative as you like, to create a truly unique and individual finish.

Stamping

Stamping is a very inexpensive technique, requiring only a little time and practice to produce many different patterns and effects. Stamping can be applied to any flat surface, the most ideal surfaces being walls, ceilings and floors. Smaller items such as tables, fitted units and decorative items such as boxes and lampshades can all be used as a surface for stamping. Avoid molded and shaped surfaces.

The choice of colors you choose is endless, as you are limited only by your imagination, and in this case, experimentation is the keyword. Once you have planned out and marked the positions of your stamp, completing a room can take comparatively little time, but remember that being too hasty can result in mistakes.

The most common pitfall is to use too much paint, creating an uneven and splotchy effect. By removing excess paint with some paper (kitchen) towel, or applying just enough paint, these mistakes are easily overcome.

To achieve perfect results, practice on some blank paper each time you reload the stamp with paint. If you happen to make a mistake, quickly wipe off the freshly stamped pattern and restamp.

You will need

Tools

• *Your design* • *Fine permanent marking pen* • *Straight edge (ruler)* • *Sharp scissors or craft knife* • *Sharp pencil* • *Foam-backed carpet* • *Wood block (for mounting design)* • *½ in. (1.2 cm.) brush* • *½ in. (1.2 cm.) bristle brush* • *Clean paper*

Materials

• *Waterproof glue* • *Acrylic paint*

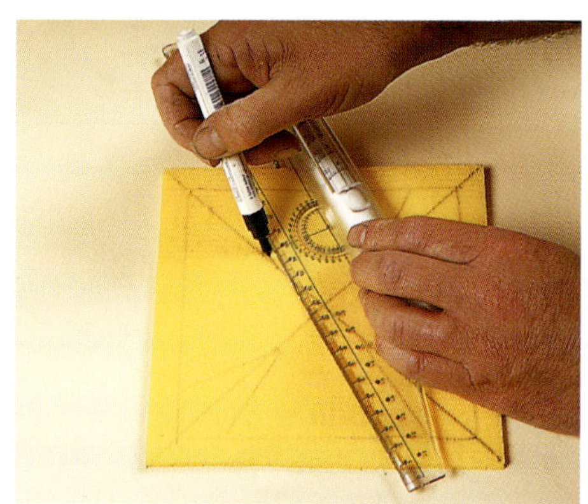

1 With a fine permanent marking pen and a ruler, transfer your chosen design to a piece of foam-backed carpet. Make the outside measurements of the design slightly smaller than the block of wood to be used in step 4.

Variation 1

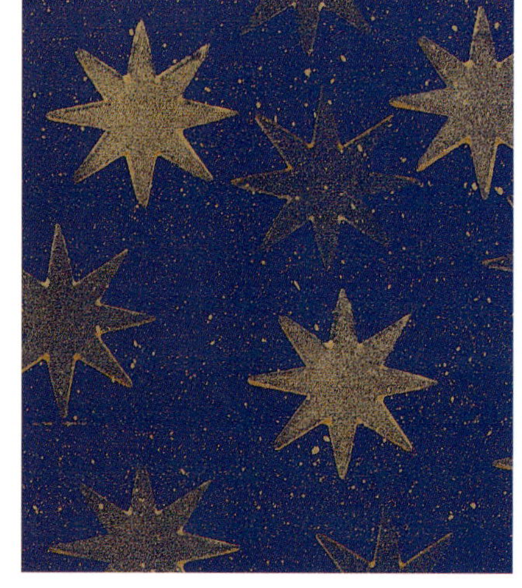

Here a romantic star-lit sky has been created from a store-bought star stamp. Acrylic gold paint was applied to the rubber star stamp, which was stamped once on paper to remove excess paint and then stamped 3 to 4 times on the basecoat of dark blue. The magical finish was completed by spattering (see p. 72) the entire surface with gold acrylic paint.

Variation 2

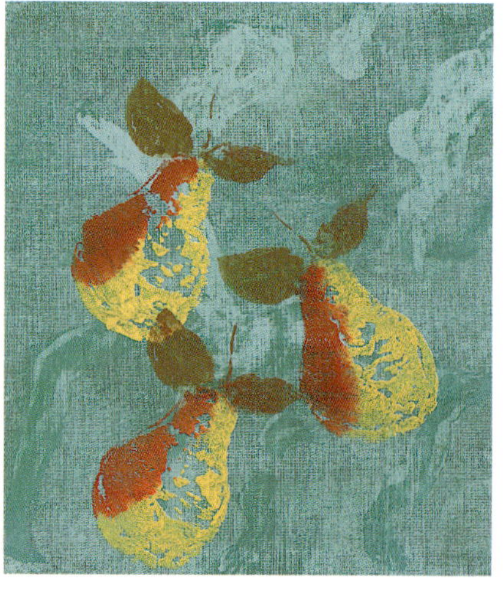

Here, a pale turquoise basecoat of semigloss latex (vinyl silk emulsion) was colorwashed (see p. 60) with a darker turquoise latex. When dry, dabs of paint were applied and left to dry then wiped off with a damp scouring pad. A potato was cut in half and a pear shape cut out. (Remove area around shape so it stands out.) Artists' acrylic paint was applied to the shape, excess paint removed, then it was stamped onto the panel and sealed.

2 With a sharp pair of scissors or a craft knife, slowly and carefully cut out all the shapes that will be printed in the final design. Throw away unwanted pieces to avoid confusion. Make sure that each shape of the design is cut out as evenly as possible.

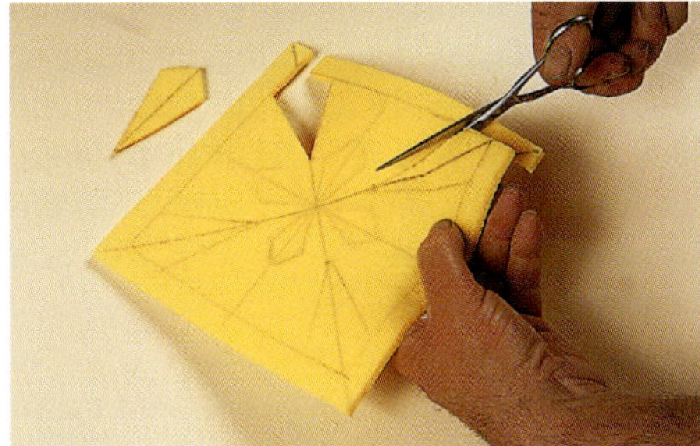

3 With the ruler and a sharp pencil, draw the design onto a smooth block of wood or medium density fiberboard. Make sure to keep the outside measurements the same as for step 1.

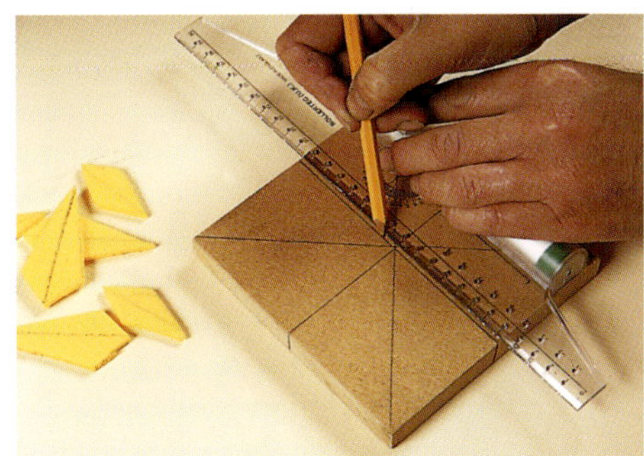

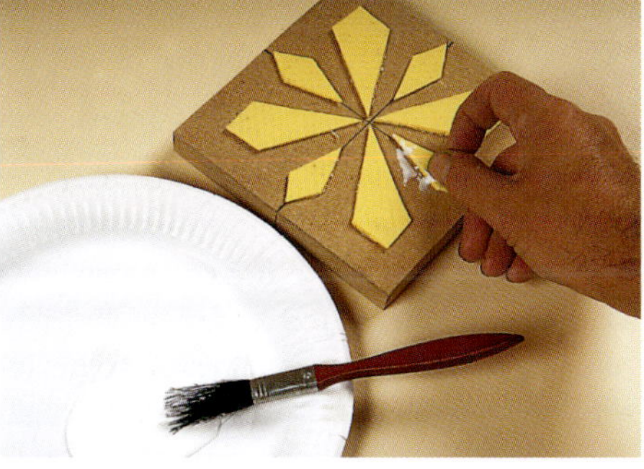

4 With a ½ in. (1.2 cm.) brush and some waterproof glue, fix the foam shapes onto the design on the wood block. Apply the glue to the outer edges of the foam pieces to avoid curling. Carefully position each section and watch that no sliding occurs before the glue has time to dry.

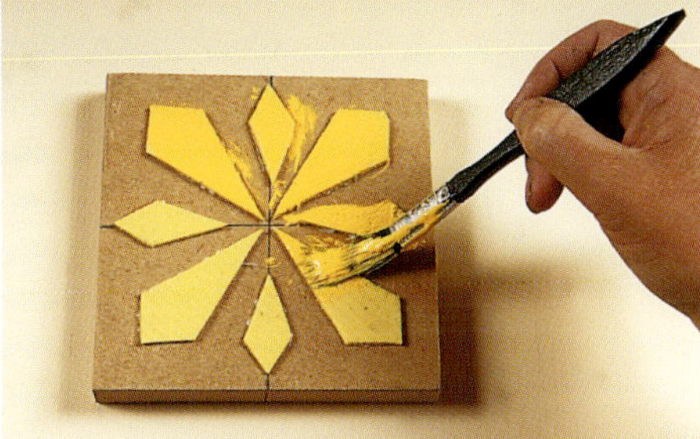

5 With a ½ in. (1.2 cm.) bristle brush, cover the surface of the printing block with paint. Apply the paint evenly and clean-up any runs with a cloth.

6 Stamp the block onto clean paper to remove excess paint before starting. Slowly and evenly press the block onto the surface. Be firm but do not apply excess pressure or this will cause the paint to squeeze out over the edges of the pattern. Remove the block quickly and evenly. Continue as required.

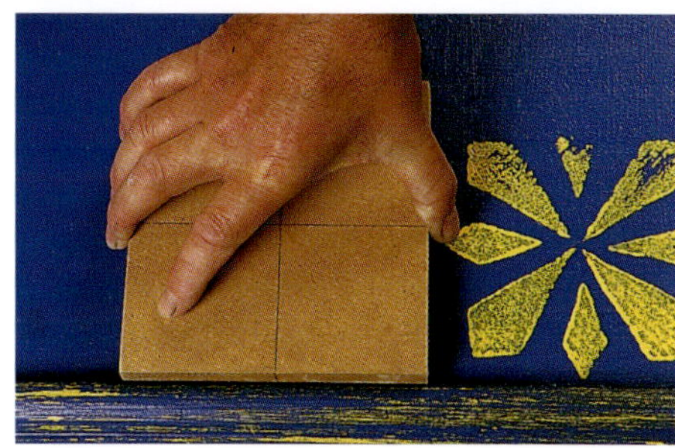

7 Stamping (below), whether using a store-bought design or making your own, allows you to create a look that is totally individual. Here the vivid yellow has transformed this wall. Stamps are fun to create and enjoyable to experiment with and stamping is only limited by your imagination.

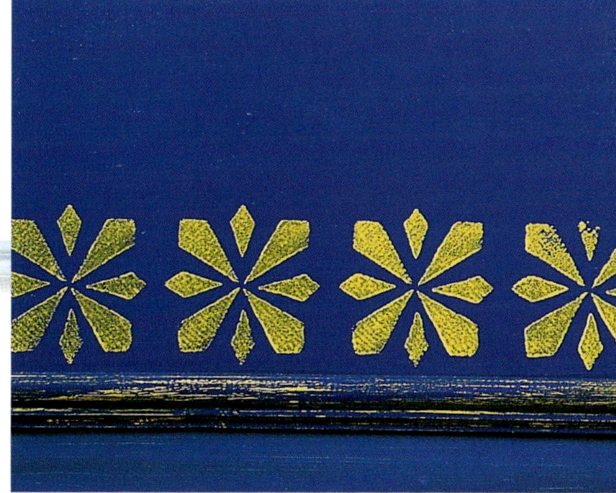

Variation 3

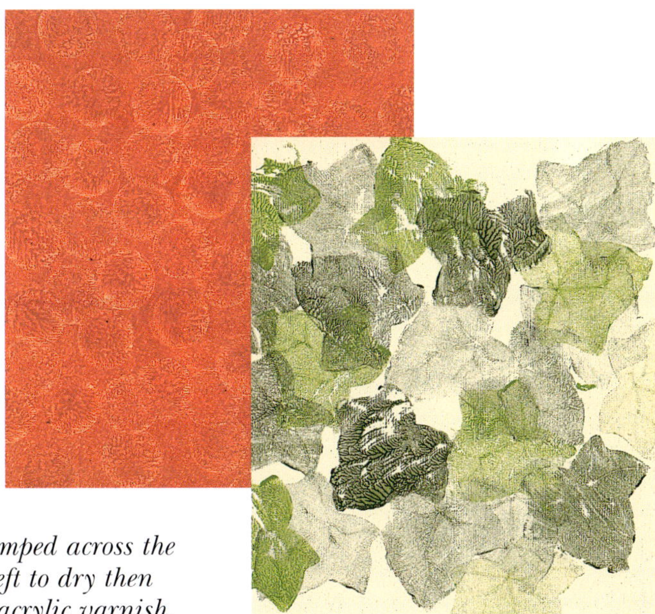

Two coats of apricot semigloss latex (vinyl silk emulsion)were applied and left to dry. A glaze of deep dusty pink artists' acrylic was mixed (1 part paint to 4 parts glaze) and used to stipple (see p. 30) away all brushstrokes. While still wet, the impression of a plastic bottle top was stamped across the surface. The glaze was left to dry then sealed with two coats of acrylic varnish.

Variation 4

Here, a basecoat of two layers of off-white semigloss latex (vinyl silk emulsion) was applied. When dry, a dark green glaze (1 part acrylic paint to 3 parts acrylic glaze) was applied using a store-bought rubber, vine leaf stamp. This was repeated using a bright green glaze. A final protective layer of acrylic varnish was applied.

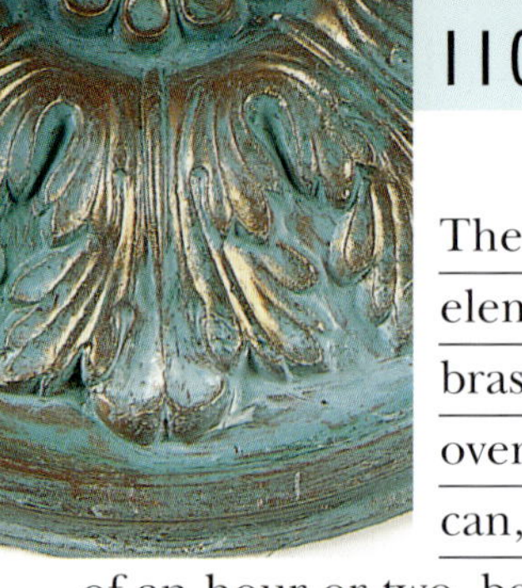

Verdigris

The effects of the elements on old brass and copper over many years can, in a matter of an hour or two, be lovingly recreated at home. The beautifully aged and weathered patina of verdigris can conjure up visions of old brass, and of bronze and copper statues brought up from the bottom of the ocean. Creating this timeless effect is an absolute pleasure when applied to such pieces as brand new plaster sconces or wall plasters.

Very inexpensive, and comparatively easy to achieve, brand new plaster or woodwork can be aged beyond recognition within hours. Although ideally suited to decorative items such as plaster busts, candlesticks, boxes and ornaments, larger areas such as cupboard doors, table tops, ceiling ornaments and chair (dado) rails can look equally attractive. Using base colors of copper or gold, traditional verdigris colors of green and blue work best, although the technique can be applied to almost any color scheme you may wish to choose.

Faults and flaws in the surface tend to enhance the effect, creating the "pitting" that only comes with years of exposure to the elements. Practice will go a long way toward helping to develop the exact "look" that you require.

Mistakes should very rarely happen, but because of the metallic nature of the basecoat, wiping the surface immediately with a damp cloth will enable you to reapply the finish. Allow the basecoat to dry completely before commencing.

You will need

Tools

• 1 in. (2.5 cm.) stiff-bristled decorating brush • Clean dishes • 1½–2 in. (3.8–5 cm.) bristle brush • Soft, lint-free cloth

Materials

• Gray undercoat • Gold paint spray or acrylic • Mid- /bright green, bright blue and white paint (acrylic) • Acrylic varnish for protection

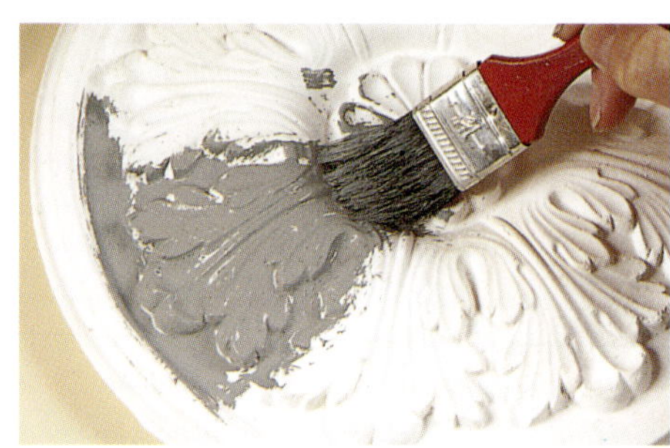

1 Prepare the surface (see *Preparation*, p. 18). Using the 2 in. (5 cm.) bristle basecoat brush apply an undercoat of dark gray semigloss latex (vinyl silk emulsion) diluted with water. Allow to dry.

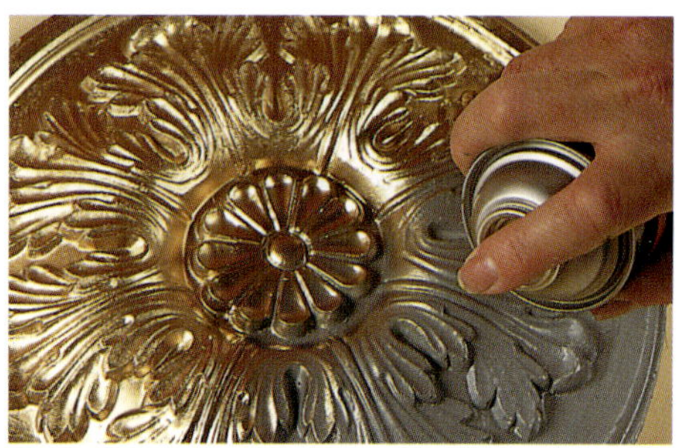

2 Paint the surface with a coat of gold acrylic paint or cover with a thin coat of gold spray paint following manufacturer's instructions. Allow to dry and apply a second thin coat of gold spray paint.

Variation 1

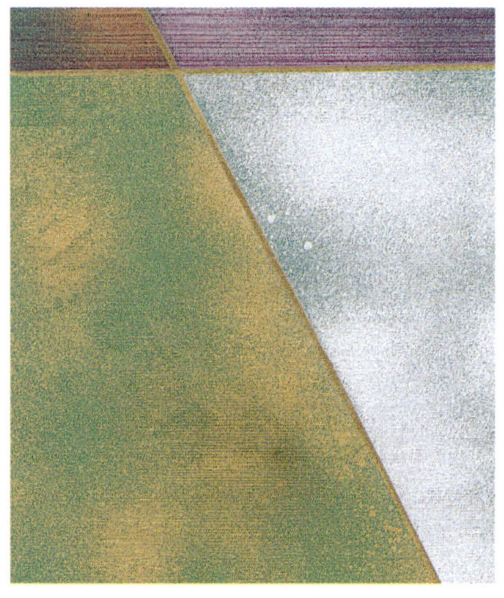

In this swatch, instead of applying the paints to the metallic surface and then removing them while still wet, the ground has been painted with a basecoat of bright green. Once dry, gold and silver paints were sprayed over the basecoat to create a far more even result. The purple dragged glaze at the top shows how well verdigris can be used in association with other effects.

Variation 2

These days because of the popularity of verdigris and other similar paint effects, more and more related products have appeared on the market. In our example a store-bought verdigris wax has been applied over a basecoat of vivid purple to create a particularly pleasing result. The wax can be used over natural woodgrain to equal effect.

3 On a clean dish place small amounts of artists' acrylic paints in mid- to bright green, bright blue and white. Add water to each color and mix to a thick, creamy consistency. The colors should not be mixed together so you may find it easier to use separate dishes.

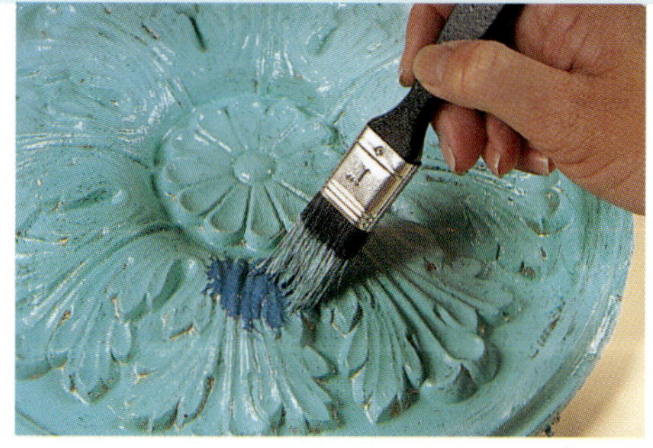

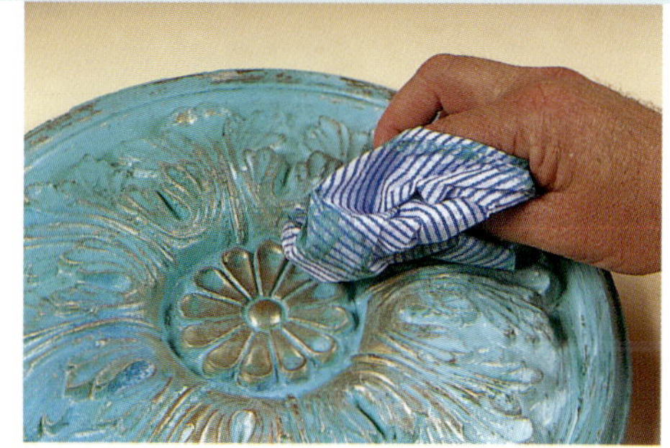

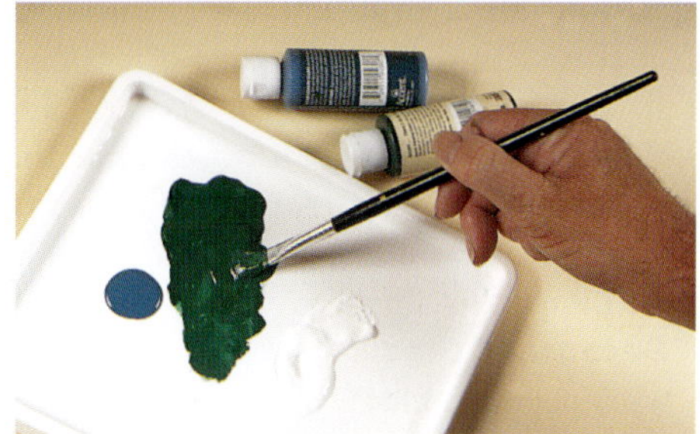

4 Paint a layer of green paint on the surface using a 1in. (2.5 cm.) bristle brush. While still wet add a layer of white paint, stippling and blending so that you achieve the characteristic verdigris color as you work.

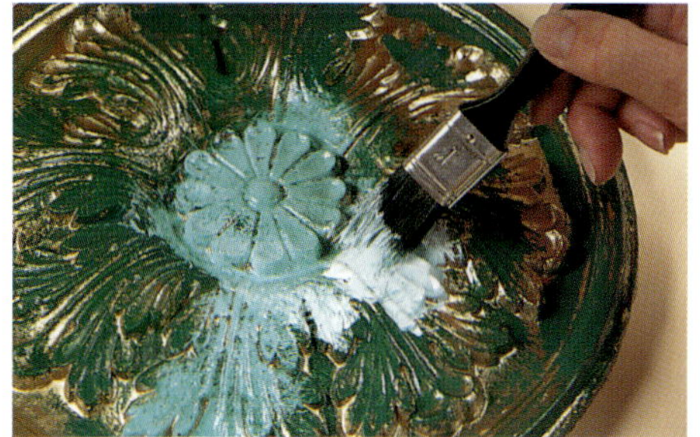

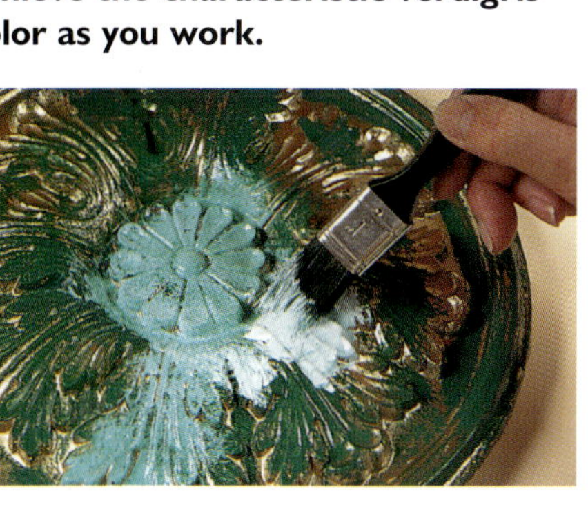

5 Once you have completely blended the green and white across the surface, leaving as many color variations as possible, highlight a few raised areas with the mid-blue. Do not over use the blue and work fairly quickly.

6 While the paint is still wet slowly wipe a clean, soft, lint-free cloth across the entire surface removing patches of the blended verdigris color to reveal the gold beneath. Continue until you have the effect you desire. Once the surface is dry, a layer of acrylic varnish can be applied to seal it if required.

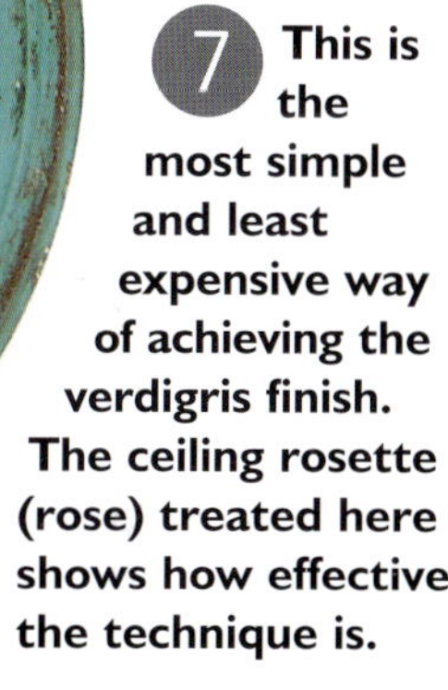

7 This is the most simple and least expensive way of achieving the verdigris finish. The ceiling rosette (rose) treated here shows how effective the technique is.

Variation 3

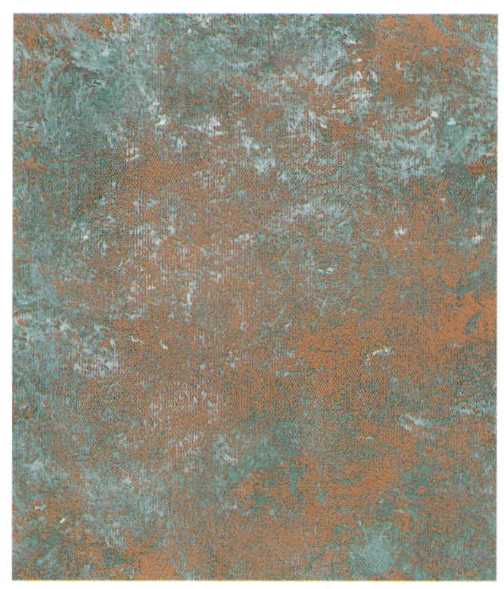

For this technique the surface was sprayed with three very thin layers of copper spray paint (follow all safety instructions) to achieve an even basecoat. When dry, some white and some viridian artists' acrylic paints were applied by dipping a crunched up plastic bag into the paint, removing the excess on some paper towel and "bagging" the surface.

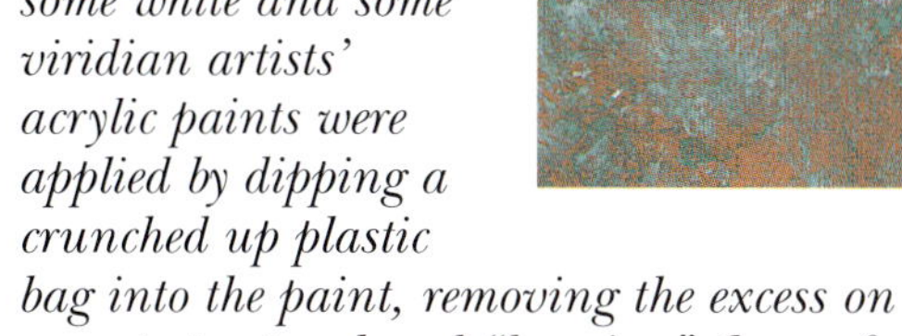

Variation 4

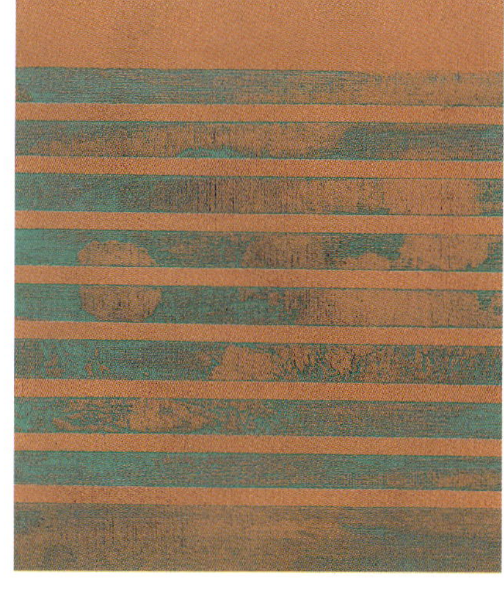

This panel was given three light sprays of copper paint, allowing each to dry between coats. Low-tack masking tape was applied to the surface using a 1 in. (2.5 cm.) band across the top. Green and white acrylic paints were mixed to achieve a verdigris color that was wiped across the surface with a soft cloth. Areas of wet paint were then "dabbed" in circular motions and left to dry a little before being removed by "buffing" with a soft cloth.

In context

Stamping is a technique that enables one to create a really individual look whether it is done formally or at random, or whether it is solid or distressed. Many different moods can be created in a very short time. The example of the use of the verdigris effect shows how good simple accessories can look with very little effort.

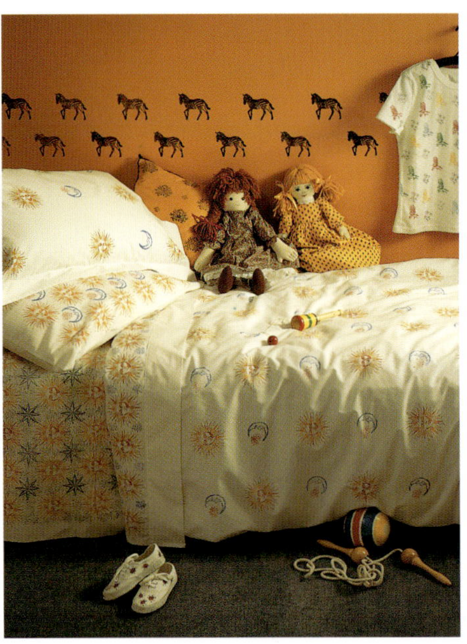

Stamping

◀ Child's bedroom

This example shows that any child's favorite images can be applied to walls as well as fabrics, making the room individual and special.

Stamping

▼ Casual living area

Over a background of hand-produced stripes, the addition of a randomly stamped fleur-de-lys motif has broken up the formality of the look yet has added points of interest. The ocher colors give a sense of warmth and cosiness to the room.

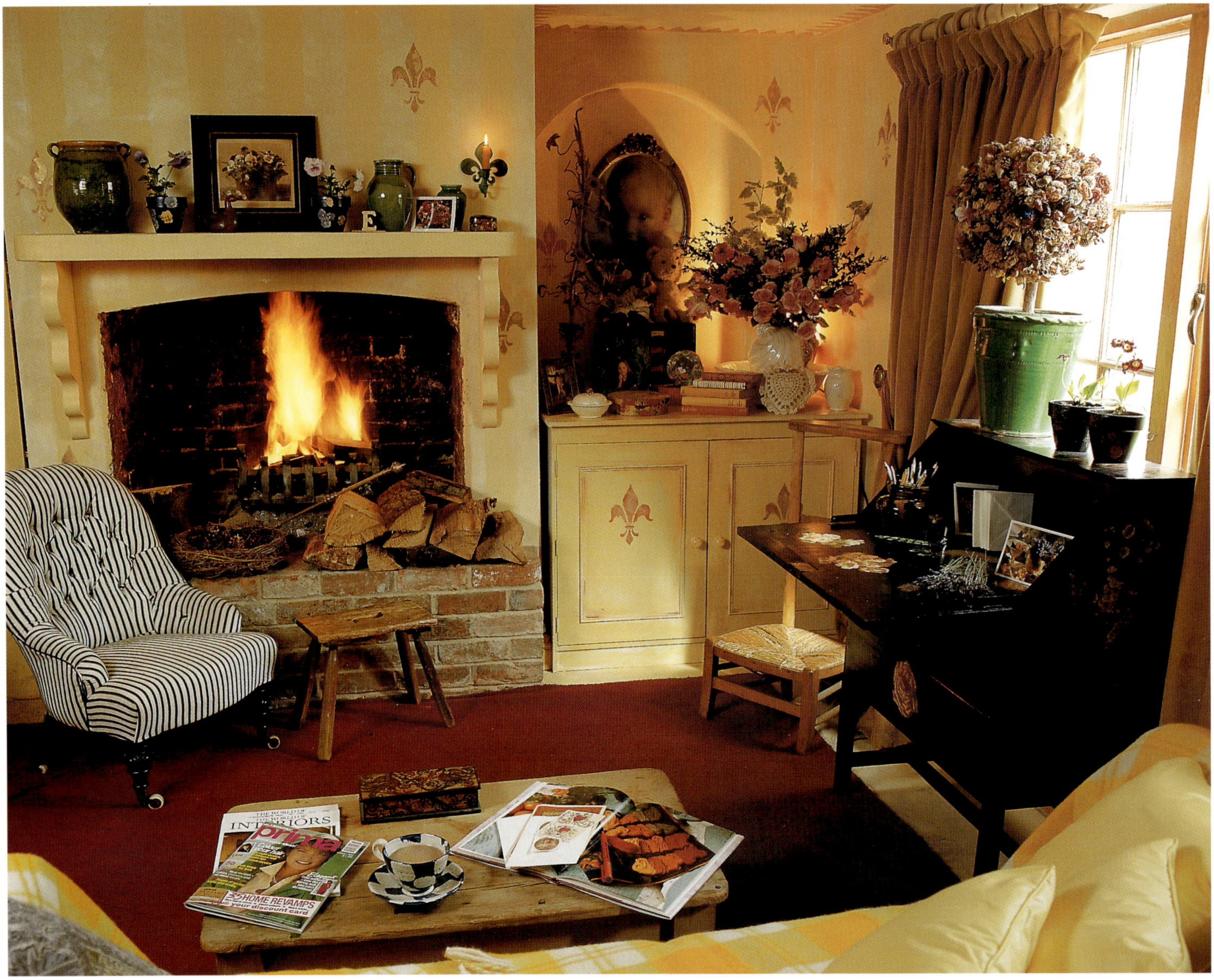

Stamping

▼ Young girl's bedroom

This tiny yet cosy room has been given a feeling of more space and openness by the use of light and airy colors and a very pretty flower and leaf stamp that has been applied to the linen as well as the walls.

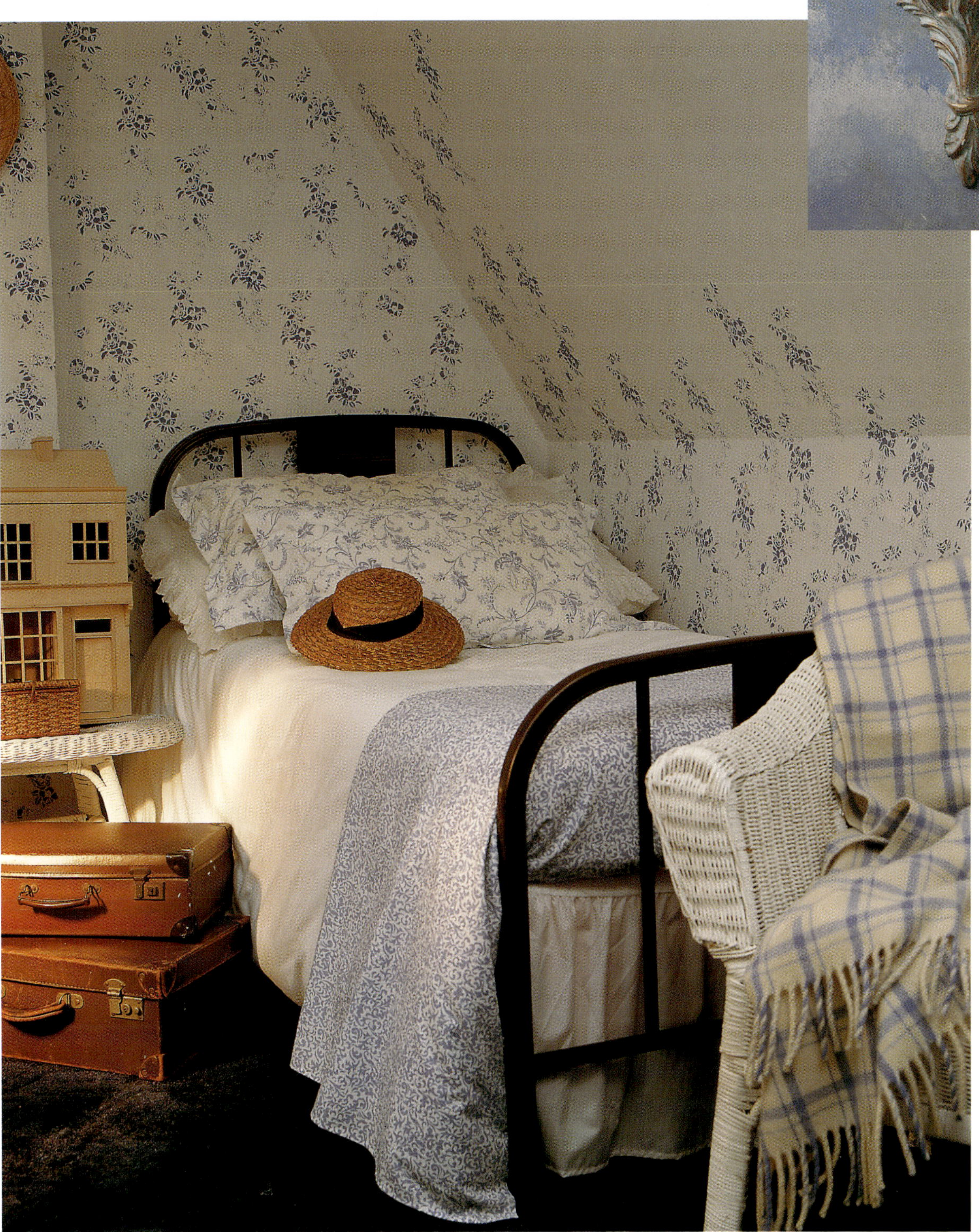

Verdigris

▲ Wall sconce and alcove

The ethereal nature of this setting has been created by very carefully applied sponging and clouding. The acanthus leaf wall sconce has been given a verdigris finish and topped by a pure white cherub.

Old stone

Old stone often conjures up pictures of fairytale castles with flagstone hallways and country kitchen floors. It is a very romantic technique to produce.

Producing an old stone effect, whether it be on floors, walls, cabinet tops, mantles or corbels, is an easy and basic technique to achieve. It also looks good when applied to window and door frames. Stone is an effect that works better in more traditional or country settings than in modern ones, but it can look stunning in any setting if used imaginatively. Not only is it inexpensive, but it is also very enjoyable to tackle. Although it is better to stay with the traditional tones of gray, other colorways can be used.

In reality, real stone does contain flaws and cracks, and therefore any mistakes that are made can most easily be utilized as part of the finished result.

If you want to create a realistic finish, study a real piece of stone. Note the structure and patterns on the surface after years of exposure to the elements. An effective and realistic result is generally attributed to a good eye for detail.

You will need

Tools

• *Clean containers for mixing glazes* • *2½–3 in. (6.3–7.5 cm.) bristle brush* • *½ in. (1.3 cm.) bristle brush* • *Lint-free kitchen cloth* • *Fine artists' watercolor brush*

Materials

• *Cream, mid-gray and pale gray semigloss latex (vinyl silk emulsion)* • *PVA glue* • *Silver sand or sawdust* • *Acrylic colors in black, white, olive or moss green, yellow ocher* • *Flat (matte) acrylic varnish* • *Acrylic glazing medium*

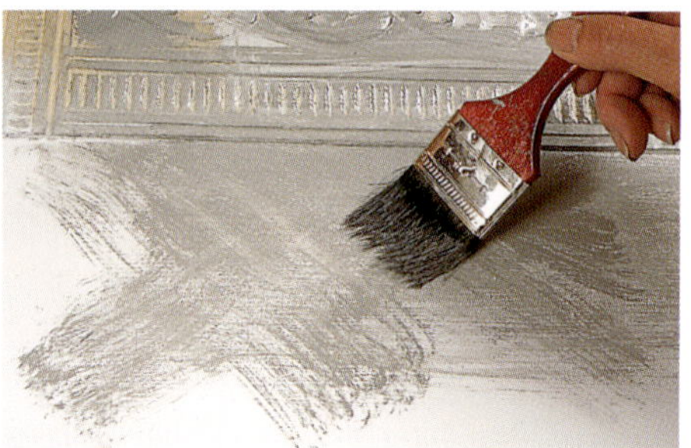

1 **Fill and sand only worst areas. Apply a basecoat of pale cream latex (emulsion). Let dry. Then apply layers of pale gray and mid-gray latex (emulsion) using random strokes in a scratchy crisscross pattern to blend with basecoat. Dry overnight.**

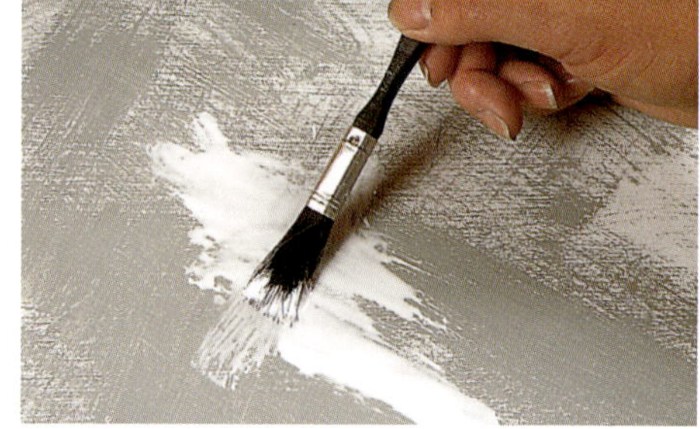

2 **Choose areas of the surface that would be particularly affected by the weather if in a natural situation and apply a generous layer of PVA glue with a ½ in. (1.2 cm.) bristle brush. Spread the glue across the surface randomly.**

Variation 1

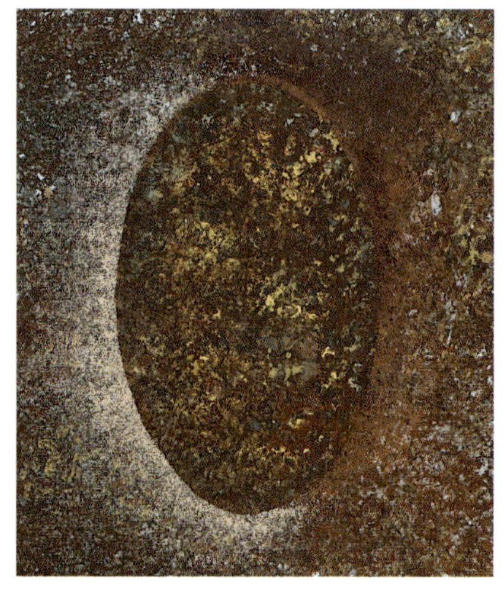

The basecoat of dark gray latex (emulsion) was heavily sponged (see p. 54) using a natural sponge. Artists' acrylic paints in dark brown, yellow ocher, terracotta and pale blue were applied with a sponge while each was still wet. An oval was cut out of stencil card and applied to the panel with spray adhesive. With a stippling brush one side of the oval was stippled (see p. 30) with light cream acrylic paint and the other with dark brown.

Variation 2

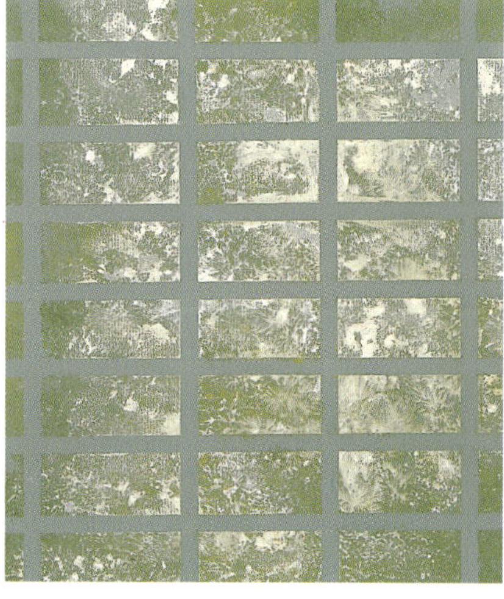

The sample here has been masked off with ¼ in. (0.63 cm.) low-tack masking tape (a stencil could be cut and used) over a basecoat of blue-gray. The entire surface was then sponged randomly with a layer of moss green glaze and allowed to dry. Following this, a mixture of fine plaster of Paris, tinted with a little yellow ocher, was applied using a soft cloth. A formal but simple wall has been created.

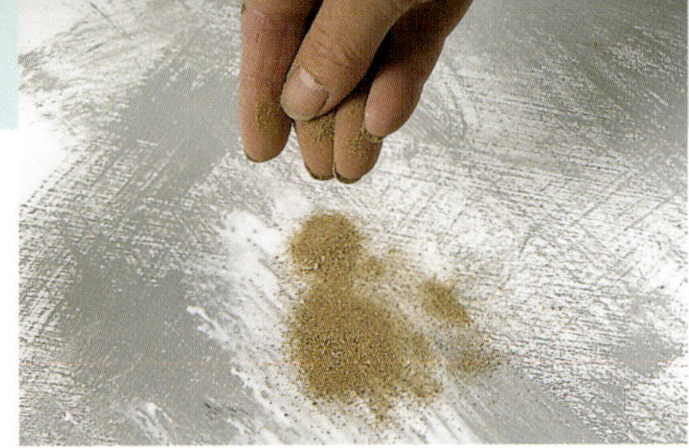

3 Apply silver sand to the wet surface, spreading it as evenly as possible and making sure that all the glue is covered. You could add sawdust or fine grit to give an even more pitted texture. Allow to dry.

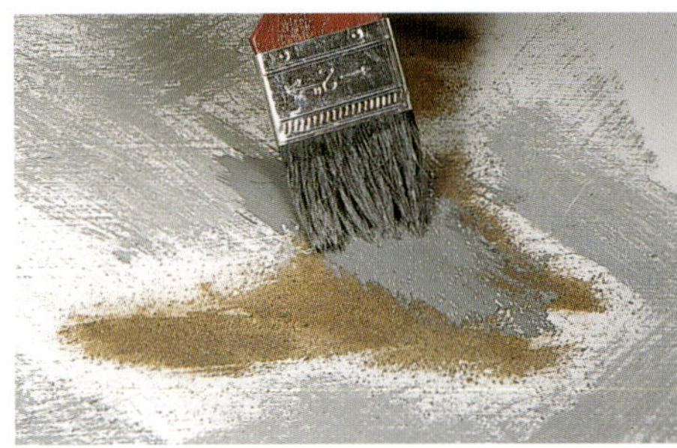

4 In separate clean containers mix glazes of moss green and white and dark gray (black and white) using artists' acrylic paints and acrylic glazing medium, following manufacturer's instructions. With water, dilute the glazes to the consistency of light cream.

Apply a layer of the dark gray glaze using the bristle brush. Make sure that it thoroughly covers all the sand. Allow to dry until tacky.

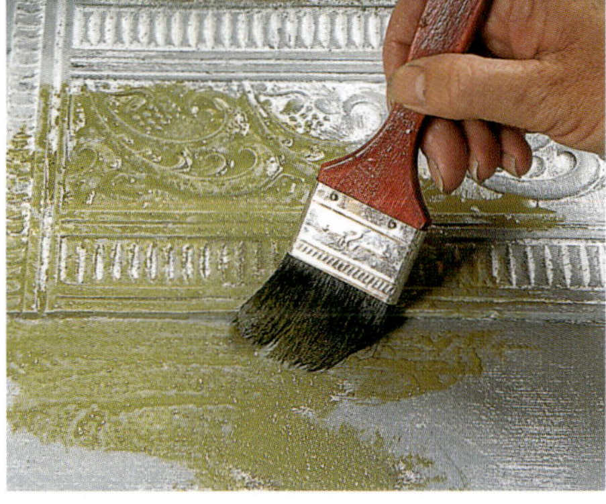

5 Apply the moss green glaze evenly using the bristle brush.

6 While the moss green glaze is still wet, randomly wipe and rub the surface with a lint-free kitchen cloth to remove part of the glaze. Highlight raised areas by exposing the gray underneath but keep the "moss" intact in all the textured areas.

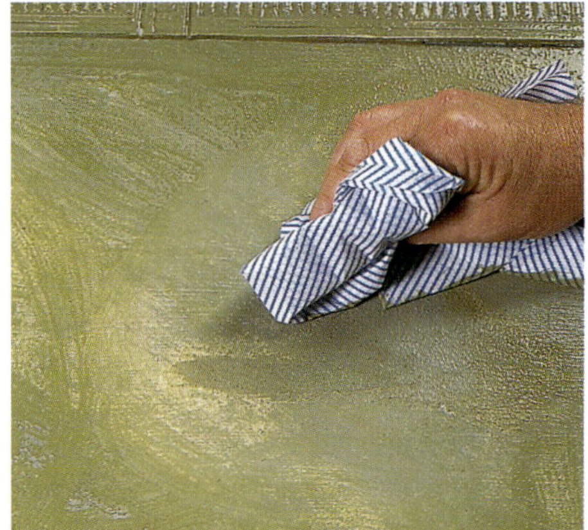

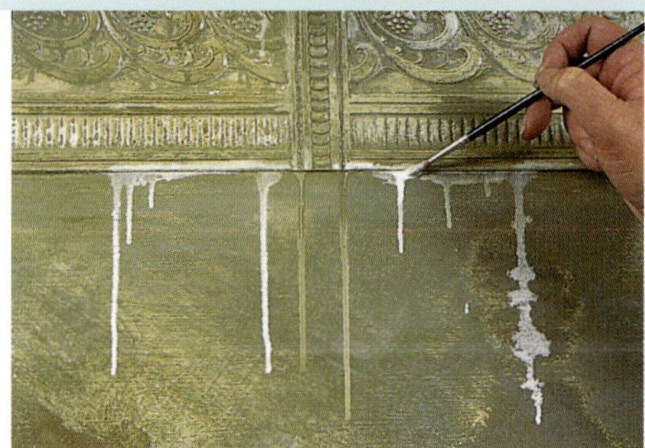

7 Mix the remaining white glaze with more water so that it is diluted to a very thin consistency. Diluted white latex (emulsion) could also be used. With a fine artists' watercolor brush, dribble the glaze down the surface to create the effect of salt on old stone.

8 Old stone can give very individual effects. Here a traditional look has been created using "carving" accentuated by the use of colors of real old, gray, stone and damp moss. Finishing off with a dead flat (matte) varnish adds to the reality of a weather-beaten, pitted surface.

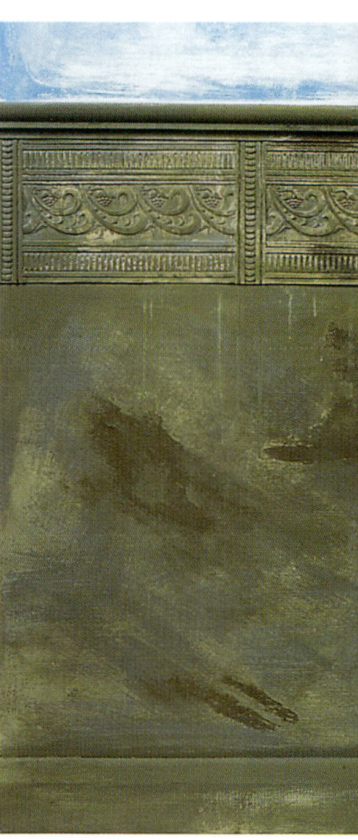

Variation 3

A background of dark blue/gray latex (emusion) was applied and left to dry. Then a layer of crackleglaze was applied following manufacturer's instructions. When touch-dry a mid-gray and moss green latex (emulsion) were applied at random using a 2 in. (5 cm.) sponge roller. Each color was applied separately while each was wet. A protective coat of oil-based varnish was applied.

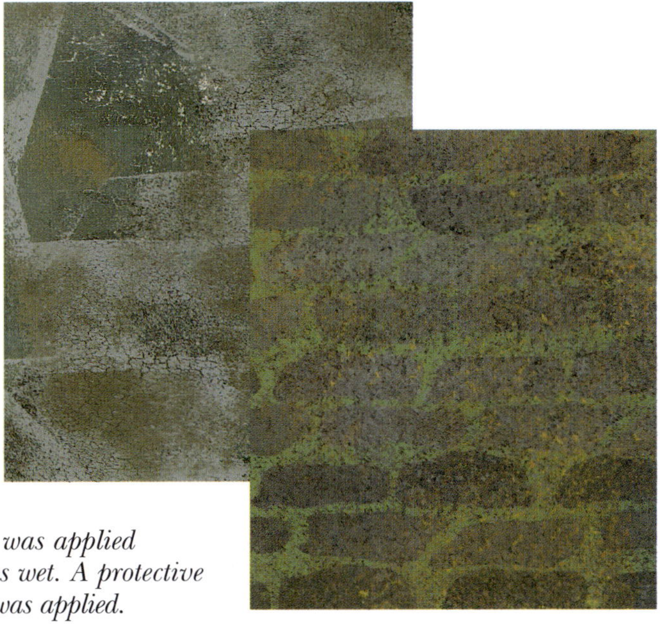

Variation 4

The effect of dry-stone walls, castle ramparts and stone cottages can easily be created using a stencil of stones. The stones were sponged in gray and black over a basecoat of moss green. After the paint had dried a little, random sponging was added in yellow and pale terracotta, effectively bringing the "wall" to life by creating the appearance of moss and lichens.

Sandstone blocking

Sandstone is a warm, textured stone reminiscent of Ancient Egypt, the Mediterranean or fairytale castles. This technique enables you to create a sandstone effect in your home with relative ease. It can be used imaginatively with other techniques such as stenciling (see p. 78), colorwashing (see p. 60) and sponging (see p. 54).

You will need

Tools

• *Good quality 3–4 in. (7.5–10 cm.) soft-bristled brush for colorwashing* • *Chalk and plumb line* • *Straight edge (ruler)* • *Natural (marine) sponge* • *Paint dishes* • *2 in. (5 cm.) glazing brush* • *Stiff 1 in. (2.5 cm.) short-bristled brush for spattering (or a toothbrush)* • *Low-tack tape ¼–½ in. (0.63–1.3 cm.) wide*

Materials

• *Acrylic glazing medium* • *Pale cream semigloss latex (vinyl silk emulsion) paint for the basecoat* • *Yellow ocher latex (emulsion) for tinting glaze* • *Artists' acrylic colors in tubes in moss green, black and white* • *Varnish for protection*

Walls, table tops, paneling, mantles, fireplace surrounds, ceiling rosettes (roses) and pillars are all possible surfaces for sandstone or sandstone blocking. In fact, most surfaces can be treated in this way. The mellow creams and warm olives used for this effect will add light and depth to the darkest corner. Sandstoning is relatively inexpensive, with minimum expense for tools and materials. The glazes can be home-made (see recipes p. 15) or bought over the counter at specialist or good decorator stores.

The key to the success of this technique is preparation and the maximum effect can be achieved with the minimum of time. Unevenness of the surface will enhance the texture of the final effect and mistakes can generally be easily incorporated into the finish as cracks and flaws in the stone. If things go wrong, make a feature of it rather than painting it out and starting again.

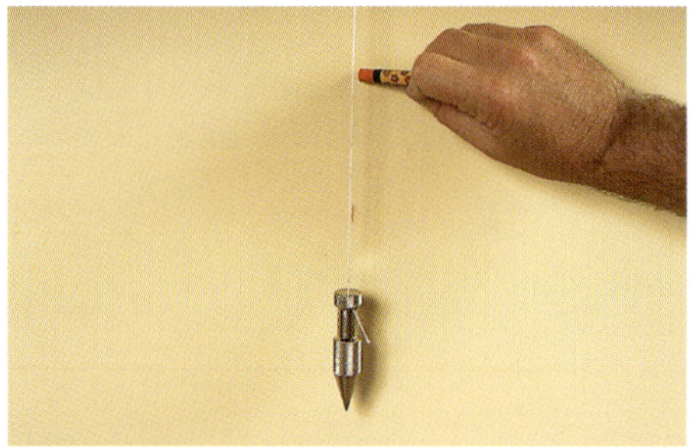

1 **Fill in only bad holes and cracks as slight imperfections will add to the effect. Apply two coats of pale cream semigloss latex (vinyl silk emulsion). Dry between coats. With a plumb line, chalk in vertical lines at 8–10 in. (20–25 cm.) intervals.**

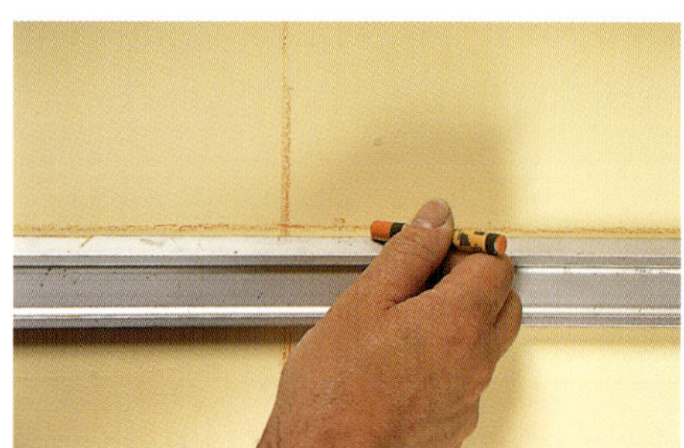

2 **From the top down, measure along each second and third vertical line a distance of around 7–8 in. (18–20 cm.) With a straight edge, or yard stick, chalk in the horizontal lines of the brick checking that each is level before you start on the next.**

Variation 1

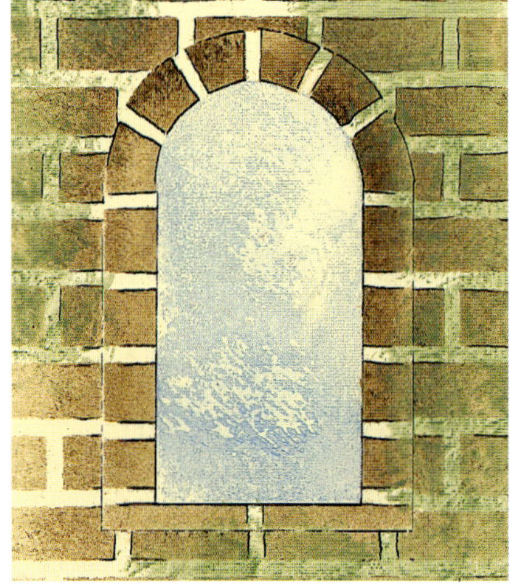

Using the taping method and artistic license, a very simple trompe l'oeil *effect has been created. The basecoat was coated in dark cream, and the center masked off with a piece of solid stencil card. Tape was used across the entire surface. A glaze of raw umber was applied, left to dry, followed by moss green. The tape was removed and blue clouding (see p. 86) added to the center. The "mortar" was highlighted with a fine, black marker.*

Variation 2

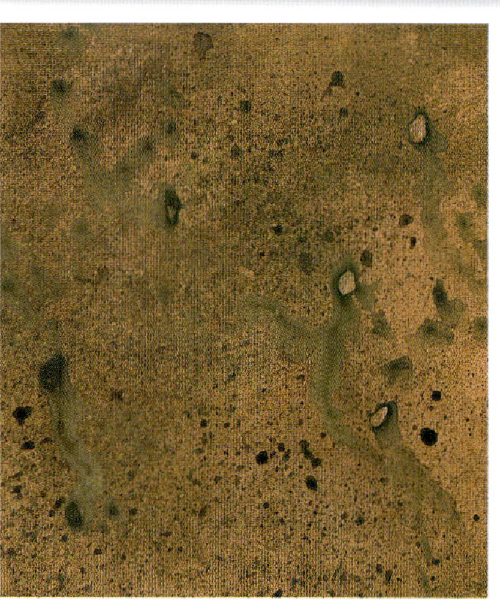

This panel was given a basecoat of two layers of pale pink semigloss latex (vinyl silk emulsion) and left to dry. A heavily diluted moss-colored acrylic paint was dabbed on the surface with a soft cloth. When dry, the surface was spattered (see p. 72) with darker green and moss green acrylic. This was left to dry and moss green paint dribbled over in puddles and dried with a hairdryer then sealed with flat (matte) acrylic varnish.

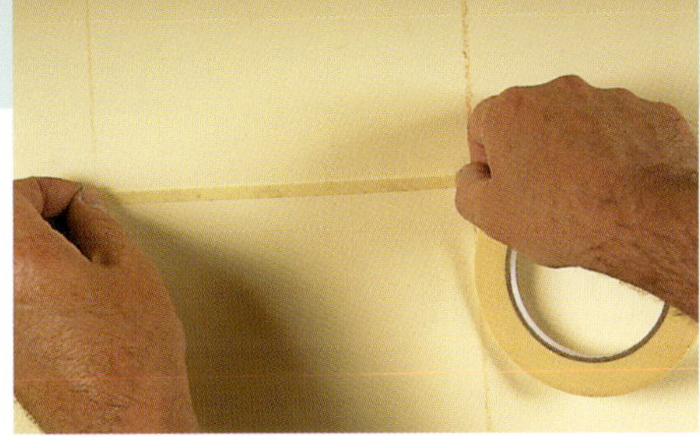

3 Fix the low-tack tape along the horizontal chalk lines. Press into position but not too firmly as the tape may remove some of the newly painted basecoat. Fix tape along the vertical lines taping over each second vertical. Make the stonework look uneven by varying the depth and width of the blocks.

4 In separate dishes mix yellow ocher latex (emulsion) and moss green artists' acrylic paint with acrylic glazing medium. Dilute with water and mix. Using a 2 in. (5 cm.) glazing brush paint the surface with yellow ocher glaze. Remove areas using a damp sponge and rework with a dry brush so some basecoat shows through.

5 Using a sponge, repeat step 4 with a little of the green glaze, highlighting areas around the tape, where the natural "mortar" would be. Using a natural sponge (see p. 54), apply a little of the green and ocher glazes at random to create a "pitted" look on the surface.

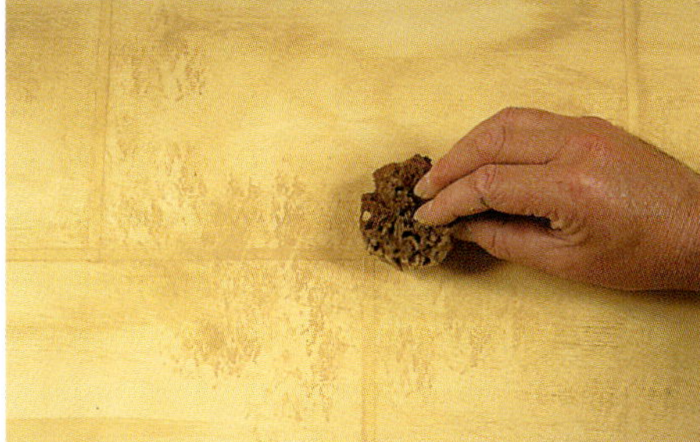

6 Using a toothbrush and some artists' acrylic paints in white and black, carefully spatter (see p. 72) certain areas across the surface. Allow to dry between spattering to avoid paint runs.

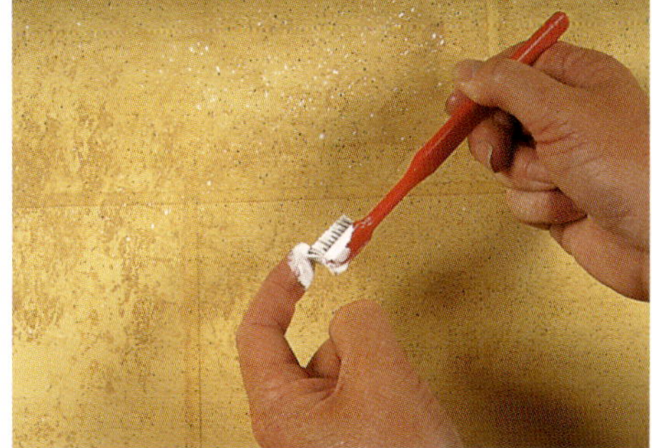

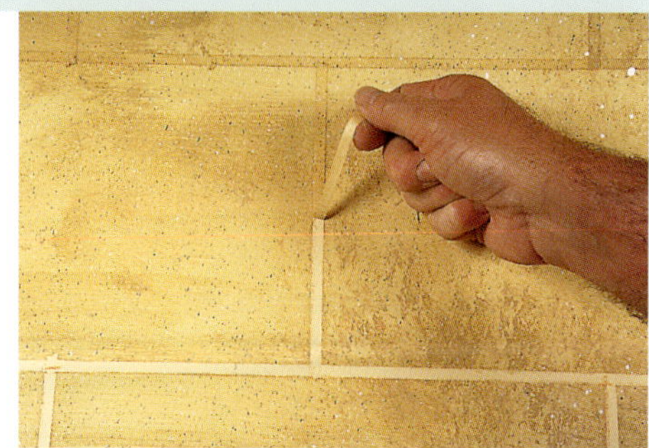

7 After the wall has been textured as you require (and you may repeat any of the previous steps), remove the tape taking care not to pull off any of the basecoat paint as you work. A sharp blade will help to gently lift each section of tape before you continue to remove it by hand. Varnish if necessary.

8 With the subtle choice of pale ochers and creams for this sandstone blocked wall, a very pleasing and warm effect has been achieved (below). The finished effect is simple and unobtrusive, which allows for other furnishings to be more extravagant and elaborate.

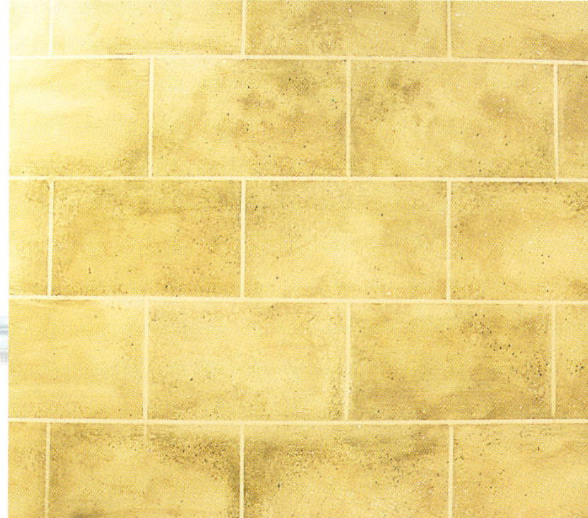

Variation 3

Pale cream semigloss latex (vinyl silk emulsion) was applied and left to dry then low-tack tape used to create a pattern before applying an acrylic glaze with terracotta and dark brown latex (emulsion) in stripes. The wet glaze was dragged with a card comb to create a layered effect. When dry, the tape was removed, yellow ocher applied and left to dry. Finally, it was sanded and sealed.

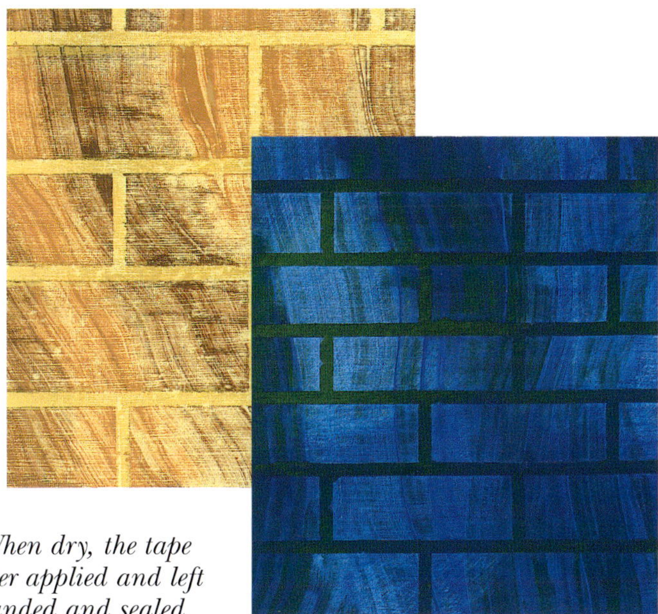

Variation 4

After painting two coats of mid-green semigloss latex (vinyl silk emulsion), ¼ in. (0.63 cm.) low-tack tape was placed in position to stop any bleeding. White and bright blue artists' acrylic paints were mixed with acrylic glaze to make three different colors. The glazes were randomly dabbed on the surface and a cardboard comb dragged across the glaze. Flat (matte) acrylic varnish was applied to protect the surface (left).

In context

This gallery shows to full effect the romantic and wonderful variations that can be created with paint when producing faux stone effects—whether it be a crisp, clean sandstone or aged brick finish. This technique can be assimilated into almost any decor, modern or traditional, and the choice of colors and variations is endless

Stone

▶ Brick paving on greenhouse (conservatory) floor

Both the color and texture of this red brick floor make it hard to believe that this result was really created by paint. It has the look of genuine age about it. Lining has been applied so effectively that it has the appearance of beautifully laid bricks.

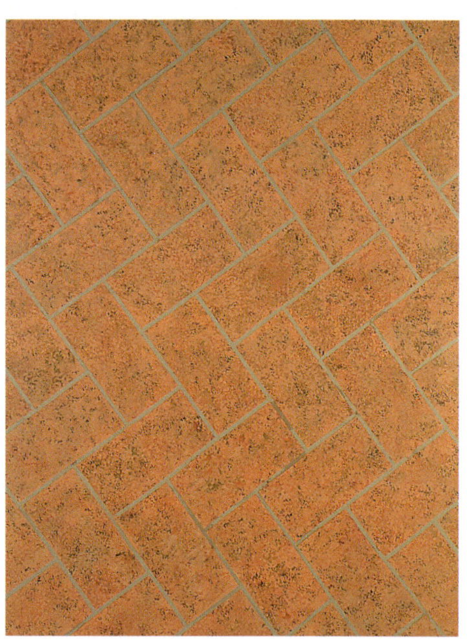

Old stone

▼ Hotel foyer

Carefully chosen colors that resemble stone have been applied over a rough plastered undulating wall. This has created a beautiful cave-like feel yet the whole area remains very open and airy.

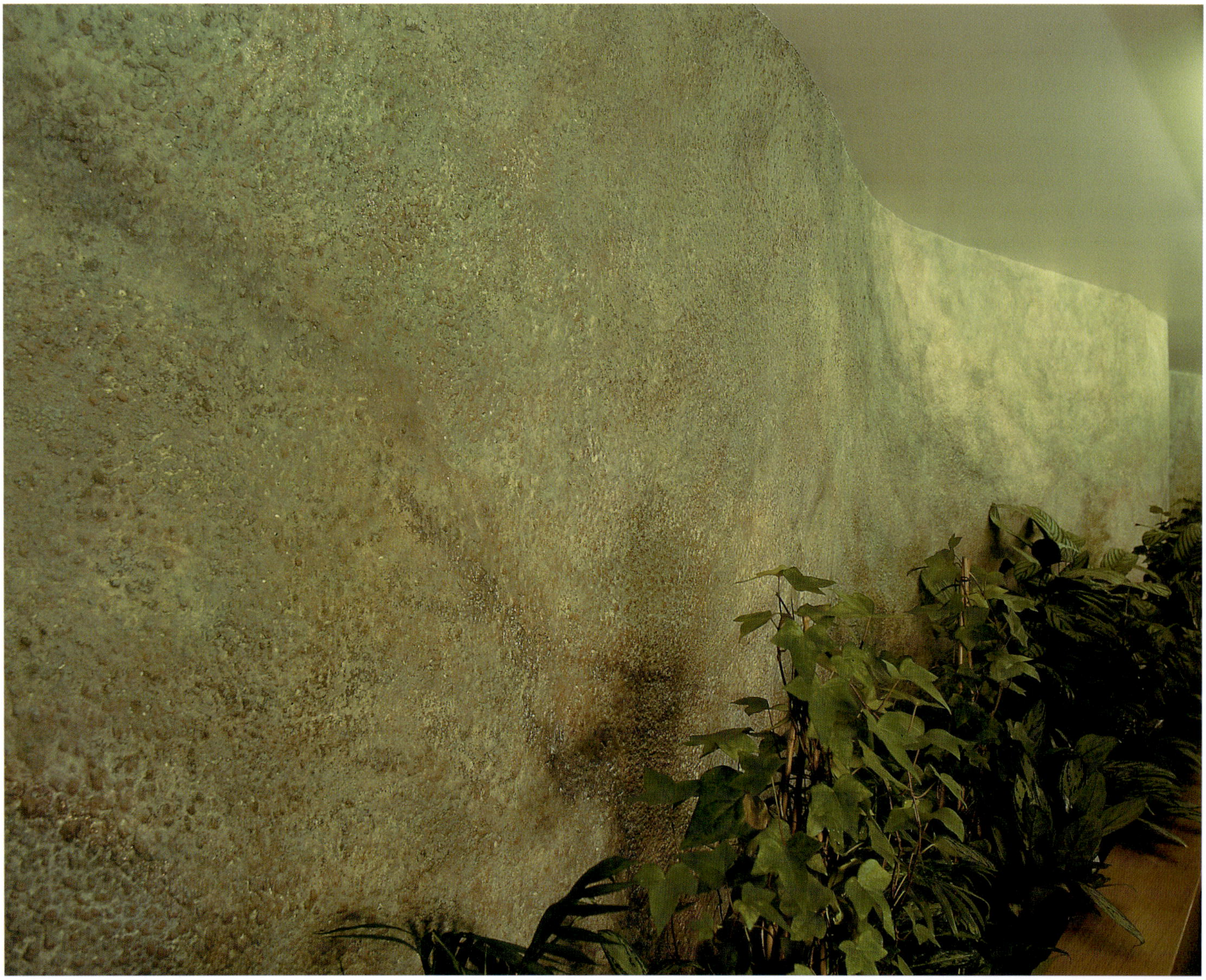

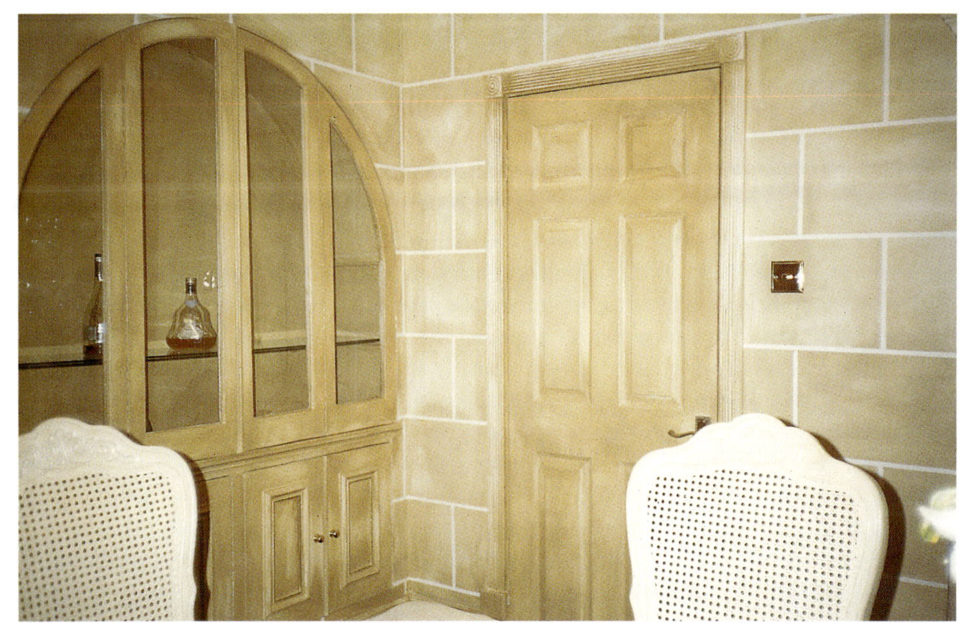

Stone

◀ Raised dining area

By incorporating the cupboards, doors and walls into this sandstone blocked dining area, a feeling of unobtrusive cosiness has been created. The light stone color has opened up the entire room yet it still retains a feeling of warmth and security.

Sand stone

▼ Hotel hallway

By using the parallel lines and the pale cream and ocher colors associated with the sandstone block effect, a long and partly enclosed hotel hallway has been given height, length and a fresh, clean openness — a result that is both calming and elegant for the guests.

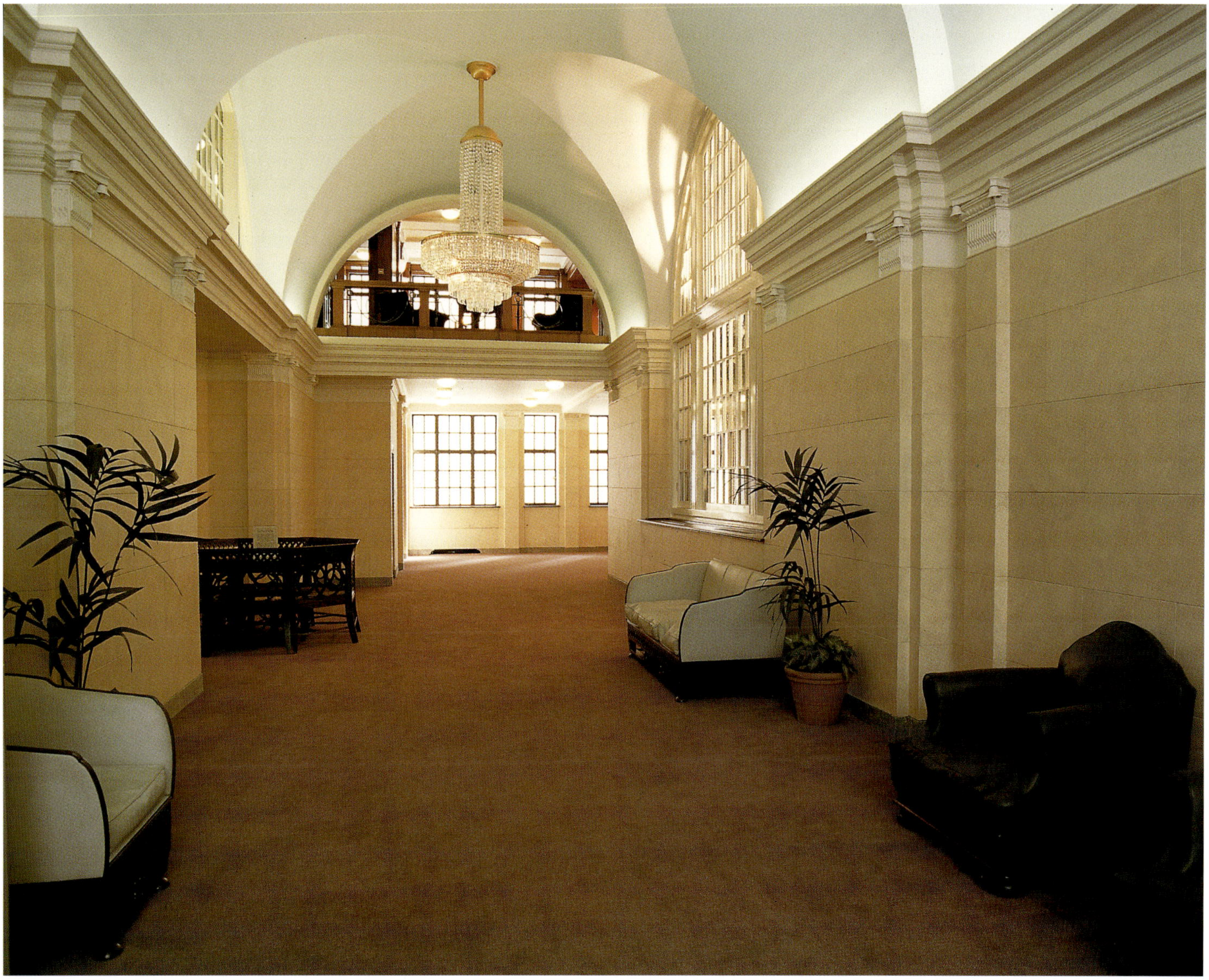

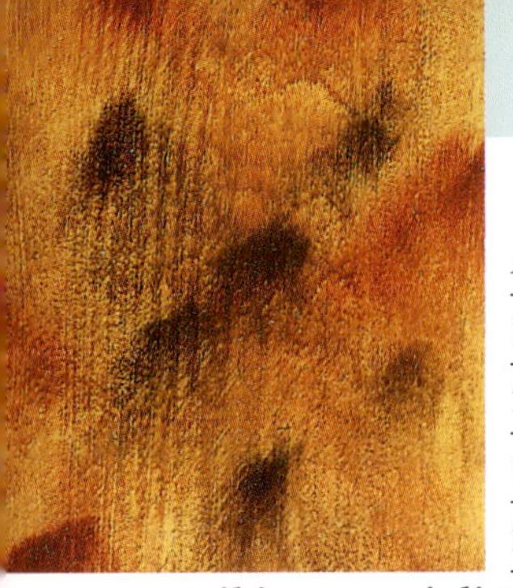

An exotic finish that originated in the Far East, tortoiseshelling is one of the most striking specialist paint finishes. Tortoiseshelling is guaranteed to look spectacular and to be a focal highlight in any room. The eye-catching final effect will give a sophisticated and stylish look to any decor.

Tortoiseshelling

Tortoiseshelling is an expensive finish to create and is therefore better suited to smaller, decorative pieces, such as lampbases, wastepaper bins and boxes, although it need not be limited to these items. When used in larger areas such as table tops, paneling and cupboard doors, it looks stunning.

Tortoiseshelling is not an easy effect to achieve, and practice on a sample board is highly recommended before attempting larger areas. As with marbling, it is a good idea to study some pictures of real tortoiseshell before attempting the effect, in order to get a feel for what it looks like.

Readily available these days are small plastic items such as combs in simulated tortoiseshell, which will help you to understand the structure and look of the real shell.

To avoid mistakes, do not attempt to complete the full finish too quickly. Visually, tortoiseshelling looks better when paneled (see p. 23) and each panel must be allowed to dry for at least 24 hours before attempting the next. If a mistake is made while the gilp (see p. 15) is still wet, careful and quick removal with a soft cloth and mineral spirits (white spirit) will overcome this, otherwise the surface must be sanded, repainted, and the effect attempted again. Patience and understanding are the secrets of success, so do not rush or be tempted to take shortcuts.

You will need

Tools

• 2–3 in. (5–7.5 cm.) bristle basecoat brush • Oil-based varnish or gilp (see p. 15) • Paint container and dishes • ¼–½ in. (0.63 cm.–1.3 cm.) artists' oil brush • 2–3 in. (5–7.5 cm.) long-bristled brush for dragging • Badger softening brush • 2 in. (5 cm.) varnishing brush • Fitch brush • Wet-and-dry sandpaper

Materials

• Yellow ocher for basecoat (eggshell) • Artists' oil tube colors in raw sienna, burnt sienna and raw umber • Oil-based varnish

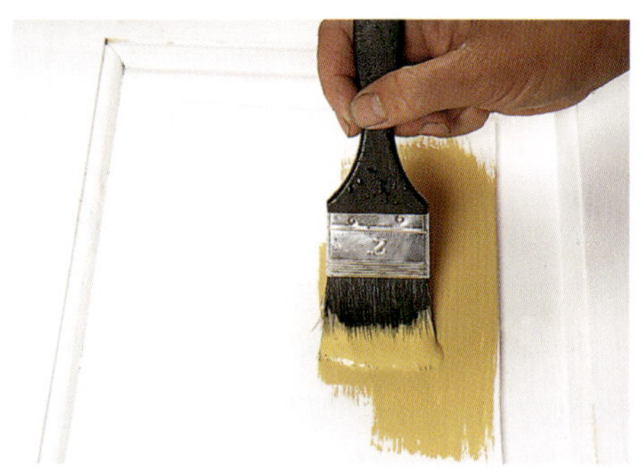

1 Prepare the surface (see *Preparation*, p. 18). With a 2–3 in. (5–7.5 cm.) bristle basecoat brush apply a coat of pale ocher eggshell paint. Allow to dry overnight. Sand down with fine sandpaper. Remove all dust with a damp cloth then apply a second coat. Allow to dry.

Variation 1

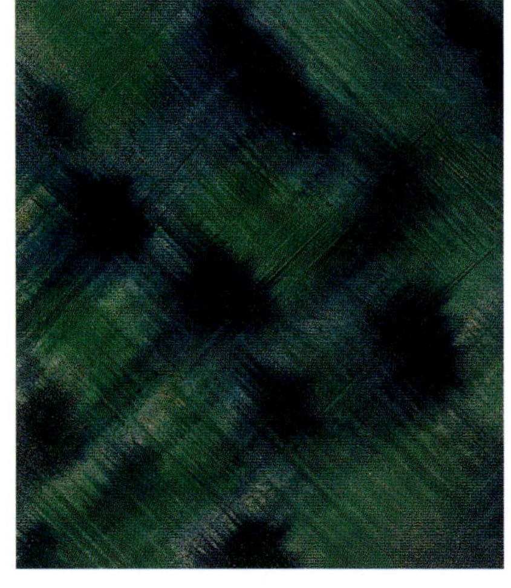

Following the gilding instructions (see p. 134) aluminum leaf was applied. When dry, a coat of clear oil-based varnish was applied, then some French ultramarine and phthalo green artists' oil paints diluted with a little mineral spirits (white spirit) were dabbed onto the surface. The effect was completed by dragging (see p. 62) with a long-bristled basecoat brush, softened a little and allowed to dry. Finally, a clear varnish was applied.

Variation 2

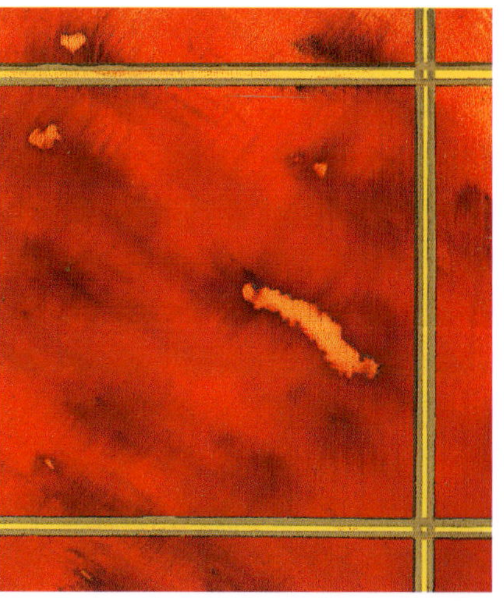

A basecoat of vivid yellow eggshell was masked off with edging stripes in low-tack tape. Varnish tinted with a little bright red artists' oil paint was applied. Small dabs of crimson artists' oil paint were added and then a softening brush was used. Heavier dabs were removed when nearly dry with a cloth and mineral spirits (white spirit). Tape was removed and the edges lined with a gold marker, fixed with a spray sealant and varnished.

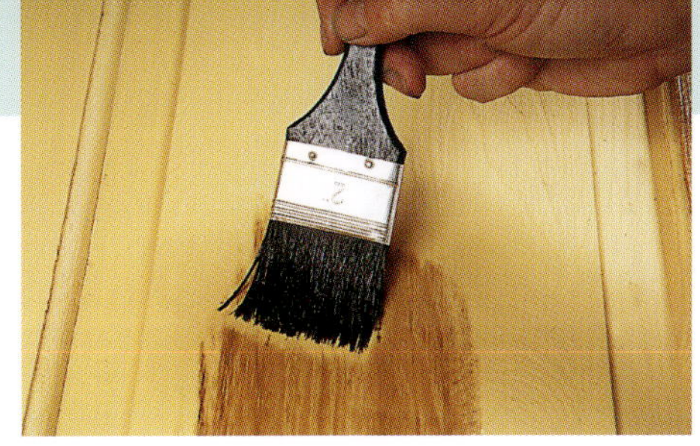

2 Pour some oil-based varnish into a container and tint with a little raw sienna oil paint. Mix enough to complete the job. (Ready mixed, mid-oak, oil-based varnish could be used.) With a 2–3 in. (5–7.5 cm.) bristle brush apply a layer of the varnish to the area being tortoiseshelled. Work quickly and evenly on an easily manageable area.

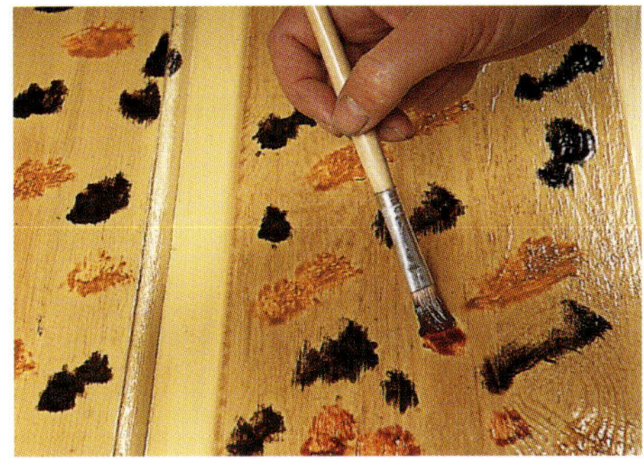

3 In three separate clean dishes pour raw sienna, burnt sienna and raw umber artists' oil paints. Thin with varnish. Using a Fitch brush dab dots of the paint across the surface in a roughly diagonal direction. Do not mix the colors. Use a clean brush for each color.

4 Carefully drag a long-bristled dragging brush diagonally across the surface in smooth, clean strokes. Repeat by cross dragging at an angle of 90 degrees. Be careful not to overdo the dragging, which will remove the spotty texture of the tortoiseshell. Add more dabs of paint and repeat the dragging until you have achieved the effect required.

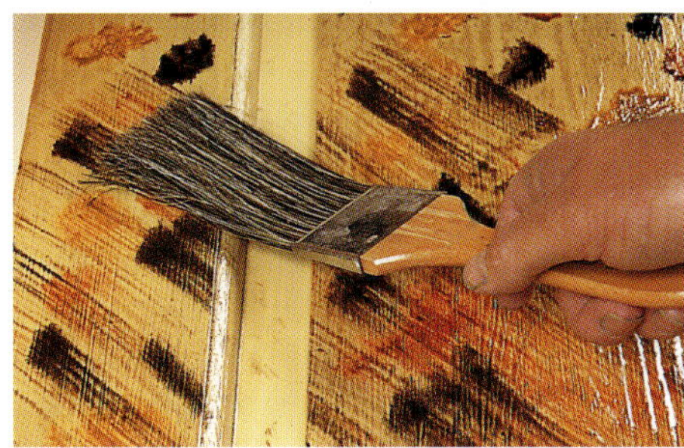

5 With a badger softening brush carefully soften the entire surface, removing all brushstrokes as you work. Work very gently, only just touching the surface. Allow to dry.

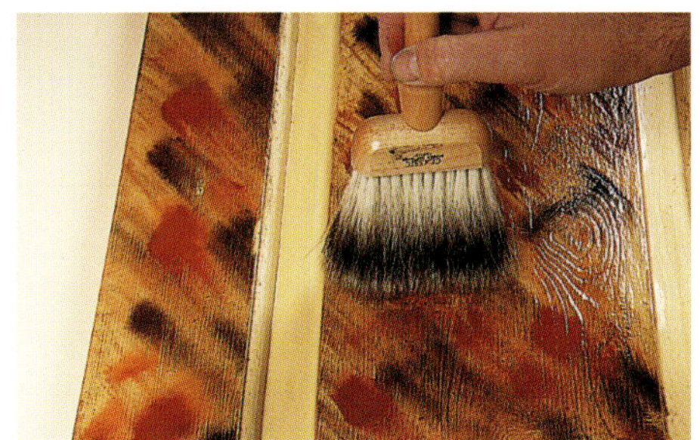

6 With a varnishing brush apply at least four coats of oil-based varnish brushing in one direction only. Carefully smooth down the surface with wet-and-dry sandpaper (see p. 25) between the last two layers to remove any imperfections in the final finish.

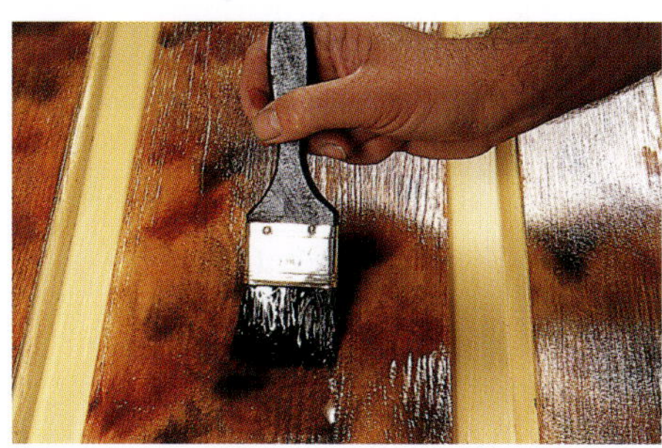

7 This is an exotic effect that creates a really beautiful and unusual result (below). Rich and sumptuous, the possibilities for its use are endless. Carefully chosen colorways can make it an attractive addition to any decorative scheme, and varnishing to a highly polished finish gives depth and clarity to a rather flat and uninteresting surface.

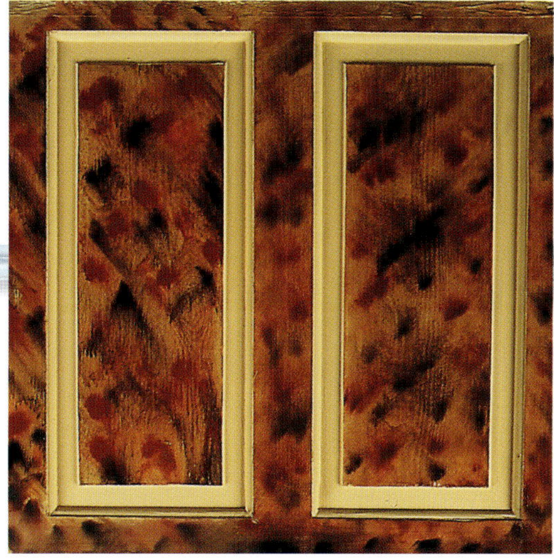

Variation 3

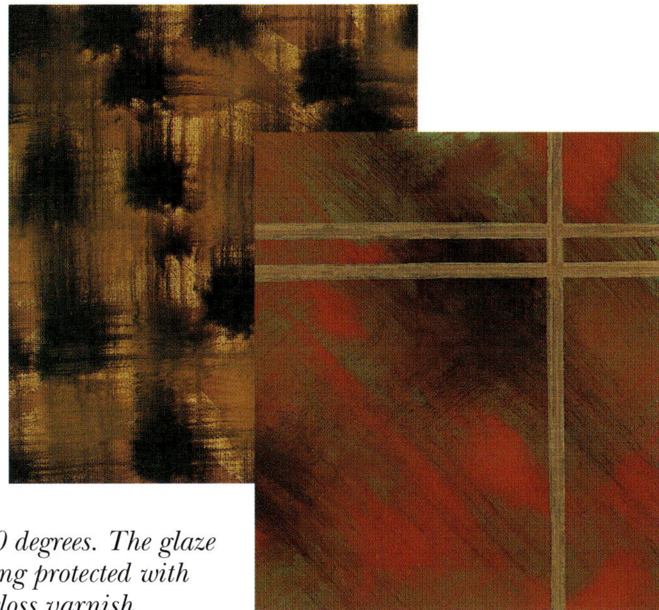

The basecoat was treated with brass leaf and bronze powder and left to dry. A covering of gilp (see p. 15) was applied and some artists' oil paint in yellow ocher and burnt umber dotted over the surface. While still wet, a dragging brush was dragged in one direction and then at 90 degrees. The glaze was left to dry before being protected with three coats of oil-based gloss varnish.

Variation 4

Because it is a luxury finish, tortoiseshelling has often been simulated with paint. This sample was done on a basecoat of mid-green and the colors used were crimson red and burnt umber. A final lining with a permanent marker created an inlaid look to the finished effect.

Shading or Fading

The look of azure skies over the Mediterranean, changing color from deep to pale blue, or exquisite sunsets over the African plains, fading from rich, deep reds to pale yellow and orange, is one that no one could help but admire. Shading or fading is an effect that creates an ambience in any setting, modern or period, and can totally lift an otherwise rather plain surface.

Shading is best suited to walls and ceilings, below chair (dado) rails and floors, but can also be used on any flat area, including table or bench tops, boxes and frames. It is simple and inexpensive to achieve, but practice on a sample board first to get used to the gradual shading of the different-colored glazes. This will eliminate any mistakes that may occur when you are working on the final effect.

Shading will show up flaws in any surface, so good preparation is necessary (see p. 18). The best quality finish is always achieved by using the best possible brushes, and with shading this is especially important as an even change of color is vital to the final finish to eliminate brushstrokes.

Ideal as a background to stenciling (see p. 78) or stamping (see p. 108), shading can create an ethereal "sky" effect before adding stenciled columns, a balustrade or urns for a simple *trompe l'oeil* effect (see p. 79). You can also create a little magic by choosing a color or colors that enhance an existing scheme. Do experiment as the results can often be very surprising and pleasing.

You will need

Tools

• *2–3 in. (5–7.5 cm.) bristle basecoat brush* • *2–3 in. (5–7.5 cm.) glazing brushes* • *Dishes* • *Low-tack tape*

Materials

• *De-greasing agent (sugar soap)* • *Undercoat* • *Acrylic glaze* • *White, dark blue and bright yellow semigloss latex (vinyl silk emulsion)*

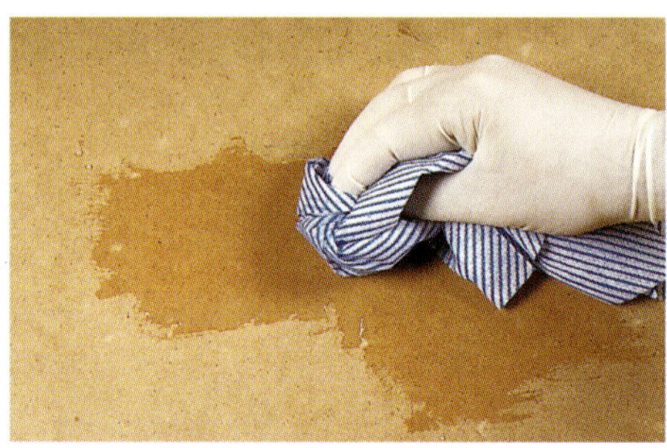

1 Clean the surface with a de-greasing agent (sugar soap) using a soft cloth (see p. 19). Wipe with a clean soft cloth and water. Sand and fill any flaws in the surface.

2 Apply a coat of undercoat with a bristle brush. Allow to dry and then apply two coats of bright yellow, semigloss latex (vinyl silk emulsion). Dry between coats.

Variation 1

Successful results with shading techniques can be readily achieved by using colors that are close in shade. Here, over a basecoat of mid-green, a heavy glaze of olive green is applied. This is then brushed horizontally using a clean, dry brush, working toward the top. After one or two brushstrokes the excess glaze is removed.

Variation 2

By combining the effect of stippling (see p. 30) interesting shading finishes can be achieved very quickly. This sample shows a bright red glaze used over a basecoat of pale cream. When stippling, remove excess glaze from your brush and continue in the chosen direction. The more you over-stipple, the more glaze will be removed, and a graduated shading will appear.

3 Pour the dark blue paint into three separate containers. To each container add varying amounts of white paint to obtain three shades of blue. Add acrylic glazing medium to each following manufacturer's instructions. Add water to achieve a pouring consistency. Make enough glaze to complete the job.

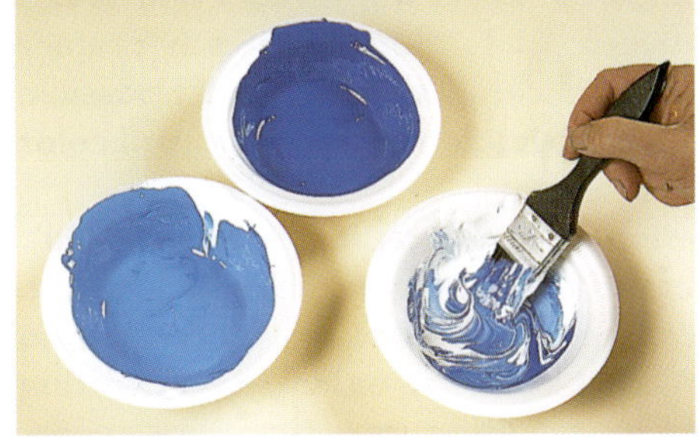

4 Use low-tack tape to seal off any areas next to the area to be painted. Make sure that the tape is pressed firmly but carefully onto the surface so that no seepage or bleeding occurs.

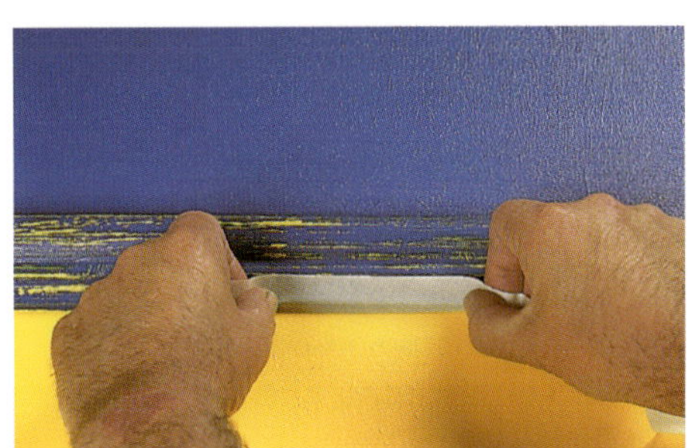

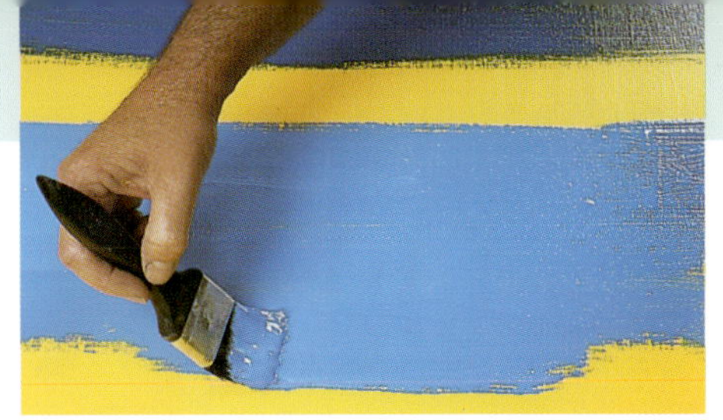

5 Working quickly (the glaze has around 15 minutes working time) apply three separate horizontal stripes of the glaze to the basecoat, using the 2 in. (5 cm.) glazing brush. Start with the dark blue at the top and end with the palest at baseboard (skirting board) level. Leave a blending area of 5–6 in. (12.5–15 cm.) between stripes.

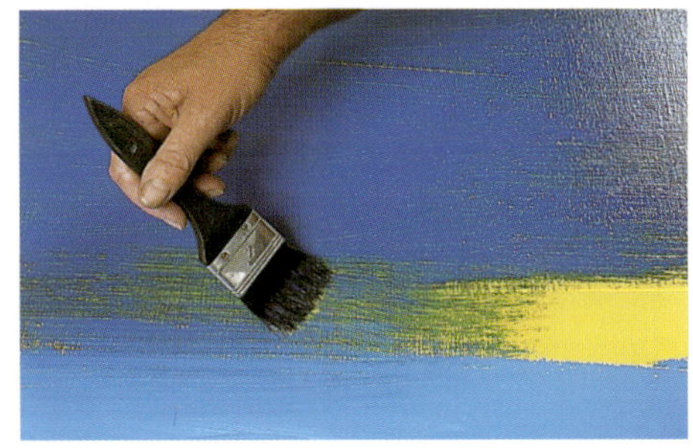

6 Working from the top down use a clean 3 in. (7.5 cm.) glazing brush to blend the stripes of color together. Use horizontal brushstrokes as quickly and as evenly as possible. Once blended, use a clean 3 in. (7.5 cm.) glazing brush to brush over the surface horizontally, eliminating any uneven areas and softening brushstrokes.

7 Here the wonders of the ocean or the magic of the sky have been created with carefully chosen shades of blue. Shading is an effective way of creating depth and mood without any previous experience in painted effects.

Variation 3

Spray paints can give some very pleasing effects, possibly none more so than metallic. Here dark green has been carefully sprayed over a basecoat of gold to achieve a very individual and extremely quick method of shading or fading. By mixing copper and gold, even greater depth can be achieved.

Variation 4

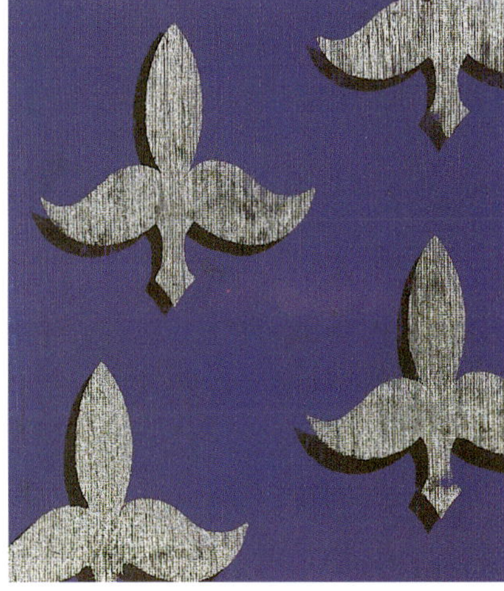

Two coats of bright blue, semigloss latex (vinyl silk emulsion) were applied and left to dry. The surface was sanded with fine-grade sandpaper. A fleur-de-lys stencil was cut from stencil card (oiled manilla board) and the pattern stenciled (see p. 78) in black acrylic. When dry, the fleur-de-lys was restenciled slightly off-center with gold size, using gilding (see p. 134). Aluminum leaf was added (see p. 134). After 24 hours it was sanded again.

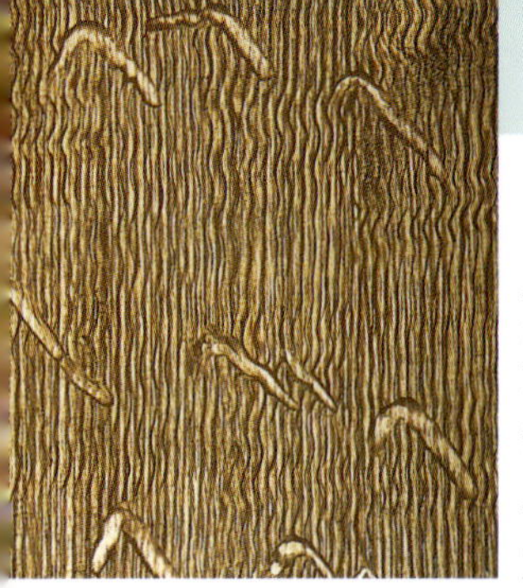

Oak woodgrain

Over the years many rare and precious woods have been simulated in faux paint effects and probably none more so than grained oak. The most beautiful of grained effects can create the look of expensive and sought-after antiques from simple everyday objects.

As with any technique that involves direct simulation of the "real thing" you should look closely at a piece of wood and become familiar with the movement of the pattern. Woodgrain is not an easy technique, but excellent results can be achieved with a little understanding and practice. Buying the relevant tools can be a little expensive to begin with, and to achieve a satisfactory effect, it is not advisable to choose cheaper alternative tools (although a much simpler effect would be achieved by making cardboard combs, see p. 40). However, once purchased and if well cared for, these tools should return their initial cost many times over.

The woodgrain effect is very effective when used in paneling, on doors, chair (dado) rails, cupboards and countertops, and is easily assimilated into both modern and traditional settings. It is best done on flat surfaces rather than on carved or ornate surfaces. For a more modern setting, you could use fantasy colors, as there is no need to be limited by tradition. Woodgraining works particularly well with marquetry (see p. 128) and lining (see p. 94).

Diligent attention to all manufacturer's instructions, and patience when following the step-by-step technique, should reduce the possibility of mistakes. However, because of the extended working time of the oil glaze (see p. 15), mistakes can be carefully and quickly removed with mineral spirits (white spirit) and a cloth. Allow the surface to dry, then reapply the glaze.

You will need

Tools

• *2–3 in. (5–7.5 cm.) basecoat bristle brush* • *½ in. (1.2 cm.) bristle brush* • *Dishes* • *Stippling brush* • *Soft, lint-free cloths* • *Steel combs* • *Eraser or eraser-tipped pencil*

Materials

• *Undercoat* • *Basecoat in magnolia or buff eggshell* • *Glaze (transparent oil)* • *Artists' oil colors in burnt umber, yellow ocher and raw umber* • *Mineral spirits (white spirit)*

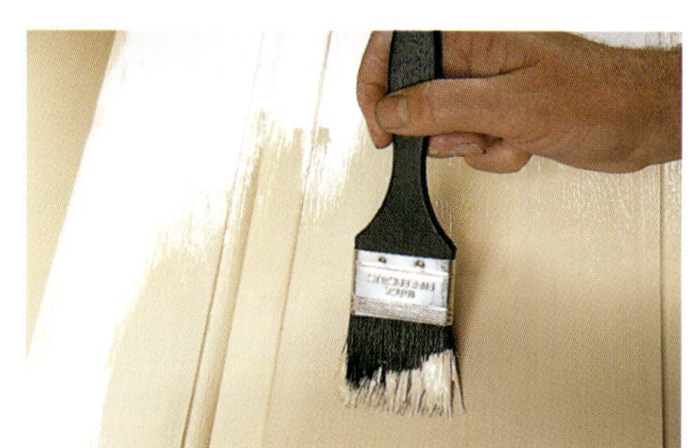

1 **Prepare the surface (see *Preparation*, p. 18). Apply an undercoat. Allow to dry. With a 2–3 in. (5–7.5 cm.) bristle basecoat brush apply at least two coats of buff eggshell paint. Allow to dry thoroughly between coats and before commencing the next step.**

Variation 1

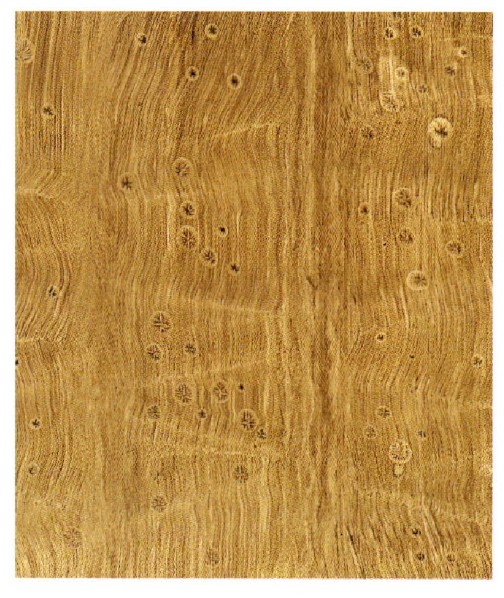

By manipulating the glaze in different ways and by varying the colorways, an assortment of wood finishes can be created. Here, a glaze of burnt umber mixed with a little raw sienna has been painted over a pale cream basecoat to create a bird's-eye maple effect. A mottler brush (see p. 12) was drawn through the glaze in a rocking motion from top to bottom. Use your knuckles to create knots to enhance the finished article.

Variation 2

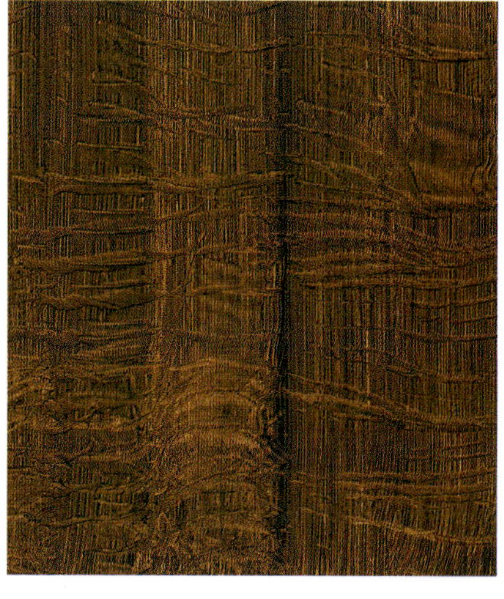

Here, the richness of ebony wood was created by over-painting the basecoat of yellow ocher with a glaze of burnt umber and a little pure color to create stripes. A mottler was dragged through the glaze, after which some medium-grade steel wool was dragged downward across the surface. The mottler was then again applied to the surface using quick, jagged strokes to create the horizontal stripes.

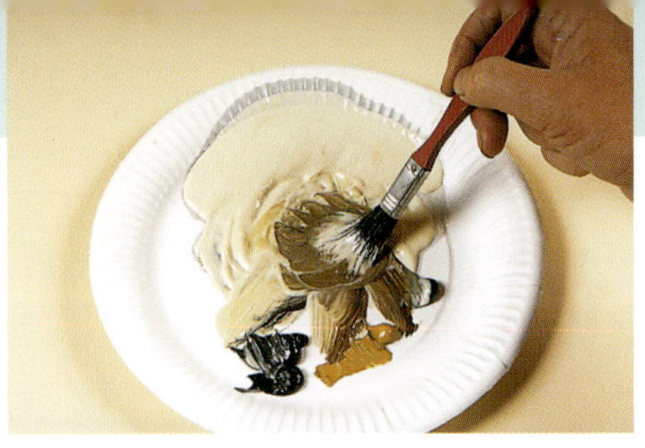

2 On a clean dish, mix some transparent oil glaze. On another dish, mix together one part raw umber, two parts yellow ocher and three parts burnt umber with a little mineral spirits (white spirit). Add the glaze and mix completely. Add a little mineral spirits to achieve a pouring consistency.

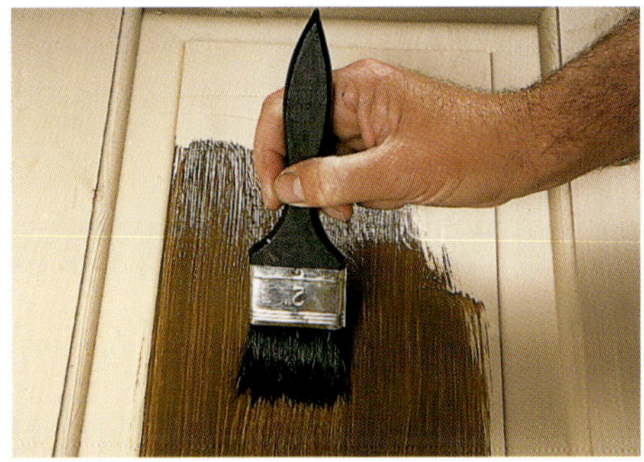

3 With a 2–3 in. (5–7.5 cm.) bristle brush apply a fairly generous layer of glaze to the surface. Cover the surface completely and use the brush in one direction only. With a stippling brush stipple out all visible brushstrokes (see *Stippling*, p. 30). Remove any excess glaze with a soft cloth.

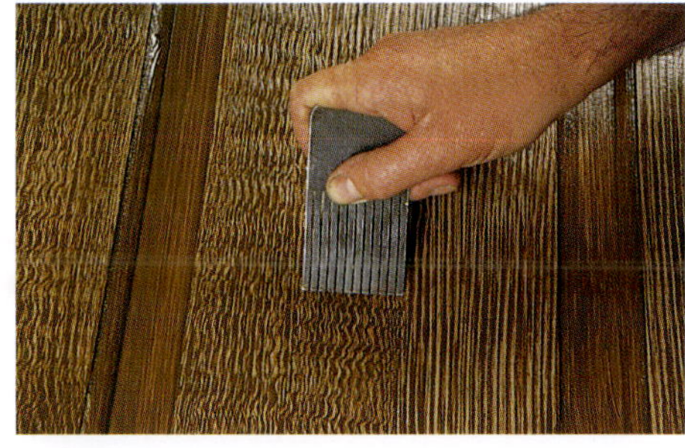

4 Drag a wide-toothed metal graining comb (see p. 40) cleanly and vertically through the wet glaze. Continue across the surface removing excess glaze from the comb with a soft, lint-free cloth as necessary. Repeat over the surface but this time ever so slightly wave the comb to create the very characteristic close oak grain.

6 The texture and density of natural oak have been achieved here using a simple combing technique (see p. 40). Both the color and the thickness of the glaze create the substance and strength of sawn oak. This texture would be enhanced by liming, which would mellow the final effect to a soft, chalky finish.

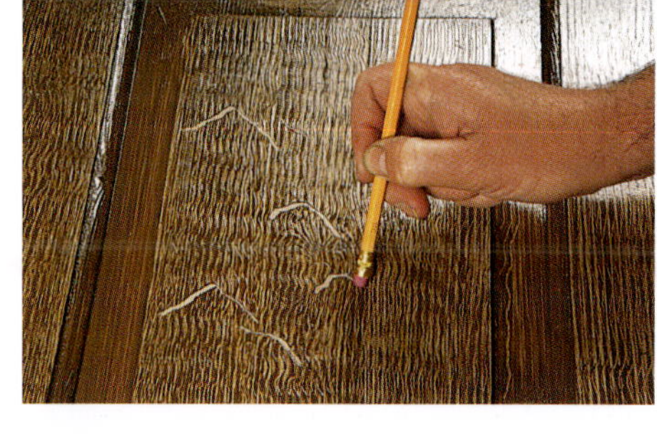

5 Using either an eraser, cloth wrapped around your finger tip or an eraser-tipped pencil, pass the eraser through the glaze in upside-down "V" shapes in roughly diagonal lines across the surface. Be careful not to over do this as the look can easily be destroyed.

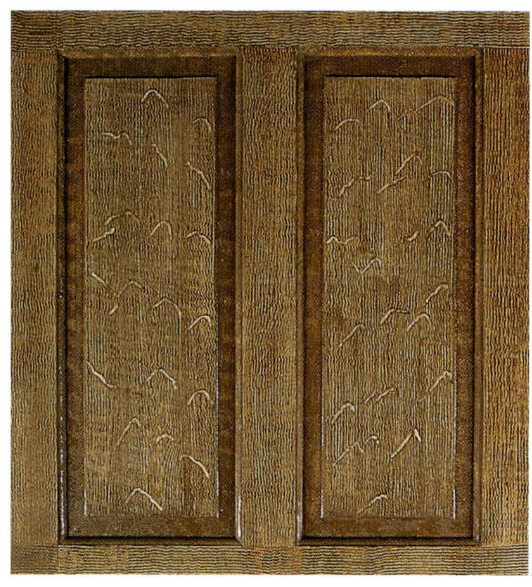

Variation 3

This oak woodgrain effect was achieved by applying a glaze of deep purple latex (emulsion) and acrylic glazing medium over a basecoat of lilac semigloss latex (vinyl silk emulsion) (1 part paint to 4 parts glazing medium).

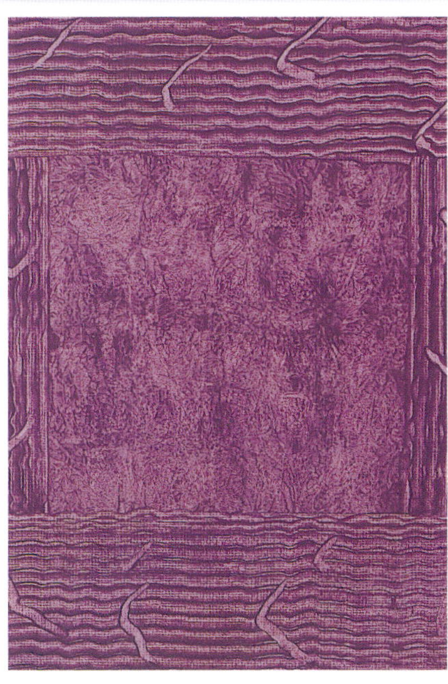

Variation 4

This panel was first painted with two coats of bright green semigloss latex (vinyl silk emulsion) and left to dry for 24 hours. A glaze of deep red artists' acrylic paint mixed with acrylic glazing medium (1 part paint to 4 parts glaze) was then applied to the whole panel. The brushstrokes were stippled out see (p. 30) and a triangular, rubber-toothed comb dragged (see p. 40) through the glaze to create a veined colorway oak grain effect.

In context

The three splendid settings here illustrate how well oak woodgrain, tortoiseshell and shading can work in larger areas. Carefully chosen colors have been used in subtle ways to create varied effects—strong and rich, and light and airy. To use the real thing in these settings would be very expensive. However, these effective simulated finishes can be created using paint for a fraction of the cost of the real thing.

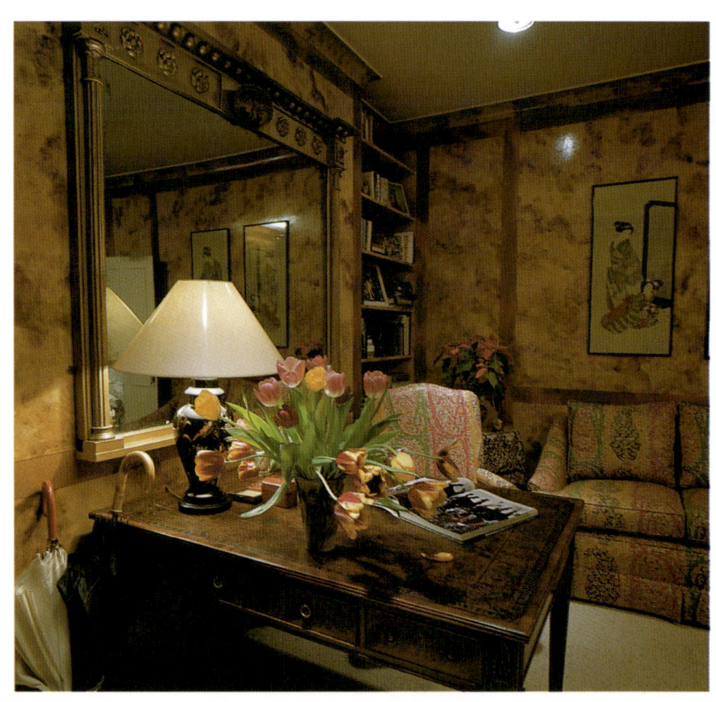

Oak woodgrain

▼ Library/sitting room

Filled with lavishly bound books, these oak woodgrained bookcases emit a simple glow that is beautifully highlighted by the rich terracotta of the very plain walls. A classic example of how simplicity is so effective.

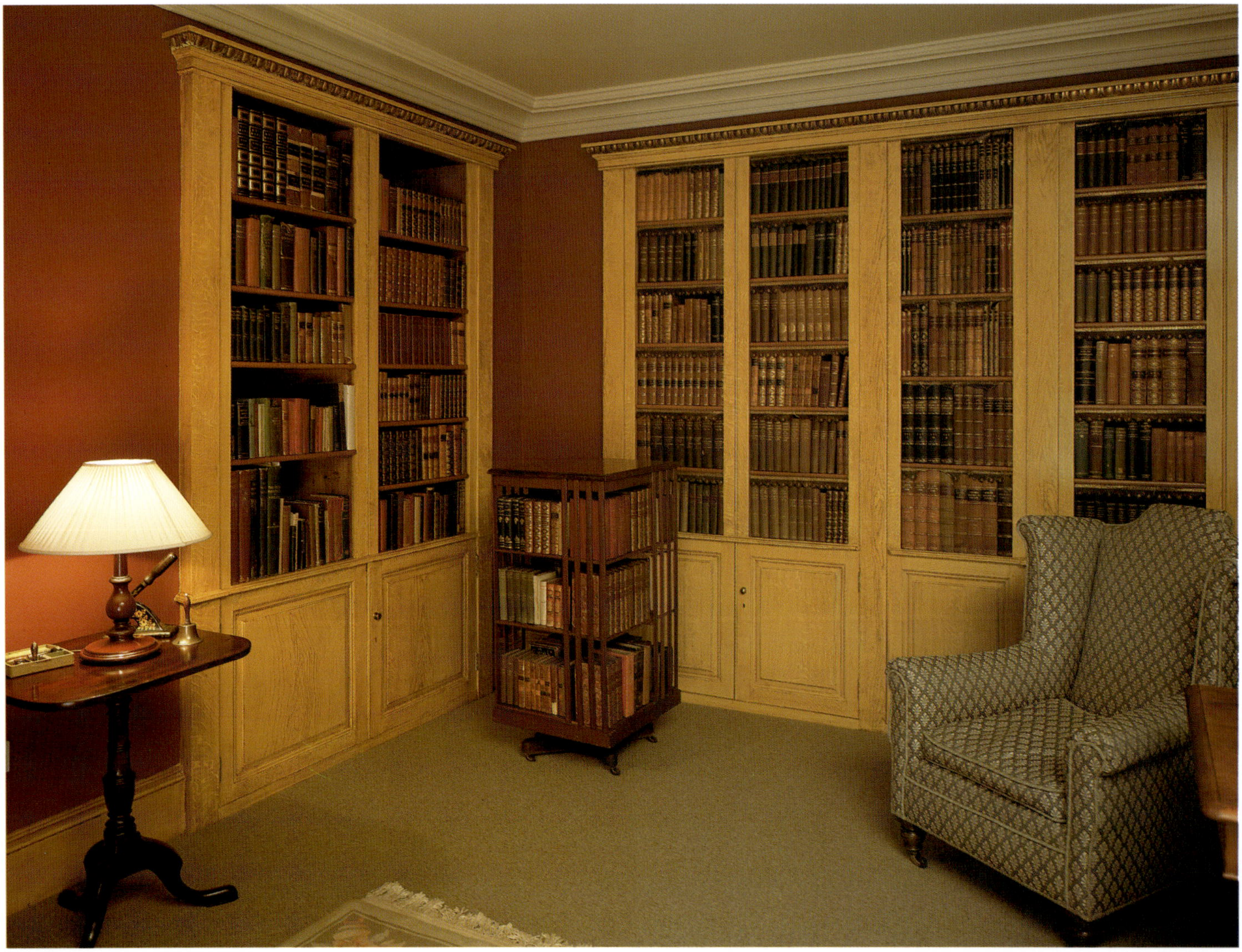

Tortoiseshell

◀ Drawing room

The exotic feel of the Far East has been exquisitely recreated here by using the rich deep colors of tortoiseshell. The glow of ocher and umber accessorized with the highly-polished surface of the desk adds warmth and richness.

Shading

▶ Living room/chimney breast

Well-chosen colors and the exquisite use of stenciling and shading has brought a wonderfully classical look to a very simple flat wall and chimney breast. The combination of shading and stenciling has resulted in a clever example of trompe l'oeil. The effect is that one is not sure about what is real and what is not.

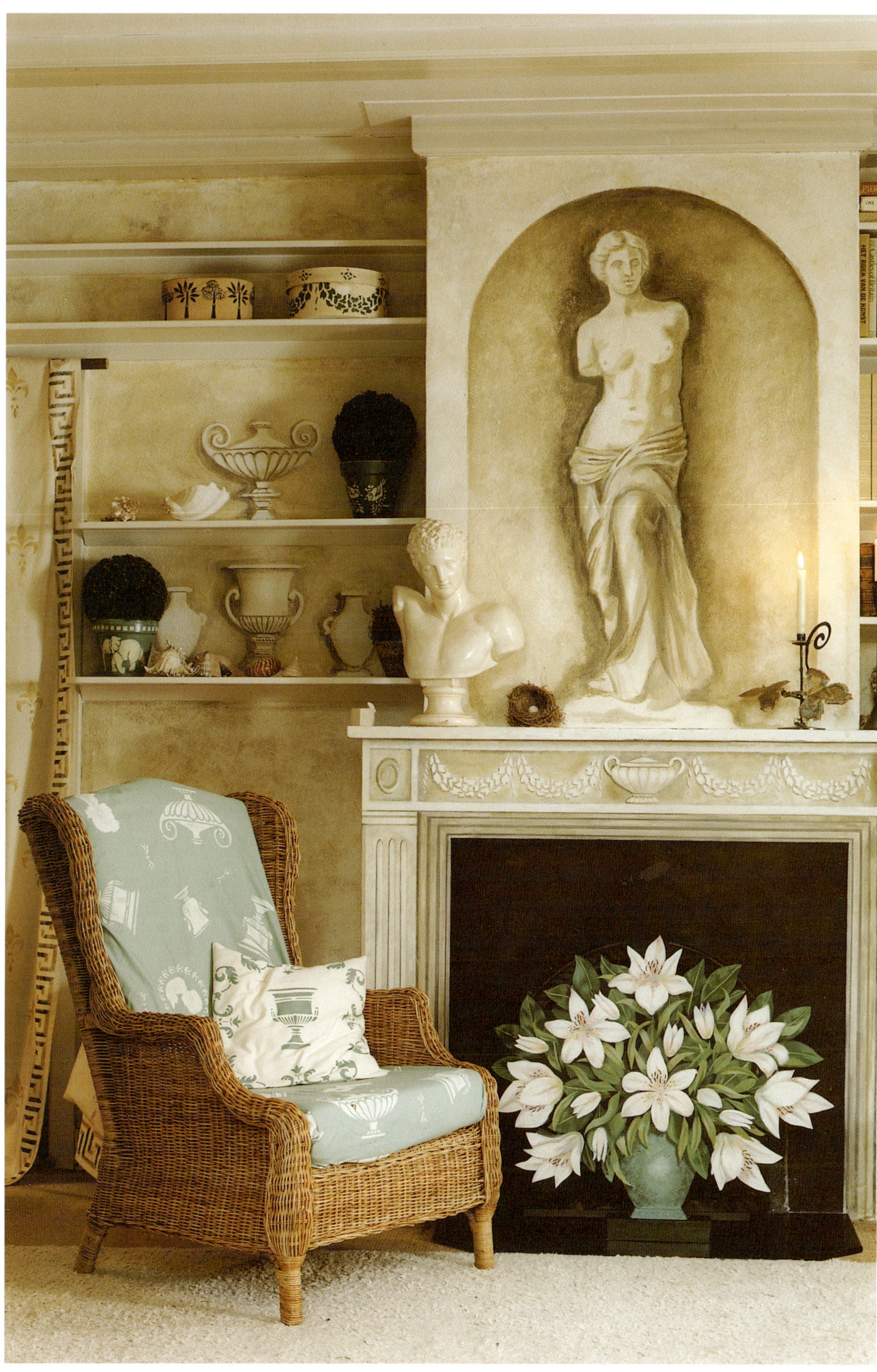

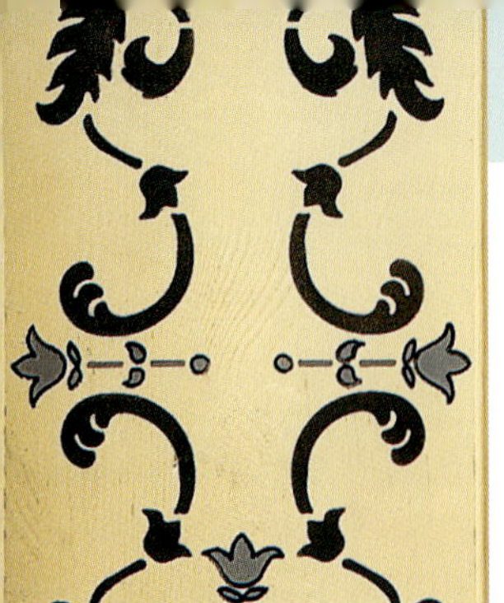

Marquetry

Creating the beautiful and exquisite patterns of marquetry, or simply using paint to emulate the effect, can result in many very individual projects. Once completed, years of immense satisfaction and pleasure will be guaranteed.

Inlaid patterns in wood will enhance any decor, modern or period. Marquetry can be applied to floors, fireplace surrounds, fitted units and doors, as well as to smaller items such as tables and boxes. Although marquetry is very inexpensive to achieve, patience and practice are necessary in order to achieve a high-quality finish.

The essence of marquetry, traditionally created by the use of many types of wood veneers, is of a very smooth surface, and so it is essential that the surface be prepared correctly. A well prepared, smooth surface, free of flaws and holes, is vital for achieving good results. Old paint and varnish must be removed completely, otherwise the paints will not be able to penetrate the wood to reveal the grain.

Once the painting is started great care should be taken, as once the paint stains the wood it is extremely hard to remove, requiring a great deal of sanding to remove the surface before reapplying the paint.

There are no limits as far as the design is concerned, it can be as simple or as complicated as you wish, and you can create a very rich spectrum of color to fit in perfectly with any decor.

You will need

Tools

• 2 in. (5 cm.) basecoat brush • Sharp pencil or ball-point pen • Tracing paper • Paint dishes • Fine and medium artists' watercolor brush • Chalk • Low-tack tape • ½ in. (1.3 cm.) bristle brush • Straight edge (ruler)

Materials

• Shellac (knotting) solution • Undercoat • Plain sketch of chosen pattern • Pale cream eggshell paint • Acrylic paints in chosen colors • Medium gold permanent marking pen • Spray sealant

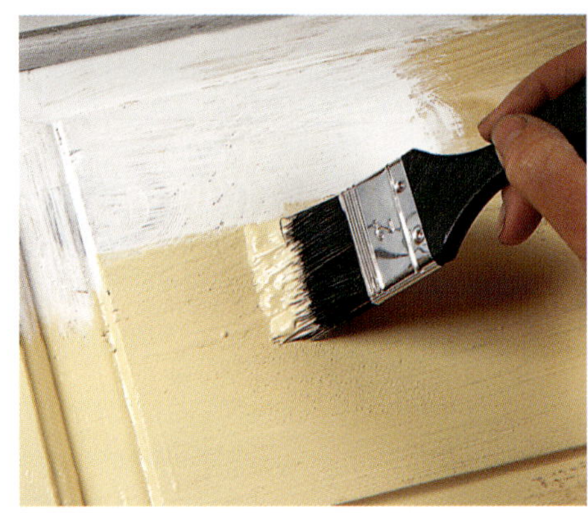

1 Fill all holes with a store-bought filler following manufacturer's instructions. Sand away all excess. Remove all dust. Seal all knots with shellac (knotting solution) and allow to dry. Using a bristle basecoat brush apply an undercoat. Allow to dry. Apply two top coats of pale cream eggshell. Allow the paint to dry completely between coats and before commencing the next step.

Variation 1

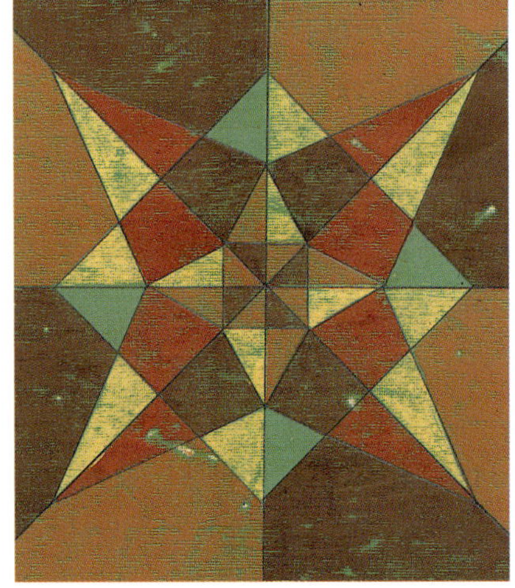

An inlay pattern was marked over a basecoat of green semigloss latex (vinyl silk emulsion). It was scored with a craft knife to avoid paint bleeding. Each area was painted with a fine brush and latex (emulsion) in chocolate brown, pale terracotta, burgundy and cream. It was left to dry then heavily sanded with fine-sandpaper and finished by lining with a fine black permanent marker, sealed and varnished with flat (matte) acrylic varnish.

Variation 2

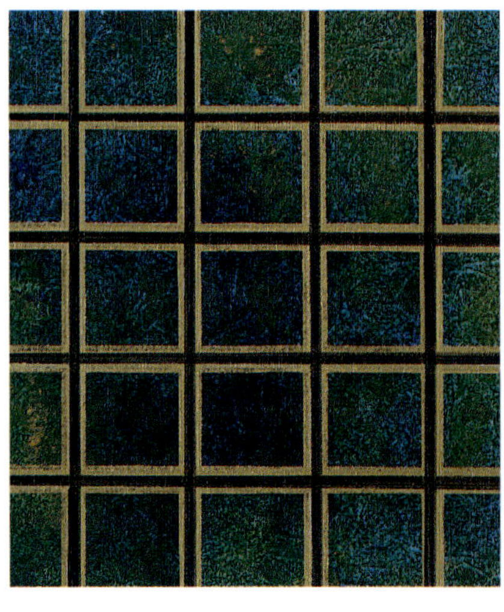

This panel was painted with a pale blue eggshell and left to dry before applying a layer of gilp, then a coat of French ultramarine and yellow ocher artists' oil paints mixed with mineral spirits (white spirit). It was then "pounced" (see p. 31) with crunched up plastic. When dry, it was lined (see p. 94) with a gold and a black permanent marking pen for a tiled effect. When dry, it was sprayed with sealant and coated with gloss varnish.

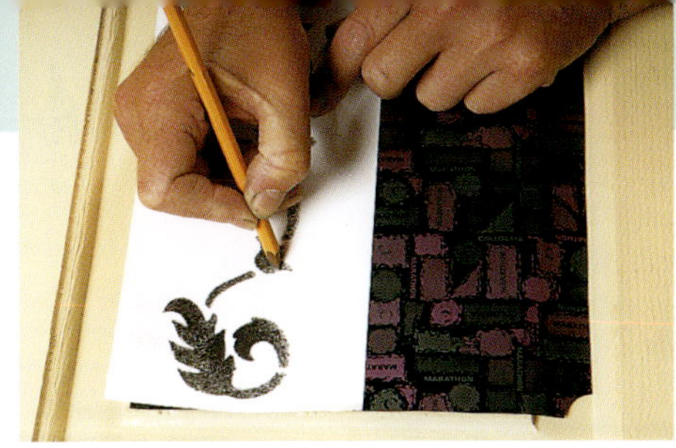

2 Enlarge or reduce the image to the required size. With a pencil or ball-point pen trace the design onto the door panel (see *Tracing*, p. 88). Check the outline is complete before removing the image.

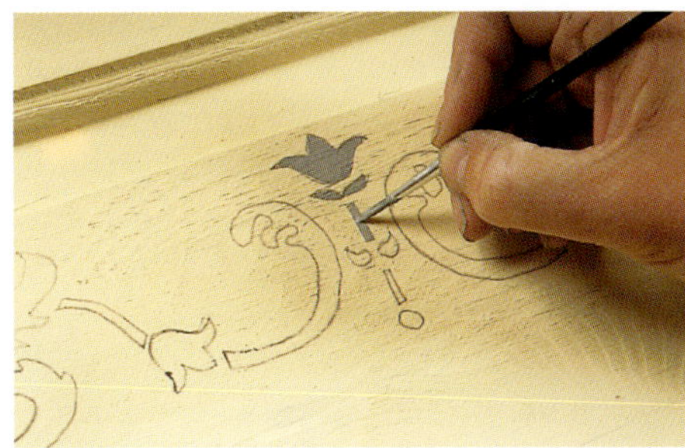

3 In separate dishes pour some artists' acrylic in black and dark gray (equal proportions of black and white acrylic). Add water until the paint achieves a consistency of pouring cream or a thickness that you find easy to paint with. With an artists' watercolor brush carefully paint in all the relevant sections of your design in the dark gray acrylic. Allow to dry. Repeat with the black paint using a clean brush.

4 Measure and mark with chalk a suitable border (see *Lining*, p. 94). Apply a line of low-tack tape along the inside edge. Leave a ¼ in. (0.63 cm.) gap and repeat with a parallel line of tape. Press both layers of tape into position to avoid seepage.

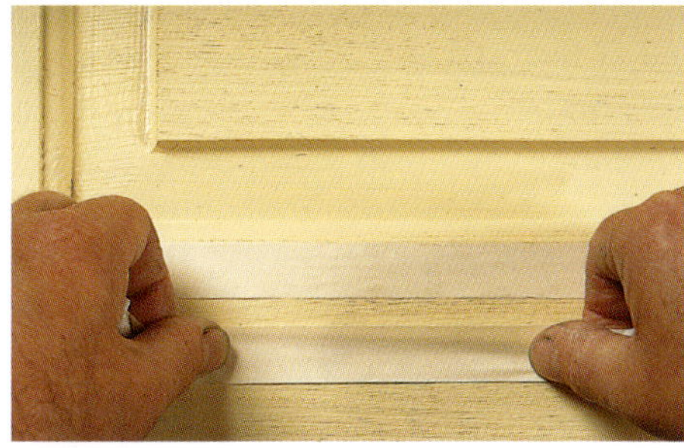

5 With a ½ in. (1.2 cm.) bristle brush paint between the parallel lines of tape with the black paint. Do not use too much paint as this will cause seepage. Allow the paint to dry before removing the tape slowly and carefully.

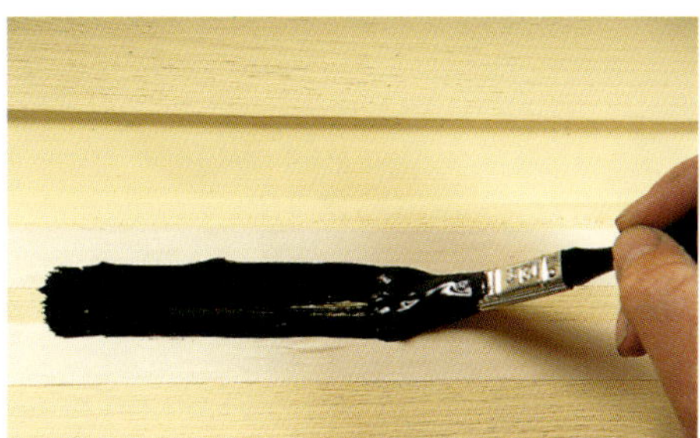

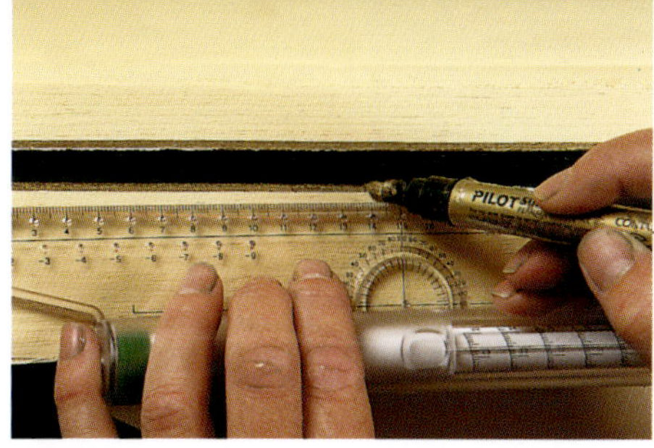

6 With a straight edge and a medium gold permanent marking pen, outline both edges of your black line. Move the pen along the straight edge quickly and evenly to avoid too much gold ink running onto the decorated surface. Use the straight edge to balance your hand if lining an awkward recess. Spray with sealant before continuing.

7 Best kept to simple patterns and designs, true inlay may be simulated using plain, flat colors. This panel has been given the look of an ebony inlay using black and white (below). Other finishes include tortoiseshell and mother-of-pearl.

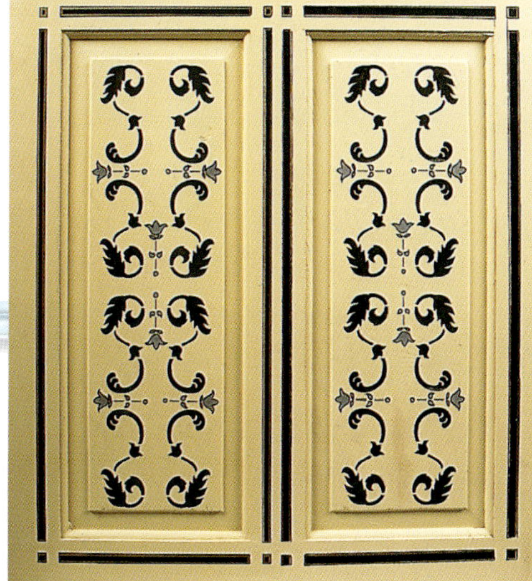

Variation 3

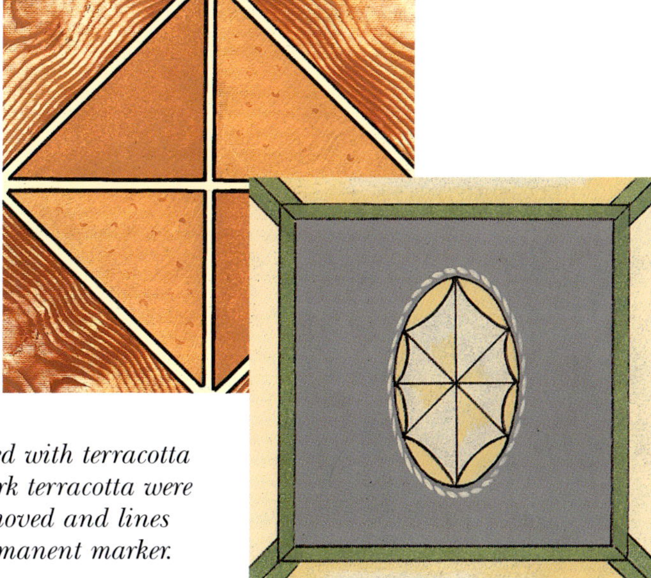

The panel was coated with cream eggshell and dried. Low-tack tape was used for the design. The triangles were painted with terracotta eggshell and oil glaze. Outside triangles were dragged and inner panels stippled. The final triangles were glazed with terracotta and dragged. Dots of dark terracotta were added. The tape was removed and lines completed with black permanent marker.

Variation 4

The creation of marquetry or inlaid effects with paint has always been a personal favorite, and the possibilities are endless. Here (left) a simple standard inlay pattern was drawn in black permanent marker over a central, oval-frame stencil. The edges of the panel were masked and stippled in green before being outlined in black.

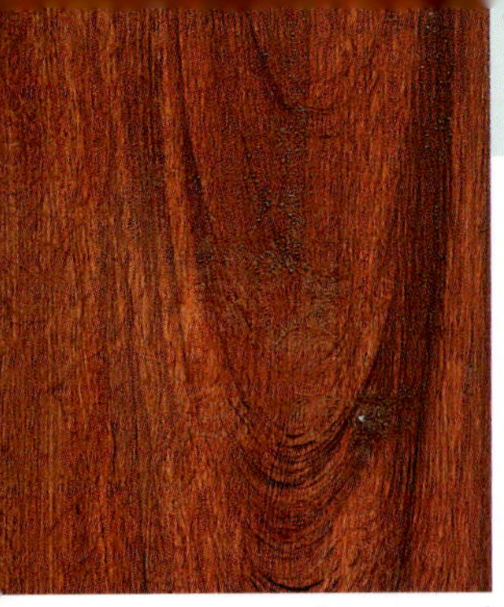

The rich color and characteristic patterning of mahogany has always made it a popular wood for craftspeople and artists to copy. Genuine mahogany is very expensive to buy, and has for centuries been used to make top-quality furniture and accessories. Now you can create the stylish look of mahogany yourself for a fraction of the price.

Flame mahogany

Moderately expensive to achieve, the effect of mahogany is used to create the look of the real wood on a base of softwood. This advanced technique needs practice but is well worth the attempt. It is suited to furniture, fireplace surrounds and boxes, and is also very effective when used in paneling and on doors, baseboards (skirting) and below chair (dado) rails. When used on larger areas such as walls, it looks best in panels and if used as a foil to other woods.

Mahogany finish looks best in a traditional setting, and works well in sitting rooms, studies and bedrooms. Although it can be used on smaller surfaces, flame mahogany is better suited to larger detailed areas. If mistakes occur remove the glaze from the basecoat with a soft, lint-free cloth dampened in mineral spirits (white spirit) and reapply the glaze. Using oil glazes extends working time for up to 30 minutes, which allows you to rework the glaze.

You will need

Tools

• *2–3 in. (5–7.5 cm.) bristle basecoat brush* • *2 in. (5 cm.) good glazing brush* • *2–3 in. (5–7.5 cm.) mottler brushes* • *Lint-free cloth* • *Satin oil varnish* • *1 in. (2.5 cm.) bristle decorators' brush* • *Softening brush* • *Dragging brush* • *Varnishing brush*

Materials

• *Undercoat* • *Transparent oil glaze* • *Artists' oil colors in burnt sienna, burnt umber, Vandyke brown and alizarin crimson* • *Mid-terracotta eggshell paint* • *Mineral spirits (white spirit)* • *Satin oil varnish*

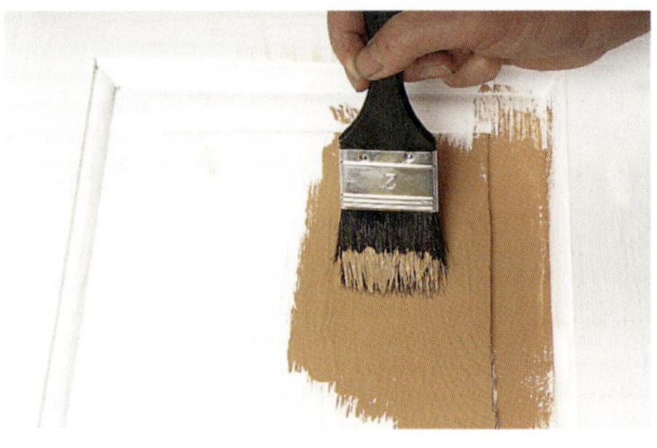

1 Prepare the surface (see *Preparation*, p. 18). Apply an undercoat. Allow to dry. Apply a coat of mid-terracotta eggshell paint using a bristle brush. Allow to dry overnight. Repeat with a second coat and dry overnight.

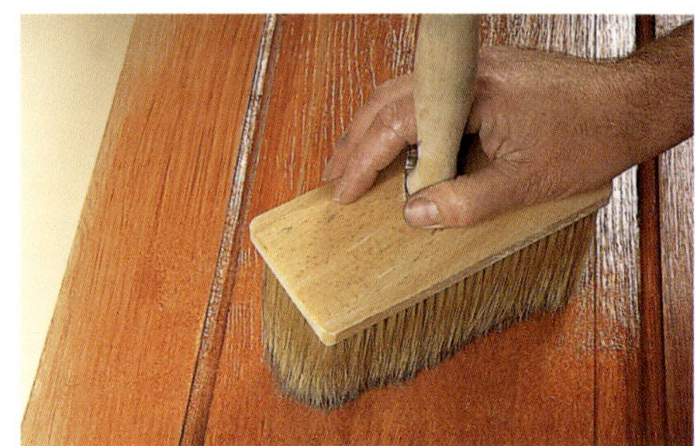

2 Mix a glaze with transparent oil glaze and equal parts of burnt sienna, Vandyke brown and burnt umber artists' oil paints. Mix with mineral spirits (white spirit) to a pouring consistency. Coat surface with glaze; stipple out brushstrokes.

Variation 1

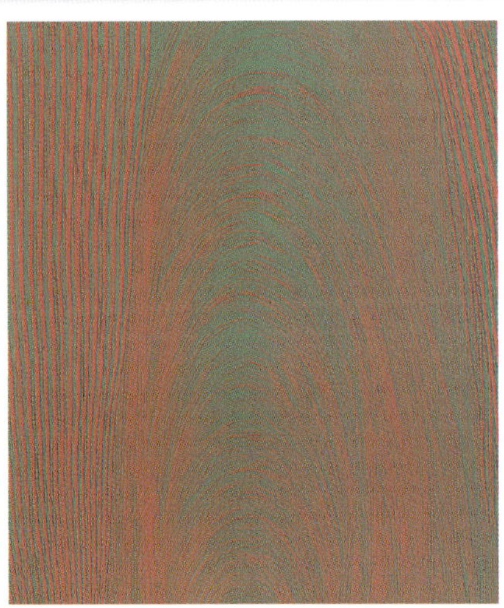

Flame mahogany is a luxurious wood to copy as shown in the step-by-step but the simulation need not end there. Fantasy colorways also work well in this variation. Here, the technique used was the same but the colors were changed. A red glaze was applied over a basecoat of mid-green resulting in a warm and surreal grained effect.

Variation 2

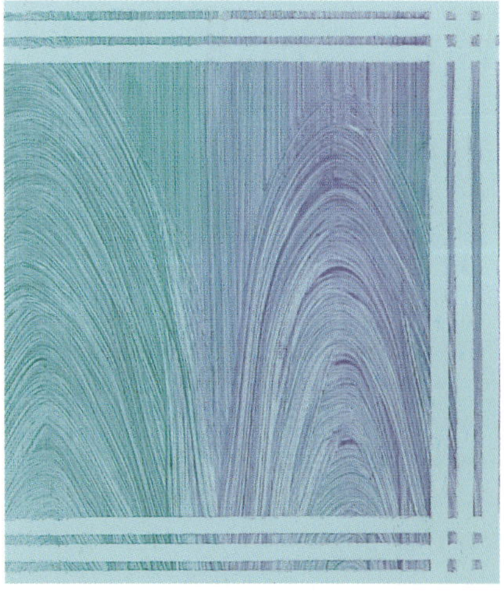

Here, low-tack tape was applied to a turquoise semigloss latex (vinyl silk emulsion) basecoat. Two separate coats of acrylic glazes of peacock green and mauve were then applied following manufacturer's instructions. A 2 in. (5 cm.) mottler brush was dragged through the glazes at an angle of 45 degrees to the surface. The glaze was allowed to dry before being sealed with two coats of flat (matte) acrylic varnish.

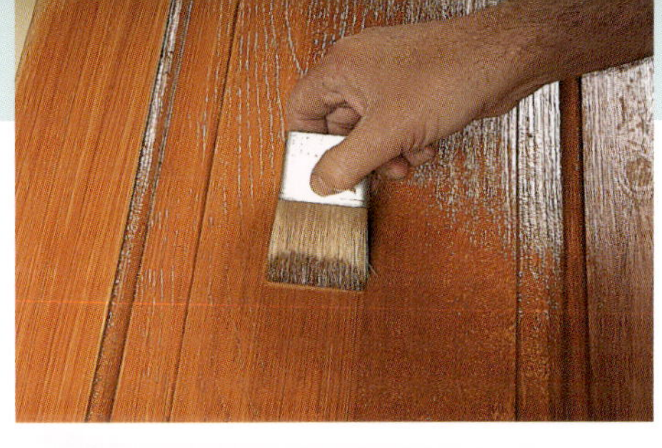

3 Drag a 2–3 in. (5–7.5 cm.) mottler brush (see p. 12) through the glaze. Follow the line of the natural grain. As you work across the surface, remove any excess glaze from the mottler with a clean cloth. Remove any glaze build-up in recessed areas with a clean, dry bristle brush. Repeat with the mottler brush across the surface creating a strong dragged pattern.

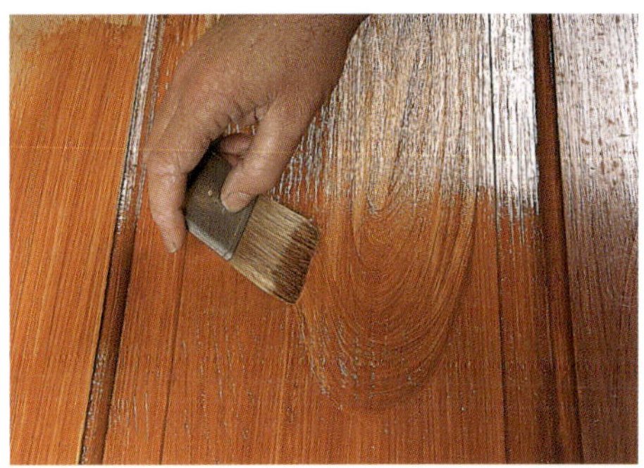

4 With a clean, dry, 2 in. (5 cm.) mottler brush, form the "feathered" age rings on the surface. Drag the mottler at a 45 degree angle through the glaze to make a vague "U" shape. Build up the size of this shape. Allow to dry.

5 Mix up a further glaze of equal parts of burnt sienna, Vandyke brown and burnt umber. Add a little alizarin crimson and dilute with mineral spirits (white spirit) as before. With the mottler overgrain the age rings with this glaze, as in step 4. Do not over do it.

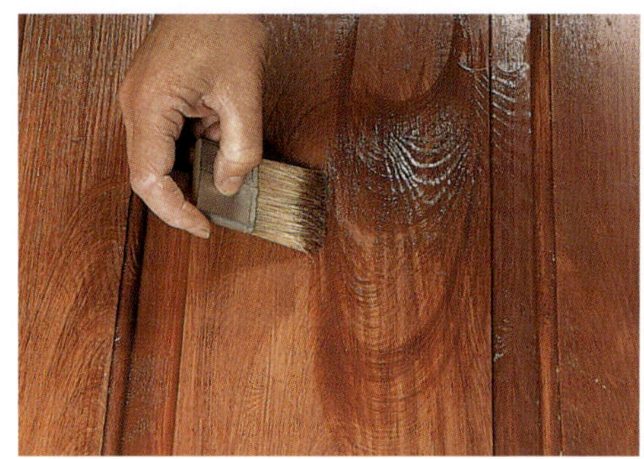

6 Pass a badger softening brush backward and forward across the surface very lightly. Allow to dry.

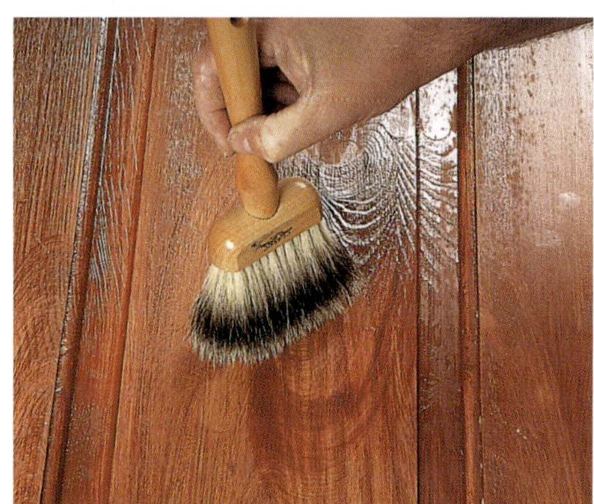

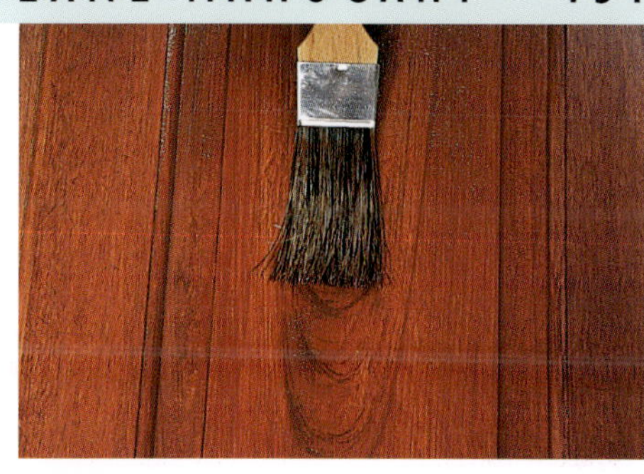

7 Mix up a glaze following step 5, but add a bit more alizarin crimson. Dilute to a more transparent consistency by adding a little more mineral spirits (white spirit). Paint glaze over the entire surface. With a dragging brush "flog" the surface gently, working the brush from the bottom to the top. Dry. Varnish with at least two coats of satin oil varnish.

8 This pine door (below) has been made to look like an expensive solid mahogany door. The layers of rich crimsons and browns characteristic of true mahogany breathe life and depth into the previously flat softwood. Polished to a beautiful, mellow patina the wood graining becomes rich and warm.

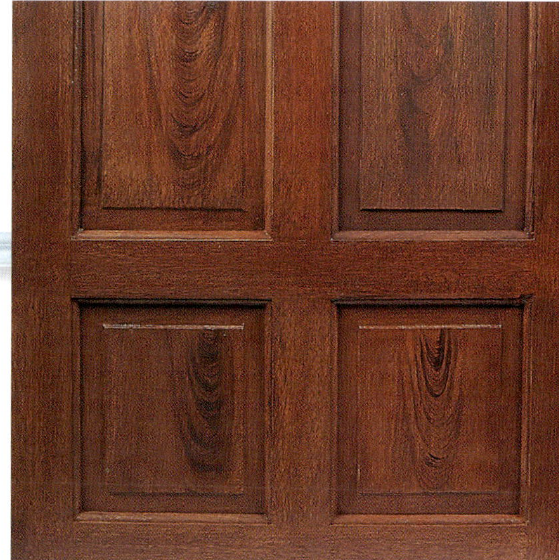

Variation 3

Using more vibrant colorways will create truly amazing results. Here, a glaze of viridian was applied over a pale blue basecoat, and the same flame mahogany technique applied. Knots were created randomly by touching the wet glaze with a knuckle very quickly (a technique used in bird's-eye maple, see p. 124), under oak woodgrain).

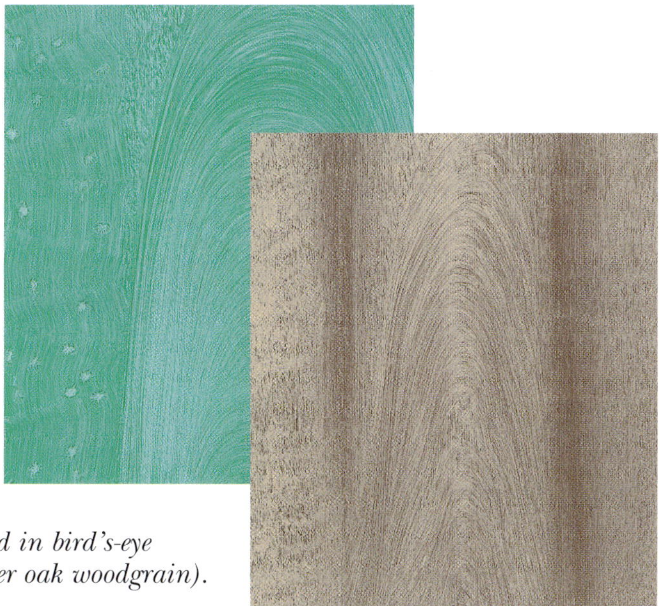

Variation 4

Keeping to more natural colors can also work well yet totally change the final effect (left). Here, the saddle-brown basecoat was overglazed with a pale cream and stippled, and then the flame mahogany technique applied.

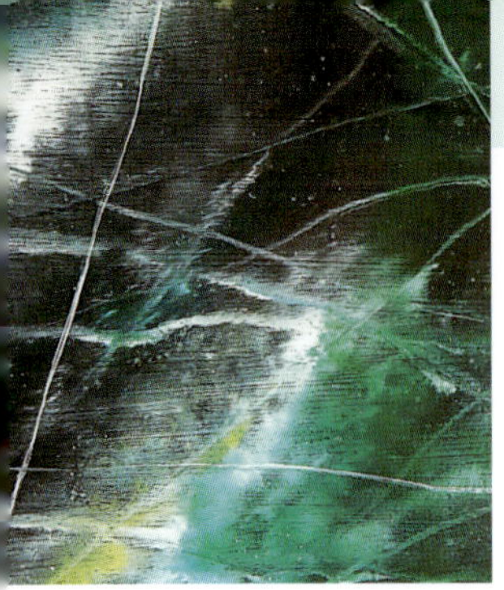

Verde antico

Verde antico, because of its striking color combinations, is an extremely popular marble to emulate. It is also one of the simpler marbles to produce, either in oil or acrylic-based paints and glazes, and using the simple techniques of sponging (see p. 54) and dragging (see p. 62).

Marbling, once mastered, is one of the most innovative and satisfying of all the paint effect techniques. Although ideally suited to floors, walls, ceilings, architectural features, table tops and paneling, marbling also can be applied to smaller decorative objects such as boxes and lampbases. Larger areas, such as walls, will look better if the effect is applied in the form of panels.

As with all projects, the best and most professional work is done with the best tools and materials possible, which means the initial investment for marbling can be moderately expensive. However, this investment will be returned many times over with the production of excellent finishes.

Pitfalls can be overcome by reading and following all step-by-step instructions. Surface preparation, including basecoat application, is important. If a mistake occurs, wipe away with a soft cloth and repaint the area.

You will need

Tools

• 2–3 in. (5–7.5 cm.) bristle basecoat brush • ½ in. (1.2 cm.) Fitch brush • Measuring tape • Chalk • Low-tack tape • Paint dish • Tack cloth • Fine, round artists' brush or swordliner for veining • Stippling brush • 2–3 in. (5–7.5 cm.) badger softening brush (or a good-quality dusting brush) • Professional quality 2–3 in. (5–7.5 cm.) varnishing brush

Materials

• Undercoat • Black oil-based eggshell paint for basecoat • Artists' tube oil paint in white, viridian and yellow ocher • Transparent oil glaze or home-made gilp • Oil-based varnish gloss for finish and protection

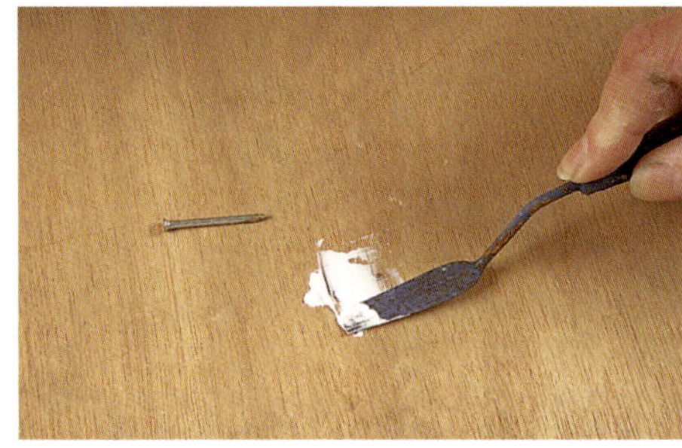

1 Prepare the surface (see *Preparation*, p. 18). Remove nails and fill holes or cracks with a store-bought filler. Sand with medium- then with fine-grade sandpaper. Dust with a brush and a damp cloth. Undercoat and dry.

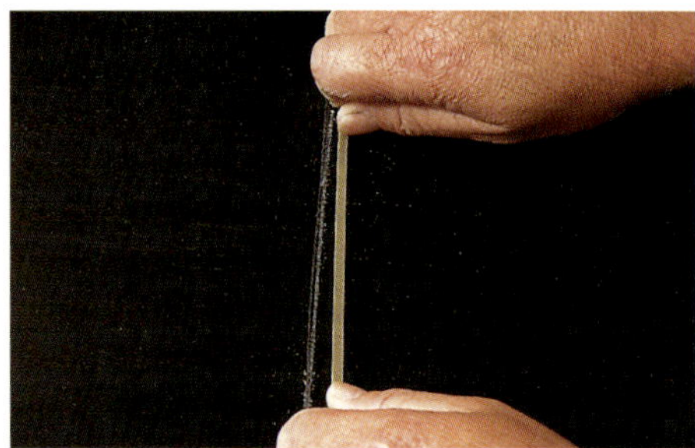

2 Using a 2 in. (5 cm.) basecoat brush apply two coats of black eggshell. Dry between coats. Measure 12 in. (30 cm.) square "tiles" and chalk in the lines. Use low-tack tape to mask off mortar lines between tiles. Press tape gently.

Variation 1

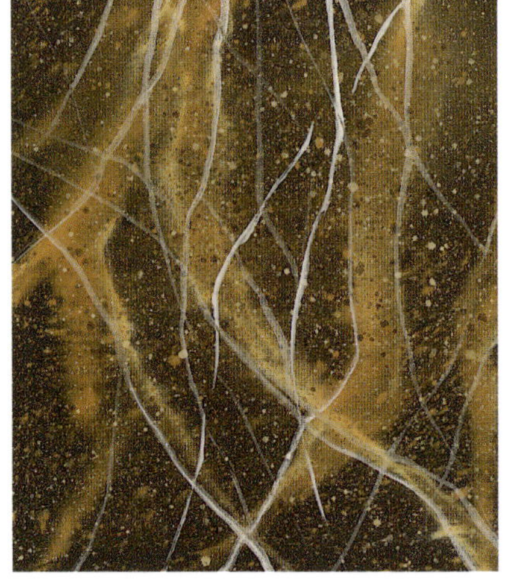

Simulated black-and-green marble, or verde antico, has a very striking and individual appearance. By varying the colorways equally good effects can be achieved. Here, yellow ocher and white veining have been applied over a basecoat of black. The wet surface was also spattered (see p. 72) with white and yellow ocher paint before being softened and coated with a clear varnish.

Variation 2

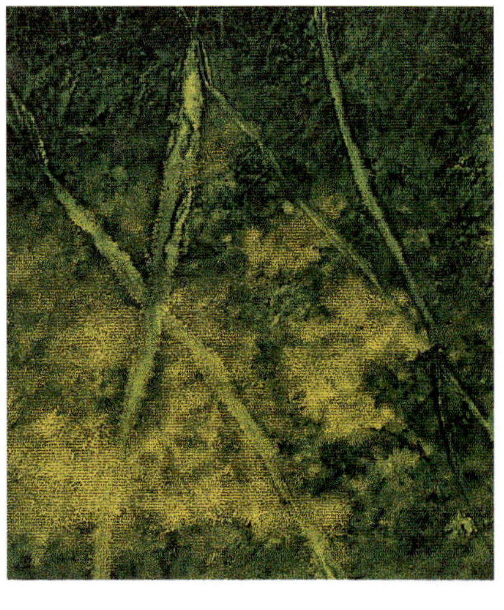

The panel was painted with yellow eggshell and left to dry. A glaze of 1 part viridian artists' oil paint and 3 parts transparent oil glaze, was sponged over (see p. 54). Before it was dry a sponge was dipped into mineral spirits (white spirit), the excess removed, and the surface sponged to separate some of the glaze. Veins were made by a lining brush dipped in mineral spirits (white spirit) drawn across surface. Once dry, it was varnished.

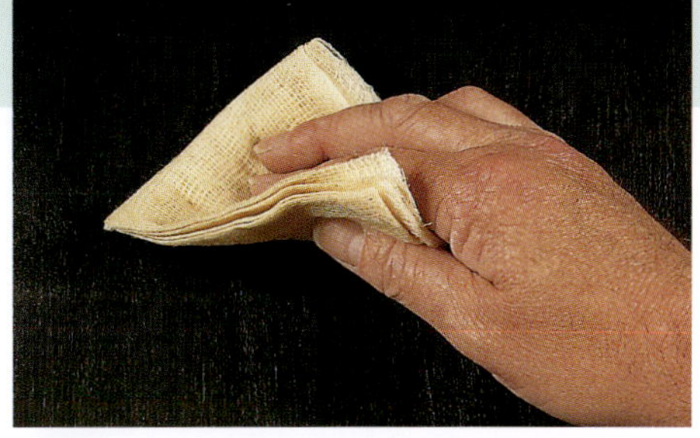

3 **On a clean dish place small amounts of artists' oil colors in yellow ocher, viridian and white, keeping each color separate. Mix each with a little transparent oil glaze or gilp (see recipe p. 15) to produce a thick pouring consistency.**

Wipe over the surface with a tack cloth (see p. 10). Using the bristle basecoat brush apply a layer of gilp or transparent oil glaze working on a convenient area.

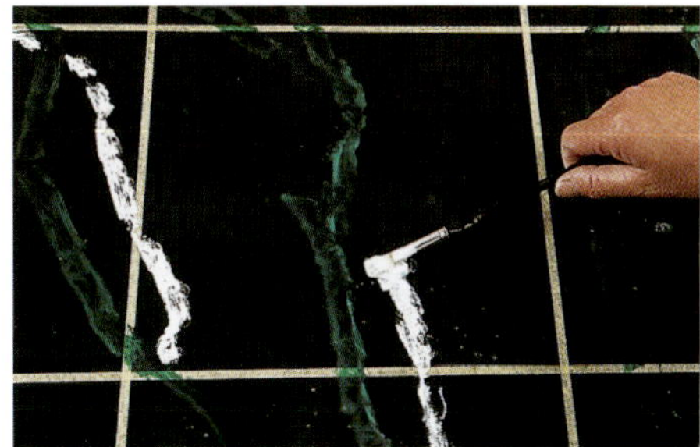

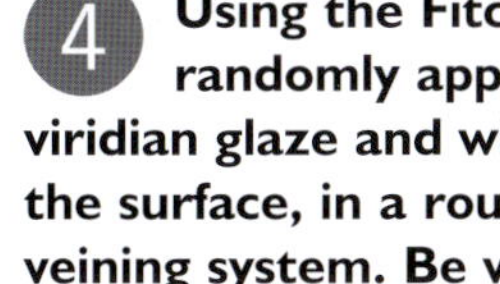

4 **Using the Fitch brush randomly apply some of the viridian glaze and white glaze across the surface, in a roughly parallel veining system. Be very careful not to overdo the effect, as more veins can always be added later.**

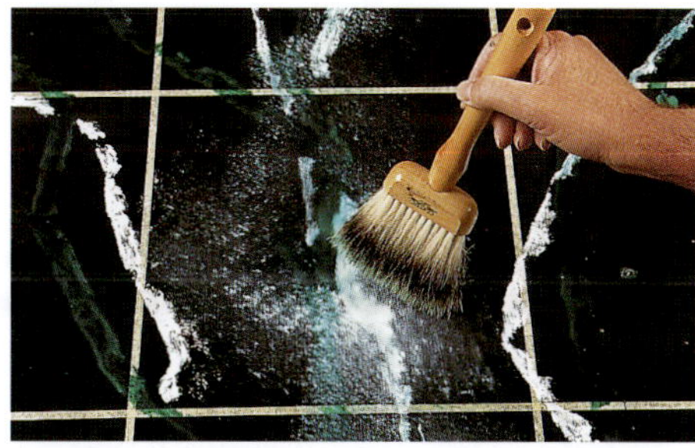

5 **Once you have achieved the look you require, stipple (see p. 30) out the veins to create a misty look and then soften with a badger softening brush. This will make the veins recede into the surface. Add more veins if wanted.**

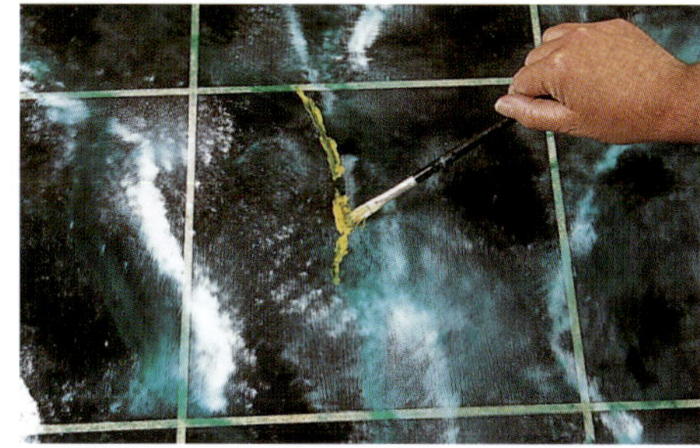

6 **Using a fine artists' brush or a swordliner, add some more fine veins with a little yellow ocher glaze. Pull the brush toward you, working it between your thumb and forefinger. Once again stipple if necessary and soften with a badger softener. Allow to dry overnight.**

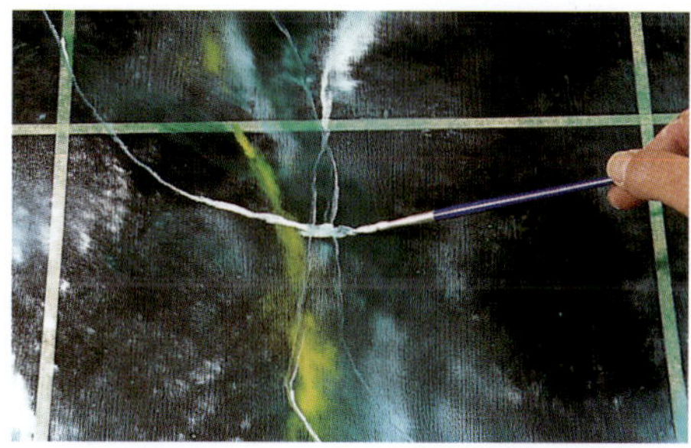

7 **Wipe the surface clean with a tack cloth and apply a layer of the gilp. Mix white artists' oil paint with a little gilp to form a light cream consistency. Apply this mix to create more veining. Allow to dry. Apply three coats of varnish.**

8 **Rich and lustrous, verde antico is one of the more popular marbles to simulate. This panel (below) has been "tiled," an effect which will add character and style to any floor . By using tinted varnishes on each alternate square, the effect has become three-dimensional.**

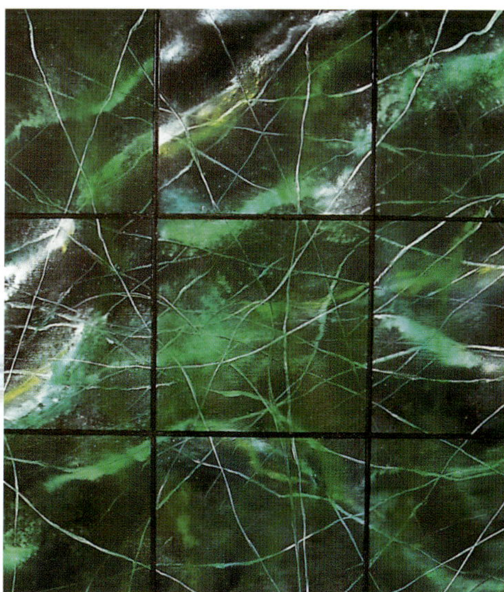

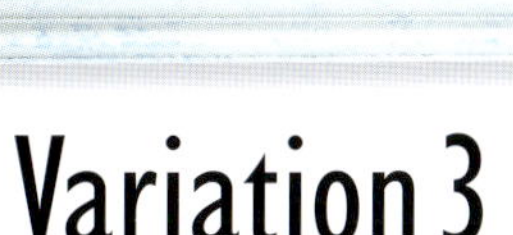

Variation 3

Over a basecoat of dark gray latex (emulsion), a glaze of 1 part gold acrylic stencil paint to 4 parts acrylic glaze was applied. The texture was created using frottage (see p. 28). While the glaze was still wet, a little bronzing powder was dropped onto the surface from a soft brush. When dry, it was sealed with a spray sealant and varnished with a satin acrylic varnish.

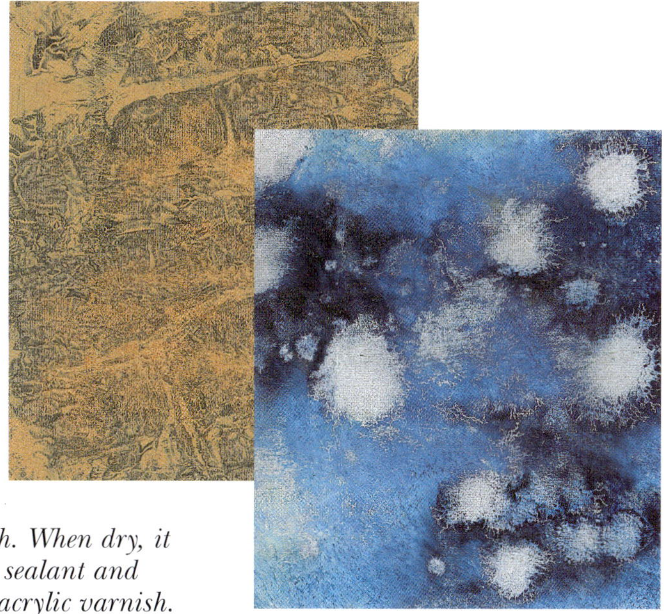

Variation 4

Two glazes were stippled (see p. 30) over aluminum leaf while each was still wet. The topcoat glaze was mixed from 1 part artists' oil paint to 3 parts transparent oil glaze (white and French ultramarine were the colors used). While still wet, mineral spirits (white spirit) was spattered on and left to dry. Oil-based gloss varnish was used to seal the surface (left).

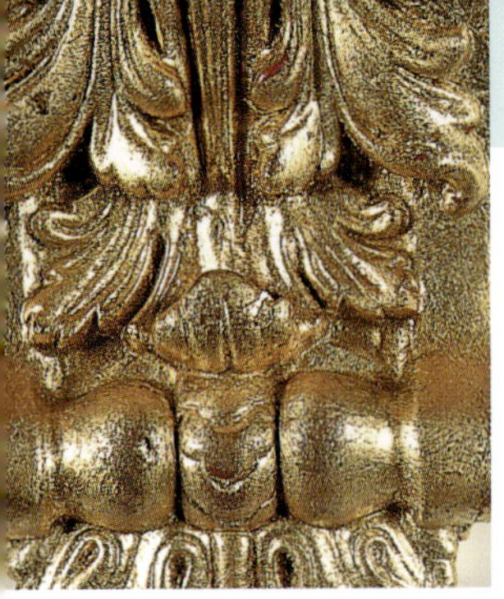

Most of us have admired the look of burnished gold on frames and the gilded embellishments on many of our most beautiful buildings. Achieving this wonderfully rich and stunning effect is certainly possible in the home. Just a little gilding here and there throughout the home will add a look of luxury and warmth, and provide visually interesting focal points in any style of interior.

Simple gilding

Gilding is ideally suited to smaller items such as boxes, lampbases, tables and picture frames, but can also be used on chair (dado) rails and molding, ceiling rosettes (roses) and furniture. Walls and ceilings can be gilded, depending on the effect required. Although the cost is reasonably high, most notably when using real gold leaf, the results are a designer's dream, and when used on smaller projects, the average outlay becomes reasonable. Gilding is ideally suited to traditional decor but can work very well in most modern settings.

For successful gilding, practice is essential. Begin with a flat surface such as a small box and progress to bigger projects. A common mistake is lack of preparation. Generally a smooth surface is required for gilding, as the leaf will show up any faults or flaws, even basecoat brush strokes. Follow instructions and if it goes wrong remove the mistake with fine steel wool and begin again.

You will need

Tools

• *1–2 in. (2.5–5 cm.) bristle basecoat brush basecoat* • *½–1 in. (1.2–2.5 cm.) soft-bristle brush to apply size* • *French chalk* • *Scissors* • *Gilders' brush to apply leaf* • *Soft artists' brush* • *Dust mask* • *Fine-grade steel wool* • *Varnishing brush*

Materials

• *Semigloss latex (vinyl silk emulsion)* • *Gold size* • *Metal leaf* • *Bronze powders* • *Appropriate varnish*

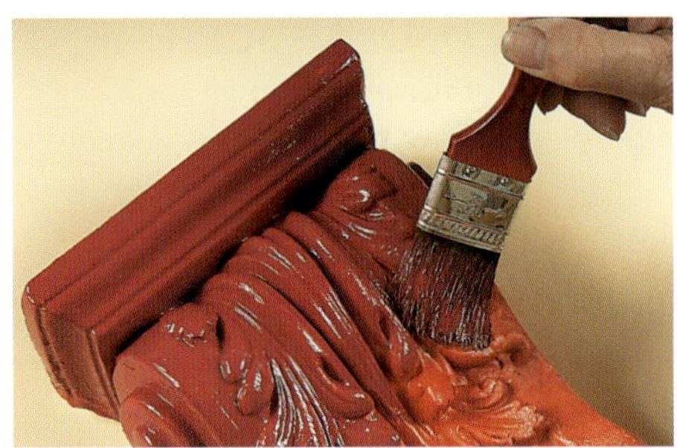

1 Gilding shows flaws, so prepare surface thoroughly. Fill all holes or cracks and sand to a smooth finish. Use a 1–2 in. (2.5–5 cm.) bristle basecoat brush to apply an undercoat. Dry. Apply two coats of crimson semigloss latex (vinyl silk emulsion).

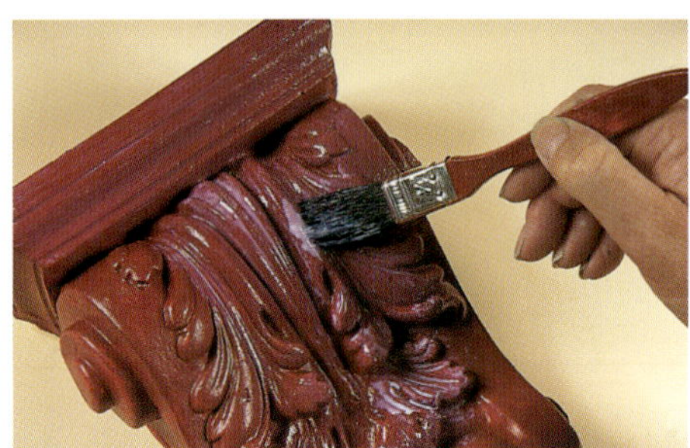

2 Using water-based gold size and a ½–1 in. (1.2–2.5 cm.) bristle brush, apply an even coat of the size. Stipple into awkward areas (see p. 30). Small areas of crimson showing through will highlight the "Florentine" look. Let size get tacky.

Variation 1

Gilding can be carried out in many ways, some a lot easier than others. Here ¾ in. (1.9 cm.) and ¼ in. (0.63 cm.) low-tack masking tape was used to create a checkered (chequered) pattern over a basecoat of olive green. With a finger wrapped in a soft, lint-free cloth, the surface was gilded with a dark and a light gold gilding wax, and finally the masking tape was removed.

Variation 2

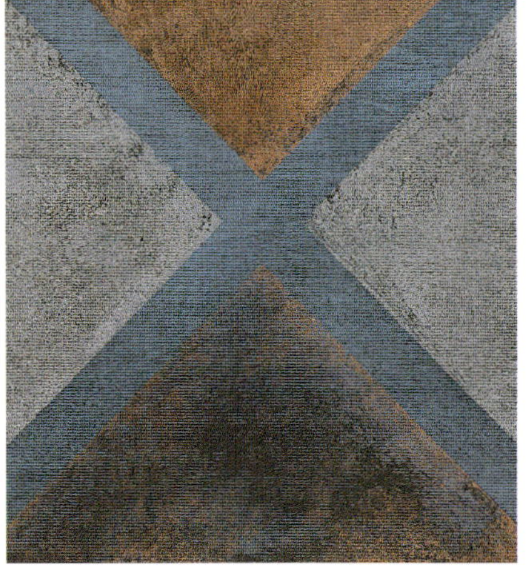

In the second variation, copper and aluminum foil have been used following the instructions for applying Dutch metal. The masking tape, which was used to create a quartered effect, was removed, and the whole surface distressed with country blue antiquing fluid, used more heavily in some areas than others.

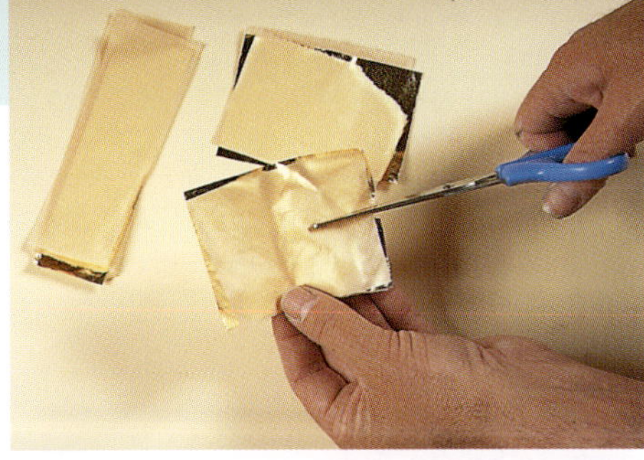

3 Lightly cover your hands with a little French chalk. Cut the sheet of gold leaf into manageable pieces for applying to awkward areas of the surface. For this purpose transfer leaf is easier to handle than the loose leaf, although it is slightly more expensive.

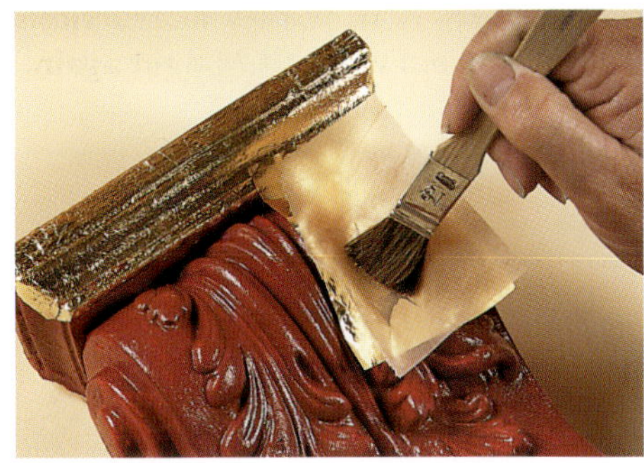

4 Once the size has gone tacky or touch dry, use a soft gilding brush to carefully place the leaf, section by section, over the surface. Press against the backing sheet to press the leaf onto the surface. Smooth down slowly and with care. Continue across the complete surface.

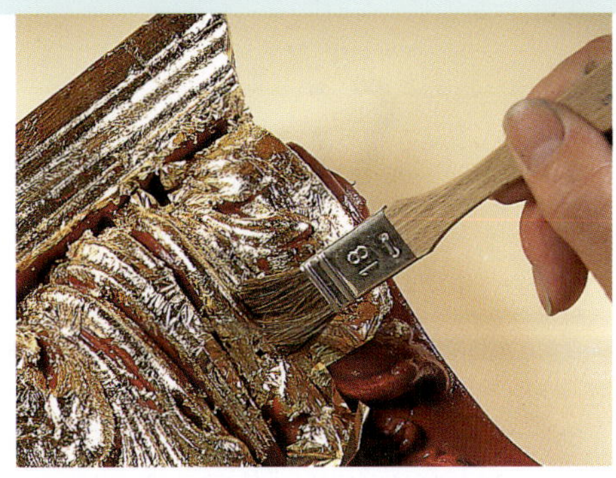

5 Once you have completed a workable area remove the backing sheet. Using a soft gilding brush, carefully and methodically smooth down any lumps or loose pieces of the gold leaf.

6 Apply a little bronzing powder in deep gold to the surface with a soft artists' brush. Use a mask to protect yourself from stray particles. Allow to dry overnight.

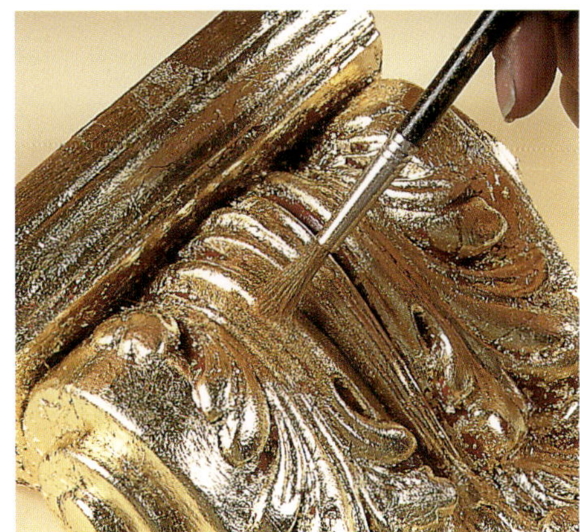

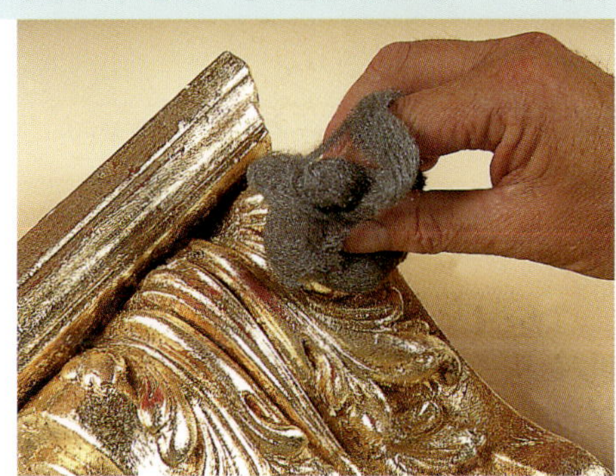

7 If required, use very fine steel wool (0000 grade) to gently distress the surface (see p. 36) by allowing the underneath layer of crimson basecoat to show through. Seal the surface with varnish. Gilt or bronzing powders should be sealed with an oil-based varnish.

8 Gilding, once considered a specialist paint finish, is now possible for us all to do successfully. Complete gilding or simple highlighting creates a look of opulence with only the minimum of practice. Rich and special, gilding highlights and enhances any surface as this plaster corbel shows (below).

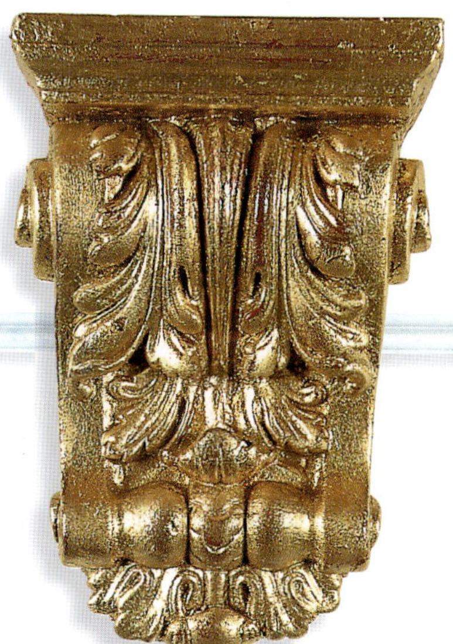

Variation 3

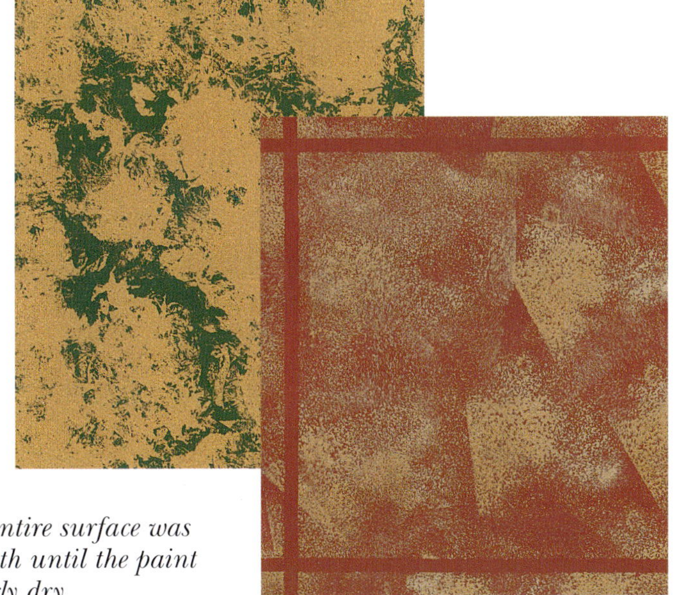

Color variation can always create totally different results. In the third variation, the surface has been painted with a basecoat of dark green and allowed to dry thoroughly. With a soft, lint-free cloth, liquid gold leaf was carefully and randomly applied to the surface. Then, the entire surface was dabbed with a clean cloth until the paint was dispersed and nearly dry.

Variation 4

The fourth variation is one of the simplest, resulting in a textured result (left). A synthetic (cellulose) sponge was dipped into acrylic gold paint, the excess removed with paper towel, and the sponge randomly dashed across the crimson basecoat to create defined edges and a geometric pattern.

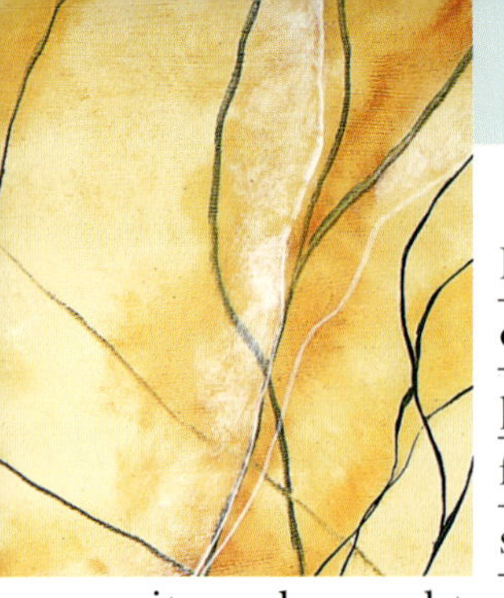

Sienna marble

Marbling is one of the most popular of the faux finishes simply because it can be used to create so many spectacular effects. Sienna is the most copied marble and is therefore one of the most popular to incorporate into different decorative schemes.

The look of marble is one of luxury and expense, but for only a moderate outlay a very effective reproduction of marble can be created in paint. The effect is best suited to columns, countertops, table tops, fireplace surrounds and smaller decorative objects. When used in large areas such as floors and walls, it is best in panels or on borders or inlay effects. It works well with other marbles (see pp. 132 and 138) and looks striking with stenciling (see p. 78).

Used as a form of inlay, marble can look well placed in both traditional and modern settings in any room in the home. Avoid placing the marble effect in a situation where it would most probably not occur naturally.

Care should be taken when handling solvent-based products and follow all instructions carefully. It is best to practice on a board first. If mistakes happen, remove with a little mineral spirits (white spirit) on a soft cloth and repaint.

You will need

Tools

• 2–3 in. (5–7.5 cm.) bristle basecoat brush • ½ in. (1.2 cm.) bristle brush • Fine lining brush • Tack cloth • Fitch brush • Stippling brush • Softening brush (badger) • Paint scraper

Materials

• Cream eggshell basecoat • Transparent oil glaze or gilp • Artists' oils in burnt umber, raw sienna, burnt sienna, black, Prussian blue, white • Oil varnish • Mineral spirits (white spirit)

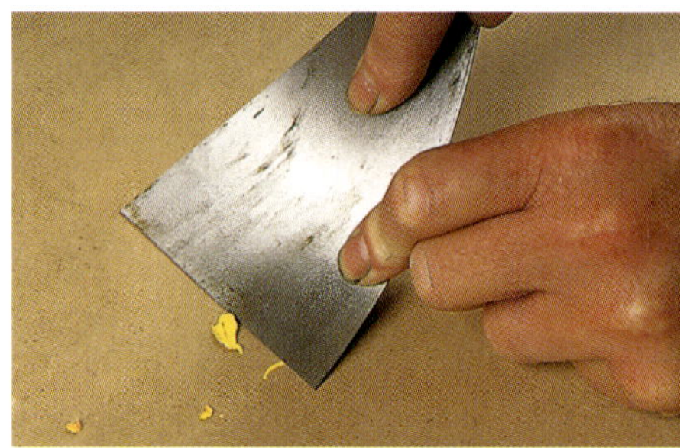

1 With a paint scraper remove flaky material from surface. Be careful not to gouge the surface as you work. Fill holes and sand to a clean surface. Apply undercoat and let dry. Apply two coats of cream eggshell drying between coats.

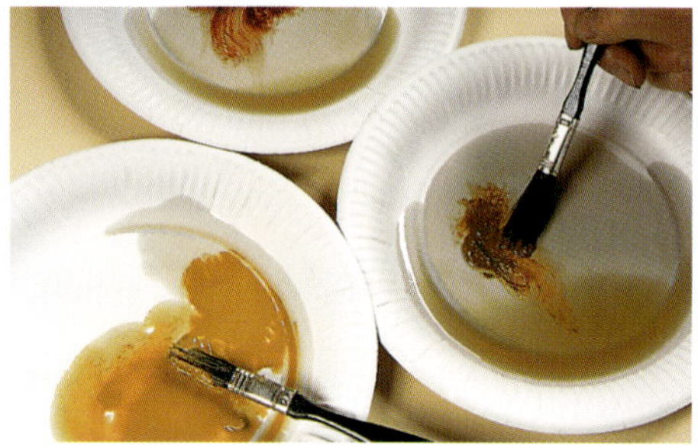

2 Mix up enough gilp (see p. 15) to complete the job. In three separate dishes mix a little of the gilp with some artists' oil paint in raw sienna, burnt sienna and burnt umber.

Variation 1

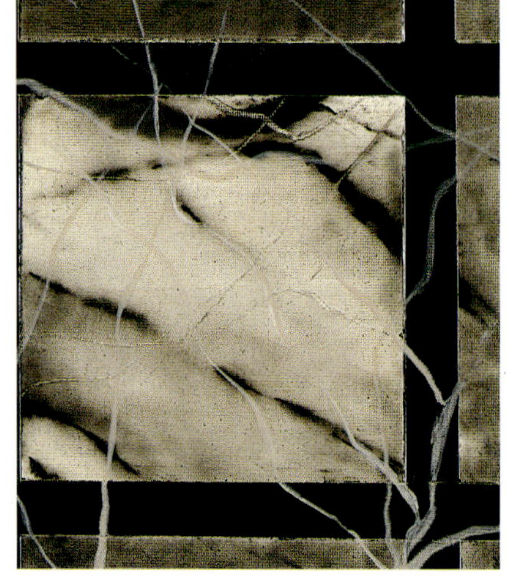

This technique creates a "fantasy" finish. The surface has been painted with a base-coat of black, and left to dry before applying masking tape. The gilp was then applied to the basecoat, and the marbling created using white oil paint and by heavily softening the whole effect. After drying, the masking tape was removed and the area thinly veined with white using a no.1 artists' lining brush. Finish with at least 3 coats of gloss varnish.

Variation 2

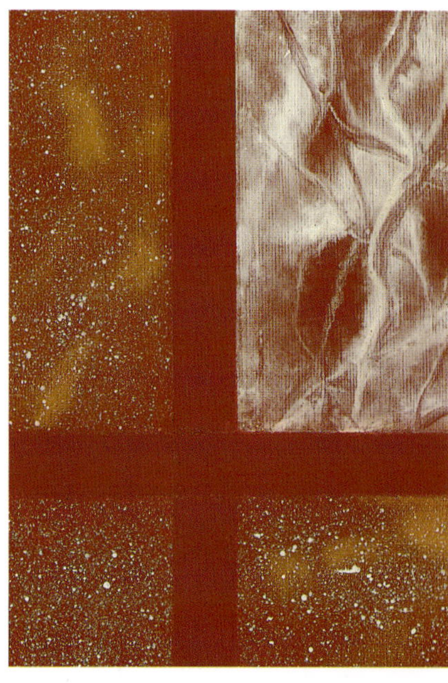

This time we masked off a basecoat of crimson and used white for the marbling effect. The outer edges were dabbed with yellow ocher, softened and then spattered randomly with the white oil paint. The whole effect was finished with a coat of gloss varnish.

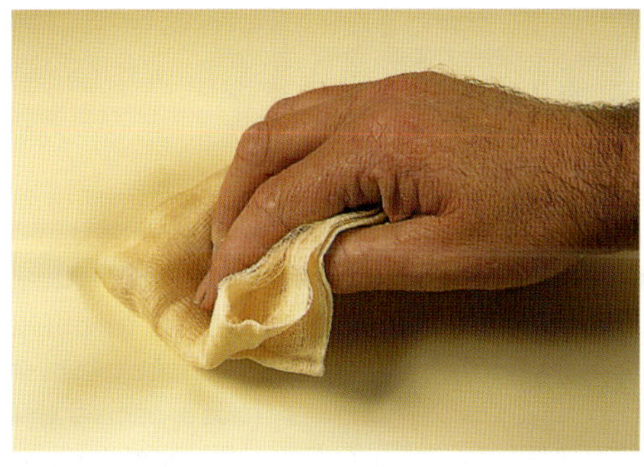

3 With a tack cloth thoroughly wipe the surface to remove any traces of lint or dust completely. With a bristle basecoat brush apply a fairly generous layer of gilp to the surface.

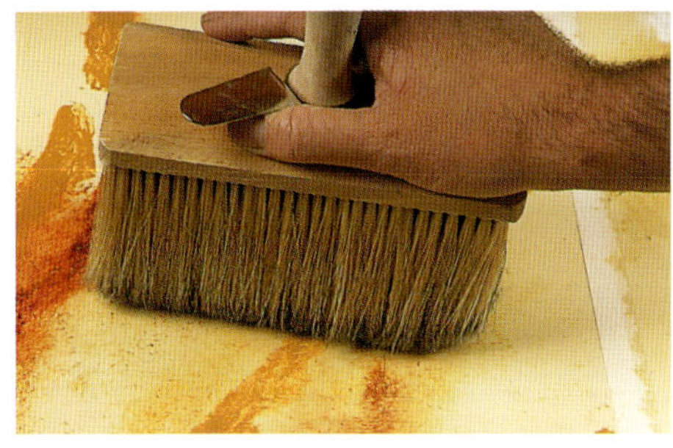

4 Using a Fitch brush (see p. 12) squiggle veins of your three colors across the surface in a roughly parallel formation. With a stippling brush (see *Stippling*, p. 30) spread the veins unevenly and create cloudy areas along the length of the veins.

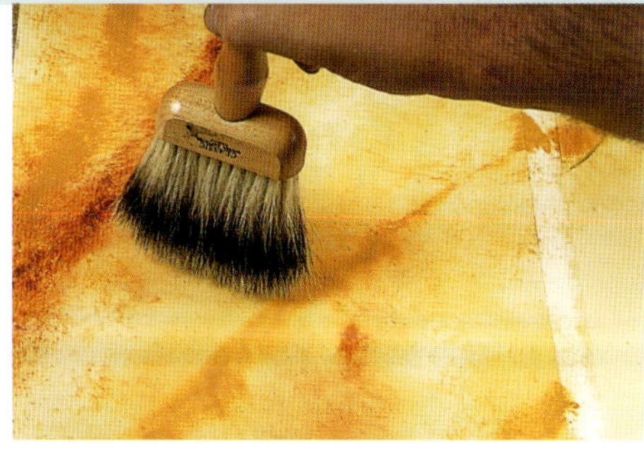

5 With a good quality badger softening brush soften the stippled surface to create the appearance of the veins receeding deep beneath the surface. Add more squiggles, stipple and soften if necessary. Allow to dry overnight.

6 Mix black artists' paint with a touch of Prussian blue. Add gilp to increase flow and achieve a creamy consistency. Wipe the surface with a tack cloth and apply a little gilp. Using a fine artists' brush draw the brush toward you across the surface rolling it occasionally to form the dark surface veins. Dry.

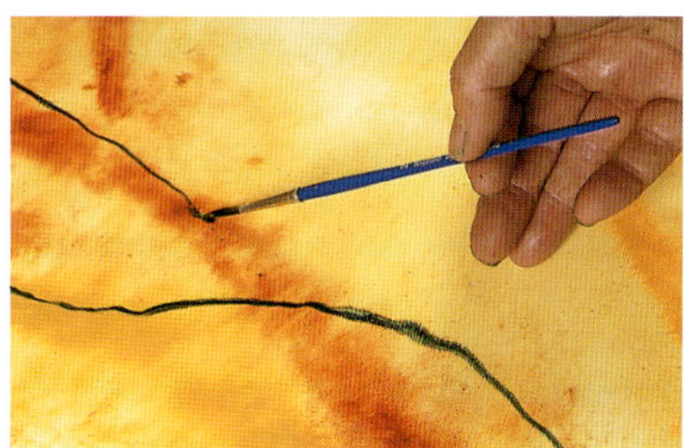

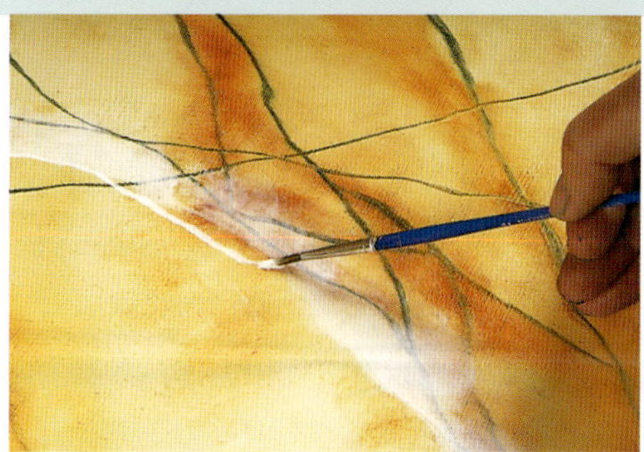

7 Wipe surface with a tack cloth. Mix white artists' oil paint with gilp until it resembles heavy cream. Stipple and soften as in step 5 and outline with crisp, white veins. Dry. Wipe again. With a lining brush, create veins in white oil paint diluted with gilp. Add veins from black and Prussian blue artists' oil paint.

8 The warm earthy tones of sienna marble make it a popular finish to simulate (below). The veins and natural structure of the pattern and color formation create a surface that is soft, warm and solid. The highly polished finish enhances and lightens any setting.

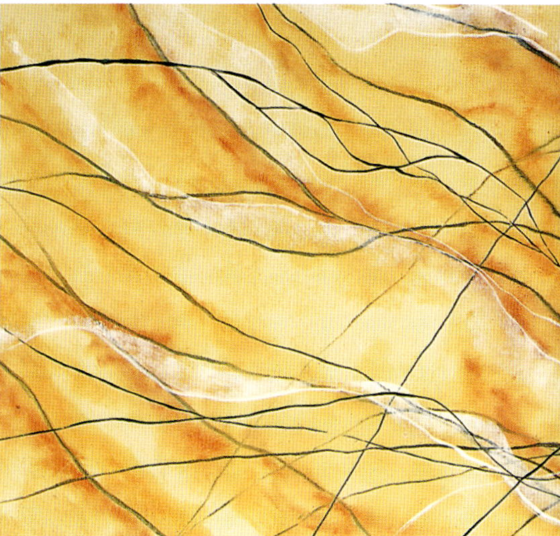

Variation 3

This variation has a textured finish. The surface was given a coat of emerald green and left to dry before applying the gilp and marbling, using only white. The first layer was softened before the veins were applied in white oil (diluted with mineral spirits [white spirit]) using a feather. As the gilp was drying the surface was spattered with mineral spirits (white spirit) to create the pitted look.

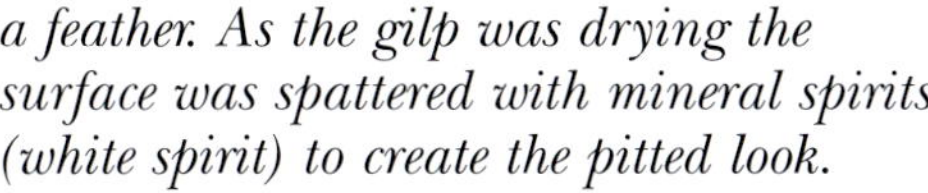

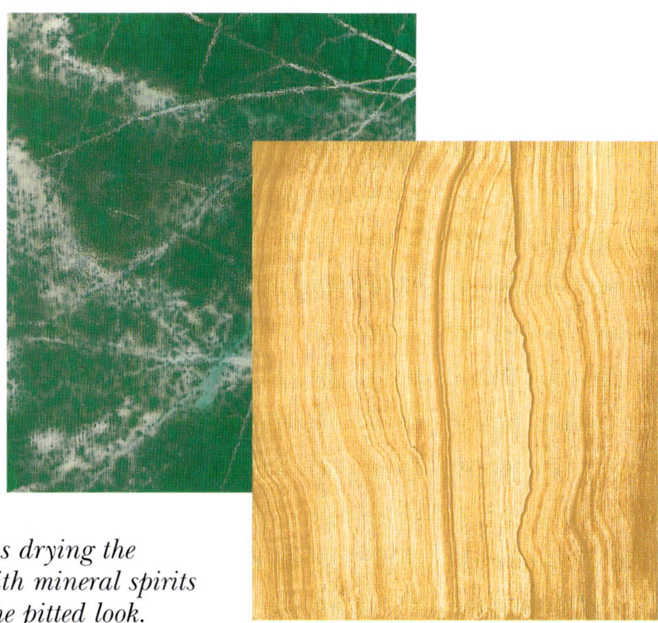

Variation 4

Over a basecoat of two layers of very pale cream semigloss latex (vinyl silk emulsion), was applied a glaze of yellow ocher latex and acrylic glazing medium (1 part paint to 3 parts glaze). After stippling out the brushstrokes (see p. 30), a cardboard comb was dragged (see p. 40) through the glaze and wobbled. The surface was sealed with satin acrylic varnish (left).

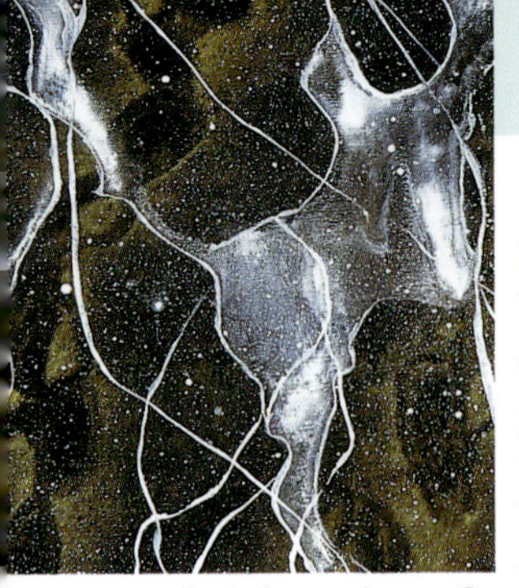

Portoro marble

Marble in any context creates a very decorative finish much copied by paint finish artists. One of the most striking and definitely the boldest is the black and gold marble commercially referred to as Portoro marble. It is an effect that is so striking, and so rich in texture and depth, that can add a feel of extravagance to both modern and traditional rooms.

Portoro marble is not an easy technique because each step must be taken slowly and each layer must be allowed to dry before the next one is applied. Practice is important. As with any marble or semi-precious stone imitation, it is best suited to smaller items. If applied to walls and ceilings, it is best to use it in panels or as a border for other techniques. It works as an inlay or as slabs on a floor. It has a rich effect unsuited to country kitchen-type decor.

This technique can be enhanced by the use of gold with techniques such as stenciling and stamping. By following manufacturer's instructions and allowing each stage to dry before the next, mistakes should be limited. If something goes wrong it can be removed with a soft cloth dampened in mineral spirits (white spirit) and the surface allowed to dry before continuing. If a mistake cannot be removed then repaint the basecoat, allow this to dry and start again.

You will need

Tools

• 2–3 in. (5–7.5 cm.) basecoat bristle brush • ½ in. (1.2 cm.) Fitch brush • Stippling brush • Badger softening brush • Unsharpened pencil or eraser • Lint-free cloth • Swordliner • Feather (optional) • 2 in. (5 cm.) varnishing brush • Wet -and-dry sandpaper • Toothbrush • Tack cloth

Materials

• Black eggshell paint • Transparent oil glaze • Artists' oil colors in yellow ocher and white • Mineral spirits (white spirit) • Gilp • Oil-based gloss varnish

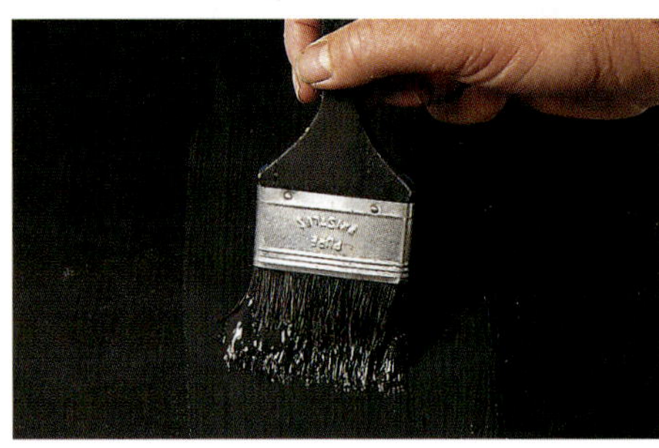

1 Prepare the surface (see *Preparation*, p. 18.) Apply an undercoat. Allow to dry. Then apply two coats of black eggshell paint. Allow at least 24 hours drying time between coats and before commencing the next step.

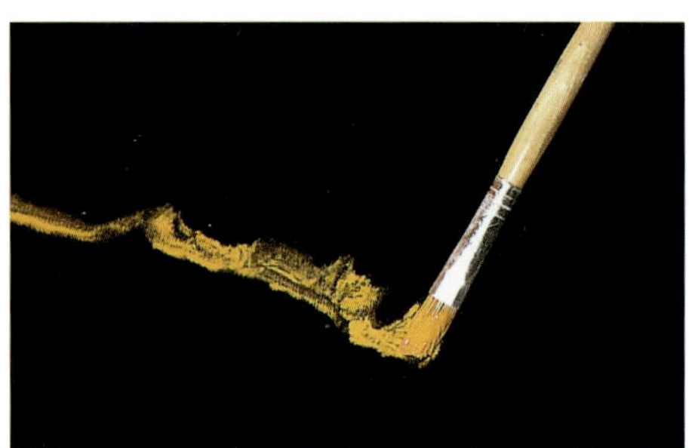

2 Clean surface with tack cloth. Mix some gilp (see p. 15) and apply an even coat. Using a ½ in. (1.2 cm.) Fitch brush, squiggle some yellow ocher artists' oil paint on the surface in a roughly parallel, veined pattern. Vary amount in each vein.

Variation 1

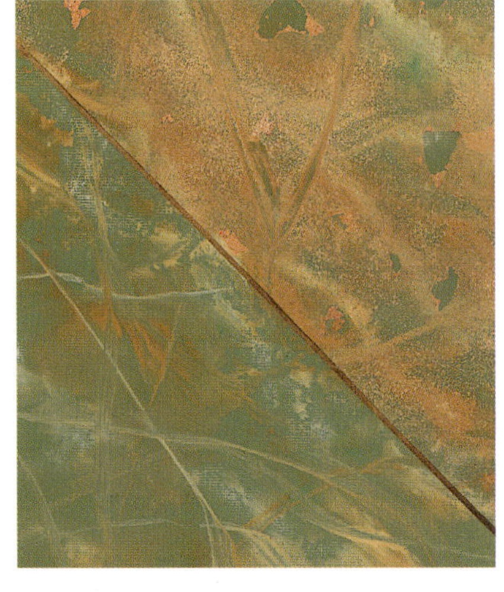

Metallic finishes always look rich and exciting when used in conjunction with other paint techniques. Here, a basecoat of mid-green has been marbled in yellow ocher and white. After masking off the bottom section carefully, a fresh, clear layer of gilp was applied, and while it was going tacky, copper powder and small fragments of copper leaf were added. It was finished with a coat of clear gloss varnish to stop tarnishing.

Variation 2

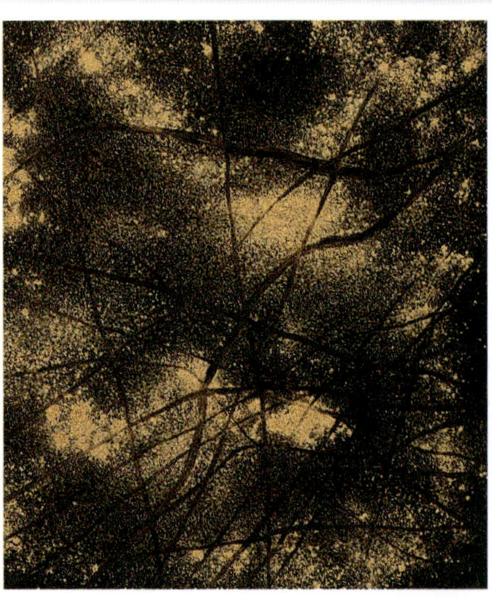

In this example a black basecoat was given a coat of clear gilp before gilt powder was dusted over and carefully softened. The veins were then applied using a fine lining brush dipped in mineral spirits (white spirit) and pulled randomly across the entire surface. After drying it was finished with a coat of gloss varnish to stop tarnishing. A copal or polyurethane varnish was used to tint the final effect with the characteristic yellow.

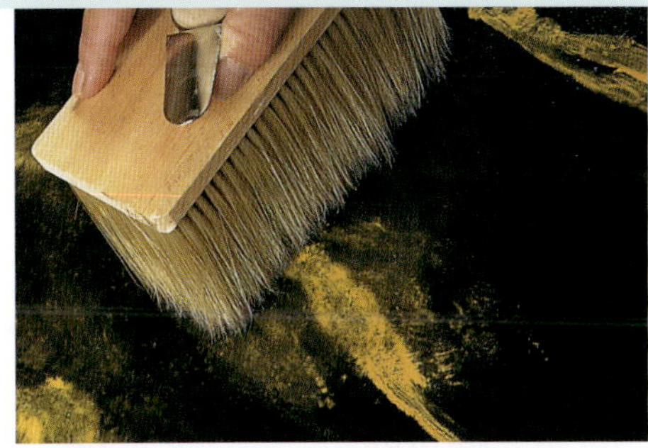

3 With a stippling brush carefully stipple (see *Stippling*, p. 30) out the veins creating a very cloudy but uneven effect within each vein. Work on one or two veins at a time making sure that each continues across the surface in a random pattern. Soften with a badger softening brush.

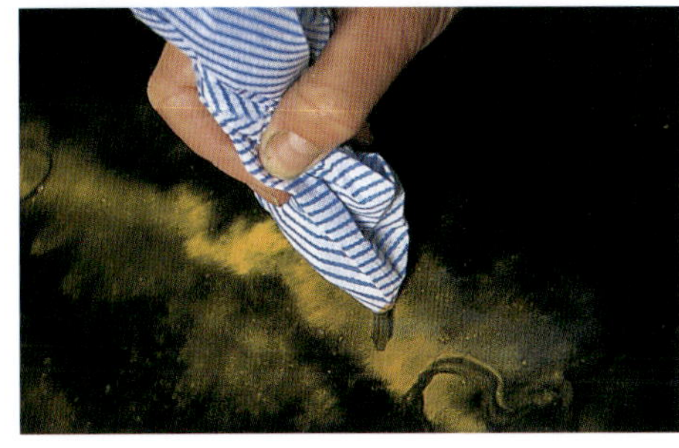

4 Using an unsharpened pencil or an eraser wrapped in lint-free cloth, work along each vein, rubbing out oval sections to form a chain-link pattern. Use a clean piece of cloth each time. Soften edges with a badger softening brush. Dry.

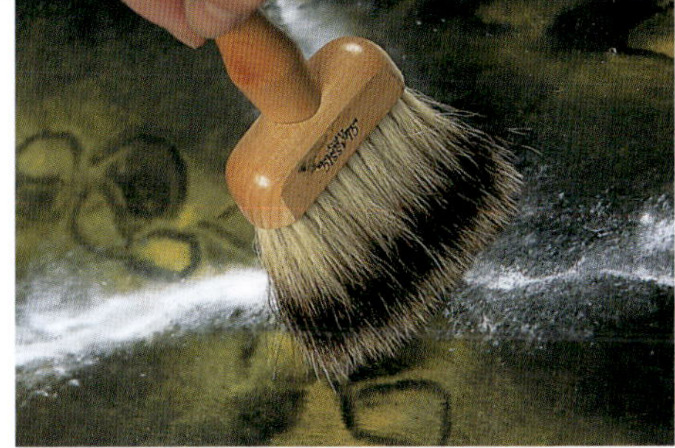

5 Apply a fresh layer of gilp. Mix white artists' oil paint with mineral spirits (white spirit) to increase the flow. With a Fitch brush create white veins by squiggling the brush across, between and over the ocher veins. Stipple, soften and dry.

6 Mix some artists' white oil paint with mineral spirits to a pouring consistency. With a fine swordliner brush outline ovals and sections of the softened white veins. Overvein the surface with more white veins by pulling the lining brush across the surface. You can use a feather for this. Allow to dry.

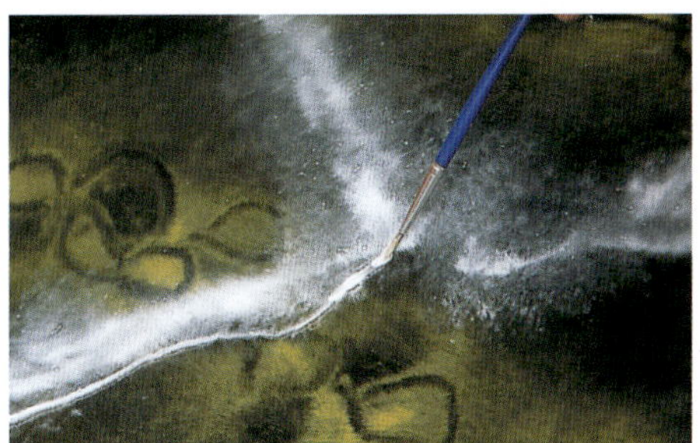

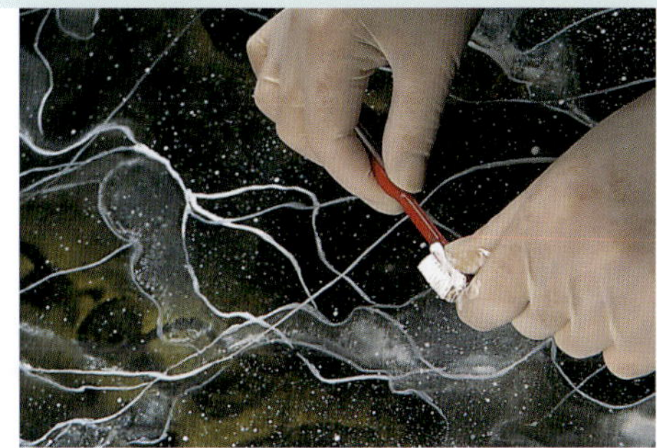

7 Carefully spatter (see p. 72) the surface at random with some white oil paint slightly diluted. Do not dilute too much as the paint will only form unsightly puddles. Allow to dry. Varnish with at least 4 coats of oil-based gloss varnish. Smooth down the last two coats with wet-and-dry sandpaper (see p. 25) between coats to help achieve a glass-like finish.

8 Marbles are always attractive displaying depth and movement in a natural way. Here, a very striking effect is achieved using black and gold (ocher). The web of veins both on and below the surface create an effect of stunning beauty and individuality (below).

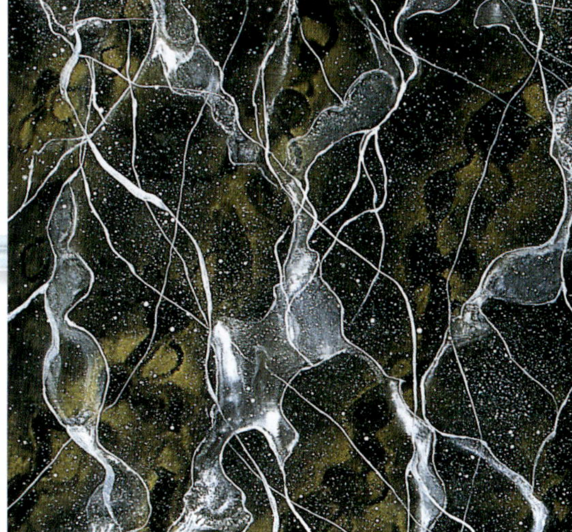

Variation 3

This panel was gilded with aluminum leaf (see p. 134) and when dry, art masking fluid applied randomly across the surface using a fine brush. When dry a foam roller was used to cover the surface with black acrylic paint and left to dry. The surface was rubbed with a cloth and the rubbery masking fluid removed. Spray gloss spray varnish was added to seal.

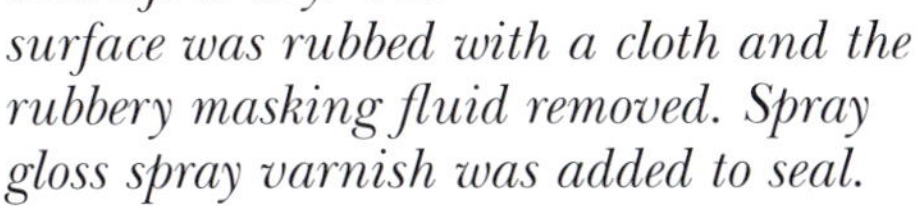

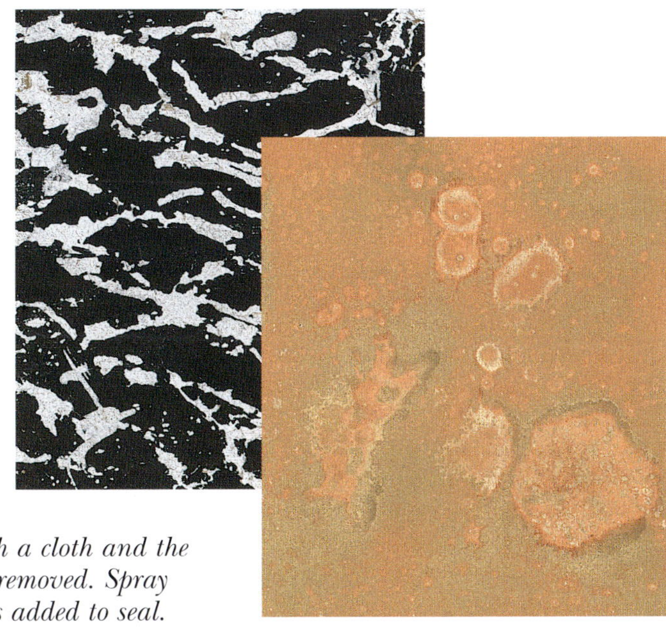

Variation 4

This watery, marbled effect was achieved by spraying gold metallic paint over a basecoat of copper. While still wet the surface was generously spattered (see p. 72) with mineral spirits (white spirit) creating the crater-like effect. The surface was then sealed with a spray gloss varnish (left).

In context

Marble has always been the most copied of all precious and semi-precious woods and stones. Not only does it look luxurious but it is also an effect that can complement any chosen decor—the use of color and style is almost limitless. It can, as shown here, work in many varied situations from the most stately to the most humble.

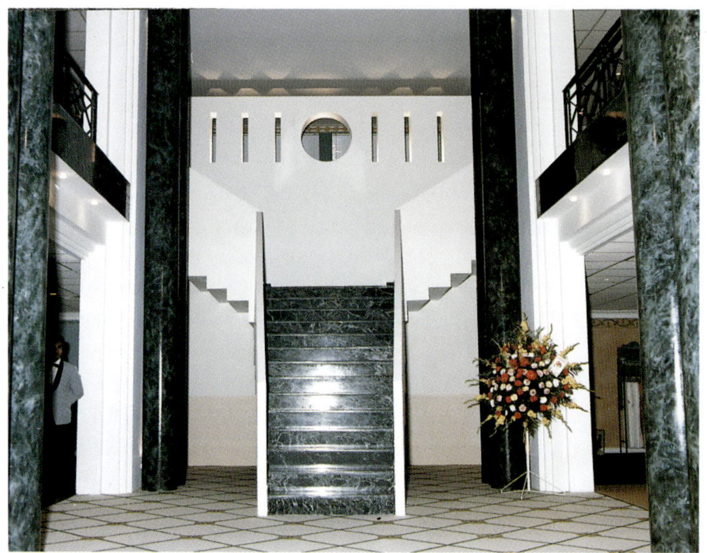

Marble

◀ Entrance hall to a public building

The most beautiful combination of black, white and green marbles on different surfaces has created a very stylish, crisp and smart feel to this entrance foyer. It is quite simple yet open and inviting.

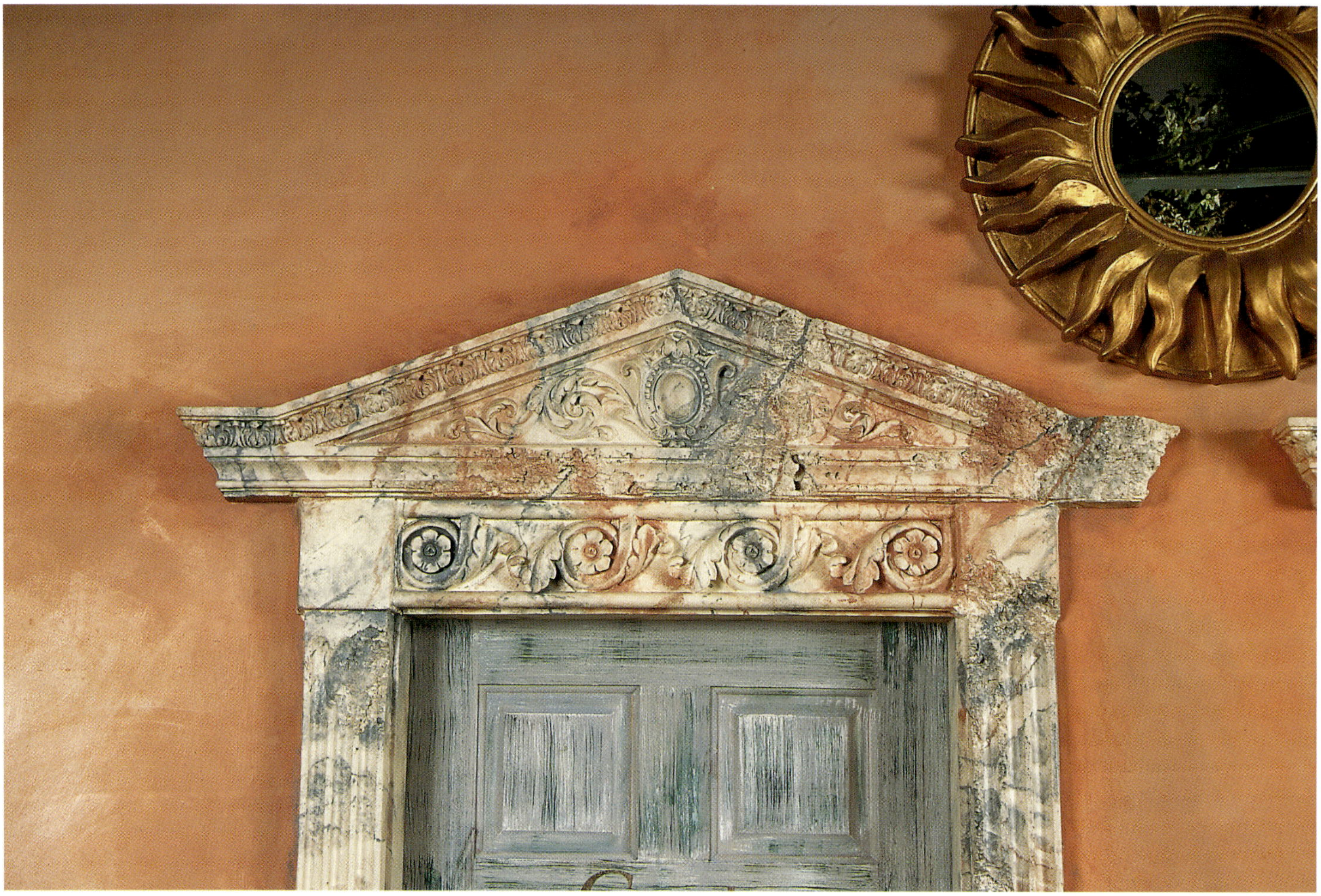

Marble

▲ Doorframe and pediment

The fantasy marble here successfully creates a warm and lavish look—fun and slightly theatrical. A welcoming and glowing environment emerges that is accentuated by the warm terracotta, colorwashed walls and gold accessories.

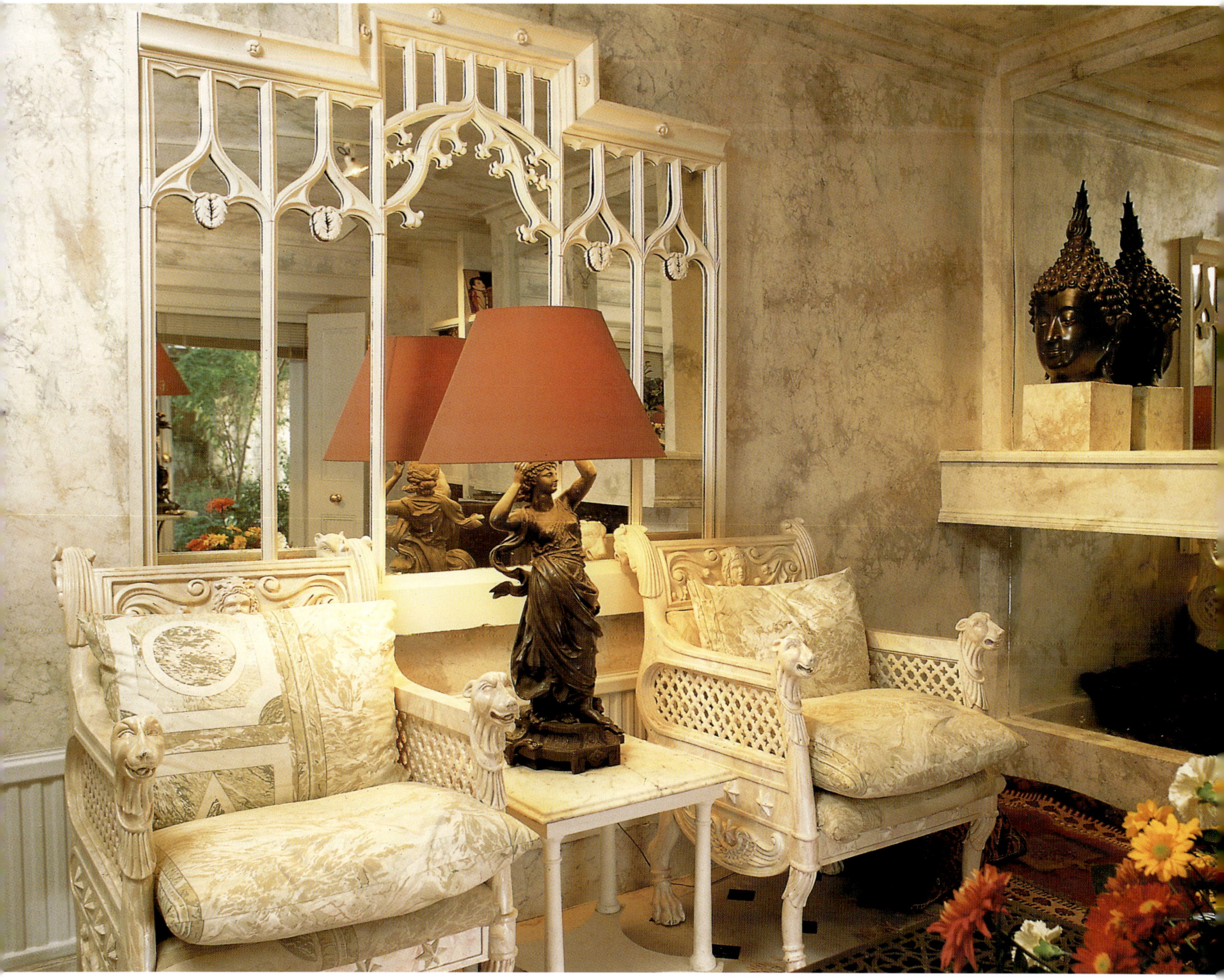

Marble

▲ Walls in a very formal sitting room

The muted colors of the marbled walls and ceilings are highlighted by the cream and white furniture in this sitting room setting. It shows how well larger surfaces can work if they are carefully designed. The lighter colors open up the room aided by the reflective surfaces of the mirrors.

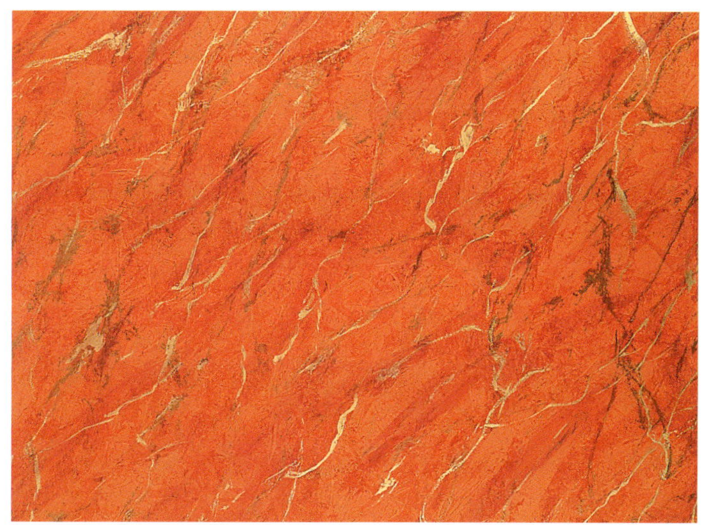

Marble

◀ Counter and table tops

Rich reds, highlighted by cream and gold show the true characteristics of marble. The many layers and patterns really bring to life the table and counter tops, that constantly reflect movement and depth.

INDEX

Page numbers in *italics* refer to illustrations

Credits

Quarto would like to acknowledge and thank the following for providing pictures used in this book. While every effort has been made to acknowledge copyright holders we would like to apologize should there have been any omissions.

Key; t=top b=below
c=centre l=left r=right

Abode p.39, p.56(b), p.92(r), p.93; Ray Bradshaw p.38(l&br), p.119(t), p.127, p.140; Brushstrokes of Oxford p.47(b), p.80(br); B&Q Plc. P.103(r); Crown Paints p.57(bl), p.64(t), p.102(tr); Davies Keeling Trowbridge Ltd p.118(b), p.119(b); E.W.A p.6. p.7, p.17, p.38(tr), p.65(t), p.92(l), p.112(b), p.113(b), p.126(t), p.141(t); ICI/Dulux p.2, p.3, p.46(b), p.57(t), p.64(b); J.H Ratcliffe p.126(b), p.140(t); Plaid Enterprises Inc. p.102(l); The Stencil Library p.81; The Stencil Store p.47(t).

This book is dedicated to Patricia Bradshaw.

The author would like to thank the following people for all their patience, help, support and hard work in producing this book: Tony Smith, Elizabeth Kangurs, Gerrie Purcell, Sally Bond, Honor Head, Jean Coppendale, James Lawrence, Martin Norris

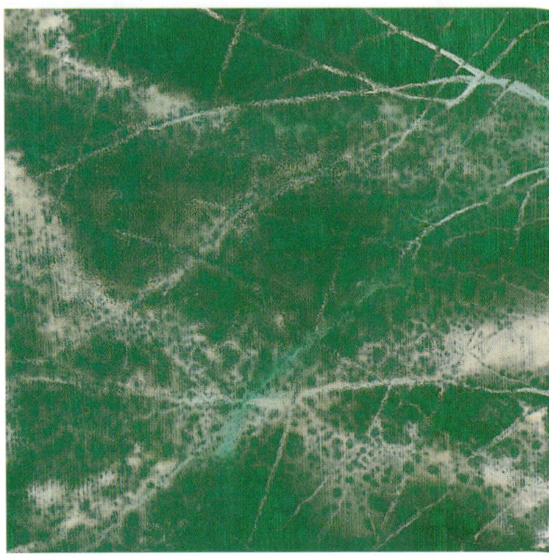

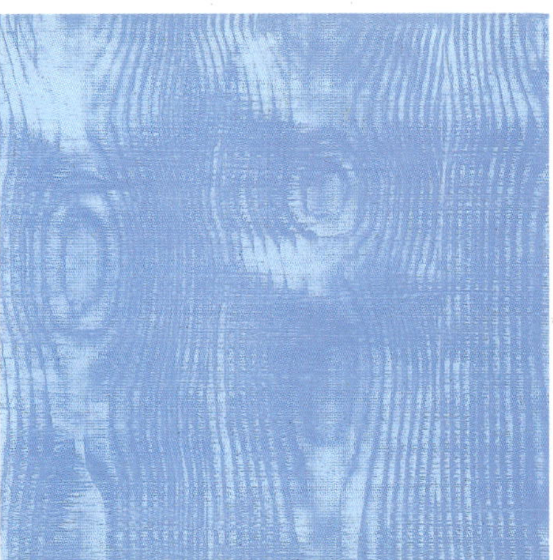

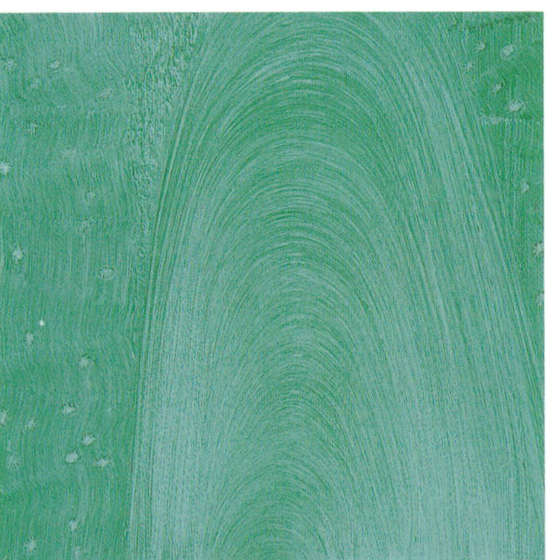

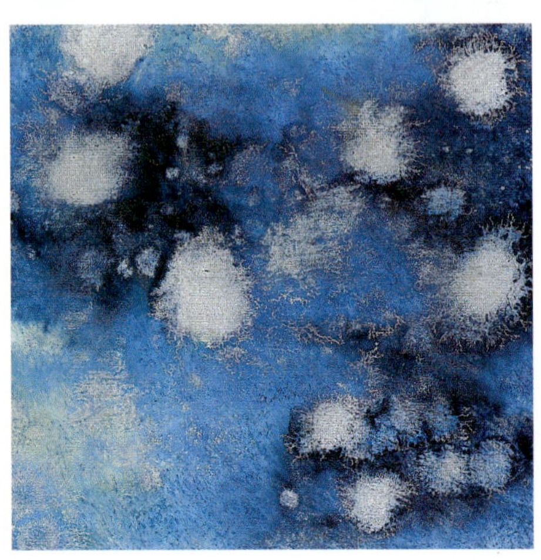